FROM THEORY TO PRACTICE IN PRIVATE INTERNATIONAL LAW

This book, compiled in honour of the work and life of Professor Jonathan Fitchen, brings together preeminent scholars from across the private international law world to address a wide spectrum of subject matter in the discipline. It offers substantial new insights into our understanding of private international law – from theory to practice.

The contributions in the book analyse a variety of conceptual and substantive problems in private international law and consider current developments in the discipline, from conceptual analyses of the evolving nature and scope of private international law to substantive problems across a range of longstanding issues on which there is insufficient scholarly analysis. These include contemporary problems of great political importance, such as environmental protection, gender-based discrimination, asymmetries of private power, and the proper delineation of public and private intervention. The authors also address emerging problems in commercial law, such as cryptocurrencies, longstanding definitional concerns in family law, and broader emerging systemic concerns, such as the treatment of authentic instruments and the place of human rights protection in global supply chains.

The book is a valuable resource for the judiciary, legal practitioners, policy makers, and scholars and students of private international law.

From Theory to Practice in Private International Law

Gedächtnisschrift for Professor Jonathan Fitchen

Edited by
Justin Borg-Barthet
Katarina Trimmings
Burcu Yüksel Ripley
and
Patricia Živković

•HART•
OXFORD • LONDON • NEW YORK • NEW DELHI • SYDNEY

HART PUBLISHING

Bloomsbury Publishing Plc

Kemp House, Chawley Park, Cumnor Hill, Oxford, OX2 9PH, UK

1385 Broadway, New York, NY 10018, USA

29 Earlsfort Terrace, Dublin 2, Ireland

HART PUBLISHING, the Hart/Stag logo, BLOOMSBURY and the Diana logo are trademarks of Bloomsbury Publishing Plc

First published in Great Britain 2024

A catalogue record for this book is available from the British Library.

A catalogue record for this book is available from the Library of Congress.

Library of Congress Control Number: 2023950681

ISBN: HB: 978-1-50995-664-7
ePDF: 978-1-50995-666-1
ePub: 978-1-50995-665-4

Typeset by Compuscript Ltd, Shannon

To Kathrin, Thomas and Sofia, with love and gratitude.

Professor Jonathan Fitchen (1969–2021)

PREFACE

It is a great honour to write the preface to a volume commemorating Professor Jonathan Fitchen, even if honour seems misplaced considering the sadness of his passing at a far too young age in January 2021. The reactions from the international academic community when this sad news was announced and the contributions to this book show how appreciated Jon was as a researcher, a professor, a mentor, a colleague and a friend. Even after time elapsing since I learned about his serious condition and his passing, I find it difficult to summon the right words.

While I have never been a direct colleague of Jon, I deeply respected him and his academic work. I got to know him as a passionate and very dedicated researcher, particularly when working on the volume on the Brussels I recast Regulation (edited by Andrew Dickinson and Eva Lein) in 2013 and 2014. He was extremely helpful in aligning our work and in giving me a better understanding of the intricate topic of the recognition and enforcement of authentic instruments. His ability to analyse such a technical matter in great depth is also evidenced by what later would be his last extensive work to be published, the voluminous book 'The Private International Law of Authentic Instruments' (Hart Publishing, 2020). But he was equally devoted to other less technical and humanistic topics, including gender (equality) and private international law.

I have had the pleasure to work with him on several other occasions and invited him a number of times to contribute to the Dutch journal on private international law. His last contribution for that journal dealt with the implications of Brexit for private international law, a topic that was difficult for him considering how he felt about that. But not only was he a rigorous and passionate researcher, he also excelled as a speaker at international conferences, where he shared his knowledge and presented his observations with enormous vigour, precision, and a relentless sense of humour.

That sense of humour, passion and compassion was also evident from the email exchanges I had the pleasure to be a part of. Whether it concerned our academic work, events or family matters, he had a way with words that would hit the right spot. His love for photography was shared when having to cancel his participation in a conference due to heavy snowfall, and delays in work or having to finish off an email conversation were sometimes jokingly and benevolently attributed to his wife ('my better half') and his children. Going through the individual and group mails that I was able to retrieve for this purpose often made me laugh. Once, when I shared a personal story causing substantial work delays, his short comment made my day – and it is one that I will always be grateful for.

The contributions to the present book only give a glimpse of his wide academic interests and of the personal impressions Jon has left behind. Even more than enlightening the academic community with this book, I hope it will give a little bit of solace to his beloved wife and children, knowing how much he was also appreciated as a colleague and friend by his academic peers.

Having struggled trying to find the right tone and to manage downsizing the high standards I had set for myself for this last brief tribute, I will end by giving Jon the last word. This is quoting a phrase from one of the emails in a group exchange, showing how he mastered words, his sense of humour and nuance, and how he appreciated and valued others.

'I too support a plurality of opinions – mine (which of course are always right – especially when I change my mind) and everyone else's.'

– Jonathan Fitchen

Xandra Kramer
Rotterdam, November 2023

TABLE OF CONTENTS

LIST OF CONTRIBUTORS

Justin Borg-Barthet is Professor of Law at the University of Aberdeen, UK.

Laura Carballo Piñeiro is Professor of Private International Law at the University of Vigo, Spain.

Andrew Dickinson is Professor of the Conflict of Laws and a Fellow of St Catherine's College at the University of Oxford, UK.

Anatol Dutta is Professor of Private Law, Comparative Law and Private International Law at Ludwig Maximilian University of Munich, Germany.

Aude Fiorini is Senior Lecturer at the University of Dundee, UK.

Lorna Gillies is Associate Professor of Law at Edinburgh Napier University, UK.

Xu Huang is a PhD candidate at Wuhan University Institute of International Law, China.

Thalia Kruger is Professor of Private International Law at the University of Antwerp, Belgium.

Alex Mills is Professor of Public and Private International Law at University College London, UK.

Carmen Otero García-Castrillón is Professor of Private International Law at Complutense University of Madrid, Spain.

Burcu Yüksel Ripley is Senior Lecturer at the University of Aberdeen, UK.

Giesela Rühl is Professor of Law at Humboldt-University of Berlin, Germany.

Zheng Tang is Professor of Private International Law at Wuhan University Institute of International Law, China.

Katarina Trimmings is Professor of Law and Director of the Centre for Private International Law at the University of Aberdeen, UK.

Patricia Živković is Lecturer in International Dispute Resolution at the University of Aberdeen, UK.

1

Introduction

JUSTIN BORG-BARTHET, KATARINA TRIMMINGS,
BURCU YÜKSEL RIPLEY AND PATRICIA ŽIVKOVIĆ

This book, in honour of Professor Jonathan Fitchen, is, first and foremost, a gift to the three people Jonathan loved best: his beloved wife, Kathrin and their wonderful children, Thomas and Sofia. We compiled this collection to distil in it some of the immense esteem and affection in which our dear friend and mentor – your husband, your father – was held. Amidst the grief of Jonathan's passing on Friday 22 January 2021, we were comforted by the overwhelming volume of heartfelt messages we received from colleagues across the globe. Jonathan was an extremely well-respected scholar. That much is readily visible in the work he produced, and in its enduring importance to the study of private international law. More importantly, however, he was a thoroughly decent man whose warmth reached into the hearts of so many private international lawyers across the world with whom he interacted over the years, including the contributors to this collection.

I. About Professor Jonathan Fitchen and his Work

To us, Jonathan was not only a colleague but also a mentor and friend. He had been the Director of the University of Aberdeen's Centre for Private International Law for a little over two years, but a mentor to us since the beginning of our careers at the University of Aberdeen. He was always generous with his time, knowledge of the law and understanding of the challenges of academic life. Chance encounters with Jonathan tended quickly to turn to research, whether his or ours. He was equally enthused by projects we were developing as he was by his own work. Remarkably, he seemed to have equally useful insights too. He shared them generously, even if he was forever apologetic about imparting analysis and data which he assumed, often incorrectly, others might already know and understand.

At the time of his passing, Jonathan had recently completed a major work on the *Private International Law of Authentic Instruments* (Hart Publishing, 2020), and not long since been promoted to a Personal Chair at the University of Aberdeen. His monograph is an exceptional piece of private international law scholarship which showcases his grasp of detail and his innate understanding of its importance. The quality of the work is all the more impressive when considering that Jonathan was a common law scholar exploring unfamiliar civilian concepts with exceptional precision and clarity. Jonathan was not satisfied merely to understand and explain the principles which private international law sought to further. His work explores the extent to which those overarching aims are given effect in a fashion that is conducive to sound governance and the sensible allocation of decisional power between private actors and the state.

In addition to his love of legal scholarship, Jonathan had a dizzying array of interests: chess, astronomy, German language, literature and music, his extensive collection of guitars, and photography. The cover image of this collection is a photograph which Jonathan took on a family outing to the Ythan Estuary in the north-east of Scotland. As with the entirety of this collection, Jonathan's presence is felt both in the framing of the image, and in the comforting familiarity of his shadow. Private international law scholarship will continue to feel that presence, and to benefit from his unique ability to compose a picture, for many years to come.

II. About this Collection

This collection consists of three parts, encompassing issues from theory to practice in private international law. Part I deals with the evolving nature and scope of private international law, a reflection of the fact that the Centre for Private International Law turned to asking these questions under Jonathan's leadership. In Part I, contributors approach conceptual concerns from a number of different but related angles. Part II focuses on civil and commercial matters in private international law, which was the focus of most of Jonathan's published work. It is unsurprising that a book in his honour should include extensive treatment of both long-standing and emerging concerns regarding the evolution of that aspect of the discipline. Part II provides a snapshot of the state of the art. It shows that our discipline continues to merit exploration of its foundational principles as it interacts with the evolution of international trade. Equally, international liberalisation requires more sustained scrutiny of private international law as a system of governance. Part III then turns to the private international law of the family, an area with which Jonathan's published work engaged occasionally insofar as it related to broader themes in his scholarship, such as the status of authentic instruments. Here too, the need for more effective technical systematisation is evident, as is the need for conceptual clarity.

In Part I, the discussion begins with Alex Mills in chapter two, on the relationship between private international law and legal pluralism. Mills offers rich insights into a multifaceted relationship which is fundamental to our understanding of the nature of our discipline and the tensions within it. He begins by explaining the origins of private international law as a regulatory system in the (public) international system, noting that private international law is a product of and a response to the uncertainties born of diversity. Notwithstanding regional and international efforts to harmonise private international law, however, the discipline remains diverse in substance and philosophy.

Thalia Kruger, in chapter three, also engages with the problem of pluralism in private international law, albeit through a quite different lens. She considers the nature of mediated settlement agreements from a technical and conceptual perspective, noting their varied treatment in national laws. Insofar as mediated settlements are treated as private agreements by the relevant national law, the traditional view in private international law has been that they should not be capable of automatic enforcement. The Singapore Convention on International Settlement Agreements Resulting from Mediation, therefore, marks a departure from the traditional view in that it sets aside the territorial limitations of authenticity and enforceability. Kruger concludes that the furtherance of autonomy is to be welcomed in principle but emphasises the importance of mechanisms to ensure the safeguarding of vulnerable parties in both domestic law and private international law.

Lorna Gillies, in chapter four, takes on the broader problem of vulnerability in private international law as its central focus. Gillies analyses the role of private international law in recognising and addressing the concept of vulnerability from the perspective of both theory and practice (technique) in cross-border cases by mapping a normative approach. She first looks at the concept of vulnerability and identifies the affected parties in private international law as well as the causes of vulnerability. This is followed by an analysis on the extent to which private international law considers vulnerability of parties in cross-border cases in its theory (through appropriateness, conflicts justice, pragmatism and effectiveness) and in its technique (through characterisation, connecting factors, capacity and party autonomy). She argues, in her chapter, that by applying Fredman's asymmetrical substantive equality reflexively, the theory and technique of private international law will be better equipped in future to deal with the inherit risk of vulnerability in cross-border cases.

Discussion then turns to a specific iteration of the problem of private international law's uneasy relationship with equality. Justin Borg-Barthet and Katarina Trimmings discuss, in chapter five, the failure of private international law consistently to engage with sex-based vulnerability and related feminist scholarship. They begin by considering the effects of structural inequality on women in the private international law of family and corporate life. Then they proceed to consider feminist analyses of the law in related disciplines with a view to identifying feminist private international law's place in the broader debate. They conclude that private international law merits more sustained scrutiny from feminist perspectives, and that the consciousness raising function of feminist analysis is an essential element in the realisation of a more equitable discipline.

Part II opens with Andrew Dickinson's discussion of the nature of 'damage' for the purposes of private international law in chapter six. He approaches his chapter as Jonathan might have, by adopting a meticulous, systematic and thoughtful approach to the identification of the meaning of crucial terms to practitioners and scholars' understanding and application of the law. Dickinson shows that, despite its centrality to EU private international law, the concept of damage remains poorly defined and poorly understood. He then engages in an ambitious systematisation of case law through a much needed explanation of the contours of damage. Dickinson's analysis and organisation of the case law therefore provides an essential taxonomy of 'damage' through which the law can be taught, understood and applied.

Burcu Yüksel Ripley, in chapter seven, also explores essential definitional questions in our discipline. Here, however, the discussion turns to how private international law's traditional techniques cope with disruptive technologies. Yüksel Ripley analyses characterisation, in conflict of laws, of cryptocurrency transfers in distributed ledger technology (DLT)-based systems. She considers that the suggestions that have been put forward for characterisation thus far have mainly attempted to characterise cryptocurrencies as a thing/property, leading to the application of the *lex situs*, or as a claim transferrable by way of assignment, leading to the potential application of conflict of laws rules on assignment of claims to cryptocurrency transfers. Given that neither of these suggestions are considered satisfactory for cryptocurrency transfers in DLT-based systems, she explores a new perspective on the issue of characterisation by utilising an analogy to electronic funds transfers and funds transfer systems under unitary and segmented approaches and considers the potential effects of both approaches on the law applicable to cryptocurrency transfers.

Laura Carballo Piñeiro, in chapter eight, develops discussion of another essential theme of Jonathan's research through which Jonathan sought to systematise essential features of transnational justice, namely the effectiveness of collective redress mechanisms. Carballo Piñeiro observes that access to justice in environmental matters appears to be restricted in most jurisdictions. She notes that a common EU approach to private enforcement of environment protection remains lacking. She assesses, in the chapter's concluding remarks, that all has been too quiet at the EU legislative level as regards enhancing environmental protection. Although judicial activism has shown the way forward, private international law is compelled to support sustainable development by providing mechanisms capable of ensuring transnational corporate accountability and the application of the polluter-pays principle.

Sustainability is a recurring theme of discussion. Carmen Otero García-Castrillón, in chapter nine, analyses the interrelation between international trade agreements and private international law. She examines the traditional division between public and private international law and the place of the study of international trade agreements in this division as well as the need for a stronger private international law attention for areas which are traditionally left to public international law despite their significance for private transactions. She further considers World Trade Organization (WTO) and free trade agreements in this context and argues that private international law could be better integrated into the analysis of international trade agreements with a pragmatic view which would, inter alia, promote international cooperation in achieving the United Nations Sustainable Development Goals.

The interactions of private international law with instruments of public law and public international law are also of concern to Giesela Rühl in chapter ten. Her chapter deals with the German Act on Corporate Due Diligence Obligations for the Prevention of Human Rights Violations in Global Supply Chains, also known as the Supply Chain Due Diligence Act (Lieferkettensorg-faltspflichtengesetz – LkSG). This new law establishes mandatory human rights due diligence obligations and requires German companies to protect human rights in their supply chains. Rühl considers whether private international law may help to effectuate the new provisions in a cross-border context. She concludes that the interactions of the new law with private international law merit further attention. In its current form, the law does not engage effectively with the place of private law and private international law in the upholding of human rights standards. As the European Union seeks to build on the German intervention, legislators would be well advised to be mindful of private international law's role in transnational regulation.

Patricia Živković, in chapter eleven, also explores the blurred lines between public and private governance, concerning the technical distinctions between the determination of substantive law in international commercial arbitration and the determination of substantive law in national courts. Živković notes the phenomenon of 'creeping' substantive review in international commercial arbitration, citing the broad interpretation of public policy by national courts, as well as national courts' review of choice of law based on the parties' objections to arbitral tribunals' determination of the issue. While lamenting the uncertainty arising from inconsistent treatment, she notes the complexities associated with ensuring uniform treatment. In conclusion, she suggests that international legislative intervention is needed to resolve the matter.

Zheng Tang and Xu Huang, in chapter twelve, analyse authentic instruments in Chinese private international law as an area which has not received much attention in the academic writing despite its importance and practical relevance, particularly in the absence of any international uniform regime regulating authentic instruments. They look at the concept of an authentic instrument in the People's Republic of China (PRC), legalisation of foreign notarised documents as well as the effect of foreign authentic instruments in the PRC. They identify areas with a scope for improvement in Chinese law and practice and make some suggestions for consideration for China.

Part III opens with Aude Fiorini, in chapter thirteen, which focuses on the decision of the US Court of Appeals of the Tenth Circuit in *Pope v Lunday*. Fiorini seeks to highlight the risk of importing subconscious elements into the judicial decision-making process in situations where the court has a wide degree of discretion. She begins with identifying the questions that need to be addressed in cases of alleged wrongful retention of newborns under the 1980 Hague Child Abduction Convention, and then contrasts this with the approach that was taken by the first instance court in *Pope v Lunday*.

Anatol Dutta discusses, in chapter fourteen, the concept of private divorce under the Brussels IIter Regulation. He explores three questions in particular. First, what is the scope of the recognition rule in Article 65(1) and does it cover private divorces? Second, what are the precise legal consequences triggered by Article 65(1)? Third, how does Brussels IIter, in particular, the rule in Article 65(1) prevent a private divorce tourism within the European Union?

This collection was not born of a specific academic design. Jonathan's published work is so distinct in its subject matter that we could not possibly have drawn together a volume which spoke specifically to authentic instruments, for example. His unique contribution to our understanding of the law in that space – the magnitude of the loss to academia – is perhaps clearest in that we could never have considered replicating the outline of his imprint on our discipline. We trust, however, that the work would have been of interest to Jonathan, and we know that much of it benefits from the intellectual impression he leaves on private international law scholarship. Taken together, the chapters in this collection show that our discipline is at a fascinating juncture in its development, one which requires both meticulous technical analysis, and critical engagement with principle. Jonathan provided both in abundance, and we are quite certain that he would have read each of this collection's chapters with great interest.

III. Thanks

We are thankful to our research assistants, Konstantina Kalaitsoglou, Raiyan Chowdhury, Benedetta Lobina and Magdalena Zabrocka. Konstantina, Raiyan and Benedetta benefited from Jonathan's vocation to teaching across a broad spectrum of law, and their own interest in legal research owes much to Jonathan's work. We also owe a deep debt of gratitude to Roberta Bassi, Sinead Moloney, Verity Stuart, Anne Bevan, Linda Goss and all at Hart Publishing. They embraced this project with extraordinary empathy, and with their usual exceptional professionalism and flexibility. Professor Greg Gordon, Head of School at the University of Aberdeen School of Law, has also been especially supportive of this project, in addition to being intellectually and emotionally available to each of us at a particularly difficult time. Equally, of course, we are grateful to the authors of each of the chapters of this book. Each chapter has been a joy to read, and we are deeply grateful for such wonderfully supportive colleagues.

Finally, we are thankful to and for Jonathan. He enriched our lives, and our scholarship. We hope that this collection stands as a fitting tribute to a brilliant scholar, a thoroughly engaging teacher, and a truly wonderful man. Thank you, Jonathan.

PART I

The Evolving Nature and Scope of Private International Law

2

Private International Law and Pluralism

ALEX MILLS

I. Introduction

Private international lawyers are often, but not invariably, 'pluralist' in their outlook. This reflects a common, but not uncontested, understanding of private international law as engaged with coordinating the harmonious coexistence of diverse systems of private law. A happy side effect of this outlook is a community spirit among private international lawyers around the world – a sense of openness and common purpose which transcends the diversity of backgrounds and traditions from which they (we) come. Professor Jonathan Fitchen, in whose tribute this chapter is offered, epitomised this in his personal generosity and collegiality, and in his work on authentic instruments.[1] Although they are unknown to common law systems, European private international law opened up the possibility that foreign authentic instruments were capable of legal effect in the UK, and Jonathan did more than anyone to ensure that these mysterious devices and their effects were properly understood. This chapter offers some thoughts on the relationship between pluralism and private international law, suggesting that the complexity and evolution of this relationship has highlighted the potential power of private international law. It considers the relationship between private international law and pluralism through three lenses: private international law as a product of pluralism; the pluralism of private international law; and pluralism as a product of private international law.

II. Private International Law as a Product of Pluralism

Private international law may be understood as a product of 'pluralism' – a response to the challenges it presents. Rules of private international law may, in

[1] Including his magnum opus, J Fitchen, *The Private International Law of Authentic Instruments* (Hart Publishing, 2020).

this light, be seen as a technique or technology which has developed to address the potential negative impacts of the coexistence of multiple legal orders.[2] In particular, they address the concern that a single dispute, relationship or act might be subject to inconsistent regulation under multiple orders. Inconsistent regulation is undesirable both for individual parties, who may be subject to contradictory requirements which mean that it is impossible for them to comply with 'the law', and also for the legal systems themselves, as conflicting regulation may reduce their effectiveness in achieving policy goals and give rise to friction which destabilises relations between private parties and between legal orders. This idea of private international law as a product of pluralism is evidenced historically by the fact that rules of private international law have tended to emerge and be developed in contexts in which diverse private law systems have existed within a cooperative framework[3] – the city states of Renaissance Italy, or the provinces of newly unified France or the Netherlands, or the diverse states of the United States of America. The idea of 'pluralism' here is, of course, a relatively limited one, as discussed further below, and in the history of private international law its development has also at times been prompted by other forms of pluralism, such as the coexistence of religious legal orders – but the predominant context in which private international law operates is, in this conception, as a response to the plurality of territorial state systems of private law.

It is not claimed that this is the only way of viewing private international law. As discussed further below, private international law may (for example) be viewed as merely a part of national law which answers basic practical questions in relation to individual cross-border situations or cases – determining which law should govern each particular legal relationship, as well as the question of which forum will be available to resolve disputes which may arise, with a focus on ensuring that justice is fairly done between the parties. Adopting such a perspective on private international law is by no means indefensible, or indeed unusual, particularly in the common law tradition.[4] But if it is viewed as a matter of purely national law, adopted unilaterally, private international law is unlikely to be effective in achieving the regulatory goal of avoiding conflicting regulation.

This broader systemic regulatory goal is reflected in traditional objectives found across the field of private international law, and recently articulated most clearly in the European Union. Strict rules of *lis pendens* and judgment recognition in the Brussels I Regulation, for example, strive to achieve this goal by reducing instances of overlapping jurisdiction between Member States, based on the argument that 'In the interests of the harmonious administration of justice it is necessary to minimise the possibility of concurrent proceedings and to ensure that irreconcilable

[2] See generally, eg, R Michaels, 'Global Legal Pluralism and Conflict of Laws' in PS Berman (ed), *The Oxford Handbook of Global Legal Pluralism* (Oxford University Press, 2020).

[3] See generally, A Mills, 'The Private History of International Law' (2006) 55 *International & Comparative Law Quarterly* 1.

[4] See further, eg, A Mills, 'The Identities of Private International Law: Lessons from the US and EU Revolutions' (2013) 23 *Duke Journal of Comparative & International Law* 445.

judgments will not be given in different Member States'.[5] The harmonisation of choice of law rules in the European Union similarly aims to ensure decisional consistency, based on the argument that:

> The proper functioning of the internal market creates a need, in order to improve the predictability of the outcome of litigation, certainty as to the law applicable and the free movement of judgments, for the conflict-of-law rules in the Member States to designate the same national law irrespective of the country of the court in which an action is brought.[6]

In private international law scholarship, this is traditionally known as the objective of 'decisional harmony', as it is focused on ensuring that any available dispute resolution processes lead to the same outcomes, but the principle is not limited to disputes – it equally provides essential clarity for parties in understanding the legal extent of their cross-border rights and obligations.

Thinking of private international law in this way requires the adoption of a perspective which examines the function and effects of private international law *internationally*, viewing it as a regulatory *system* rather than as just another aspect of national law.[7] For much of its history, this was indeed the dominant way in which private international law was conceived – it was developed as part of a broader law of nations, and was understood as being international in both its functions and its sources (as it tended to be derived from natural law principles or rather thin Roman law foundations).[8] At the end of the nineteenth century, with increasingly diverse systems of national private law emerging, there was a reaction which emphasised the need for the international codification of principles of private international law, particularly reflected in a series of conferences on private international law which were held in the Hague in 1893 and over the following decade.

As discussed further below, this codification movement was at best partially successful, and in reality rules of private international law experienced substantial divergence over the course of the twentieth century. In the latter parts of the century, however, there was (and has since continued to be) a rediscovery of the public and systemic perspective on private international law, which has been particularly sparked by developments within federal systems.[9] Perhaps the

[5] Regulation (EU) No 1215/2012 of the European Parliament and of the Council of 12 December 2012 on jurisdiction and the recognition and enforcement of judgments in civil and commercial matters, [2012] OJ L351/1, Recital 21.

[6] Regulation (EC) No 593/2008 of the European Parliament and of the Council of 17 June 2008 on the law applicable to contractual obligations (Rome I), [2008] OJ L177/6, Recital 6; and (identically) Regulation (EC) No 864/2007 of the European Parliament and of the Council on the law applicable to non-contractual obligations (Rome II), OJ L199/40, Recital 6.

[7] See generally, A Mills, *The Confluence of Public and Private International Law: Justice, Pluralism and Subsidiarity in the International Constitutional Ordering of Private Law* (Cambridge University Press, 2009).

[8] See generally, eg, Mills, 'The Private History of International Law' (n 3).

[9] See generally, eg, Mills, 'The Identities of Private International Law' (n 4); Mills, *The Confluence of Public and Private International Law* (n 7).

most well-known developments are in the European Community and its successor the European Union, already noted above. Before the European Community private international law had, over the course of the twentieth century, developed a significant variety in the different laws of the different Member States. But over recent decades, private international law has been transformed, initially through treaties like the Brussels Convention and Rome Convention, and now through EU Regulations. In the last decade, a regime of European private international law has been established through the Brussels I and II Regulations, and the Rome I, II and III Regulations. As noted above, the harmonisation of these rules strives to achieve traditional systemic objectives of private international law – allowing parties to easily predict where litigation may take place, reducing the risk of conflicting judgments, and ensuring that the same single law will govern their legal relationship regardless of where in the European Union their dispute may be litigated.

This wave of European private international law regulation is more significant than just reflecting a change in the source of private international law, from national to international[10] or EU law. It also reflects a fundamental change in the character of private international law itself, or rather, a renaissance of its traditional vision. In the European Union, private international law (at least to the extent that it has been regulated as part of EU law) is no longer part of the 'private' law or the 'procedural' law of national Member States, but part of European *public* law, clearly reconceived as about defining the relationship between Member State legal orders – the distribution of regulatory authority between Member States. In both Australia and Canada, the last 30 years have seen similar developments to those in the European Union, although driven by the courts rather than by statutory regulation – the recognition that private international law serves a federal constitutional function of ordering the regulatory authority between the constituent federal provinces or states, balancing the needs of centralised ordering with the pluralism of their distributed regulatory arrangements.[11] The rules of private international law which have been adopted by the courts in Australia and Canada have been understood to reflect the requirements of these federal systems – the need to accommodate the diversity of provincial laws in an ordered federal structure. Private international law in each of these contexts may thus be understood as a product of pluralism – rules which have been generated in response to the existence of legal diversity in an attempt to manage the risks created by that diversity.

These developments have also prompted a broader reconsideration of the role of private international law – whether it can and should be viewed as serving a

[10] The Brussels Convention and Rome Convention might better be characterised as treaty arrangements rather than EU legal instruments, albeit with a regional character; the Lugano Convention which extends the Brussels I Regulation regime to EFTA states is a similar and continuing regional treaty arrangement.

[11] See generally, Mills, *The Confluence of Public and Private International Law* (n 7) 74–114.

public regulatory function as part of the international legal order.[12] The unification of private international law on the international plane does not quite have an equivalent to the European Commission or Court of Justice, or to the constitutional courts of Australia and Canada, although it does have the Hague Conference on Private International Law.[13] This organisation has, since 1955, been the institutionalised embodiment of the internationalist movement in private international law which led to the original codification conferences at the end of the nineteenth century. It is dedicated to the international harmonisation of rules of private international law, which also means implicitly and more deeply that it is dedicated to the internationalisation of the conception of private international law itself. The adoption of this global perspective and its focus on international systemic goals supports the idea of private international law as a potential response to global pluralism in private law.

III. The Pluralism of Private International Law

Despite the persistence of an internationalist and systemic perspective on private international law, as discussed above, for much of the nineteenth and twentieth centuries this view of private international law was somewhat neglected or marginalised. It declined in favour of an alternative view which placed emphasis on the idea of private international law as *national private* law. Private international law was considered to be *national* law, because it was viewed as part of the law of each state – as private international law matured as a subject, national courts and legislatures were increasingly active in its development, but this also meant that it increasingly reflected the national policies and objectives and national conceptions of justice and fairness which those agencies (at least primarily) serve. The result was (and is) not just a pluralism of national laws (of private international law), but a pluralism of different visions for the subject, different conceptions of its purpose, not just between states but also within them and across the global community of private international lawyers. As Patrick Glenn observed, private international law, as a response to diverse fragmenting national legal orders in the nineteenth century, itself became subject to the same processes of fragmentation that it was developed to resist.[14] Private international law was also considered to be *private* law, because (particularly in the pragmatic common law tradition) the development of private international law rules was driven by ideas of meeting the expectations of the parties and the fair and efficient resolution of individual cross-border disputes. In this tradition, the emphasis was not placed on systemic

[12] See, eg, H Muir Watt, 'Jurisprudence Without Confines: Private International Law as Global Legal Pluralism' (2016) 5 *Cambridge Journal of International Law* 388.

[13] See: www.hcch.net/.

[14] HP Glenn, 'Harmonization of law, foreign law and private international law' (1993) 1 *European Review of Private Law* 47, 50.

objectives, but on ensuring that each individual dispute ends up in the appropriate court, with the appropriate law. In the latter part of the twentieth century, private international law was sometimes thought of as simply part of the law of civil procedure. Indeed, the common law rules on jurisdiction, which might be viewed as providing the very foundations and limits of the regulatory power of the English courts in private law matters, are set out in the Civil Procedure Rules, and in significant part as merely a 'Practice Direction' to those Rules.

The development of modern private international law thus also has a very different relationship with pluralism. Instead of private international law being understood as a product of pluralism, it is often understood as itself being a 'subject' of (or subject to) pluralism. Diverse national traditions of private international law have developed and in large part have themselves had to learn how to coexist, relying generally on principles such as comity (in the absence of coordinating rules analogous to those provided by private international law itself under its systemic conceptualisation).[15] But there are significant difficulties in providing for cooperation or coordination between national actors serving distinct national legal/cultural traditions, however internationally minded they are. The examples noted above of legal systems in which private international law has (re)developed a systemic approach all involve systems in which certain actors have the capacity to impose a unified framework on the presented diversity – the constitutional courts of Canada and Australia, or the more complex law-making institutions and processes which have led to the various EU legal instruments. While local judges in these systems may have a primarily local function – they serve as part of the courts of Quebec, New South Wales, or Belgium – they nevertheless are also able to understand their function in a broader sense, as part of their identity and their conception of whose interests they serve is also Canadian, Australian, or European. In a legal sense, they may consider themselves as serving (and may indeed swear an oath to serve) a unifying concept such as 'the sovereign';[16] alternatively, the collective interest may become intertwined with the local, where (for example) a duty to uphold Belgian law becomes understood to include EU law. Extrapolating this sense of commonality or shared identity beyond such 'regional' systemic contexts undoubtedly presents greater challenges – it is perhaps of particular interest whether the experience of the United Kingdom in being part of a systemic EU approach to private international law is something which survives Brexit, for example, when it comes to interpreting retained EU instruments (the Rome I and II Regulations), or perhaps in a modified form through greater engagement with the work of the Hague Conference on Private International Law, or whether there is a reversion to a more traditional unilateral approach. The Hague Conference has itself faced challenges in overcoming the diversity in the way in which private international law itself has evolved, such as the divide

[15] At one time *renvoi* was potentially understood as serving such a function, as it enables a court to align its choice of law rules with those applicable in a foreign court, but the disadvantages of this approach are now widely considered to outweigh the limited benefits.

[16] See, eg, Oaths Act 1900 (NSW), Fourth Schedule.

between civil and common law systems, as well as overcoming more generally the idea that private international law is reflective of national values and traditions in a way which should be preserved.

For private international law to perform such a global governance function well, it needs to be 'internationalised', or 'universalised', so that different national courts act in a coordinated and consistent way. This presents something of an apparent paradox. For private international law to act in support of legal pluralism, it needs to abandon its own pluralism – the distinctive national traditions of private international law which have developed in different states around the world. To provide an effective response to the problems created by diverse rules of private law, private international law needs to act and be understood to act at a higher level, serving a higher order of interests – to detach itself from its local context (even if local interests retain overriding representation through mandatory rules or considerations of public policy). This is undoubtedly a challenging idea, and one whose implementation through domestic courts must invariably be to some extent compromised by the range of other duties to which judges are subject. It may also be noted, however, that national court judges already, in varied contexts, accept the need for a special 'internationalist spirit'[17] when it comes to problems of private international law, recognising that their function extends beyond the traditional confines of their domestic constitutional role.

The apparent paradox described above is not a contradiction in private international law itself, but a contradiction in the impulses to which it is subject. On the one hand, private international law is understood as international, and as needing to be unified to serve its global purposes – as a product of pluralism. On the other hand, private international law is understood as domestic, as a reflection of local values, interests and traditions – as a subject of pluralism. This conflict of identities is part of why private international law has struggled to develop and maintain a clear sense of its own function, extending even to the interminable debates over the title of the discipline. The conflict (not of laws, but of conceptions of conflict of laws) is also, however, part of the richness of private international law, which is eternally debating its own relationship with globalisation and international law, as well as its connection with both local and global substantive legal goals and values. This debate may also be understood through the ambivalence of the relationship between private international law and pluralism.

IV. Pluralism as a Product of Private International Law

Despite their opposing perspectives, the two lenses on private international law and pluralism examined above have something important in common. They view private international law in relatively passive terms – as either the product

[17] *Raiffeisen Zentralbank Osterreich AG v Five Star General Trading* [2001] EWCA Civ 68, [2001] 2 WLR 1344, [26].

of a pluralist context, or as a part of law which is itself subject to pluralism. More recently, private international lawyers have increasingly recognised that these perspectives underestimate the potential of private international law as an agent of change in the world.

It has, for example, been recognised that private international law has a unique and critical role to play in the European legal order. Private international law imposes a degree of order on the diverse private law systems of the different Member States which nevertheless constitute a single unified market and legal order – it enables coordination of that diversity. In so doing, it acts as a support not only for the market itself, but for the diversity it is accommodating – it makes it less necessary to adopt substantive European rules to prevent the risk of conflicting regulation. Indeed, it may even create incentives for certain states to resist substantive harmonisation, as they may gain a competitive advantage from having their particular rules benefit from mutual recognition throughout the European Union. Viewed in this way, private international law is not just implicated in the horizontal distribution of regulatory authority between Member States, but also the *vertical* distribution of regulatory authority between the institutions of the European Union and the Member States. Private international law is thus no less than one of the foundations of European legal pluralism in private law – it is not (or not just) that European pluralism generates private international law, but that private international law generates and supports European pluralism.

Extrapolated to the international plane, as a technique for coordinating diverse systems of national private law, private international law can similarly act to support and preserve that diversity, which we might call 'interstate legal pluralism'. It can take away the pressure to harmonise, and allow diversity to flourish, at least in the limited context of a plurality of territorial states. It is true that pressures or impulses to harmonise may nevertheless arise from other sources, such as competition between legal orders or from their more spontaneous interactions[18] – but that pressure is at least alleviated by private international law rules which reduce the costs of maintaining diversity.

In so doing, private international law does not just reflect the identity of the actors with which it engages, but also shapes and constructs that identity. Even outside the context of a systemic approach, private international law (at least as traditionally understood) requires a judge to step outside their normal role, and recognise other legal systems of the world as equivalent to their own. Depending on the circumstances, in a private international law case an English judge might stay proceedings in favour of the German courts, recognise a French judgment, or apply Saudi Arabian family law. Any foreign legal order can, in effect, end up regulating the resolution of disputes or the distribution of property in England – the starting point at least is a cosmopolitan perspective that every legal order is equally valid. Inevitably, private international law does not just preserve pluralism

[18] See, eg, MG Maduro, 'So Close and Yet So Far: The Paradoxes of Mutual Recognition' (2007) 14 *Journal of European Public Policy* 814.

between states, it introduces or accommodates pluralism within them, and in so doing it makes judges agents of pluralism.

This has a further important implication – that private international law has a role in determining not just the existence of pluralism, but its scope and limits. One traditional limit on pluralism is public policy, operating as an exception to the application of foreign law or a defence to the recognition and enforcement of a foreign judgment. The limits of public policy thus define one of the boundaries of the acceptance of diversity within private international law – how much difference it is possible to accept.[19]

Another deeper challenge for private international law is whether and to what extent this acceptance of difference should involve recognising the fundamental insight of 'legal pluralist' scholars, that state law is not the only source of the laws, rules or other normative principles which guide people's lives.[20] The rules which shape our lives are not only those which bind or protect us as citizens, or even those which confer rights on us as humans, but also a diverse range of rules which apply to us as members of a variety of different communities. Our identities are not solely those of citizens, or even residents of a territory, but may also be as members of a religious group, or a club or society, or a professional or business association, or a variety of other forms of social or cultural ordering. The rules or customary practices of those groups may shape our behaviour as much as state law. In some cases, the rules of those groups may conflict with state law, and yet people may find those rules so compelling that they accept the risk or even likelihood of a breach of state law and consequential punishment rather than breaching those other rules. A religious pâtissier may refuse to decorate a cake for a same-sex wedding (an issue which has led to Supreme Court decisions in both the United States[21] and United Kingdom);[22] business practices in a particular commercial context may be viewed by participants as binding even if they are merely a codification of community norms which departs from potentially applicable state law.

The claim that this complexity represents *legal* pluralism is always vulnerable to the argument that the rules provided by other forms of social organisation are not *law*, but there is more than a hint of definitional circularity about such arguments. We could choose to define 'law' in such a way as to include only state-sanctioned rules, and it is true that there is something distinctive about such rules which requires particular treatment, and indeed justifies the predominance of

[19] See further, generally, A Mills, 'Dimensions of Public Policy in Private International Law' (2008) 4 *Journal of Private International Law* 201.

[20] See, eg, H Muir Watt, 'Conflicts of Laws Unbounded: The Case for a Legal-Pluralist Revival' in PS Berman (ed), *The Oxford Handbook of Global Legal Pluralism* (Oxford University Press, 2020); MA Helfand, *Negotiating State and Non-State Law: The Challenge of Global and Local Legal Pluralism* (Cambridge University Press, 2015); PS Berman, *Global Legal Pluralism: A Jurisprudence of Law Beyond Borders* (Cambridge University Press, 2012); R Michaels, 'Global Legal Pluralism' (2009) 5 *Annual Review of Law & Social Science* 243.

[21] *Masterpiece Cakeshop, Ltd v Colorado Civil Rights Commission*, 584 US __ (2018).

[22] *Lee v Ashers* [2018] UKSC 49, [2020] AC 413.

such a concept of law in legal scholarship. Under traditional 'positivist' definitions of law as the command of a sovereign,[23] non-state law would clearly not satisfy the criteria for being 'law'. Modern theorists, however, including modern 'positivists', frequently take the view that the legal status of a norm is conferred through a collective understanding of a community that the norm is binding. These approaches emphasise the importance of the 'internal perspective' (how a norm is viewed by a member of the affected community) rather than relying solely on identifiable objective characteristics of the norm.[24] We cannot define our way out of the reality that non-state forms of rules are felt by many individuals to be just as compelling as, and sometimes more compelling than, state law. If lawyers are concerned with law as a matter of social reality, rather than institutional form, then the existence of non-state law is impossible to deny as a social fact (which does not preclude the possibility that state law would wish to be resistant to that social fact). These non-state forms of law are, importantly, not necessarily constrained by national boundaries[25] – the 'social practices' they describe are not necessarily those of national societies, or sub-groups within a single state, but may themselves be global or regional or entirely deterritorialised (particularly as communications technologies have enhanced the possibility of delocalised social interactions). Non-state law may thus not only reflect a legal pluralism within the state, but potentially beyond it.

In its openness to the application of other sources of law, private international law *could* mean not just applying foreign law, but non-state law. This has traditionally only been permitted in the context of arbitration, but it is expressly permitted under the (soft law) Hague Principles on Choice of Law in International Commercial Contracts, approved by the Hague Conference in 2015.[26] Private international law is thus potentially a gateway to the broader universe of law recognised by scholars of legal pluralism.[27] It offers a possible way in which national legal systems might be receptive not just to foreign law but to law beyond the state. The decision whether and to what extent to open that gateway – to embrace or resist pluralism? And what pluralism? – is a challenge faced by all legal systems. These questions also, of course, arise in a purely domestic context in which private international law issues would not ordinarily be considered. But private international law may in any case be adapted as a mechanism to mediate between different forms of legal ordering, rather than only between potentially applicable forms of state law, and as such may become utilised as a mechanism for opening or closing off the recognition of non-state law within the state. Where

[23] Most closely associated with J Austin, *The Province of Jurisprudence Determined* (J Murray, 1832).

[24] Perhaps most closely associated with HLA Hart, *The Concept of Law* (Oxford University Press, 1961).

[25] See, eg, W Twining, *General Jurisprudence: Understanding Law from a Global Perspective* (Cambridge University Press, 2009).

[26] See: www.hcch.net/en/instruments/conventions/full-text/?cid=135. For discussion, see generally, A Mills, *Party Autonomy in Private International Law* (Cambridge University Press, 2018) 491–520.

[27] See, eg, Muir Watt, 'Conflicts of Laws Unbounded' (n 20).

a relationship or situation crosses borders, the argument for the application of non-state law is, however, potentially strengthened as the case for the application of any particular state law is weakened by the cross-border connections, and the non-state law may by contrast cut across national boundaries (as in the case, for example, of many forms of religious law). Such an argument has been particularly successful in the context of arbitration because many arbitrators may view the process of arbitration itself as institutionally detached from state law.[28] The application of non-state law in such cases potentially opens up another avenue for the substantive harmonisation of private law and avoiding regulatory conflict – not through a coordinated selection of a single state law, but through the shared acceptance that commonly accepted forms of non-state law should instead govern the legal relationship, that is, of legal pluralism beyond the state.

V. Conclusions

This chapter began with an observation that private international lawyers are often, but not invariably, pluralist in their outlook. Although true (or at least defensible), this observation risks masking the deep complexity and ambivalence of the relationship between private international law and pluralism.[29] Private international law may be understood as a product of a limited form of interstate pluralism – as a set of rules generated by the coexistence of national systems of private law, which seeks to minimise the risks of conflict created by that diversity. It may thus be understood as serving a systemic function, whether regional or international, which requires private international law rules themselves to be harmonised and operate on a higher level. Private international law may also, however, be understood as itself a subject of pluralism – part of the diverse law of each national system, reflecting the culture and values of that system, and potentially embracing a plurality of approaches and values, not just between states but also within them. These opposing perspectives may also be countered by a third lens, which views private international law as playing a more active role, not just shaped by its context but also in turn shaping that context. In situations where pluralism may be under challenge by impulses to centralise or harmonise, private international law may support pluralism through allowing for the coexistence of order and diversity. Private international law may ask judges to act in service of

[28] See further, eg, K Boele-Woelki, 'Party Autonomy in Litigation and Arbitration in View of the Hague Principles on Choice of Law in International Commercial Contracts' (2016) 379 *Recueil des Cours* 35, Ch V; Helfand (n 20); G Saumier, 'The Hague Principles and the Choice of Non-State "Rules of Law" to Govern an International Commercial Contract' (2014) 40 *Brooklyn Journal of International Law* 1; M Pryles, 'Application of the Lex Mercatoria in International Commercial Arbitration' (2003) 18 *International Arbitration Report* 21; TE Carbonneau (ed), *Lex Mercatoria and Arbitration: A Discussion of the New Law Merchant* (Kluwer, 1998).

[29] See further, eg, VR Abou-Nigm and MBN Taquela (eds), *Diversity and Integration in Private International Law* (Edinburgh University Press, 2019).

values and interests beyond those of their particular local order, to recognise the equal value of foreign legal systems. And private international law may finally shape pluralism itself, by determining how open a legal system is to diversity, and whether this extends to rules of non-state law. The difficulty of these questions is reflected in the uncertainties around the function of private international law as a discipline – but their richness is also reflected in the diversity of perspectives adopted by private international law scholars and scholarship.

3

The Private International Law of Mediated Settlement Agreements

THALIA KRUGER

Tribute

Jonathan Fitchen is the master of authentic instruments. His book,[1] which was published shortly before his untimely death, is a testimony to his excellent academic skills: his knowledge of languages, his attention to detail, his care in analysis, his inquisitive mind, his ability to find information in the most obscure places, and his clarity of expression.

It is unfortunate that he did not have the opportunity to dig into the wonderous world of mediated settlement agreements, their relation to authentic instruments and their recognition across borders. Jonathan would have been able to straddle both commercial and family agreements, as he had done for authentic instruments. When reading for this chapter, I sorely missed being able to discuss the intricacies and contradictions with Jonathan. He would have been able to write this chapter better than I can.

I. Introduction

The idea of this chapter is to build on the work that Jonathan has done on authentic instruments in private international law. It starts with the question what mediated settlement agreements are. They have different natures. These differences have an effect even if the agreements do not migrate to other legal systems, but a cross-border element inflates the differences. Whether the agreements are authentic instruments or something else will determine how they travel across borders, how they are accepted or recognised in the places they travel to, and which papers they need for their travels.

[1] J Fitchen, *The Private International Law of Authentic Instruments* (Hart Publishing, 2020).

For the purposes of this contribution, the distinction between mediation and conciliation is not material. Conciliation can also lead to a settlement agreement. Such agreement would raise the same questions from a private international law perspective as settlement agreements after mediation would. Thus, the contribution consistently uses mediation as a broad term to include conciliation and other similar processes under which an independent third party assists the disputing parties in coming to an amicable solution.

After an attempt at clarifying what mediated settlement agreements are, the analysis below will turn to the question how these can be enforced.

II. What are Mediated Settlement Agreements?

The first difficulty is to find a definition of a mediated settlement agreement. In essence, such agreement is not very different from any other type of agreement. The difference is not in the result, but in the process that led to the agreement. If parties managed to negotiate the agreement themselves, without the assistance of a mediator, why should they be at a disadvantage as compared with parties that achieved the exact same result with the help of a mediator? For the purposes of recognition and enforcement, the parties with an agreement that they negotiated themselves will often be in the same position as those with an agreement reached through mediation, ie, they have a (new) contract that can be enforced as a contract.[2] But the Singapore Convention does place the parties who used a mediator in a better position.[3]

One might then wonder whether the distinction lies in the fact that some agreements are the result of a settlement after a dispute, while others are just an agreement to do or not to do something. A mere agreement is, generally speaking, not immediately enforceable (but this point is elaborated further below). Parties agree to do something. If one of them does not keep their promise, a dispute arises and then they go to court or to an arbitral tribunal, or they seek to settle their dispute in another way (alternative dispute settlement), ie, through negotiation or mediation.

Various policymakers on national, EU and international levels have sought to encourage people to settle their disputes amicably and to stay out of the courts.[4]

[2] See the general overview by E Sussman, 'The Final Step: Issues in Enforcing the Mediation Settlement Agreement' (2008) 2 *Contemporary Issues in International Arbitration and Mediation: The Fordham Papers* 343.

[3] United Nations Convention on International Settlement Agreements Resulting from Mediation, adopted 20 December 2018, entered into force 12 September 2020 (Singapore Convention).

[4] See, for instance, different approaches in 11 EU Member States, discussed by G De Palo et al, '"Rebooting" the Mediation Directive: Assessing the Limited Impact of its Implementation and Proposing Measures to Increase the Number of Mediations in the EU' (European Parliament, 2014), available at: www.europarl.europa.eu/RegData/etudes/etudes/join/2014/493042/IPOL-JURI_ET(2014)493042_EN.pdf; G De Palo, 'A Ten-Year-Long "EU Mediation Paradox" When an EU Directive

There are various reasons for this policy: amicable forms of dispute settlement are cheaper for the persons involved and for society, it assists in decluttering courts with long waiting times, and agreements are more inclined to bring sustainable solutions, as they are supported by the parties and have not been imposed on them from some authority. Even though these agreements are more likely to be adhered to by parties, policymakers also want to ensure that the parties walk away with something enforceable. If not, they would be worse off than parties who used the court system. So, it would be a bit strange for policymakers to keep people out of court only for them to be stuck with a weak result and possibly a need to later turn to a court after all.

For this very reason, as early as in 2008, the EU Mediation Directive sought to ensure enforceability.[5] The Directive requires EU Member States to make sure that the outcome of mediation can be enforceable nationally.

Once it is enforceable nationally, international enforcement would ensue in the domains in which EU instruments regulate cross-border enforcement. These domains cover many civil and commercial matters.[6]

However, *how* these agreements can be enforced across borders depends on *what* the agreements are.

A. Are they Authentic Instruments?

Jonathan Fitchen explained in his book what authentic instruments are. First, he distinguished between private and public documents. Private documents bear no evidentiary value.[7] Authentic instruments are a sub-category of public documents, because they are drawn up by a public official or issued by a public office.[8] Such

Needs To Be More … Directive' (European Parliament, 2018), available at: www.europarl.europa.eu/RegData/etudes/BRIE/2018/608847/IPOL_BRI(2018)608847_EN.pdf.

[5] Directive 2008/52/EC of 21 May 2008 on certain aspects of mediation in civil and commercial matters [2008] OJ L136/3.

[6] Regulation (EU) No 1215/2012 of 12 December 2012 on jurisdiction and the recognition and enforcement of judgments in civil and commercial matters (Brussels Ia); Regulation (EC) No 4/2009 of 18 December 2008 on jurisdiction, applicable law, recognition and enforcement of decisions and cooperation in matters relating to maintenance obligations (Maintenance Regulation); Regulation (EC) No 2201/2003 of 27 November 2003 concerning jurisdiction and the recognition and enforcement of judgments in matrimonial matters and the matters of parental responsibility (Brussels IIa); Regulation (EU) 2019/1111 of 25 June 2019 on jurisdiction, the recognition and enforcement of decisions in matrimonial matters and the matters of parental responsibility, and on international child abduction (Brussels IIb); Regulation (EU) No 650/2012 of 4 July 2012 on jurisdiction, applicable law, recognition and enforcement of decisions and acceptance and enforcement of authentic instruments in matters of succession and on the creation of a European Certificate of Succession (Succession Regulation); Regulation (EU) 2016/1103 implementing enhanced cooperation in the area of jurisdiction, applicable law and the recognition and enforcement of decisions in matters of matrimonial property regimes (Matrimonial Property Regulation); Regulation (EU) 2016/1104 implementing enhanced cooperation in the area of jurisdiction, applicable law and the recognition and enforcement of decisions in matters of the property consequences of registered partnerships (Partnership Property Regulation).

[7] Fitchen (n 1) 30.

[8] ibid, 21.

'public office' could be a notary, a person not working as an official but exercising a public function attributed to them by the state.

Turning to mediated agreements, they could be authentic instruments if they are officialised by a notary. The fact that the notary signs and stamps the agreement gives it authenticity. This serves an evidentiary purpose: the agreement now carries a presumption that its content is true. The notary confirms that the parties have agreed to this particular resolution of their dispute. The notary, unlike a court, does not establish or attribute the rights of the parties. The notary only confirms what the parties have said their rights are.[9] They will have difficulty to later contest that they had said that these were the rights. However, they (or someone else) could still contest the legality of what was decided. In other words, the notary has not made a final decision about the rights and parties may still turn to a court for this purpose. What they can request of a court after they have mediated an agreement, is a question for domestic procedural law and falls beyond the scope of this contribution.

However, the signature of a mediator does not turn a mediated settlement agreement into an authentic instrument, as a mediator generally is not an official or a person exercising an official duty such as a notary.

B. Are they Court Settlements?

In some instances, mediation takes place within the ambit of formal court proceedings. This can take place at various stages. Domestic procedural law can either require judges to refer parties to mediation or in some cases court structures have mediation chambers embedded. It is also possible that parties in the course of the proceedings decide themselves that a settlement might be possible and that they opt for mediation with such a goal.

If the parties reach a mediated agreement while the court proceedings are still pending, they might be able to enter this into a settlement judgment. A court settlement is not the same as a judgment, since the judge did not determine the rights and obligations of the parties, but only noted that the parties agreed about this themselves. In the EU instruments on recognition and enforcement, court settlements are mentioned separately from judgments, alongside authentic instruments and judgments.[10] Yet, apart from setting the condition of enforceability at the place where the court settlement was made, the Regulations contain no separate conditions; they refer to the same procedure as for the enforcement of judgments. The important test is thus the status of the court settlement at its place

[9] Notaries can also confirm that a person holds a particular legal status, but this function falls beyond the scope of the present chapter.

[10] See, for instance, Brussels Ia Chapter IV (Arts 58–60); Maintenance Regulation Chapter VI (Art 48); Matrimonial Property Regulation Chapter V (Arts 58–60); Partnership Property Regulation Chapter V (Arts 58–60); Succession Regulation Chapter V (Arts 59–61).

of origin. The Hague Choice of Court and Judgment Conventions follow the same approach.[11] The Hague Maintenance Convention simply provides that settlements and agreements are covered by the same recognition and enforcement regime as court decisions.[12] The Brussels IIb Regulation pays more attention to authentic instruments and 'agreements', but no longer refers to 'court settlements' or 'settlements'. It defines an agreement as a document that is not an authentic instrument but that has been concluded by the parties and has been registered by a public authority.[13] Member States must communicate to the European Commission the public authorities that can register such agreements.[14] The Commission will make this information available on its e-justice portal.[15]

Not all court settlements are the same. In some cases, a judge has to check the agreement before it can actually have any effect between the parties. This might be the case for instance when children are involved and the judge has to verify that the agreement does not infringe the best interests of the children.[16] The question then arises whether the mediated settlement agreement that becomes a court settlement changes its nature: does it, after being checked by a judge, enter into the realm of judgments? The answer under Brussels IIb is 'no': a separate set of rules applies. However, the answer is not always this clear in other domains. This question becomes of particular pertinence when the mediated settlement agreement has to travel across borders, as will be explained below.

C. Are they Mere Agreements?

If the mediated settlement agreement does not take the form of an authentic instrument or of a court settlement, it is nothing more than a mere contract. As explained, the only difference is that this agreement came about after a dispute, while other agreements are generally made when there is no dispute. On the contrary, people enter into agreements to get something from someone they trust or to cooperate with a seemingly reliable counterparty.

[11] Hague Convention of 30 June 2005 on Choice of Court Agreements, entered into force 1 October 2015 (Hague Choice of Court Convention) Art 12; Hague Convention of 2 July 2019 on the Recognition and Enforcement of Foreign Judgments in Civil or Commercial Matters, not yet in force (Hague Judgments Convention) Art 11.

[12] Hague Convention of 23 November 2007 on the International Recovery of Child Support and Other Forms of Family Maintenance, entered into force 1 January 2013 (Hague Maintenance Convention) Art 19(1).

[13] Brussels IIb Art 2(2)(3).

[14] Brussels IIb Art 103(1)(a).

[15] ibid, Art 103(4). The information is not yet available, presumably because the Commission will publish all information on all Member States at the same time.

[16] Brussels IIb Regulation contains specific certificates for authentic instruments and agreements: Annex VIII for divorce and Annex IX for parental responsibility. The court or competent authority can only issue the Annex IX certificate if there are no indications that the agreement is not contrary to the best interests of the child (Art 66(3)).

This characteristic of being a post-dispute agreement makes a mediated settlement agreement special. However, for enforcement purposes an agreement is an agreement and not enforceable without going to court again.[17] The advent of the Singapore Convention changed this legal logic. As Schnabel notes, this Convention created a 'new category of legal instrument on the international plane, elevating what would otherwise be a mere contract to a sui generis status'.[18] Schnabel adds that this approach was controversial.[19] At the same time, mediated settlement agreements do not lose their status as contracts and parties can still rely on aspects of contract law.[20]

For scholars of private international law this raises characterisation issues. For us, it must be clear when something is a 'mere' agreement and when it is a post-dispute agreement. How will we know? Who will tell? Must there be an agreement to mediate?[21]

III. Enforcement

It is said that mediated settlement agreements are most often respected,[22] because parties have reached the agreement themselves and therefore feel a sense of ownership along with their responsibility to do as they promised they would. However, the greater the number of mediation agreements that exist, the larger the risk becomes of some of them not being respected and needing enforcement with the help of a state authority. Moreover, if there is no certainty that the result actually has legal weight, why would anyone spend their time and energy on a process that takes more out of them than laying their disputes at the door of someone else?[23] National and EU legislators are increasingly encouraging parties by various methods to stay out of court and try using mediation or other forms of amicable settlement to achieve that.[24] But what kind of justice is that if parties walk away with an empty promise, only to have to go to court anyway? Even though parties will not always need to use the enforcement mechanism, the fact that it exists can incentivise mediation and provide parties with the peace of mind that justice will be done.[25]

[17] Sussman (n 2).

[18] T Schnabel, 'The Singapore Convention on Mediation: A Framework for the Cross-Border Recognition and Enforcement of Mediated Settlements' (2019) 19 *Pepperdine Dispute Resolution Law Journal* 1, 9.

[19] ibid.

[20] ibid, 11.

[21] Not under the Singapore Convention. This was apparently deliberately left out to avoid complication; see ibid 14.

[22] Sussman (n 2) 344.

[23] See also, Schnabel (n 18) 2–3.

[24] See, as a recent example, Brussels IIb Recital 43. See also Sussman (n 2) 343–44, indicating the encouragement of, as well as the popularity and growth of, mediation already by 2008.

[25] Schnabel (n 18) 4 explains that the Singapore Convention, by ensuring enforcement, would provide an incentive to mediate.

Turning then to cross-border enforcement, this is even more challenging.[26] To start with, it is perhaps worth stating what used to be obvious: something (whatever it may be) can only be enforced in a foreign country if it is enforceable in the place where it was created. This very basic premise is true for authentic instruments and for judgments. It is only once enforceability has been established under domestic law that private international lawyers can consider how the document can travel across state borders. Even if enforceable domestically, parties might still face an extra hurdle when trying to enforce their mediated settlement agreements internationally.[27]

The question of *how* a document can travel, has two sub-questions. First, through which legal (legislative or treaty) means, and second, though what kind of process.

A. The Legal Instruments

On the international level, the United Nations General Assembly adopted the Singapore Convention on International Settlement Agreements Resulting from Mediation in 2018.[28] After 46 states signed the Convention on the day that it was opened for signature (7 August 2019),[29] various other states have also ratified it. It entered into force on 12 September 2020 between the first ratifying states (Fiji, Qatar and Singapore) and ratifications are increasing. The European Union has yet to decide whether it will ratify the Convention. The Member States cannot ratify it individually as the matter of mediation belongs to the external competence of the European Union.[30] In the United Kingdom, the Ministry of Justice held a consultation about possible ratification.[31]

Additionally, UNICTRAL has amended its Model Law on International Commercial Mediation and International Settlement Agreements Resulting from Mediation[32] (previously the Model Law on International Commercial Conciliation).[33] The amended version contains a new section on international

[26] SI Strong, 'Realizing Rationality: An Empirical Assessment of International Commercial Mediation' (2016) 73 *Washington & Lee Law Review* 1973, 2054 states that her survey indicated that the perceived degree of difficulty to enforce mediated settlement agreements is markedly higher for international than for domestic situations.

[27] Schnabel (n 18) 3.

[28] United Nations General Assembly Resolution A/RES/73/198 of 20 December 2018.

[29] See: www.singaporeconvention.org/jurisdictions.

[30] The EU has competence to regulate on Mediation – see Consolidated Version of the Treaty on the Functioning of the European Union [2008] OJ C115/50 (TFEU) Art 81(2)g) (The EU has taken up its competence to regulate on the matter internally, by way of the Mediation Directive and various regulations on cross-border enforcement (see above (n 5).) The Singapore Convention, from its side, permits participation by regional economic integration organisations (Art 12).

[31] The consultation was open from February to April 2022, see: consult.justice.gov.uk/.

[32] Amended version adopted in 2018, see: uncitral.un.org/sites/uncitral.un.org/files/media-documents/uncitral/en/annex_ii.pdf.

[33] Previous version adopted in 2002, see: uncitral.un.org/sites/uncitral.un.org/files/media-documents/uncitral/en/03-90953_ebook.pdf.

settlement agreements and their enforcement.[34] The lack of such enforcement mechanism was a source of major criticism against the previous version of the Model Law.[35]

The Singapore Convention is to some extent modelled on the successful New York Convention on the Recognition and Enforcement of Foreign Arbitral Awards of 1958.[36] The Singapore Convention applies to international settlement agreements. 'International' is defined with reference to the parties and the place of performance of the agreement.[37] The place where the agreement is concluded is irrelevant. This is different from the New York Arbitration Convention, which is aimed at 'foreign' arbitral awards, thus issued in a different state from where enforcement is sought. While the New York Arbitration Convention does the private international law exercise of ensuring that something that is enforceable in one state becomes enforceable in all other Contracting States, the Singapore Mediation Convention operates in a different way. It aims to make agreements enforceable irrespective of the place where the mediation took place. The New York Convention applies to arbitral awards issued in other states. It is not limited to awards concluded in other Contracting States, although states can make a reservation that they will only apply the Convention to fellow Contracting States, ie, restrict the Convention to a reciprocal application.[38] But rather than being merely transnational, the Singapore Convention defies borders: it contains no concept of a mediation seat. Therefore, enforcement cannot be determined according to what would be the situation in some states of origin as there does not seem to be a State of origin.[39] This makes understanding it from a private international law perspective challenging, as will become clear in the next section.

Outside the Singapore Convention, the international enforcement of mediated settlement agreements can only be achieved by changing their nature into something enforceable such as a court judgment or an arbitral award.[40] On the EU level, many Regulations govern cross-border enforcement in various domains of civil law.[41] These Regulations work in the way described above, ie, through the mechanism of authentic instruments or court settlements,[42] or in the case of Brussels IIb 'agreements'.

[34] UNCITRAL Model Law 2018 (n 32) s 3.

[35] Sussman (n 2).

[36] Entered into force 7 June 1959 (New York Convention). This Convention is successful in the sense that more than 160 States are party to it, see: uncitral.un.org/en/texts/arbitration/conventions/foreign_arbitral_awards/status2.

[37] Singapore Convention Art 1(1).

[38] New York Convention Art I(3).

[39] Schnabel (n 18) 21.

[40] E Chua, 'Enforcement of International Mediated Settlements without the Singapore Convention on Mediation' (2019) 31 *Singapore Academy of Law Journal* 572 discusses these options in international, regional and domestic law.

[41] See the instruments mentioned in (n 6) above.

[42] See C Esplugues and JL Iglesias, 'Mediation and private international law: improving free circulation of mediation agreements across the EU' in 'The Implementation of the Mediation Directive, Compilation of In-depth Analyses for the European Parliament's Committee on Legal Affairs' (European

B. The Process for Enforcement

The Singapore Convention's scope relating to instruments covered by the instrument is restricted to mediated settlement agreements in the narrow sense. It excludes court settlements that can be enforced as judgments and settlement agreements recorded as arbitral awards and enforceable as such.[43] Judgments can be enforced through other international instruments, such as the Hague Choice of Court Convention[44] and the Hague Judgments Convention.[45] For arbitral awards we have the New York Convention. It makes sense that a settlement agreement should not simultaneously fall under various regimes of enforcement, as this might undermine procedural efficiency and legal certainty. If a court settlement is not regarded as a judgment and thus cannot be enforced through this route, it seems that the Singapore Convention remains available. The qualifier for enforceability as a court judgment refers to the legal position in the state of the court.[46] Therefore, if the mediated settlement agreement has the same weight as a court judgment in that state, the Singapore Convention route is unavailable. This remains so even if there is no international convention applicable to the international enforcement of the settlement-turned-judgment. For arbitration the qualifier is different: enforceability is not to be assessed from the point of view of the law of the state of the seat (where the arbitral award was legally speaking created) but the law of the state where enforcement is sought.[47]

Settlements that the parties have reached themselves without a mediator are not covered by the Singapore Convention either.[48] Here again, a scholar of private international law might get a bit nervous by the blurriness of the category: what if the mediator was involved at the start, the process broke down, but one of the parties subsequently had a change of heart and conceded some points in order to get to a settlement after all?

The Singapore Convention does not require double exequatur, ie, that the agreement must first be declared enforceable by the court of the place where it was made.[49]

The Convention does not call for any form of authenticity of the mediated agreement. It is only required that the agreement resulted from the settlement

Parliament, 2016) 70, available at: www.europarl.europa.eu/RegData/etudes/IDAN/2016/571395/IPOL_IDA%282016%29571395_EN.pdf. See also, I Kunda and M Tičić, 'Authentic Instruments and Court Settlements under the Twin Regulations' in L Ruggeri, A Limante and NP Vogrinc (eds), *The EU Regulations on Matrimonial Property and Property of Registered Partnerships* (Intersentia Online, 2021).

[43] Singapore Convention art 1(3). According to Schnabel (n 18) 24, the exclusion of mediated settlement agreements that can be recognised as judgments was very important for the EU.

[44] Above (n 11).

[45] ibid.

[46] Singapore Convention Art 1(3)(a)(ii).

[47] Schnabel (n 18) 27.

[48] Schnabel, ibid, 18–19, explains that the Working Group discarded the option of including all settlements in their Convention.

[49] Concerning this choice, see ibid, 13.

of a commercial dispute, that it was signed by the parties, and that a mediator was involved.[50] The settlement agreement does not even have to be contained in a single document.[51] The involvement of a mediator must be proved at the time when enforcement is sought and can be done by the mediator's signature on the agreement, a written declaration by the mediator, or an attestation by the mediation institution where the mediation was carried out.[52] This list is not exhaustive, and any other means of proof may be used.

Interestingly, the Singapore Convention imposes no further requirements concerning the mediator.[53] The mediation might have been institutional, which means that some quality check could take place by the institution (for instance working with lists of accredited mediators, requiring training to be placed on the list). However, the nature of those quality controls is entirely in the hands of the institutions. At the same time, mediations do not have to be institutional. Mediators do not have to be accredited. Mediations do not have to be a structured process in order to benefit from the enforcement regime of the Singapore Convention. The Working Group that drafted the Convention did consider suggestions to limit the Convention to structured mediation processes but decided not to do so as it was not clear what this limitation would exactly entail.[54]

Even if national legislators impose quality controls, these do not apply under the Singapore Convention, exactly because the Convention does not work through the requirements of national law. For instance, a requirement that mediators have to be licensed does not translate into the Singapore Convention. The fact that the mediator was not licensed will not constitute a ground to regard the agreement as null and void and, consequentially, a refusal to enforce it.[55] It is possible that an agreement cannot be enforced in the place where it was drawn up but can be enforced elsewhere if it complies with the minimum requirements of the Convention. This again defies private international law and the 'obvious' statement above that a document can only be enforceable elsewhere if it is enforceable in the place where it was created.

When considering quality controls, the grounds for refusing enforcement of the mediated settlement agreement are also relevant. Regarding the quality standards for the mediator, the authority addressed may refuse enforcement if the party opposing enforcement proves that '[t]here was a serious breach by the mediator of standards applicable to the mediator or the mediation without which breach that party would not have entered into the settlement agreement'.[56] Three reasons why this quality control is not very strong are: (i) that it only applies if

[50] Singapore Convention Arts 1(1) and 4.
[51] ibid, Art 2(2); Schnabel (n 18) 28.
[52] Singapore Convention Art 4(1).
[53] The Working Group did discuss independence and qualifications, but in the end did not include this in the Convention; Schnabel (n 18) 19.
[54] Schnabel, ibid, 15–16.
[55] Under the Singapore Convention Art 5(1)(b)(i); see Schnabel, ibid, 44.
[56] Singapore Convention Art 5(1)(e).

the party opposing enforcement invokes and proves it; (ii) the provision does not regulate what the applicable standards are; and (iii) the standards only become relevant under the high threshold that the breach of the standard was so serious that without it the party would not have entered into the settlement agreement.

The next possible quality control is that the mediator was not impartial or independent and failed to disclose this, to the extent that the failure to disclose 'had a material impact or undue influence on a party without which failure that party would not have entered into the settlement agreement'.[57] This ground for refusal should also be raised and proved by the party opposing enforcement. It is good that this quality control is there, but its bar is high.

If enforcement would be contrary to public policy, it may also be refused, even on the requested authority's own motion.[58] This provision is similar to that of the New York Convention,[59] and other international instruments on recognition and enforcement.[60] It is widely accepted that the provision on public policy must be interpreted restrictively.[61] Interestingly, though, the Singapore Convention does not use the shorthand for this restrictive interpretation that has become a custom in the Hague Conventions (and in EU instruments), namely the word 'manifestly'. This does not seem to mean a lower threshold for invoking public policy as a ground for refusal; the drafters used the words of the New York Convention and expect the same high standard to apply.[62]

C. Recognition and/or Acceptance

The Singapore Convention also applies to the recognition of mediated settlement agreements, but its drafters deliberately refrained from using the word 'recognition'. During the negotiation of the Convention, the European Union opposed the inclusion of recognition of mediated settlement agreements, on the basis than 'recognition' is reserved for acts of states (such as judgments).[63] The Convention uses the word 'relief' to refer to enforcement and the type of recognition that is necessary in order to get to enforcement. Concerning recognition, for *res iudicata*-type purposes, the Convention allows a party to 'invoke the settlement agreement

[57] ibid, art 5(1)(f).

[58] ibid, art 5(2)(a).

[59] Above (n 36) Art V(2)(b).

[60] See, for instance, the Hague Choice of Court Convention Art 9(e); Hague Judgments Convention Art 7(1)(c).

[61] F Garcimartín and G Saumier, 'Explanatory Report to the Hague Convention of 2 July 2019 on the Recognition and Enforcement of Foreign Judgments in Civil or Commercial Matters' (HCCH, 2020) available at: www.hcch.net/en/instruments/conventions/publications1/?dtid=3&cid=137, para 259; T Hartley and M Dogauchi, 'Explanatory Report to the Hague Convention of 30 June 2005 on Choice-of-Court Agreements' (HCCH, 2013), available at: www.hcch.net/en/instruments/conventions/publications1/?dtid=3&cid=98, paras 153 and 189.

[62] Schnabel (n 18) 54.

[63] ibid, 35.

in accordance with its rules of procedure and under the conditions laid down in this Convention, in order to prove that the matter has already been resolved'.[64] In this way, the Convention avoids the word 'recognition' so as to circumvent the debate on what can or cannot be recognised, while it does provide a mechanism to prevent litigation of a settled dispute.

Over the years, the European Union has moved from 'recognition' of authentic instruments to 'acceptance' of such. The difference in wording indicates that recognising a judgment is subject to fewer checks than required for authentic instruments. The difference is very clear in the recent Brussels IIb Regulation: while a recognising authority does not check the jurisdiction of the court that issued a judgment, it does check the jurisdiction in the case of an authentic instrument.[65]

IV. Conclusion

It is a good idea that parties take matters into their own hands and settle their disputes out of court. However, out of a concern for persons in a vulnerable position, some national legislators have imposed certain safeguards and quality controls. Under EU Regulations in the field of civil and commercial matters, enforcement of mediated settlement agreements takes place through national quality controls: enforcement in another state is only possible if the agreement is enforceable in the place where it was drawn up. It must qualify either as a court settlement or an authentic instrument.

If a mediated settlement agreement is an informal agreement that parties reached with the help of a neutral third person (thus qualifying under the definition of 'mediation'), it will not automatically be enforceable. This seems logical from a private international law perspective: it is impossible to recognise more than what exists where it was created.

The Singapore Convention, however, does not follow such private international law logic. It goes beyond the questions of what is enforceable and authentic. It goes beyond the territorial question of where an agreement was reached. The Singapore Convention will not only lead to more enforcements of mediated settlement agreements, but also pose a new challenge for scholars of private international law.

[64] Singapore Convention Art 3(2). Schnabel (n 18) 39 states that the provision contains a functional definition of recognition without using the word.

[65] Brussels IIb Art 64 provides that the section on the recognition and enforcement of authentic instruments and agreements only applies to such instruments and agreements in that they have been formally drawn up or registered in compliance with the Regulation's jurisdiction rules.

4

Vulnerability and Private International Law: Mapping a Normative Approach Towards Asymmetrical Substantive Equality

LORNA E GILLIES

I. Introduction

The first two decades of this century have already witnessed an increasing range of inequalities between individuals across borders. These inequalities have common aspects. There are a variety of reasons for inequality which manifest as vulnerability. The first reason is that inequality often arises from socio-legal or socio-economic challenges. Operating at the level of the individual, micro examples of inequality and vulnerability arise in a wide range of civil, commercial, private and family relationships including matters of private rights and status. Operating at the level of the state, macro examples of inequalities are the protection of the environment, the preservation of fundamental human rights, the stability and regulation of global markets (finance, food, fuel), and access to justice.[1] The second reason is that inequality is not restricted by geography, but is very frequently cross-jurisdictional in its scope and impact.[2] The third reason is that inequality increases parties' vulnerability by exposing them to greater risk of detriment or harm based on status or the context of a legal relationship.

[1] United Nations General Assembly, Seventy-fourth session, Agenda item 19(a), Sustainable development: implementation of Agenda 21, the Programme for the Further Implementation of Agenda 21 and the outcomes of the World Summit on Sustainable Development and of the United Nations Conference on Sustainable Development, Resolution Adopted by the General Assembly of 15 October 2019 74/4. Political declaration of the high-level political forum on sustainable development convened under the auspices of the General Assembly, para 20, p 4 available at: documents-dds-ny.un.org/doc/UNDOC/GEN/N19/318/21/PDF/N1931821.pdf?OpenElement.

[2] H Muir Watt, 'Jurisprudence Without Confines: Private International Law as Global Legal Pluralism' (2016) 5 *Cambridge International Law Journal* 388.

The consequences of inequality and vulnerability can be wide ranging, rendering norms and laws inappropriate and ineffective in theory and unjust, unconscionable[3] and manifestly unfair in practice.[4] Furthermore, these consequences magnify when inequality occurs across borders where different norms, laws and enforcement mechanisms apply directly or indirectly. This inequality-vulnerability spectrum presupposes two points. The first is the need to conceptualise and recognise vulnerability as a consequence of a normative, substantive or procedural inequality. The second is that the risk of vulnerability can result in harm or detriment to individuals in cross-border relationships and disputes arising from them.

Therefore, in order to mitigate against the risk of vulnerability, it is important to consider private international law's approach and response. At the policy level, we are reminded of Remien's point that it is 'the duty of the State to balance social or economic inequalities between its citizens or to make access to justice easier for those in particular need of it'.[5] At the legislative and pragmatic levels, the technique of private international law differs in the recognition of vulnerability in a wide range of cross-border situations. Some illustrative examples include jurisdiction for maintenance proceedings, the return of cultural objects,[6] rules of recognition to secure the prompt return of the abducted child,[7] proposals for protection of vulnerable adults,[8] mental health and capacity,[9] cross-border divorce,[10] cross-border succession,[11] delicts,[12] insolvency,[13] and jurisdiction and choice

[3] R Banu, 'Conflicting Justice in Conflict of Laws' (2020) 53 *Vanderbilt Journal of Transnational Law* 461.

[4] Case C-307/19 *Obala I lučice d.o.o v NLB Leasing d.o.o* [2021] ILPr 21, Opinion of AG Bobek, para 133.

[5] M Reimann, 'American Private Law and European Legal Unification: Can the United States be a Model?' (1996) 3 *Maastricht Journal of International and Comparative Law* 217.

[6] Council Regulation (EU) No 1215/2012 of the European Parliament and of the Council of 12 December 2012 on jurisdiction and the recognition and enforcement of judgments in civil and commercial matters (recast), [2012] OJ L351/1 (Brussels I Recast) Art 7(4).

[7] Convention of 25 October 1980 on the Civil Aspects of International Child Abduction, entered into force 1 December 1983 (Hague Child Abduction Convention) Art 3.

[8] In 2022, the European Commission conducted an Open Consultation of the Hague Convention on the International Protection of Adults. In 2023, the European Commission issued a proposal for an EU Regulation on Jurisdiction, Applicable Law, Recognition and Enforcement of Measures and Cooperation in Matters Relating to the Protection of Adults together with a Annex to the Regulation proposing that EU Member States adopt the Hague Convention on the International Protection of Adults 2000: COM (2023) 280 FINAL 2023/0619 (COD) 31.05.2023. See also P Beaumont and P McEleavy, *Anton's Private International Law*, 3rd edn (W Green, 2011) para 18.02.

[9] Mental Capacity Act 2005.

[10] Council Regulation (EU) No 1259/2010 of 20 December 2010 implementing enhanced cooperation in the area of the law applicable to divorce and legal separation, [2010] OJ L343/10.

[11] Council Regulation (EU) No 650/2012 of the European Parliament and of the Council of 4 July 2012 on jurisdiction, applicable law, recognition and enforcement of decisions and acceptance and enforcement of authentic instruments in matters of succession and on the creation of a European Certificate of Succession, [2012] OJ L201/107.

[12] Council Regulation (EC) 864/2007 of the European Parliament and of the Council of 11 July 2007 on the law applicable to non-contractual obligations (Rome II), [2007] OJ L199.

[13] Council Regulation (EU) No 2015/848 of the European Parliament and of the Council of 20 May 2015 on Insolvency Proceedings (recast), [2015] OJ L141, Recitals 10, 11, 17.

of law rules to protect consumers, employees and insureds.[14] There is a broader question as to how far private international law recognises vulnerability through its techniques of characterisation, connecting factors, party autonomy, mandatory rules and public policy. However, to date, there has been little consideration of how vulnerability has been recognised and addressed through both the *theory and technique* of private international law. If vulnerability is not given due recognition through theory and technique of private international law, the purpose of private international law is diminished and its potential in responding to vulnerability is not fully realised.

The aim of this chapter is to consider the role of private international law in recognising and addressing the concept of vulnerability from the perspective of theory and practice (technique) by mapping a normative approach. Rather than framing a party, state or context *as vulnerable*, it is necessary to assess existing theoretical and technical approaches in private international law which support all three (party, state, context). The objective of this chapter is structured around three sections. Following this introductory section, the next section considers the concept of vulnerability. The third section reviews how the theory of private international law through appropriateness, conflicts justice, pragmatism and effectiveness engages with vulnerability. It then turns to consider the extent to which the 'universal'[15] concept of vulnerability operates through techniques of private international law. Finally, the fourth section of the chapter provides a response premised on Fredman's four 'pillars' of asymmetrical substantive equality.[16] Taken together, each of these pillars can be used to support private international law's role in dealing with vulnerability in cross-border cases. By applying asymmetrical substantive equality, the theory and technique of private international law will be better equipped in future to engage with the inherent risk of vulnerability in cross-border cases.

II. Vulnerability: Mapping the Concept and the Parties in Private International Law

The purpose of this section is to identify the concept of vulnerability and the parties affected in private international law. It will be considered how vulnerability arises in cross-border cases involving parties and states.

A. The Concept of Vulnerability

It is the role of norms and laws to underpin and enact rights and protections in the territorial jurisdiction. Where applicable, rules of recognition seek to recognise

[14] Regulation (EU) 1215/2012 (n 6) Arts 17–23.
[15] J Henning, *Law and the Relational Self* (Cambridge University Press, 2019).
[16] S Fredman, *Discrimination Law* (Oxford University Press, 2011).

and respect norms, law and judgments in other territorial jurisdictions. The shared objective is that the rule of law is respected and access to justice can occur regardless of individual status or territorial connection to a sovereign state. The concept of vulnerability connects to the broader relationship between public international law, human rights, and private international law.

Vulnerability has been categorised as legal, political, social or economic. It arises in a variety of circumstances and varies across different fields. In response, public international law deals with the issue of vulnerability through conventions which may recognise vulnerability to persons, states and in different contexts. The European Convention on Human Rights (ECHR) provides inalienable rights which engage with private international law; the right to a fair trial (Article 6), the right to respect for private and family life (Article 8), the right to freedom of expression (Article 10), the right to marry (Article 12), the right to an effective remedy (Article 13), and prohibition of discrimination (Article 14).[17]

Vulnerability is a universal concept.[18] Henning reminds us that '(W)e are all equally vulnerable in our human nature. We should all be seen as equally vulnerable'.[19] In addition, vulnerability can be both contextual[20] and particular. For example, the Opinion of the European Human Rights Agency on Business and Human Rights identifies 'persons in situations of vulnerability, such as women, persons with disabilities, indigenous people and children'.[21] An insight into the most recent scope of vulnerability – in the context of business and human rights – is through the recommendations of the Parliamentary Assembly of the Council of Europe. In 2019 it proposed to extend business and human rights to include 'gender-based human rights abuses ... vulnerable population groups [and] whistle-blowers'.[22]

This chapter draws on Peroni and Timmer's concept of vulnerability, which is also from a human rights perspective. In their paper, the authors assessed the concept of vulnerability through international human rights law and European Court of Human Rights (ECtHR) jurisprudence. Peroni and Timmer explain that

[17] European Union Agency for Fundamental Rights, 'Improving access to remedy in the area of business and human rights at the EU level – FRA Opinion 1/2017' (10 April 2017), available at: fra.europa.eu/sites/default/files/fra_uploads/fra-2017-opinion-01-2017-business-human-rights_en.pdf.

[18] M Neal, '"Not Gods but Animals": Human Dignity and Vulnerable Subjecthood' (2012) 33 *Liverpool Law Review* 177, 186–87.

[19] Henning (n 15).

[20] The European Law Institute's report also includes migrant workers, reflecting the consequences of serious human rights violations which they rightly identify as 'often more egregious, including harm to life and limb, property, or the environment'; European Law Institute, 'Report on Business and Human Rights: Access to Justice and Effective Remedies' (2022), available at: www.europeanlawinstitute.eu/fileadmin/user_upload/p_eli/Publications/ELI_Report_on_Business_and_Human_Rights.pdf, 31.

[21] FRA Opinion (n 17) 8.

[22] Council of Europe, Parliamentary Assembly, 'Human rights and business – what follow up to Committee of Ministers Recommendation CM/Rec (2016) 3?', Recommendation 2166, para 1.9, Resolution 2311, para 8.4.6, and Reply to Recommendation 15015, available: at pace.coe.int/en/files/28298.

vulnerability is 'not a label, but a layered concept'.[23] Vulnerability arises due to actual or potential harm to a natural or legal person or a state. In turn, vulnerability can be caused by the actions of a state, a third party or a combination of actions of both the third party and state. In order to engage further dialogue about the treatment and application of vulnerability in the theory and technique of private international law, this chapter takes a holistic approach. It follows Peroni, Timmer and Henning's 'universal' concept of vulnerability by considering the causes of vulnerability due to actions of the state, a third party or combination.

B. Who is a Vulnerable Party in Private International Law?

Having recognised that vulnerability is a universal and layered concept, three broad examples will be used to demonstrate a vulnerable party in private international law. First is vulnerability of a natural person. Vulnerability may arise as a result of a natural person's status, relationships or circumstances. Vulnerability can arise prior to or as a result of a cross-border dispute. Recognising the status or circumstances of parties as vulnerable can have important practical benefits. For example, the Hague Child Abduction Convention 1980,[24] the Hague Convention on the International Protection of Adults 2000,[25] and the EU Regulation on mutual recognition of protection measures in civil matters[26] recognise the concept of the abducted child, the status of the vulnerable adult and the protection of a person's 'life … integrity, liberty [and] security'[27] respectively.

Legal persons may also be subject to harms leading to inequality and vulnerability. Small and medium sized enterprises (SMEs) compete and operate at a commercial and competitive disadvantage to other legal entities such as corporations and limited liability partnerships. SMEs do not fall within the category of the traditional consumer. Unsecured creditors, such as employees and consumers, are also vulnerable to the actions of the debtor business.

Whilst it may be beneficial to recognise vulnerability to parties on a case-by-case basis, there is a tension in this general approach. It has been argued that rather than framing individuals or groups 'as' vulnerable – which may potentially subject individuals or groups to unwarranted or unnecessary 'stigma, stereotyping, humiliation or violence' – it is necessary to first identify those *at risk of vulnerability within* existing norms and laws. The effect of norms and laws may threaten, reduce or negate an individual's or group's status, protection, rights and remedies

[23] L Peroni and A Timmer, 'Vulnerable groups: The promise of an emerging concept in European Human Rights Convention law' (2013) 11 *International Journal of Constitutional Law* 1056.

[24] Above (n 7).

[25] Convention of 13 January 2000 on the International Protection of Adults, entered into force 1 January 2009.

[26] Council Regulation (EU) No 606/2013 of the European Parliament and of the Council of 12 June 2013 on mutual recognition of protection measures in civil matters, [2013] OJ L181/4.

[27] Regulation (EU) 606/2013, ibid, Recital 6. Words removed and added for syntax.

in comparison to other individuals or groups. The imbalance may result in an inequality. In turn, and in response to the risks to individual rights and protections, vulnerability 'within' norms and laws must become a greater part of discussions and debates in private international law than has occurred previously.

Second is vulnerability of a state. For example, the United Nations (UN) Sustainable Development Goals (SDG) Declaration 2015 states that if the aim of sustainable development is a 'just, equitable, tolerant, open and socially inclusive world' then to achieve this 'needs of the most vulnerable are met'.[28] The concept of vulnerability is at the heart of many global issues such as migration, human rights, access to essential services, access to justice and remedies. Two SDGs can be provided by way of short example. SDG 10 is concerned with reducing inequalities, and SDG 16 provides for securing peace, justice and strong institutions. The mixed technique of private international law has been shown to add value in discussions on 'remedies for human rights violations and environmental damage',[29] first through the combined influence of judicial authority and its increasing effect on cross-border commercial and family cases in a human rights context; second, legislative authority derived the relationship between the Hague Conference on Private International Law (HCCH) and its constituent members and other international organisations such as the United Nations and the United Nations Conference on Trade and Development (UNCTAD); and, third, policy orientation and priorities through shared pragmatic objectives in securing jurisdiction, choice of law and recognition of judgments.

Having identified the categories of vulnerable parties in private international law, the three causes of vulnerability can now be considered. These are actions of a state, the actions of a third party, or the actions of the state and third party in combination. The effect of these causes/sources will now be considered for each of the parties in the previous section. The purpose of this subsection is to illustrate how vulnerability is both universal in its reach and contextual in its impact.

C. Vulnerability of Natural Persons

The causes of vulnerability of natural persons will now be considered. The first cause of vulnerability to a natural person may be the actions of a state. The state's first order law and/or policy may result in inequality, imbalance, lack fitness for purpose or adequate protection for parties. In private international law terms, the imbalance may extend through the scope, interpretation or absence of a particular ground of jurisdiction, choice of law or enforcement of judgment.

One example of the actions of the state may be through its regulatory, legislative and/or judicial response to new and emerging activities. New technologies,

[28] UN General Assembly Resolution A/RES/70/1 of 21 October 2015, para 8.

[29] eg, European Law Institute Report (n 20) 43; and most recently, *Jalla v Shell International Trading and Shipping Co* [2021] EWCA Civ 1559.

such as artificial intelligence, smart contracts and blockchain, are good examples. These new technologies invite us to return to Kessedjian and Boele Woelki's two questions from the not too distant past.[30] These two questions are 'which court decides?' 'Which law applies?' These two key questions continue to resonate in disputes concerning artificial intelligence,[31] smart contracts,[32] blockchain and post Brexit approaches to data privacy. In international sales contracts, there is a continued tension between appropriateness of law,[33] conflicts justice and material justice in securing access to justice and consumer enforcement cooperation in different countries.

Another example may be where the state seeks to specifically protect parties through human rights and non-discrimination. In the context of human rights, the concern is the 'heightened vulnerability and marginalisation'[34] of vulnerable parties who have been subjected, and continue to be subjected, to serious 'business related human rights abuses'.[35] In the context of non-discrimination, a recent example is the recognition of foreign same and opposite sex civil partnerships. Another example is the role of choice of law in the international protection of adults. Schedule 9, paragraph 13 of the Mental Capacity Act (Northern Ireland) 2016 illustrates that 'where a protective measure is taken in one country, the conditions for implementation are governed by the law of the other country'.[36] The forum's mandatory rules may also override the parties' choice of state law. There should be alignment between the state's rules of recognition and its public policy. Whilst the state may or may not permit, by its own laws, legal relationships as same or opposite-sex civil partnership or marriage, surrogacy or adoption, the state of recognition should not use its public policy to deny recognition of such relationships.

The second cause of vulnerability to a natural person may be the actions of a third party. There may be a prior existing relationship or a degree of proximity between the parties. The prior existing relationship may be civil and commercial, in contract, tort or delict. One party might act in breach of an agreement on jurisdiction or choice of law. The relationship may instead be of a family or private nature, such as one between spouses, partners, parents, legal representatives and children.[37] The parties may be connected by virtue of proximity of the third-party actions, such as harm arising from business conduct and activities in the jurisdiction.

[30] K Boele-Woelki and K Kessedjian (eds), *Internet: Which Court Decides? Which Law Applies?* (Kluwer Law International, 1997).

[31] LE Gillies, 'Artificial Intelligence, International Private Law and the Application of Law: Which Court Decides? Which Law Applies?' on file with author.

[32] The Law Commission of England and Wales has recently undertaken a review of the application of smart contracts in English Law, see: www.lawcom.gov.uk/project/smart-contracts/.

[33] R Brownsword, *Law 3.0* (Routledge, 2020).

[34] European Law Institute Report (n 20) 8.

[35] ibid.

[36] Mental Capacity Act (Northern Ireland) 2016, sch 9, para 13.

[37] *In Re B (A Child) (Care Proceedings: Jurisdiction)* [2013] EWCA Civ 1434, [2014] 2 WLR 1384 [37].

The third cause of vulnerability to a natural person is where a combination of state and party activity results in vulnerability to that natural person. For example, tactical procedural remedies available in one state may be used by one party against another party. For example, a court may grant an anti-suit injunction to restrict commercial proceedings abroad.[38] A court may grant a freezing (Mareva) injunction to preserve proceedings in the forum, and to avoid the risk or threat of 'unjustified dissipation of assets'.[39] A court may grant a Hemain injunction in divorce proceedings[40] to prevent proceedings in the other state. The combination of state and third-party activity may cause vulnerability to the natural party in matters of jurisdiction (scope, exclusions, connecting factors), choice of law (validity) or in seeking to secure recognition and enforcement of a foreign judgment.

D. Vulnerability of Legal Persons

The causes of vulnerability of legal persons will now be considered. The first cause of vulnerability of a legal person is the action of the state. In jurisdictional terms, the application of the centre of main interests (COMI) is a double-edged concept. It supports the interests of creditors by distinguishing between main and secondary insolvency proceedings. However, the ability of a legal entity to change its seat/right of establishment on the basis of COMI may result in a commercial disadvantage, increase risk and vulnerability of third party 'local'[41] creditors.[42] For choice of law, the theory of establishment/incorporation determines if an entity in one country can change seat, or establish a branch, agency or subsidiary in another country. The theory of incorporation enables a legal entity to forum shop by moving seat, resulting in a corresponding risk to third-party creditors.[43]

The second cause of vulnerability of a legal person is through the actions of a third party. For example, the vulnerability will depend on the civil or commercial relationship between the parties. Jurisdiction and choice of law rules in contract and tort may be a consideration, including the mandatory rules of the forum if not the state concerned.

The third cause of vulnerability of a legal person is the combined action of a state and third party. For example, there may be a situation where the action of the state prefers to support, through its jurisdiction and choice of law rules, the

[38] Case C-159/02 *Turner v Grovit* [2005] 1 AC 101.

[39] *Fundo Soberano de Angol v Jose Filomeno dos Santos* [2018] EWHC 2199 (Comm) [86].

[40] *ER v FB* [2018] EWFC 18; *cf Lachaux v Lachaux* [2021] EWHC 1797 (QB), [2022] EMLR 2 [33] on the recognition of a foreign judgment despite a Hemain injunction having been granted against the foreign state.

[41] M Tsimplis, 'Modified Universalism and Cross-Border Insolvency of Shipping Companies' [2020] *Journal of Business Law* 345, 346.

[42] MT Epeoglou, 'The Recast European Insolvency Regulation: a missed opportunity for restructuring business in Europe' (2017) 6 *UCL Journal of Law and Jurisprudence* 31, 44.

[43] ibid, 44.

third party over the legal entity. There may be a connection between this cause of vulnerability and the treatment of the legal entity under its theory of incorporation of its choice of law rule for particular harms suffered by the legal entity such as in tort for breach of competition, anti-competitive practice, privacy and data protection, or environmental damage. Similar to the previous example, regulatory arbitrage may result in vulnerability of the legal entity to harm caused by the action – or inaction – of the state in addition to, or compared with, the other party.

E. Vulnerability of States

The three causes of vulnerability of states will now be considered. The first cause of vulnerability of states is through the actions of another state or group of states. The actions of a state may be legislative, judicial, constitutional or political. There is a broader connection between private and public international law. To begin with, three examples may illustrate the point.

The first example is the effect of external competence of supranational institutions on states. For example, the EU's external competence arose out of Article 65 of the Treaty of Amsterdam.[44] It has directly or indirectly influenced both the Europeanisation of private international law and the laws of EU (and non-EU) Member States since. One consequence of external competence has been where the European Union has 'leverag[ed]'[45] non-EU Member States to adjust to EU approaches. Writing prior to Brexit, Mills suggested that a supranational legal system such as the EU's may indirectly influence the relationship between the EU Member State and its relationship with non-EU Member states. The EU's recent decision refusing to approve the UK's request to join the Lugano Convention is a pertinent post Brexit example – consequence – of the (in)direct influence of the European Union on the United Kingdom as a non-EU Member State.[46]

The second example is the tension between the legitimacy of anti-suit injunctions in cross border disputes and the principle of territoriality in international law. Dickinson has recently identified this as the 'interference paradox'.[47]

[44] J Basedow, 'The Communitarisation of the Conflict of Laws Under The Treaty of Amsterdam' (2000) 37 *Common Market Law Review* 687, 698–99; O Remien, 'European Private International Law, The European Community and its Emerging Area of Freedom, Security and Justice' (2001) 38 *Common Market Law Review* 53, 74–75; CT Kotuby Jr, 'External Competence of the European Community in the Hague Conference on Private International Law: Community Harmonization and Worldwide Unification' [2001] *Netherlands International Law Review* 1, 3–4 and 17–18; considered in the context of cross-border consumer protection beyond the EU in LE Gillies, *Electronic Consumer Contracts and International Private Law A Study of Electronic Consumer Contracts* (Ashgate, 2008) 59–62.

[45] A Mills, 'Private International Law and EU External Relations: Think Local, Act Local Global or Think Global, Act Local?' (2016) 65 *International & Comparative Law Quarterly* 541, 573.

[46] European Commission, 'Assessment on the application of the United Kingdom of Great Britain and Northern Ireland to accede to the 2007 Lugano Convention' COM(2021) 222 final.

[47] A Dickinson, 'The Interference Paradox' [2020] *Law Quarterly Review* 569, 574, considering the consequences of the English Court of Appeal decision in *SAS Institute Inc v World Programming Ltd* [2020] EWCA 599, [2020] 1 CLC 816.

The paradox is that whilst there may be a general justification for granting an anti-suit injunction, the recent Court of Appeal case *SAS Institute Inc v World Programming Ltd* highlights an overarching concern about 'improper interference with sovereignty'[48] of the foreign state. Dickinson's response is that the English court has two choices: continue with the existing approach in granting anti-suit injunctions, or grant them only if there is evidence of genuine risk of '"unwarranted" judicial interference' by the foreign system in English proceedings.[49]

The third example is the law of state immunity. The European Convention on State Immunity 1972, the State Immunity Act 1978, and the UN Jurisdictional Immunities Convention 2005 all apply a 'restrictive theory'[50] which uphold state immunity for (civil)[51] claims brought against it by other states. However, as the recent conflict in Ukraine demonstrates, this does not extend to criminal acts. Furthermore, any changes to the legal or political relationship a state has with another state or group of states, such as Brexit, may impact the policy[52] and legislative approach.

Turning now to the second cause of vulnerability of states. Here we can consider the actions of a third party. The third parties referred to here are multinational enterprises (MNEs) with a seat in one jurisdiction operating globally via subsidiaries, branches or agencies. The activities of the third party may impact the state on matters such as data protection, competition, environmental damage and so on. The state's jurisdiction and choice of law rules may be challenged by the regulatory arbitrage between state regulation and self-regulation. The consequence of regulatory arbitrage raises challenges not just for the state, but also its citizens. The example is the 'big five' MNEs in the technology sector which have been involved in litigation concerning, inter alia, abuse of a dominant position,[53] data protection,[54] privacy[55] and patent infringement[56] which has directly or indirectly impacted states and their citizens.

The third cause of vulnerability to a state is due to the combined action of another state and third party. This is similar to the discussion above, when a state, through *lis pendens*[57] or anti-suit injunction,[58] affects the sovereignty of another state.

[48] Dickinson, ibid, 574.

[49] ibid.

[50] Beaumont and McEleavy (n 8) para 6.13.

[51] s 16 of the State Immunity Act 1978 confirms that Part 1 of the Act, applicable to proceedings brought in the UK by or against other States, does not apply to criminal proceedings.

[52] At the time of writing, there is an ongoing debate about the future scope and terms of the EU–UK Northern Ireland Protocol and the corresponding risk of breach of international and trade law should the UK government decide to unilaterally vary it.

[53] Case T-167/08 *Microsoft Corp v European Commission* [2012] 5 CMLR 15.

[54] Case C-131/12 *Google Spain SL v Agencia Espanola de Proteccion de Datos* (AEPD) [2014] QB 1022.

[55] Case C -311/18 *Data Protection Commissioner v Facebook Ireland Ltd* [2021] 1 WLR 751; Case C-498/16 *Schrems v Facebook Ireland* [2018] 1 WLR 4343.

[56] *Samsung Electronics Co Ltd v Apple Retail UK Ltd* [2014] EWCA Civ 376.

[57] *West Tankers Inc v Allianz SpA (The Front Comor)* [2012] EWCA Civ 27, [2012] Bus LR 1701.

[58] *Turner* (n 38).

As above, it is also similar to where a state legitimises the actions of a third party which may impinge on another state.

The next section of the chapter considers the extent to which current theoretical approaches in private international law taken account of vulnerability in cross border cases.

III. Vulnerability and the Theory and Techniques of Private International Law

The theory of private international law is based, in broad terms, on four key concepts: appropriateness; conflicts justice; pragmatism; and effectiveness. The purpose of this section is to consider two things. First, is the extent to which the theoretical framework of private international law considers vulnerability of parties to cross-border disputes. Considering the concept of vulnerability in this way lends itself to the universal idea of vulnerability and balances the interests of vulnerable parties and states in cross-border disputes. The second part of this section broadly maps the techniques of private international law through consideration of selected techniques and examples.

A. Appropriateness

The first concept is appropriateness. Along with conflicts justice,[59] appropriateness is the principal basis upon which a court exerts its judicial authority in a cross-border case. One example which reflects the concept of appropriateness is the doctrine of *forum non conveniens*. Throughout the United Kingdom and common law jurisdictions, the doctrine has been used to determine whether another court is more appropriate to hear the dispute, in the interests of the parties and the ends of justice. However, is it evident that *forum conveniens* recognise and respond to inequalities and vulnerability and if so, how does it do so? The doctrine has increased in significance for a range of reasons. There has been application of the doctrine in determining whether a vulnerable person has been wrongfully removed from their habitual residence.[60] There has been recent consideration of the doctrine in relation to establishing jurisdiction for damages against business for human rights abuses.[61] In the United Kingdom, the European Union

[59] P Beaumont, '"Great Britain"' in J Fawcett (ed), *Reform and Development of Private International Law* (Oxford University Press, 2002) 208–09.

[60] *O (Court of Protection: Jurisdiction)* [2013] EWHC 3932 (COP), [2014] Fam 197.

[61] *Vedanda Resources Plc v Lungowe* [2019] UKSC 20, [2020] AC 1045, considered by M Cornaglia, 'Vedanta Resources Plc v Lungowe [2019] UKSC 20 (Case Comment)' [2019] *European Human Rights Law Review* 309, 315.

(Withdrawal Agreement) Act 2020 removed the EU system of civil and commercial jurisdiction after the end of the Brexit transition period, leaving questions of jurisdiction over EU and non-EU defendants to be determined by the Civil Procedure Rules (CPR)[62] for proceedings in England, Schedule 8 to the Civil Jurisdiction and Judgments Act 1982 for proceedings in Scotland and *forum conveniens* in both cases. Arzandeh explains that the role of *forum conveniens* is twofold. First, it enables the court to assert its own jurisdictional competence, and second, it seeks to promote the state's 'jurisdictional values'.[63] *Forum non conveniens* may apply either in service out cases or where the defender seeks the court's discretion to sist/stay under section 49 of the Civil Jurisdiction and Judgments Act 1982. Arzandeh's historical analysis of the doctrine presents two broad points which provide an insight into the connection between appropriateness and vulnerability. The first point is that the traditional judicial application of the doctrine applied a broadly balanced approach. However, the second point made by Arzandeh is that a series of cases from *St Pierre* to *Spiliada* demonstrate that the doctrine was used to support a 'pro-plaintiff' stance,[64] favouring the English court over the foreign court and 'generat[ing] legal uncertainty and … economic inefficiency for litigants'.[65] Assessing the doctrine in this manner suggests a potential increased risk of vulnerability to litigants. Arzandeh concludes that in future it may be worth applying the doctrine 'on a more restrictive basis'[66] akin to what constitutes injustice under Article 6(1) ECHR.[67]

However, the pre-Brexit and post-Brexit jurisprudence of the UK courts has demonstrated that *forum conveniens* will continue to have a prominent role in determining whether UK courts are the appropriate place for the case against a foreign defender to be heard.[68] The doctrine continues to be considered across a wide spectrum of civil, commercial and private law disputes. For example, in *Stylianou v Toyoshima v Suncorp Metaway Insurance Ltd*,[69] the claimant had sustained substantial injury abroad and raised proceedings there. However, due to the seriousness of the injuries, she was unable to participate in proceedings abroad.

[62] *Brownlie v FS Cairo (Nile Plaza) LLC*; also known as *Cairo (Nile Plaza) LLC v Lady Brownlie* [2021] UKSC 45, [2021] 3 WLR 1011; A Briggs and A Dickinson, 'Reframing Jurisdiction: A New Scheme?' 2022 41(4) CJQ 317.

[63] A Arzandeh, *Forum (Non) Conveniens in England Past, Present and Future* (Hart Publishing, 2018) 8.

[64] ibid, 140.

[65] ibid, 119.

[66] ibid, 109.

[67] ibid, 131.

[68] LE Gillies, 'Appropriate Adjustments Post Brexit: Residual Jurisdiction and Forum Conveniens in UK Courts' [2020] *Journal of Business Law* 161; see also L Merrett, 'International Employment Law Cases Post Brexit: Choice of Law, Territorial Scope, Jurisdiction and Enforcement' (2021) 50 *Industrial Law Journal* 343, 346.

[69] *Stylianou v Toyoshima v Suncorp Metaway Insurance Ltd* [2013] EWHC 2188.

She sought service out to bring proceedings in England. The specific feature of the case was that the extent of the claimant's injuries rendered her vulnerable and unable to continue litigation abroad and that seeking to commence proceedings in the English courts, after liability had been admitted, the court was satisfied that this was not an abuse of process.

The doctrine also has application in family law cases. *Forum conveniens* has recently been applied by the English High Court in a case concerning the acute welfare of a 'highly vulnerable' child who had been brought to the United Kingdom by her father.[70] After protracted proceedings, the English court established jurisdiction under Regulation EC 2201/2003 Brussels IIbis on the basis of the child's habitual residence in the United Kingdom. The English court ordered the child's return to the United States.

Forum conveniens was also considered by the English court in determining a father's application for a stay of English wardship proceedings, brought by the mother, in favour of the Singaporean court instead. As a consequence of previously attempting to remove the child from Singapore, the mother was detained and subsequently deported from Singapore. The English court said that it was appropriate to refuse the stay. In doing so it was permitted to account of the mother's 'perception of vulnerability … and … great concern' if the English proceedings were stayed.[71] A further example of *forum conveniens* and habitual residence arose in the case *Chai v Peng*.[72] In determining a party's habitual residence, the court took account of expert evidence which referred to the connection between the party's vulnerability and the need for the 'continuity of case … in his social environment'.[73]

B. Appropriateness and *Lis Pendens*

Another example which relates to appropriateness of jurisdiction is *lis pendens*. Where proceedings relating to the same subject matter are raised in different jurisdictions, the principle of *lis pendens* may enable the court first seised to take jurisdiction. For example, the current Brussels Ibis Regulation (EU 1215/2012) on jurisdiction in civil and commercial matters operates *lis pendens* on the 'principle of allocation'.[74] As *lis pendens* supports the concept of forum selection, this may be to the defender's detriment, increasing their risk of defending proceedings in a state which may assert jurisdiction on a 'first past the post' basis.[75]

[70] *Re X (Care Proceedings: Jurisdiction and Fact Finding* [2020] EWHC 2742, [2021] 2 FLR 449 [46].
[71] *MB v GK, KF, GG* [2015] EWHC 2192 (Fam), [2016] 2 FLR 132 [110].
[72] *Chai v Peng* [2014] EWHC 3518 (Fam), [2015] 2 FLR 424.
[73] ibid, [19].
[74] Gillies, 'Appropriate Adjustments Post Brexit' (n 68) 166.
[75] Beaumont and McEleavy (n 8) para 8.121.

The golden thread that runs between appropriateness, conflicts justice, pragmatism and effectiveness is the 'parties' conflict interests'.[76] Parties conflicts interests is addressed by conflicts justice *and* material justice, as the next section will consider.

C. Conflicts Justice

The second concept is conflicts justice. As readers will already be aware, conflicts justice is concerned with 'appropriateness'[77] through the 'application of the law of the proper state'.[78] Two points must be considered. The first is the parties' conflicts interest and the second is respect for material or substantive[79] justice.

By parties' conflicts interest, we mean that each party has their own, individual expectations of which court and law applies to their relationships and any disputes arising from them.[80] However, parties' knowledge of their substantive rights remains subjective, which may contribute towards increased vulnerability. Vonken provided an objective response that a party may be only expected to be aware of the 'essential principles of justice … of their own law'.[81] However, this response does not fully address a range of issues such as lack of information symmetry between the parties and the challenge of pleading and proving foreign law.[82] To ensure the appropriate application of state law, conflicts justice must take account of material[83] or substantive[84] justice.

Since private international law follows the first order rules of the state,[85] material justice must also be respected.[86] Material justice is focused on ensuring that

[76] APMJ Vonken, 'Balancing Processes in International Family Law, On the determination and weighing of interests in the conflicts of laws and the "openness" of the choice of law system' in TM De Boer, *Forty Years On: The Evolution of Post War Private International Law in Europe, Symposium in Celebration of the 40th Anniversary of the Centre of Foreign Law and Private International Law, University of Amsterdam*, 27 October 1989 (Kluwer, 1990) 171–73.

[77] SC Symeonides, 'Material Justice and Conflicts Justice in Choice of Law' in P Borchers and J Zekoll (eds), *International Conflict of Laws for the Third Millennium: Essays in Honor of Friedrich K Juenger* (Transnational Publishers, 2001).

[78] ibid.

[79] R Michaels, 'Private International Law and the Quest for Universal Values' in F Ferrari and DP Fernández Arroyo (eds), *Private International Law Contemporary Challenges and Continuing Relevance* (Elgar, 2019).

[80] Vonken (n 76) 178.

[81] ibid.

[82] *Brownlie* (n 62).

[83] Symeonides, 'Material Justice and Conflicts Justice in Choice of Law' (n 77) 13–14.

[84] Michaels (n 79).

[85] HLA Hart, *The Concept of Law* (Clarendon Press, 1961); A Mills, *The Confluence of Public and Private International Law: Justice, Pluralism and Subsidiarity in the International Constitutional Ordering of Private Law* (Cambridge University Press, 2009) 9–20.

[86] SC Symeonides (ed), *Private International Law at the End of the 20th Century: Progress or Regress?* (Kluwer Law International, 2000) 44–45.

the applicable law – and its *differences* compared with other substantive laws[87] – is identified. The purpose of this exercise is to ensure that the proper result – 'equal treatment'[88] of foreign and domestic law – is achieved. Symeonides' example that 'statutory choice of law rules'[89] which rely on connecting factors as techniques to link to the dispute to the relevant territory has proved correct. In EU private international law, connecting factors have been the principle 'methodological'[90] norm which set out – as well as limit/control – jurisdiction, choice of law and enforcement of judgments in furtherance of EU internal market objectives.

D. Pragmatism

The fourth concept is pragmatism. The purpose of pragmatism is to enable coherent, practical application of private international law.[91] Beaumont and McEleavy remind us that it is an 'anti-theor[etical]' construct in that it seeks to assess the operation of private international law with other jurisdictions, akin to comparative law.[92] For example, the English courts frequently consider 'pragmatism' as part of their assessment of the second limb in service out cases.[93] To that extent, pragmatism is about 'practicability and efficiency in doing justice in the present situation'.[94] Another valuable response to the theory of pragmatism is provided by Whincop and Keyes. These authors stated that 'pragmatism *means* policy'.[95] With this approach, the aims of pragmatism have been described as 'anti-foundational … forward looking … facilitating meaningful choice and action'.[96] Therefore, pragmatism is practical and policy orientated. To support a pragmatic approach, it is possible to implement 'choice influencing factors'[97] of legal certainty, predictability and uniformity. These three factors support the management of disputes as well as their avoidance. For example, choice of law for immovable property, *lex situs* regarded as an example of the 'principle of effectiveness'.[98]

[87] Banu (n 3) 521.
[88] Beaumont and McEleavy (n 8) para 2.95; M Bogdan, *Private International Law as Component of the Law of the Forum* (Martinus Nijhoff Publishers, Hague Academy of International Law, 2012) 80–81.
[89] Symeonides, *Private International Law at the End of the 20th Century* (n 86).
[90] C Semmelmann, 'The European Union's Economic Constitution under the Lisbon Treaty: Soul Searching Among Lawyers Shifts the Focus to Procedure' [2010] *European Law Review* 516, 532.
[91] MJ Whincop and M Keyes, *Policy and Pragmatism in the Conflict of Laws* (Ashgate, 2001).
[92] Beaumont and McEleavy (n 8) para 2.92.
[93] eg, as part of the assessment of evidence under the second limb to grant of service out under English Civil Procedure Rules: *Kaefer Aislamientos SA de CV v AMS Drilling Mexico SA de CV Atlantic Tiburon 1, The* [2019] EWCA Civ 10, [2019] 1 WLR 3514 [78].
[94] Beaumont and McEleavy (n 8) para.2.96.
[95] Whincop and Keyes (n 91) 2.
[96] Whincop and Keyes (n 91) 2–3.
[97] Beaumont and McEleavy (n 8) para 2.71; P Hay, O Lando and RD Rotunda, 'Conflict of Laws as a Technique for Legal Integration' in M Capelletti, M Seccombe and J Weiler (eds), *Integration Through Law*, Vol 1, Book 2, (Walter de Gruyter, 1986) 194.
[98] Beaumont and McEleavy (n 8) para 21.19.

As a choice influencing factor, legal certainty is often used by institutions and legislators as both an aim and a justification of a proposed convention, instrument or other legislation. In private international law, the aim of legal certainty is to enable the court, or state law, with the closest or most appropriate territorial connection to a dispute to apply. Justification for a legislative measure may be to secure legal certainty in furtherance of a policy objective or a societal need, such as vulnerability of parties, states or a particular context. Predictability of result is intended to enable parties to ascertain with reasonable certainty which court has jurisdiction and crucially which law applies.[99]

Legal certainty and predictability of result are high-level aims, which may or may not be experienced by parties in practice. Furthermore, in the absence of recognition of vulnerable parties or states, rules on standing and applicable law may result in detriment to vulnerable parties. For example, the recent FRA Report explains that in claims against businesses for human rights violations, burden of proof, representation or legal standing and applicable law are three of the most significant barriers to access to justice. There is a general demand that an individual plaintiff demonstrates a causal link between the activity, the harm caused and the damage. Not all states permit collective proceedings for such claims. General choice of law rule based on the place of damage restricts those proceedings – and damages – to that place.[100]

Therefore, how should pragmatism recognise and respond to vulnerability arising from cross-border relationships? There are three points to be made here. The first is that a dialogue should begin as to how various aspects of vulnerability of parties and states have been recognised in cross-border disputes to date. This means that *policy has a role to play in agenda setting and practice has a role to play* in mapping the issues and contributing responses. However, to be meaningful – thus avoiding 'unbridled methodological pluralism'[101] – a dialogue should begin on recognition of vulnerability in private international law. In doing so, we can be (re)introduced to Vonken's question – 'should conflicts law respond, and if so to what extent, to the social changes reflected in the evolution of contemporary private law?'[102] We should be beyond that question by asking how private international law should, in tandem with public international law and human rights law, respond to social changes reflected through vulnerable persons and states.

This links to the third point, namely the pragmatic response. The objective of pragmatism is to support 'unification and harmonisation and coordination'.[103] It is submitted that the first step should be coordination as a means of facilitating

[99] This is to be contrasted with predictability of decision, when legal certainty is favoured over discretionary-based judicial decision-making.

[100] European Union Agency for Fundamental Rights, 'Business and Human Rights – Access to a Remedy' (Luxembourg, 2020) 6, 8–9 and 13–14, available at: fra.europa.eu/sites/default/files/fra_uploads/fra-2020-business-human-rights_en.pdf.

[101] Vonken (n 76) 172.

[102] ibid.

[103] Beaumont and McEleavy (n 8) para.2.97.

Whincop and Keyes' forward-thinking, choice and action. The previous points on appropriateness, conflicts justice, pragmatism and effectiveness can provide the theoretical framework. The second step is to identify how techniques in private international law engage with vulnerability. The next section of the chapter considers examples from a range of techniques from characterisation of a dispute through to choice of law. Then taking Beaumont and McEleavy's approach of 'practicality and simplicity',[104] the penultimate section of this chapter suggests a four-step approach based on asymmetric substantive equality – participation, transformation, redistribution and recognition. Such an approach would reflect the 'open character of the conflicts law system … accommodate various adaptations and differentiations [whilst containing] methodological pluralism within acceptable limits'.[105]

E. Techniques of Private International Law

The next section broadly considers some selected techniques of private international law in cross-border cases and the extent to which these techniques recognise and address vulnerability of parties in cross-border disputes. The selected techniques are characterisation, connecting factors, capacity and party autonomy.

i. Characterisation and Connecting Factors

Characterisation or classification is the first step in a private international law dispute. It is the general role of the *lex fori* to classify the 'true issue or issues thrown up by the claim and defence'.[106] This exercise applies an 'internationalist spirit'[107] to identifying the issue, rather than a purely national approach which may have the effect of restricting or excluding the claim. In that sense, characterisation has an important role to play in supporting the recognition of vulnerability relative to the parties, the state or the context of the dispute as outlined in section III.

Connecting factors are an important technique in private international law. Their primary purpose is to determine a party's personal law.[108] Their secondary purpose is to determine the relevant legal system for the purposes of either jurisdiction, choice or law or both. Broadly speaking, connecting factors may be traditional and 'doctrinal',[109] such as domicile or religion.[110] Alternatively,

[104] ibid, para 2.94.
[105] Vonken (n 76) 173.
[106] *Macmillan Inc v Bishopgate Trust (No.3)* [1996] 1 WLR 387 (CA) per LJ Auld at 407A-B, cited in *Fiona Trust and Holding Corp. v Privalov* [2010] EWHC 3199 [152].
[107] *Atlantic Telecom GmbH, Noter* 2004 SLT 1031, [31] (Lord Brodie), quoting *Macmillan Inc*, ibid, 407B.
[108] Beaumont and McEleavy (n 8) paras 7.01 and 7.03.
[109] ibid, para 7.03.
[110] ibid.

connecting factors may be policy-orientated and 'contemporary',[111] such as habitual residence and nationality. Whilst it is beyond the scope of this chapter to examine in detail the benefits and limitations of both categories, these connecting factors have an important role to play in supporting the exercise of individual rights across borders. This role is more so when there is a risk of vulnerability to parties and the connecting factor – habitual residence in particular – must be established.

ii. *Connecting Factors and Capacity*

There have been recent cases where the recognition of party vulnerability has arisen relative to the connecting factor applicable to disputes concerned with abducted children and vulnerable adults.

With regard to the Hague Convention on the Civil Aspects of International Child Abduction 1980, it is two of the four defences to return of the child to the court of their habitual residence that are relevant. The purpose of these two defences is concerned with the child's 'risk' of being returned and their 'objection' to return. Specifically, Article 13(c) is the defence that returning the child would place that child in grave risk (or otherwise subject them to an intolerable situation). Article 13(d) is the defence that the child has reached a degree of maturity and objects to return. As readers know, these are fact-specific tests so turn on the circumstances of each individual case. Vulnerability is neither a term of art in the Convention itself or the original official supporting documentation of the HCCH.[112] However, at the time of writing, a search of the HCCH's INCADAT database shows that in the period from 1990 to 2021 approximately 67 decisions from Contracting States referred to the concept of the vulnerable party or vulnerability in international child abduction. In view of the chapter's focus on vulnerability, and the reader's patience, it is prudent to focus on a few of the most recent examples from the UK courts. In *W v A*,[113] the Scottish Inner House of the Court of Session upheld an appeal against the return of a child to Poland. The Court was satisfied that a 'child-centric'[114] approach should have been followed by the court and once the 'gateway'[115] of the child's objection was met, the defence was established, and return should not have been ordered. In this case, the first instance court had erred in law by placing greater weight on the Polish court's

[111] ibid.

[112] E Perez-Vera, 'Explanatory Report on the Convention on the Civil Aspects of International Child Abduction' (HCCH) and 'Actes et Documents de la Quatorzième Session' (6–25 October 1980, HCCH), both available at: www.hcch.net/en/instruments/conventions/specialised-sections/child-abduction.

[113] *W v A* [2020] CSIH 55, 2021 SLT 62.

[114] ibid, [10]–[11], citing Lady Hale in *Re M (Children) (Abduction: Rights of Custody)* [2007] UKHL 55, [2008] 1 AC 1288.

[115] *W v A* (n 113) [11].

decision and its disregard by the reclaimer (appellant). In *Re V and W (Hague Return Order: Lithuania)*[116] the English court was satisfied that the child's prior vulnerability – anxiety – justified an order to refuse return to its former habitual residence. In *Re S*,[117] the court followed the basis for grave risk in *Re C* that there must be 'clear and compelling evidence of a grave risk of harm or other intolerability which must be measured as substantial, not trivial, and of a severity which is much more than is inherent in the inevitable disruption, uncertainty and anxiety which follows an unwelcome return',[118] and was satisfied that there would be grave risk to the children and refused to order their separation and return. These very recent examples serve as illustrations that the defences are crucial to the effectiveness of the Convention on the one hand, the continued need to balance interests of parties and Contracting States on the other[119] and the recognition of the child – and on occasion the parent's – inherent and continuing vulnerability in such cases.

With regard to the Convention on the International Protection of Vulnerable Adults 2000, a range of cases highlight the relationship between the Convention's aims, habitual residence, *forum conveniens* and international comity of courts. In *Re MN* the question arose whether a foreign judgment could be enforced to enable a woman who lacked capacity to return to California.[120] The court held that the Mental Capacity Act 2005, Schedule 3, point 4 ensured that a person who lacked capacity had their best interests and affairs dealt with in the country of their habitual residence. The court held that party's habitual residence, and authority for its change, were key to the enquiry. The court held that the assessment of such authority should be according to California law.

The Hague Convention on the International Protection of Adults 2000 is applied in England through the provisions of Schedule 3 to the Mental Capacity Act 2005. There have been cases brought before the English courts which demonstrate how the court assesses, in the matter of a vulnerable adult, if there has been a change of habitual residence. In *O (Court of Protection: Jurisdiction)*, the question was whether a vulnerable adult who lacked capacity should be returned to England from Scotland.[121] The Scottish court had previously granted an interim welfare guardianship order on the basis of the adult's presence in the jurisdiction. The English court was asked to order the return of the adult to England. The English court confirmed that a change to habitual residence could be made on the basis of authority. Such authority could be justified on the grounds of necessity, provided the act was done in good faith and in the vulnerable person's best interests. On that basis, the English court held that the vulnerable adult was habitually resident in Scotland and that matters relating to welfare ought to be dealt with by the Scottish

[116] *Re V and W (Hague Return Order: Lithuania)* [2022] EWHC 739 (Fam).
[117] *Re S* [2020] EWHC 2940 (Fam).
[118] ibid.
[119] Perez-Vera (n 112) paras 9 and 41; *AD v SD* [2023] CSIH 17.
[120] *Re MN* [2010] EWHC 1926 (Fam).
[121] *O (Court of Protection: Jurisdiction)* [2013] EWHC 3932 (COP), [2014] Fam 197.

court. This approach was followed similarly in *AB v XS*.[122] The English court said it would be an 'inherent misuse of jurisdiction'[123] to order the return of a vulnerable adult who had been moved to Lebanon and had been habitually resident there for the past seven years. These two key issues, authority to change habitual residence on the grounds of necessity and integration as the test of habitual residence, were both considered in the case *In Re QD (Jurisdiction: Habitual Residence)*.[124] The English Court of Protection held that the vulnerable adult was integrated into life in Spain and therefore habitually resident there. The Court also held that there was no authority to remove the vulnerable adult to England on the basis of necessity. Instead, the Court held that the 'covert plan'[125] to remove the adult from Spain to England had been done 'by stealth'.[126]

These cases show two important points regarding the habitual residence of a vulnerable adult. The first point is that compared with cases involving children, there is no equivalent to the concept of parental responsibility for vulnerable adults. The second point is that the test for a change of habitual residence of a vulnerable adult is integration.[127] Both of them point to the need for future discussion on how private international law can build on existing protections for vulnerable adults, so as to be compatible with the best interests of the vulnerable adult and their human rights.

iii. *Party Autonomy: Commercial Contracts*

With regard to party autonomy, there appear to be differing opinions regarding its application to commercial and private law disputes. Most of the literature broadly accepts that parties should be entitled, as with any other terms which can be agreed, to select the jurisdiction and choice of law they see fit to meet their commercial and personal relationships.

From a policy perspective, the tension between vulnerability and jurisdiction can be summed up as occurring due to the overarching preference for party autonomy over protection; the category of cases excluded; where vulnerability is within the rule already versus where it is not; the risk of parallel proceedings and the criteria used to determine if the court can decline jurisdiction in favour of another foreign court.

In terms of the policy towards jurisdiction, vulnerability may manifest as 'litigation risk':[128] that is, the risk of legal proceedings occurring between parties to a commercial transaction. Whilst parties can manage litigation risk through

[122] *AB v XS* [2021] EWCOP 57, [2022] 4 WLR 13.
[123] ibid, [35] (Leiven J).
[124] *In Re QD (Jurisdiction: Habitual Residence)* [2019] EWCOP 56.
[125] ibid, [29].
[126] ibid.
[127] *AB v XS* (n 122) [27].
[128] R Fentiman, *International Commercial Litigation*, 2nd edn (Oxford University Press, 2015) 41.

party autonomy and negotiate contractual terms, there may be a continued – and elevated – transaction risk. These transaction risks are examples of universal vulnerabilities. We all recognise that (in no particular order) in the commercial context, regulatory compliance, competition/anti-competitive practices, inflation, pricing, energy costs, distribution, sustainability, environmental impact, and harms and employment rights are the most prevalent, universal concerns.

By comparison, the individual (natural person) in a private international law case is extremely limited in their ability to negotiate a choice of forum clause. The litigation risk may not be recognised (identified) or fully understood. These transaction risks are examples of the natural person/private consumer's universal vulnerabilities. The natural person's transactional risk ranges across regulatory compliance and arbitrage, the effect of competition on individual consumers/collective interests, sustainability and the environmental impact, pricing, data protection and privacy, remedies and dispute resolution.

One common example from the above is in the context of sustainable development. Kruger has recently reviewed UN SDG 10 – reducing inequalities – and proposes a mid-ground on party autonomy in this context. She accepts the party autonomy principle with two provisos: first, that 'the principle should not reinforce existing inequalities'; and second, that 'the rule should be tempered for vulnerable parties'.[129] Kruger presents an interesting conclusion that connecting factors might not be appropriate in the context of SDG 10. She also concedes that there should not be a departure (where it applies) from the *actor sequitur* principle and suggests that a *forum necessitasis* rule should be devised instead. These are most interesting points on how inequality should be part of debates concerning party autonomy in the context of SDG 10's aims. Whilst not all countries have an *actor sequitur* rule, a *forum necessitasis* rule may be feasible. However, *it* would need to be very specifically drafted for it to achieve the pragmatists' goal of political support and practical benefit.

In terms of the policy towards vulnerability, choice of law, or applicable law, fairs better. The Rome I Regulation EC 593/2008 for Contracts and Rome II Regulation EC 864/2007 for Non Contractual Obligations – both instruments continue to apply in the United Kingdom post Brexit – are still intrinsically premised on party autonomy. The same concerns that occur with jurisdiction agreements apply to agreements on choice of law. There may be a lack of recognition of vulnerability within the choice of law rule which prohibits parties from selecting a non-state, religious or secular law. There may also be vulnerability in either enabling parties to modify their initial choice(s) or through the concept of *dépeçage* – or splitting – of the applicable law.

[129] T Kruger, 'The Private Side of Transforming our World – UN Sustainable Development Goals 2030 and the Role of Private International Law – SDG 10: Reduced Inequalities' (Intersentia Online, 25 November 2021), available at: www.intersentiaonline.com/publication/the-private-side-of-transforming-our-world-un-sustainable-development-goals-2030-and-the-role-of-p/12, para 5.2.

The same scope for recognition of vulnerability applies to consumer and employee contracts, and in specific delicts concerned with product liability, breach of competition and environmental damage. However, there may be scope for giving greater recognition to vulnerability through the operation of mandatory rules which cannot be derogated from by contract or where they are a mandatory law of the forum.

Choice of law rules for 'protected'[130] consumer contracts may reflect the vulnerable interests of consumers. However, these rules are narrowly drafted to protect only those parties to which the measure applies. For example, choice of law rules for consumers only applies to 'final, private consumers' and does not extend to SMEs who may be conceptually distinct but experience similar economic or legal vulnerabilities with consumers in practice.

Both EU Regulations on contractual and non-contractual obligations contain choice of law rules which apply mandatory rules irrespective of party choice. These rules enable the law of a third state or the forum to override party choice where that rule is mandatory in character. Mandatory rules tend to be restricted to the territory of the sovereign state and are characterised as a rule to meet the political, social or economic objectives of that state. There may be scope to further examine, define and interpret the concept of vulnerability within these rules when the EU Commission conducts their review of the operation of these Regulations.

iv. Party Autonomy: Family Matters

However, the literature shows that there are quite different opinions regarding the justification for party autonomy for cross-border family law disputes. Beaumont and McEleavy are of the view that forum shopping and the risk to vulnerable parties are two reasons which explain why party autonomy is not a principle suited to family law disputes.[131] Carruthers has also thoroughly questioned the role of party autonomy in the regulation of adult relationships. She invites us to consider the extent to which party autonomy should be used to support party 'privilege or right'[132] to 'self-determination' as a matter of policy and regulation[133] on the one hand, and 'within the limits prescribed by law'[134] on the other. In favouring choice of law in family law which have a 'sufficient[ly] appropriate … connection to the parties' should be permitted subject to the 'normal control of forum public policy'.[135]

[130] P Stone, *EU Private International Law*, 3rd edn (Edward Elgar, 2014) 125.

[131] Beaumont and McEleavy (n 8) para 7.12.

[132] J Carruthers, 'Party Autonomy in the Legal Regulation of Adult Relationships; What Place for Party Choice in Private International Law' (2012) 61 *International & Comparative Law Quarterly* 881, 883.

[133] ibid, 884.

[134] ibid.

[135] ibid, 912.

IV. Vulnerability in Private International Law: Recognition Through Asymmetrical Substantive Equality

As mentioned earlier, Fredman's asymmetrical substantive equality is premised around what this author terms as four 'pillars. These pillars are 'participation, transformation, redistribution and recognition'. By applying these pillars reflexively, there is potential for private international law to take greater account of vulnerability to parties, countries and contexts in future through asymmetrical substantive equality. This can be achieved through ensuring vulnerability is central to private international law policymaking, legislative drafting, the judicial reasoning of national and supranational courts, and practice.

A. Participation

The four pillars start with participation. Participation is understood to be a wide-ranging concept which begins with engaging private international law in the debate and towards the representation of vested interests. We must consider how private international law ensures effective representation of vulnerability through the theory and techniques of private international law explored in this chapter. The theoretical influences of appropriateness, conflicts justice, pragmatism and effectiveness must be tempered with the techniques of private international law – classification, connecting factor, capacity and party autonomy. This pillar is closely connected to the second pillar.

B. Transformation

Participation is closely connected to the second pillar of 'transformation'. Transformation should 'respect and accommodate difference, removing the detriment but not the difference itself'.[136] In legislative terms, this means ensuring policies – and the evidence contained in them – are designed to identify a detriment and deal with it. This may become more significant as the United Kingdom continues to develop its own policies and legislation in private international law post Brexit. Following the previous section, in private international law terms, this should entail revisiting the various theories and techniques considered in sections three and four.

[136] Fredman (n 16) 30.

C. Redistribution

The third concept is redistribution. Redistribution is intended to improve efficiencies and reduce detriment. In private international law terms, this would mean improving existing policy, legislative and judicial approaches to enable parties being prevented from participating in or securing any justice due to rules of substance and procedure, as outlined in sections two, three and four.

D. Recognition

The fourth concept is recognition. Recognition means the ability to 'promote and redress' the balance *within* the rule. This is aligned with private international law as a second order legal norm.

Recognition may operate at the level of the state – ie, giving recognition to the laws of the foreign legal system and judgments of the foreign court. Here we are reminded of Kegel's 'altruistic state' concerned with the 'just ordering of private life … seeking the best and fairest solutions for all'.[137] Here the balancing exercise is in respecting state sovereignty but including vulnerability when seeking to balance the interests of parties with little, or tenuous, prior connections to states. This links to another example of recognition.

Recognition may also operate at the level of the party, ie, recognition of the status of the party or their legal relationship and how the rule is designed to reflect – recognise – that status or relationship. In addition to the examples in section IV, good examples can be found in cross-border family law. The Civil Partnership Act 2004 and the subsequent Marriage and Civil Partnership Acts 2013 and 2014 in England and Scotland respectively enabled same-sex civil partnerships to be converted into marriages. Furthermore, the recent introduction of the Civil Partnership (Scotland) Act 2020, section 3, provides recognition of cross-border civil partnerships as overseas relationships between parties of different sex.[138]

V. Conclusion

The aim of this chapter was to consider the role of the theory and technique of private international law in recognising and addressing vulnerability. It proposed an approach which can contribute towards securing conflicts justice whilst recognising and addressing vulnerability in cross-border cases.

[137] G Kegel, *International Encyclopedia of International Law, Volume III/1 'Fundamental Approaches'* (Mohr Siebeck, 2011).

[138] Following the UK Supreme Court's decision in *R (on the application of Steinfield) v Secretary of State for Education* [2018] UKSC 32, [2020] AC 1.

The objective of this chapter was to begin more explicit dialogue between vulnerability and private international law by mapping a normative approach. Rather than framing a party, country or context as vulnerable, it was shown that it is necessary to assess existing theoretical and technical approaches in private international law which recognise the risk of vulnerability of natural persons, states and legal entities. The objective of this chapter considered the concept of vulnerability and reviewed the theory of private international law through appropriateness, effectiveness, conflicts justice and pragmatism. It then considered the extent to which the Henning's 'universal' concept of vulnerability operates through techniques of private international law. The final section of the chapter provided a response premised on Fredman's four 'pillars' of asymmetrical substantive equality. Taken together, each of these pillars can be used to support private international law's role in dealing with vulnerability in cross-border cases. By applying asymmetrical substantive equality, the theory and technique of private international law will be better equipped in future to engage with the inherent risks of vulnerability in cross-border cases.

5

Private International Law as the Final Frontier for Feminist Scholarship?

JUSTIN BORG-BARTHET AND KATARINA TRIMMINGS*

I. Introductory Remarks

Shortly after Jonathan Fitchen took on the leadership of the Centre for Private International Law at the University of Aberdeen, the Centre membership turned to discussing areas in which our discipline would benefit from fresh perspectives. Inspired in part by our colleagues' work on the feminist judgments project,[1] we alighted on the problem of private international law scholarship's failure consistently to engage with gendered difference. With his *magnum opus* on authentic instruments approaching completion,[2] Jonathan embraced the idea of working together on a monograph analysing private international law from a feminist perspective – a considerable pivot from his more recent work.

Regrettably, a coronavirus pandemic and Jonathan's illness meant that the monograph was never to be. Still, our discussions had progressed sufficiently for a number of questions and problems to be identified. In the first instance, we noted that private international law suffered from a degree of rigidity which often made it somewhat unresponsive to the vulnerabilities of disadvantaged groups.[3] This was especially evident where the law had benefited from international or regional harmonisation which engendered a degree of entrenchment. If our discipline were to be more responsive to those needs, we asked, what systemic or targeted changes might be necessary?

* The authors are thankful to Benedetta Lobina and Magdalena Zabrocka for their invaluable research assistance. The usual disclaimer applies.

[1] See generally, The Scottish Feminist Judgments Project, available at: www.sfjp.law.ed.ac.uk/.

[2] J Fitchen, *The Private International Law of Authentic Instruments* (Hart Publishing, 2020).

[3] For a robust critique of the inherent contradictions in private international law's professed neutrality, see H Muir Watt, 'The Relevance of Private International Law in the Global Governance Debate' in H Muir Watt and DP Fernandez (eds), *Private International Law and Global Governance* (Oxford University Press, 2014).

Feminist legal theory has had a profound impact on our understanding of much of the law, challenging long-standing constructs of what is with new questions about whether it ought to be so. In public international law, for example, feminist scholars have critiqued the failure of the international system to account for male privilege and its marginalisation of women in the international system.[4] Similarly, private lawyers observe the influence of male heteronormativity in a broad array of private relationships, particularly as they pertain to the family,[5] but also in relation to male dominance in the market.[6] Others note barriers to justice for women arising from deficiencies in civil procedure.[7] With so much feminist analysis in private international law-adjacent disciplines, it is somewhat surprising that private international law has, perhaps uniquely, escaped sustained scrutiny with reference to gendered understandings of power and its entrenchment in the law.

Our discipline has tended instead towards a preference for objectivity which results in a degree of indifference to gendered experience. This is not to say that women are entirely unseen by the law, however. Indeed, Ralf Michaels and Ivana Isailović observe that 'PIL has always dealt with questions related to gender justice'.[8] By way of example, the initial intention of the Hague Child Abduction Convention[9] was to address the mischief of paternal child abduction.[10] Moreover, the Convention includes provision for derogation from rules on return in the event of exposure to domestic violence.[11] Equally, the Hague Maintenance Convention 2007 establishes a system of recovery of family maintenance obligations, designed to provide expeditious, low-cost routes for family members who are reliant on others.[12] In the context of existing family economic dynamics, women and children are the usual beneficiaries.[13] Still, in general terms, international and European instruments remain predominantly gender neutral in language and design.

[4] See, eg, for extensive discussion, H Charlesworth and C Chinkin (eds), *The Boundaries of International Law: A Feminist Analysis* (Manchester University Press, 2000).

[5] See, eg, ND Hunter, 'Marriage, Law, and Gender: A Feminist Inquiry' [1991] *Law and Sexuality* 9.

[6] See, eg, M Eichner, 'Market-Cautious Feminism' (2016) 69 *Studies in Law, Policy and Society* 141.

[7] Gema Fernández Rodríguz de Liévana, 'The fallacy of gender-neutral procedure is limiting women's access to justice' (*LSE Blogs*, 25 May 2017), available at: blogs.lse.ac.uk/wps/2017/05/25/the-fallacy-of-gender-neutral-legal-procedure-is-limiting-womens-access-to-justice/.

[8] Max Planck Institute for Comparative and International Private Law, Hamburg, 'Gender and Private International Law' (2019), available at: www.mpipriv.de/gender-and-pil.

[9] Hague Convention of 25 October 1980 on the Civil Aspects of International Child Abduction.

[10] See, eg, L Silberman, 'The Hague Child Abduction Convention Turns Twenty: Gender Politics and Other Issues' (2000) 33 *International Law and Politics* 221.

[11] See, eg, K Trimmings and O Momoh, 'Intersection between Domestic Violence and International Parental Child Abduction: Protection of Abducting Mothers in Return Proceedings International' (2021) 35 *International Journal of Law, Policy and the Family* 1.

[12] Hague Convention of 23 November 2007 on the International Recovery of Child Support and Other Forms of Family Maintenance.

[13] For evidence of the gendered understanding of the mischief which the Convention sought to address, see Hague Conference on Private International Law, *Convention of 23 November 2007 on the International Recovery of Child Support and Other Forms of Family Maintenance. Explanatory Report by Alegría Borrás and Jennifer Degeling* (HCCH, 2013) paras 568–69.

Often, scholarly work is equally inclined to preserve the orthodoxy of policy neutrality.[14] There is, of course, considerable merit in the argument that private international law should be neutral. The argument proceeds on the basis that private international law must be apolitical if it is to operate as a mediator between divergent policy choices. In this construct, the purpose of private international law is to provide methods to identify appropriate connections to courts and laws. Save to the extent that carve-outs are provided for public policy and mandatory rules, substantive policy outcomes and the articulation of values underlying those outcomes are matters for other disciplines. This neutrality, in turn, enables the harmonisation of private international law with a view to providing predictability in an increasingly interconnected, pluralist world.

Important notable exceptions to the scholarly orthodoxy do exist, however. Mary Keyes laments the lack of engagement with gender in private international law, and argues persuasively that the discipline's professed policy neutrality tends towards the entrenchment of conservative assumptions of gender roles.[15] Similarly, Mirela Župan and Martina Drventić observe the tendency of private international law to disregard structural inequalities between women and men in transnational family and economic relationships.[16] Karen Knop, Ralf Michaels and Annelise Riles illustrate the potential of the conflicts process to illuminate gendered and cultural conflicts of laws.[17] Roxana Banu advocates reference to relational feminism as a route to reimagining the transnational individual to account for asymmetries of power without disregarding women's individualism.[18] Gülüm Bayraktaroğlu-Özçelik examines private international law through the lenses of UN Strategic Development Goal 5 concerning gender equality.[19] In addition, there is a significant body of literature concerning child abduction and surrogacy which adopts a gendered approach to legal criticism without necessarily expressing critiques in overtly feminist terms.[20] Analyses of jurisdictional rules in divorce and

[14] See M Keyes, 'Women in private international law' in S Harris Rimmer and K Ogg (eds), *Research Handbook on Feminist Engagement with International Law* (Elgar, 2019) 104. Accepted manuscript available at: Keyes218230Accepted.pdf (griffith.edu.au).

[15] ibid, 104–17.

[16] M Župan and M Drventić, 'Gender Issues in Private International Law' in G Carapezza Figlia, L Kovačević and E Kristofferson (eds), *Gender Perspectives in Private Law* (Springer, 2023).

[17] K Knop, R Michaels, A Riles, 'From Multiculturalism to Technique, Feminism, Culture, and the Conflict of Laws Style' (2012) 64 *Stanford Law Review* 589.

[18] R Banu, 'A Relational Feminist Approach to Conflict of Laws' (2017) 24 *Michigan Journal of Gender & Law* 1.

[19] G Bayraktaroğlu-Özçelik, 'SDG 5: Gender Equality' in R Michaels, V Ruiz Abou-Nigm and H van Loon (eds), *The Private Side of Transforming our World: UN Sustainable Development Goals 2030 and the Role of Private International Law* (Intersentia Online, 2021).

[20] See, eg, Trimmings and Momoh (n 11) 1; Silberman (n 10) 221; MH Weiner, 'International Child Abduction and the Escape from Domestic Violence' (2000) 69 *Fordham Law Review* 593; K Trimmings et al (eds), *Domestic Violence and Parental Child Abduction* (Intersentia, 2022); B Quillen, 'The New Face of International Child Abduction: Domestic-Violence Victims and Their Treatment under the Hague Convention on the Civil Aspects of International Child Abduction' (2014) 49 *Texas International Law Journal* 621; J Lewis, 'The Hague Convention on the Civil Aspects of International

marital separation also evidence awareness of the disparate effects of ostensibly neutral rules.[21] However, these remain exceptions. The overall tenor of the discipline tends towards a collective shrug of the shoulders in the face of widespread sex-based inequity.

This chapter sets out to deepen a nascent conversation about how private international law could benefit from fresh analysis with a view to exposing the deficiencies of a discipline which congratulates itself on its neutrality.[22] It does so, in part, by looking to the organisation of rules concerning family and corporate life, particularly in the European Union, focusing especially on the effects of private international law's blindness to gendered financial inequality. It begins in section II and section III by considering the effects of structural inequality on women in the private international law of family and corporate life. Section IV then considers feminist analyses of the law in related legal disciplines with a view to identifying feminist private international law's place in the broader debate, and seeks to further discussion concerning adequate theoretical bases for the articulation of a more gender-aware discipline. We conclude that further and more sustained feminist legal analysis of private international law is needed to pierce the false assumptions of neutrality and to enable more structured awareness of the law's divergent effects.

II. Family Life

It is perhaps easiest to see the potential for feminist critiques of the law in the context of the family. After all, the practice of family law remains very much concerned with opposite-sex relationships. Still, however, private international law tends to favour neutrality, often resulting in unlike situations being treated as though they were objectively alike. Equally, the treatment of decisional autonomy reveals a paternalistic tendency and a degree of imperviousness to feminist critiques of the law. This section illustrates these concerns with reference to dissolution of marriages in section A, parent–child relationships in section B, and international surrogacy arrangements in section C.

Child Abduction: When Domestic Violence and Child Abuse Impact the Goal of Comity' (2000) 13 *Transnational Law* 391; K Trimmings and PR Beaumont, 'International Surrogacy Arrangements: An Urgent Need for Legal Regulation at the International Level' (2011) 7 *Journal of Private International Law* 627; S Bassan, 'Can Human Rights Protect Surrogate women in the Cross-Border Market?' in M Jänterä-Jareborg and H Tigroudja (eds), *Women's Human Rights and the Elimination of Discrimination* (The Hague Academy of International Law, Martinus Nijhoff Publishers, 2016); A Donchin, 'Reproductive tourism and the quest for global gender justice' (2010) 24 *Bioethics* 323.

[21] See, eg, P McEleavy, 'The communitarization of divorce rules: what impact for English and Scottish law?' (2004) 53 *International and Comparative Law Quarterly* 605; M-C Foblets, 'Migrant Women Caught between Islamic Family Law and Women's Rights: The Search for the Appropriate "Connecting Factor" in International Family Law' (2000) 7 *Maastricht Journal of European and Comparative Law* 11.

[22] See Muir Watt (n 3).

A. Divorce, Legal Separation and Annulment

The Brussels II*ter* Regulation[23] provides a particularly compelling example of the failure of private international law to account for gendered asymmetry of power in marriage and its dissolution. This is especially evident in relation to the opportunities for forum shopping afforded by Article 3 of the Regulation which delimits the courts in which an action for divorce, separation or annulment can be lodged:

> In matters relating to divorce, legal separation or marriage annulment, jurisdiction shall lie with the courts of the Member State
>
> (a) in whose territory:
>
> (i) the spouses are habitually resident,
>
> (ii) the spouses were last habitually resident, insofar as one of them still resides there,
>
> (iii) the respondent is habitually resident,
>
> (iv) in the event of a joint application, either of the spouses is habitually resident,
>
> (v) the applicant is habitually resident if he or she resided there for at least a year immediately before the application was made, or
>
> (vi) the applicant is habitually resident if he or she resided there for at least six months immediately before the application was made and is a national of the Member State in question; or
>
> (b) of the nationality of both spouses.

Article 3 is the product of an elaborate compromise between different legal and policy traditions, and ultimately grants equal status to a significant range of approaches to the establishment of jurisdiction.[24] There is no hierarchy between the seven grounds of jurisdiction – once any of the courts identified in Article 3 is seised of a case, all other courts subsequently seised of a claim are required to decline jurisdiction.[25] In other words, the claimant is empowered unilaterally to fix the place in which divorce, separation or annulment litigation will proceed. While none of the grounds is exorbitant when viewed in abstract terms, the extent of choice affords claimants significant latitude to engage in forum shopping. The Brussels II*ter* Regulation contains no corrective provision which would constrain the deployment of jurisdictional rules to exact an advantage or to vex the other party. If any of the connecting factors required for relevant jurisdictional grounds is present, a court is required to exercise jurisdiction regardless of the circumstances of the parties or of the claimant's motivation for seising a particular court. Litigants would be well advised, therefore, to seize the initiative and lodge a claim in the courts which suit them best.[26]

[23] Council Regulation (EU) 2019/1111 of 25 June 2019 on jurisdiction, the recognition and enforcement of decisions in matrimonial matters and the matters of parental responsibility, and on international child abduction (recast).

[24] See McEleavy (n 21 617–20.

[25] Council Regulation (EU) 2019/1111 (n 23) Art 20.

[26] J Borg-Barthet, *Jurisdiction in Matrimonial Matters: Reflections for the Review of the Brussels IIa Regulation* (European Parliament Committee on Legal Affairs (JURI), 2016) 12.

Unsurprisingly, Article 3 is framed in neutral terms with no overt advantaging or disadvantaging of either sex. This, however, masks the underlying reality of economic power asymmetries as between men and women in most marriages. Families in which the male partner is the sole or main financial provider remain the norm throughout Europe, particularly in households with children.[27] It follows that, typically, the male partner is better placed to procure costly legal advice which would enable them to win any race to seise a court whose exercise of jurisdiction they deemed advantageous. Potential for exploitation of economic disparity is exacerbated by a legal profession which is mindful of the benefits which may accrue from jurisdictional advantage.[28] Far from advising clients to seek consensual outcomes, the law is framed in terms which require lawyers to enable clients to seek the advantage of unilateral action.[29]

The jurisdictional design of Article 3 is also noteworthy insofar as it provides no legal force to prorogation agreements, save to the extent that paragraph (a)(iv) accounts for the possibility of joint applications in a Member State in which either spouse is habitually resident. While the parties are at liberty to agree a forum in which to litigate from among those available in Article 3, and to uphold that agreement, stringent jurisdictional rules do not afford any acknowledgement to agreement.[30] The retention of jurisdictional rules which encourage an adversarial process at the outset is especially surprising when considered in the context of an emerging global consensus that marital disputes should be resolved in as amicable a manner as possible.[31] Viewed from a feminist perspective, this constitutes significant regression from a family law system which privileges problem-solving in the domestic sphere. The empowerment of parties, particularly women, to exercise self-determination in the resolution of family disputes, which is encouraged in domestic cases through mechanisms such as mediation,[32] is undermined by a transnational order which encourages, and arguably necessitates, aggressive forum shopping.

Furthermore, while the potential for vexatious use of jurisdictional rules is problematic in and of itself, it is especially alarming when considered in the

[27] McEleavy (n 21) 627–28.

[28] Borg-Barthet, *Jurisdiction in Matrimonial Matters* (n 26) 19.

[29] ibid.

[30] For discussion of potential safeguards in relation to the vitiation of consent in prorogation agreements, see Borg-Barthet, ibid, 32–33.

[31] M Antokolskaia, 'Dissolution of marriage in westernised countries' in J Eekelaar and R George (eds), *Routledge Handbook on Family Law and Policy* (Routledge, 2014) 85. Chen Wei and Lei Shi, 'Divorce procedure in China' in J Eekelaar and R George (eds), *Routledge Handbook on Family Law and Policy* (Routledge, 2014) 114–15; N Espejo-Yaksic and F Lathrop-Gómez, 'Relaxation and dissolution of marriage in Latin America' in J Eekelaar and R George (eds), *Routledge Handbook on Family Law and Policy* (Routledge, 2014) 136; A Singer, 'Parenting issues after separation: a Scandinavian perspective' in J Eekelaar and R George (eds), *Routledge Handbook on Family Law and Policy* (Routledge, 2014) 239; M Maclean and J Eekelaar, 'Institutional mechanisms: courts, lawyers and others' in J Eekelaar and R George (eds), *Routledge Handbook on Family Law and Policy* (Routledge, 2014) 373.

[32] See, eg, M Lichtenstein 'Mediation and Feminism: Common Values and Challenges' (2000) 18 *Mediation Quarterly* 19, 21.

context of domestic abuse. No mechanism is provided for a court to refuse the exercise of jurisdiction where this would exacerbate abuse which persisted during a relationship. The Regulation proceeds on the basis that the rules are neutral. While, to our knowledge, there is no empirical engagement with use of jurisdictional rules in the context of dissolution of abusive marriages, analogous evidence of the deployment of court proceedings as an instrument of spousal abuse does exist. Crosse and Millar's qualitative study of spousal abuse in the context of divorce proceedings demonstrates a worrying phenomenon of male spousal abuse in the form of threats and harassment through the legal process.[33] Of course, it does not necessarily follow that there is a widespread problem of spousal abuse through Article 3 of Brussels II*ter* specifically. Nor, however, is there any rational reason to assume that transnational law of marital disputes would be uniquely immune to abusive practices. Indeed, the deployment of private international law rules more generally to extract negotiating advantage is well documented in both the pre-litigious and litigious phase.[34] More specifically in relation to litigation arising from marital disagreements in the context of spousal abuse, there is ample evidence of intimidatory misuse of litigation in international child abduction.[35] The preponderance of evidence therefore suggests that Article 3 provides opportunities to abusive spouses of which legislators should be mindful. It follows, in our view, that courts should be empowered to guard against the misuse of jurisdictional rules through the introduction of safeguards which would blunt the sharper edges of rules designed to afford predictability in preference to all other considerations.

In sum, therefore, the overarching jurisdictional design in relation to matrimonial disputes shows little recognition of economic and experiential differences which render neutral rules far from neutral in practice. As we observe in the following sections, this is far from an isolated incident of gender blindness in the law, and in many cases is something of an unintended but unaddressed feature of private international legal design.

B. Parent–Child Relationships

Questions concerning private international law's adequacy when dealing with domestic abuse also arise in respect of parent–child relationships, specifically in the context of child abduction. The 1980 Hague Convention on the Civil Aspects of International Child Abduction (hereafter the 1980 (Hague) Convention) is

[33] R Crosse and M Millar, 'Irish Women's Ongoing Experiences of Domestic Abuse in Separation and Divorce' (2017) 58 *Journal of Divorce and Remarriage* 507.

[34] For qualitative and quantitative analysis of the use of jurisdictional litigation as a negotiating technique, see PR Beaumont, M Danov, K Trimmings and B Yüksel 'Great Britain' in PR Beaumont, M Danov, K Trimmings and B Yüksel (eds), *Cross-Border Litigation in Europe* (Hart Publishing, 2017) 84–85.

[35] See the section II.B of this chapter and the references therein.

based on the premise that the wrongful removal or retention of a child across international borders is generally contrary to the child's welfare and that, in most cases, it will be in the best interests of the child to be returned to the state of his or her habitual residence where any issues relating to the custody of or access to the child should be resolved.[36] Exceptions to the duty to secure the prompt return of the child[37] are justified only in exceptional circumstances,[38] including where 'there is a grave risk that his or her return would expose the child to physical or psychological harm or otherwise place the child in an intolerable situation'[39] (hereafter 'the grave risk of harm' defence). The Brussels II*ter* Regulation tightens the application of the grave risk of harm defence by prohibiting a non-return order on the basis of Article 13(1)(b) of the 1980 Convention if it is established that adequate arrangements have been made to secure the child's protection upon his or her return.[40] The Regulation deserves credit for reinforcing the 1980 Convention's summary return policy; however, there is a justified concern that, 'whilst sparing no effort to fulfil the ambitions of the Regulation, courts might … compromise the safety of … the returning parent'.[41] Indeed, the wording of both Article 13(1)(b) of the Convention and Article 27(3) of Brussels II*ter* makes it clear that 'it is the situation of the child which is the prime focus of the inquiry'.[42] These two provisions embody the mechanism for the protection of the child from harm in return proceedings. However, there is no consideration of the safety of the taking parent upon the return, either in the Convention or in the Brussels II*ter* Regulation.

The gendered aspect comes into play here as a matter of serious concern for two principal reasons. First, it is widely acknowledged that 'domestic violence affects women disproportionately'.[43] For example, in England and Wales, an estimated 1.7 million women and 699,000 men aged 16 years and over experienced domestic abuse between March 2021 and March 2022 – a prevalence rate

[36] E Pérez-Vera, 'Explanatory Report on the 1980 Hague Child Abduction Convention', paras 20–26, available at: assets.hcch.net/docs/a5fb103c-2ceb-4d17-87e3-a7528a0d368c.pdf (Explanatory Report).

[37] 1980 Hague Convention, Art 12(1).

[38] See 1980 Hague Convention, Arts 12(2), 13 and 20.

[39] ibid, Art 13(1)(b).

[40] Council Regulation (EU) 2019/1111 (n 23) Art 27(3).

[41] K Trimmings, *Child Abduction within the European Union* (Hart Publishing, 2013) 136.

[42] Permanent Bureau of the Hague Conference on Private International Law, '[Draft] Guide to Good Practice on Article 13(1)(B) of the Hague Convention of 25 October 1980 on the Civil Aspects of International Child Abduction, Prel Doc 3 of June 2017 [11], available at: assets.hcch.net/docs/0a0532b7-d580-4e53-8c25-7edab2a94284.pdf (hereafter Permanent Bureau 2017); and Permanent Bureau of the Hague Conference, 'Domestic and Family Violence and the Article 13 "Grave Risk" Exception in the Operation of the Hague Convention of 25 October 1980 on the Civil Aspects of International Child Abduction: A Reflection Paper' (May 2011) [140], available at: assets.hcch.net/upload/wop/abduct2011pd09e.pdf (hereafter Permanent Bureau 2011).

[43] Council of Europe Convention on preventing and combating violence against women and domestic violence (Istanbul Convention) Art 2(1). The Istanbul Convention defines domestic violence as including 'acts of physical, sexual, psychological and economic violence that occur within the family or domestic unit or between former or current spouses or partners, whether or not the perpetrator shares or has shared the same residence with the victim' (Art 3(b)).

of approximately 7 in 100 women as opposed to 3 in 100 men.[44] Second, unlike back in the 1970s when the 1980 Convention was drafted, nowadays the majority of parental child abductions (73 per cent) are committed by mothers.[45] Many of these mothers are fleeing domestic violence.[46] Although there are no comprehensive statistics on how many 1980 Convention cases involve allegations or findings of domestic violence, empirical research has confirmed that this phenomenon frequently plays a role in parental child abduction cases.[47] Indeed, available evidence suggests that domestic violence may be present in about 70 per cent of parental child abduction cases.[48] This figure suggests that over a half of the returning mothers 'may potentially be at risk of re-victimisation at the hands of their violent ex-partners'.[49] Returning mothers in child abductions committed against the background of domestic violence are subject to particular vulnerabilities. These include the risk of revictimisation upon their return to the State of habitual residence, the lack of financial and emotional support in the State of habitual residence plus probable financial dependence on the left-behind father on the return, and sometimes the lack of credibility as a respondent in return proceedings due to the failure to report the incidents of domestic violence in the State of habitual residence prior to the abduction.[50] Moreover, such abducting mothers are often exposed to 'intimidatory litigation', whereby the left-behind father abusively uses the return proceedings as a means of further harassment, rather than from a genuine desire to secure the return of the child.[51] Such 'intimidatory litigation' adds greatly to the anxiety suffered by the abducting mother who, as a survivor of an

[44] Office for National Statistics (ONS), 'Domestic abuse victim characteristics, England and Wales: year ending March 2022', 25 November 2022, available at: www.ons.gov.uk/peoplepopulationandcommunity/crimeandjustice/articles/domesticabusevictimcharacteristicsenglandandwales/yearendingmarch2022.

[45] N Lowe and V Stephens, 'A statistical analysis of applications made in 2015 under the Hague Convention of 25 October 1980 on the Civil Aspects of International Child Abduction, Global Report', September 2017 [10], available at: d0b285f1-5f59-41a6-ad83-8b5cf7a784ce.pdf (hcch.net).

[46] Permanent Bureau 2011 (n 42); and N Lowe and M Nicholls, *International Movement of Children* (Lexis Nexis, 2016) 564. See generally, I Pretelli, 'Three Patterns, One Law – Plea for a Reinterpretation of the Hague Child Abduction Convention to Protect Children from Exposure to Sexism, Mysogyny and Violence against Women' in M Pfeiffer et al (eds), *Liber Amicorum Monika Pauknerova* (Wolters Kluwer, 2021).

[47] See, eg, J Edleson et al, 'Multiple perspectives on battered mothers and their children fleeing to the United States for safety: A study of Hague Convention cases' (December 2010), available at: Multiple Perspectives on Battered Mothers and their Children Fleeing to the United States for Safety: A Study of Hague Convention Cases (ojp.gov) 2010; Reunite Research Unit (led by M Freeman), 'The Outcomes for Children Returned Following an Abduction' (September 2003) (hereafter Reunite 2003); Reunite Research Unit (led by M Freeman), 'International Child Abduction: The Effects' (2006); and S Shetty and J Edleson, 'Adult Domestic Violence in Cases of International Parental Child Abduction' (2005) 11 *Violence Against Women* 115.

[48] Reunite 2003, ibid; and S De Silva, 'The International Parental Child Abduction Service of the International Social Service Australian Branch' (2006) 11 *The Judges' Newsletter* 63.

[49] Trimmings, Child Abduction within the European Union (n 41) 152.

[50] POAM Project, 'Best Practice Guide: Protection of Abducting Mothers in Return Proceedings: Intersection between Domestic Violence and Parental Child Abduction Guide to Good Practice', 2021, 7, available at: Best-Practice-Guide_POAM.pdf (abdn.ac.uk) (hereafter POAM Guide).

[51] ibid.

abusive relationship, is likely to be overwhelmed already with the repercussions of that relationship.[52]

The grave risk of harm defence mentioned earlier is particularly pertinent to abductions committed against the background of domestic violence. Indeed, it is often raised by taking mothers opposing the return, usually on the basis of allegations involving the child as the 'direct victim', or as an 'indirect victim' where the child is exposed to the effects of domestic violence directed towards the mother.[53] The defence is, however, not easy to establish.[54] Although domestic violence against the taking mother may present an Article 13(1)(b) exception to return, '[e]vidence of the existence of a situation of domestic violence, in and of itself, is … not sufficient to establish the existence of a grave risk to the child'.[55] The key question is whether the effect of domestic violence on the child upon his or her return to the State of habitual residence will meet the high threshold of the Article 13(1)(b) exception.[56] This assessment can only reliably be carried out if a prior evaluation of the merits of the allegations of domestic violence has been undertaken by the court in the return proceedings.[57] The burden of proof that Article 13(1)(b) (or any other exception to return) applies, rests with the person opposing the child's return.[58] It is, therefore, for the taking mother to produce evidence to corroborate the defence raised.[59]

As domestic violence, by its very nature, usually occurs behind closed doors, supporting or corroborative documentary evidence can be scarce. Indeed, the absence of police or other authority intervention is not untypical of a disempowered victim of domestic violence, demonstrated by psychological conditions such as battered women syndrome. Notwithstanding this, there are cases where the alleged victim is equipped with documentary evidence, usually relating to previous proceedings in the State of habitual residence, seeking protection from

[52] ibid.

[53] Permanent Bureau 2017 (n 42) [11]. The grave risk of harm defence may also be raised where the mother is unable to return with the child due to fear of the father; the resulting separation from the primary carer may be argued to create a grave risk for the child. ibid [9]. It is to be noted that it is not mandatory for the taking parent to return together with the child, however, the mother (in particular if she is the primary carer), will typically accompany the child back to the State of habitual residence, even if it means that she has to compromise their own safety.

[54] Explanatory Report (n 36) [34].

[55] Hague Conference on Private International Law, 'Guide to Good Practice under the HCCH Convention of 25 October 1980 on the Civil Aspects of International Child Abduction – Part VI – Article 13(1)(b)', 2020 [58], available at: 225b44d3-5c6b-4a14-8f5b-57cb370c497f.pdf (hcch.net) (hereafter HCCH Guide).

[56] ibid.

[57] See POAM Guide (n 50) section 5.1.2.

[58] See, eg, *In the Matter of E (Children)* [2011] UKSC 27 [32].

[59] The court should be required to evaluate the evidence against the civil standard of proof, ie, the ordinary balance of probabilities. *In the Matter of E (Children)* (n 58) [35]. See also, *Re C (Children) (Abduction Article 13(B))* [2018] EWCA Civ 2834 [48]; and HCCH Guide (n 55) 27. See also, POAM Project Report – United Kingdom, 95, available at: research.abdn.ac.uk/wp-content/uploads/sites/15/2020/02/National-report_UK.pdf.

domestic violence. Such evidence may take the form of police and/or medical reports, previous non-molestation orders, ouster orders, non-harassment orders, child arrangement orders, or even criminal proceedings relating to specific acts of violence. Nevertheless, in the context of return proceedings, obtaining such documentary evidence in a cross-border setting, even with the support of Central Authorities, may prove challenging, and at times unsuccessful, within the strict timescales afforded to Hague Convention cases.[60] Consequently, courts in return proceedings tend to avoid undertaking an evaluation of the merits of the allegations of domestic violence and either disregard them completely as being irrelevant to the summary return procedure under the 1980 Convention, or simply proceed to considering protective measures that would facilitate the return.[61] The latter approach focuses on assessing the adequacy of protective measures as a substitute for investigating the disputed facts. Concerns over the speed of the return proceedings should, however, not take priority over the proper assessment of risk, and consideration of the safety of the child and the taking mother, especially when there is an alleged case of domestic violence which is at least prima facie credible. Indeed, the emphasis on speed may encourage courts to minimise or ignore allegations of domestic violence rather than determining them, thus leaving an unassessed risk of harm. In line with this reasoning, several commentators have condemned the above approaches as inadequate and rightly suggested that, in line with the European Court of Human Rights (ECtHR) guidance in the case of *X v Latvia*,[62] the court should consider the disputed allegations of domestic violence, with the examination leading to a ruling on 'specific reasons [for the decision] in light of the circumstances of the case'[63] ('the assessment of allegations' approach).[64] To address the concern over the speed of the return proceedings, the court should proceed carefully so as to avoid pursuing full proceedings on domestic violence. The assessment of the allegations should be carried out within the boundaries of the return proceedings, through a process of 'thorough, limited and expeditious' examination ('effective examination'),[65] while the likelihood of future coercive and

[60] 1980 Hague Convention, Art 11.

[61] See, eg, *In the Matter of E (Children)* (n 58); *Re F (A Child)* [2014] EWCA Civ 275; *In the Matter of M (Children)* [2016] EWCA Civ 942; and *GCMR Petitioner* [2017] CSOH 66.

[62] *X v Latvia* (Application no 27853/09) Grand Chamber [2013].

[63] ibid, [107].

[64] eg, POAM Guide (n 50) section 5.1.2; and A Barnett, 'Draft Guide to Good Practice on Article 13(1)(b) of the Hague Convention on International Child Abduction – a perspective from England and Wales' 18, in *Eight Letters Submitted to the United States Department of State and the Permanent Bureau of the Hague Conference on Private International Law about a Draft Guide for Article 13(1)b) and Related Draft Documents that were circulated for comment prior to the October 2017 meeting of the Seventh Special Commission on the 1980 Hague Child Abduction Convention at The Hague*, available at: law.ucdavis.edu/faculty/bruch/files/Letters-re-Hague-Convention.pdf. The assessment of allegations approach seems also to correspond with the relevant proposal in the HCCH Guide (n 55) 31. See also *Re K (1980 Hague Convention) (Lithuania)* [2015] EWCA Civ 720; *Re C (Children) (Abduction Article 13(B))* (n 59); and *Uhd v McKay* [2019] EWHC 1239 (Fam).

[65] *X v. Latvia* (n 62). See O Momoh, 'The Interpretation and Application of Article 13(1) b) of the Hague Child Abduction Convention in Cases Involving Domestic Violence: Revisiting X v Latvia

violent behaviour should suffice to meet the requirement under Article 13(1)(b), and to examine the availability of protection measures.[66]

The problem with protection measures, however, lies with their enforceability. Courts in some Contracting States routinely accept unenforceable voluntary promises made by the left-behind parent called 'undertakings'.[67] Examples of undertakings include non-molestation/non-harassment undertakings;[68] undertakings relating to the occupation of the family home;[69] undertakings relating to financial support;[70] and undertakings relating to residence or access to the child.[71] Undertakings do not always contain protective measures as such, but may instead encompass 'more light-touch' practical arrangements to facilitate and implement the child's return and enable a 'soft landing' of the child in the State of habitual residence.[72] Unenforceability of undertakings is of particular concern in child abduction cases committed against the background of domestic abuse.[73]

Courts in some Contracting States have endeavoured to alleviate these concerns by seeking to ensure that protection measures ordered in return proceedings have legal effect, for example by virtue of the 1996 Hague Convention on Jurisdiction, Applicable Law, Recognition, Enforcement and Co-operation in Respect of Parental Responsibility and Measures for the Protection of Children[74] (1996 Convention) or Regulation 606/2013 on mutual recognition of protection measures in civil matters.[75] However, the effectiveness of protection measures in the context of domestic violence has been subject to debate as such orders are

and the Principle of "Effective Examination"' (2019) 15 *Journal of Private International Law* 626, 651. For further analysis as to how to strike this difficult balance, see POAM Guide (n 50) section 5.1.3.

[66] See C Honorati, 'Il ritorno del minore sottratto e il rischio grave di pregiudizio ai sensi dell'art. 13 par. 1 lett. b della convenzione dell'Aja del 1980' (2020) 4 *Rivista di diritto internazionale privato e processuale* 815.

[67] Described as 'promises offered or in certain circumstances imposed upon an applicant to overcome obstacles which may stand in the way of the return of a wrongfully removed or retained child'. PR Beaumont and PE McEleavy, *The Hague Convention on International Child Abduction* (Oxford University Press, 1999) 30. See also, Trimmings, *Child Abduction within the European Union* (n 41) 155–61.

[68] eg, 'not to use violence or threats towards the mother, nor to instruct anybody else to do so', or 'not to communicate with the mother directly'.

[69] eg, 'to vacate the family home and make it available for a sole occupancy by the mother and the child'.

[70] eg, to pay for the return tickets for the mother and the child'.

[71] eg, 'not to seek to separate the mother from the child', or 'not to seek contact with the child unless awarded by the court or agreed'.

[72] See *Re S (A Child) (Hague Convention 1980: Return to Third State)* [2019] EWCA Civ 352 [55]; and POAM Guide (n 50) sections 3.1 and 3.2.

[73] R Schuz, *The Hague Child Abduction Convention: A Critical Analysis* (Hart Publishing, 2013) 293.

[74] Art 11 of the 1996 Hague Convention provides for the jurisdiction to issue measures based on the presence of the child on the territory of the State of refuge. There is a corresponding provision in the Brussels II*ter* Regulation (Art 15). On the utility of the 1996 Convention in return proceedings involving allegations of domestic violence, see, eg, Trimmings and Momoh (n 11) 13–14.

[75] The Regulation provides for the mutual recognition of civil protection measures across the EU by establishing 'rules for a simple and rapid mechanism for the recognition of protection measures ordered in a Member State in civil matters' Art 1. On the utility of Regulation 606/2013 in return proceedings involving allegations of domestic violence, see, eg, Trimmings and Momoh (n 11) 14–15.

commonly breached and satisfactory follow-up measures by relevant authorities may be lacking.[76] It has therefore been rightly suggested that, '[i]n the light of concerns over the effectiveness of protective measures,[77] the employment of civil protection orders with a view to making a return order should not be considered in cases where it has been established that there is a future risk of severe violence'.[78] However, in the absence of explicit recognition in the 1980 Convention of the gendered nature of parental child abductions committed against the background of domestic abuse, courts in many Contracting States often risk the safety of the returning mother and the child by making return orders conditional on unenforceable and/or inappropriate protection measures.[79]

C. International Surrogacy Arrangements

Feminist theory also offers rich insights into the analysis of the law concerning surrogacy arrangements.[80] A similar trend can be observed specifically with respect to international surrogacy arrangements as there is a growing body of literature examining surrogacy arrangements with a foreign element through the lens of gender.[81] International surrogacy is approached in this literature from various perspectives. Little attention is paid in the private international law literature to the disparity of treatment between the intended father and the intended mother in the case law of the ECtHR, however. This section highlights this disparity as a further, and particularly egregious, illustration of the propensity of the law to

[76] POAM Guide (n 50) section 4.3.3.

[77] This is partly because breaches of civil protection orders are often not criminalised. S van der Aa et al, 'Mapping the Legislation and Assessing the Impact of Protection Orders in the European Member States' 149, available at: poems-project.com/wp-content/uploads/2015/04/Intervict-Poems-digi-1.pdf.

[78] POAM Guide (n 50) section 4.4.

[79] See comment by Lady Hale (UK Supreme Court) in *In the Matter of E (Children)* (n 58) [7] where she expressed concerns about the 'too ready' acceptance by the courts of common law countries of undertakings which are not enforceable in the courts of the requesting State.

[80] eg, M Lyndon Shanley, '"Surrogate Mothering" and Women's Freedom: A Critique of Contracts for Human Reproduction' (1993) 18 *Signs* 618; R Klein, *Surrogacy: A Human Rights Violation* (Spinifex Press, 2017); WA Wiegers, 'Economic Analysis of Law and Private Ordering: A Feminist Critique' (1992) 42 *University of Toronto Law Journal* 170; C McLeod, 'For Dignity or Money: Feminists on the Commodification of Women's Reproductive Labour' in B Steinbock (ed), *The Oxford Handbook of Bioethics* (Oxford University Press, 2009); F Daunt, 'Exploitation or Empowerment – Debating Surrogate Motherhood' (1991) 55 *Saskatchewan Law Review* 415; K Lieber, 'Selling the Womb: Can the Feminist Critique of Surrogacy Be Answered? (1992) 68 *Indiana Law Review* 205; J Parks, 'Gestational Surrogacy and the Feminist Perspective' in S Skills (ed), *Handbook of Gestational Surrogacy* (Cambridge University Press, 2016); and M Becker, 'Four Feminist Theoretical Approaches and the Double Bind of Surrogacy' (1993) 69 *Chicago-Kent Law Review* 303.

[81] See, eg, Banu (n 18); S Van Wichelen, 'Law as Antikinship: The Colonial Present in Global Surrogacy' (2022) 8 *Catalyst: Feminism, Theory, Technoscience* 1; S Saravanan, *A Transnational Feminist View of Surrogacy Biomarkets in India* (Springer, 2018); and L Eriksson, 'Outsourcing problems or regulating altruism? Parliamentary debates on domestic and cross-border surrogacy in Finland and Norway' (2022) 29 *European Journal of Women's Studies* 107.

deploy neutral language where the effects of decisions are especially gendered – in this case for self-evident biological reasons which, nevertheless, are not accorded sufficient legislative or judicial attention.

The ECtHR case law in the area of international surrogacy has centred on the recognition in the country of residence of the intending parents of a parent–child relationship established in the country of birth.[82] The leading case in this field is *Mennesson v France*[83] (decided jointly with the case of *Labassee v France*).[84] The cases concerned the refusal to grant legal recognition in France to parent–child relationships that had been legally established in the United States between children born as a result of international surrogacy and their intending parents. In both cases, the intending parents were married heterosexual couples. The children were conceived using the intending fathers' sperm and donor eggs. Court orders made in California and Minnesota respectively ruled that the intending parents were the children's legal parents, and birth certificates were drawn up in the United States to reflect the terms of the court orders. The French authorities, however, refused to enter the particulars of the birth certificates in the French civil status register. The couples then took the matter to the courts. Their claims were dismissed at the final instance by the French Court of Cassation, which held that the California and Minnesota court judgments were incompatible with French international public policy as they contained provisions which conflicted with fundamental principles of French law, in particular the principle of inalienability of civil status. The Court also held that recording the particulars of the birth certificates would give effect to a surrogacy agreement which was null and void on public policy grounds under the French Civil Code.

The couples then brought the case before the ECtHR. In both cases, the Court held that there had been no violation of Article 8 of the European Convention on Human Rights concerning the intending parents' right to respect for their family life as, despite a lack of legal recognition of parenthood, the family was able to live together in a situation broadly comparable with other families and was not in danger of separation.[85] However, there had been a violation of Article 8 of the Convention concerning the children's right to respect for their private life.[86] The Court noted that there was no consensus in Europe either on the lawfulness of

[82] For a detailed overview of the case law, see K Trimmings, 'Surrogacy Arrangements and the Best Interests of the Child: The Case Law of the European Court of Human Rights' in E Bergamini and C Ragni (eds), *Fundamental Rights and Best Interests of the Child in Transnational Families* (Intersentia, 2019).

[83] *Mennesson v France*, no 65192/11, ECHR 2014 (extracts).

[84] *Labassee v France*, no 65941/11, 26 June 2014.

[85] For a criticism of such 'negative formulation of the right to respect for family life', see C Fenton-Glynn, *Children and the European Court of Human Rights* (Oxford University Press, 2021) 253, who argues that the approach creates 'a clear distinction between 'conventional' forms of reproduction and new family forms'.

[86] This approach was followed by the ECtHR in other cross-border surrogacy cases, eg, *Laborie v France*, no 44024/13, 19 January 2017; *Foulon and Bouvet v France*, nos 9063/14 and 10410/14, 21 July 2016.

surrogacy arrangements or on the legal recognition of the relationship between intended parents and children lawfully conceived abroad as a result of such arrangements. This lack of consensus reflected the fact that recourse to surrogacy raised difficult ethical issues. Accordingly, states had to be allowed a wide margin of appreciation in making surrogacy-related decisions. However, when it comes to legal parenthood, the margin of appreciation afforded to the state must be reduced. This is because legal parenthood is intrinsically linked with a person's identity, and the right to establish one's identity is in turn connected with the right to respect for private life under Article 8. The refusal to recognise in France the legal parent–child relationship that had been established in the United States 'undermined the children's identity within French society'.[87] Such refusal was considered particularly worrying where, as in the present case, 'one of the intended parents is also the child's biological parent'.[88]

The reference to a single concept of 'biological parenthood' here is, however, somewhat misleading. While automatic recognition must be given to the biological intending father, when it comes to the recognition of the legal position of the intending mother – genetically related or not – it is sufficient for her to be permitted to go through a step-parent adoption.[89] In other words, unlike in respect of a biologically related intending father, there is no obligation to recognise *ab initio* the legal parent–child relationship between the child and the intending mother. Such a gendered approach to filiation in cross-border surrogacy cases is clearly out of line with the notion of gender equality, especially when examined through the lens of the legal position of a genetically related intending mother.

III. Economic Life: Corporate Governance

Feminist analysis of private international law as it relates to economic governance has been especially lacking. There is, of course, a significant body of literature concerning substantive contract and consumer protection law, some of which

[87] *Mennesson v France* (n 83) (extracts) [96].

[88] ibid (extracts) [100]. *cf Paradiso and Campanelli v Italy* [GC], no 25358/12, 24 January 2017 (absent this genetic connection no 'family life' existed between the child and the intended parents, notwithstanding the fact that they had cared for the child for the first eight months of his life. The case concerned the separation and placement for adoption of a child conceived abroad through surrogacy and brought back to Italy in violation of Italian adoption laws; and *Valdís Fjölnisdóttir and Others v Iceland*, no 71552/17, 18 May 2021, non-recognition of parental affiliation with a non-biological child born abroad via surrogacy, while preserving bond through foster care did not violate Art 8 rights. In this case 'family life' was found to have existed as, unlike in *Paradiso*, the child had been in the uninterrupted care of the intending parents for over four years and the relationship had been strengthened not only by the passage of time but also by the legally established foster care arrangement).

[89] ECtHR, 'Advisory opinion concerning the recognition in domestic law of a legal parent–child relationship between a child born through a gestational surrogacy arrangement abroad and the intended mother', 10 April 2019. See also *D v France*, no 11288/18, 16 July 2020; and *KK and Others v Denmark*, no 25212/21, 6 December 2022.

adopts a feminist perspective.[90] Equally, in employment relations, the gender pay gap is well documented,[91] as is the disparity in the distribution and exercise of governance responsibility in corporate law and theory.[92] Little has been said about the extent to which the structure of transnational economic governance has the potential to exacerbate gender inequalities in national law or to limit the efficacy of corrective national measures, however.[93]

The private international law of companies has tended in the direction of liberalisation which results in the consolidation of existing power asymmetries in economic governance. This is true both of choice of law and jurisdictional rules. It is especially troubling given that the constitutionalisation of the private international law of companies in the European Union and elsewhere produces a significant degree of entrenchment of the very neoclassical economics which some feminist theorists decry.[94] Feminist scholars note that advocates of the notion of a free market guided by the invisible hand either pass off gender inequality as rational individual choice or as a market failure to which institutions have failed to respond.[95] It follows, from the perspective of proponents of free markets, that liberalised markets are not incompatible with gender equality at all; a truly free market would not tolerate gender inequity.[96] It is argued hereunder that, from a private international law perspective, this argument does not bear scrutiny. First, even accepting the free market approach for the sake of argument, liberalisation of private international law occurs in the context of imperfectly free markets which tolerate gender inequity. Secondly, it is submitted that the argument is intrinsically flawed when considered with reference to a broader spectrum of corporate legal theory which questions the contractual characterisation of corporate law.

[90] See, eg, L Mulcahy and S Wheeler (eds), *Feminist Perspectives on Contract Law* (Cavendish, 2005); O Gan, 'A Feminist Economic Perspective on Contract Law: Promissory Estoppel as an Example' (2021) 28 *Michigan Journal of Gender and Law* 1; MM Ertman, 'Contract's Influence on Feminism and Vice Versa' in D Brake, M Chamallas and V Williams (eds), *The Oxford Handbook of Feminism and the Law in the United States* (Oxford University Press, 2023).

[91] See, eg, P Foubert, *The Gender Pay Gap in Europe from a Legal Perspective* (European Commission, 2010), available at: ec.europa.eu/social/BlobServlet?docId=6181&langId=en.

[92] See, eg, C Villiers, 'Achieving Gender Balance in the Boardroom: Is it Time for Legislative Action in the UK?' (2010) 30 *Legal Studies* 533; E Hickman, 'Boardroom Gender Diversity: A Behavioural Economics Analysis' (2014) 14 *Journal of Corporate Law Studies* 385; SS Carlson, '"Women Directors": A Term of Art Showcasing the Need for Meaningful Gender Diversity on Corporate Boards' (2012) 11 *Seattle Journal of Social Justice* 337; S Terjesen and V Singh, 'Female Presence on Corporate Boards: A Multi-Country Study of Environmental Context' (2008) 83 *Journal of Business Ethics* 55; A Belcher, 'Board Diversity: Can Sex Discrimination Law Help?' (2005) 56 *Northern Ireland Legal Quarterly* 356.

[93] Brief consideration of the potential for private international law to limit gender-related innovation in corporate law can be found in J Borg-Barthet, *The Governing Law of Companies in EU Law* (Hart Publishing, 2012) 69–70.

[94] P England, 'The Separate Self: Androcentric Bias in Neoclassical Assumptions' in MA Ferber and JA Nelson *Beyond Economic Man: Feminist Theory and Economics* (University of Chicago Press 1993) 37; Ertman (n 90).

[95] E Braunstein, 'The Efficiency of Gender Equity in Economic Growth' (2015) The International Working Group on Gender, Macroeconomics and International Economics, Working Paper Number 7, 6, available at: lib.icimod.org/api/files/07954981-f151-43fc-95ad-7ebdb18b3792/1556.pdf.

[96] ibid.

Resistance to feminist critiques dovetails with broader assumptions which underpin the structure of transnational corporate law. To the extent that private international law scholars engage with corporate legal theory, the analysis has tended to rely on neoclassical economic accounts of the firm. In particular, authors tend to refer to Coase's work on the nature of the firm in which he noted that the establishment of firms (and, by extension, corporations specifically) was motivated by entrepreneurs' need to identify efficiencies in the organisation of business activities.[97] Coase's work says nothing explicit about the consequences of the nature of the firm, as he saw it, for corporate governance. However, the analysis proceeds on the basis of an implicit assumption that investors of capital are empowered to manage other factors of production with a view to realising efficiencies.[98] From Coase's work, other authors articulated more explicitly a view of corporate governance in which the allocation of decision-making power in corporate law is justified on the basis of the investment of capital or the exercise of management functions.[99] Insofar as private international law scholarship engages with corporate legal theory as a matter of course, the tendency has been to take neoclassical accounts of the firm at face value, disregarding more progressive analyses.[100] It follows, therefore, that private international law scholarship has tended in the direction of analyses which favour the preservation of approaches to governance which are dissonant with feminist critiques of markets.

Given the general tenor of private international law scholarship in relation to corporate law, it is unsurprising that liberalisation of choice of corporate law has acquired something of a dogmatic status in judicial and policymakers' imagination, notwithstanding diversity of theoretical opinion and practical application in the municipal sphere.[101] The European Court of Justice held in *Centros* that incorporators' decisions concerning the place of incorporation of companies, and consequently the law governing a company's internal affairs, was to be upheld by

[97] RH Coase, 'The Nature of the Firm' (1937) 4 *Economica* 386, 386–405.

[98] J Paterson, 'The Company Law Review in the UK and the Question of Scope: Theoretical Concerns, Practical Constraints and Possible Directions' in R Cobbaut and J Lenoble (eds), *Corporate Governance: An Institutional Approach* (Kluwer Law International, 2003) 145.

[99] MC Jensen and WH Meckling, 'Theory of the Firm: Managerial Behaviour, Agency Costs and Ownership Structure' (1976) 3 *Journal of Financial* Economics 305, 305–60; AA Alchian and H Demsetz, 'Production, Information Costs and Economic Information' (1977) 62 *American Economic Review* 777, 777–95; OE Williamson, *The Economic Institutions of Capitalism* (Free Press, 1985); OE Williamson, 'The Theory of the Firm as Governance Structure: From Choice to Contract' (2002) 16(3)*Journal of Economic Perspectives* 171, 171–95.

[100] For echoes of Coase's work in discussion of the economic theory of choice of corporate law, see S Lombardo, 'Conflict of Law Rules in Company Law after *Überseering*: An Economic and Comparative Analysis of the Allocation of Policy Competence in the European Union' (2003) 4 *European Business Organization Law Review* 301, 314–22; MJ Whincop, 'Conflicts in the Cathedral: Towards a Theory of Property Rights in Private International Law' (2000) 50 *University of Toronto Law Journal* 41, 52–54; EM Iacobucci, 'Toward a Signaling Explanation of the Private Choice of Corporate Law' (2004) 6 *American Law and Economics Review* 319, 319–20; FJ Garcimartín Alférez, 'Cross-Border Listed Companies' (2007) 328 *Recueil des Cours de l'Académie de Droit International* 13, 47.

[101] See Paterson (n 98) 141; J Dine, *The Governance of Corporate Groups* (Cambridge University Press, 2000) 1; A Belcher, 'The Boundaries of the Firm: The Theories of Coase, Knight and Weitzman' (1997) 17 *Legal Studies* 22; Borg-Barthet, *The Governing Law of Companies in EU Law* (n 93) 13–72.

the Member States.[102] Party autonomy was extended to cross-border incorporation in *SEVIC Systems*[103] and to cross-border transformations in *VALE*.[104] The Court of Justice did not engage with questions of corporate legal theory (and still less with feminist critiques of the law) in any of those judgments, reasoning instead on the basis of the market freedoms conferred by Articles 49 and 54 of the Treaty on the Functioning of the European Union.

There is some consideration of the diversity of theoretical thought in corporate law and governance in the Advocate General's Opinion in *Powell Duffryn*, however. This was a case concerning prorogation of jurisdiction, as opposed to choice of law. However, the outlook of the court is very much in evidence in respect of its broader approach to controversies concerning the nature and purpose of companies in transnational law. The Advocate General's acknowledgment of diversity of thought and practice was swiftly followed by dismissal of doctrinal controversy in company law with a view to resolving the matter with reference to the overarching aim of legal harmonisation through the Brussels Convention on Jurisdiction and the Recognition of Judgments in Civil and Commercial Matters 1968.[105] Ultimately, the Advocate General concluded that intra-corporate relations are contractual for the purposes of prorogation of jurisdiction.[106]

The contractual construct of the private international law of companies has a twofold effect on gender equality. In an immediate sense, liberalisation enables corporate decision-makers to choose to be governed by corporate law systems which facilitate the concentration and consolidation of decision-making power, and consequently potentially also to consolidate concentrations of economic power. In broader systemic terms, liberalisation of choice of corporate law tends to incentivise further liberalisation of substantive corporate law to the detriment of existing progressive policy, while also acting as a potential disincentive to progressive innovation.[107] Taken together, these consequences tend to exacerbate the advantages which accrue to established power, often male, from a reliance on contractual theorisation of markets which disregards the fallacy of equal bargaining power.[108]

Concerns regarding the preservation of gendered power asymmetry in choice of corporate law is exacerbated by the tendency of jurisdictional rules to pose barriers to enforcement of obligations to parties in a weaker economic position.[109]

[102] Case C-212/97 *Centros Ltd v Erhvervs-og Selskabsstyrelsen* [1999] ECR I-01459.

[103] Case C-411/03 *SEVIC Systems AG* [2005] ECR I-10805.

[104] Case C-378/10 *VALE Építési kft* ECLI:EU:C:2012:440; Case C-106/16 *Polbud – Wykonawstwo sp. z o.o.* ECLI:EU:C:2017:804.

[105] See AG Tesauro in Case C-214/89 *Powell Duffryn plc v Petereit* [1992] ECR I-01745, para 4.

[106] ibid.

[107] Borg-Barthet, *The Governing Law of Companies in EU Law* (n 93) 69–71.

[108] See CA Mackinnon, *Toward a Feminist Theory of the State* (Harvard University Press, 1994) 237; R Cohen, 'Feminist Thought and Corporate Law: It's Time to Find Our Way Up From the Bottom (Line)' (1994) 2 *American University Journal of Gender, Social Policy & the Law* 1, 6.

[109] See generally, FM Farrington, 'A Return to the doctrine of forum non conveniens after Brexit and the implications for corporate accountability' (2022) 18 *Journal of Private International Law* 399, and the references therein.

Here too, the law's preference for contractual orthodoxy tends to exacerbate disparities by shielding the party in a stronger economic position from enforcement of obligations. Again, the assumption of contractual negotiating equality tends not to withstand contact with the realities of risk transfer from dominant actors to those in a weaker economic position,[110] serving instead to consolidate existing patterns of control, including as they regard gendered distribution of economic power.

IV. Conclusions: Private International Law and the Taxonomy of Feminist Legal Thought

We argued in the foregoing sections of this chapter that, across its various subdisciplines, private international law has a gender problem. It follows that there is some urgency for our discipline to draw on feminist legal thought to correct its course and address the manner in which its rules may have profoundly discriminatory effects on women. Given the paucity of feminist engagement with private international law, and consequently the absence of developed bespoke theoretical grounding, it is instructive to consider how to situate private international law in the context of existing feminist analyses of the law. Of course, feminist legal theory is diverse in method and ideological grounding. Accordingly, we do not propose here to provide a comprehensive account of relevant scholarship. Nor do we seek to advance a definitive or comprehensive feminist theory of private international law. Instead, we look to general themes in existing scholarship to identify the extent to which feminist private international law can rely on better-developed narratives to infuse the discipline with a healthy dose of self-criticism in relation to the law's effects on women. We look particularly to public international law and private law as the principal disciplines with which private international law interacts.

Historically, several feminist scholars argued that international law creates a false dichotomy between the public and private sphere, and that this results in states expressing little interest in the affairs of women.[111] The argument proceeded on the basis that women's experiences are especially distinct in the domestic, interpersonal sphere, whereas international law concerns itself principally with male-dominated areas of activity.[112] Even accepting, for the sake of argument, that women are to be found in the domestic sphere, the relevance of this critique to private international law is limited. Indeed, to the extent that much of private international law is built on international agreements, that critique of public international law may have required some qualification at the outset; states have long concerned themselves in their relations with one another with matters which are

[110] See SE Woodward, 'Limited Liability in the Theory of the Firm' in DA Wittman (ed), *Economic Analysis of the Law. Selected Readings* (Blackwell Press, 2003).

[111] See K Engle, 'After the Collapse of the Public/Private Distinction: Strategizing Women's Rights' in D Dallmeyer (ed), *Reconceiving Reality: Women and International Law* (ASIL, 1993).

[112] ibid.

intimately related to interactions of particular concern to women. In addition to agreements of a classical public international law nature such as the Convention on the Elimination of all Forms of Discrimination Against Women and general human rights instruments (which are widely acknowledged in feminist discourse),[113] the Hague Conference and European Union have adopted instruments across a vast swathe of matters affecting family life.[114]

Nevertheless, it remains true that international relations are principally 'peopled by men',[115] and this is also the case for much of the historical development and application of private international law instruments.[116] It is arguable that this results in private international law failing consistently to address questions of equality with a view to attaining substantive outcomes. Often, it preserves differences. At worst, it provides opportunities for private actors to avoid equality-oriented substantive law through jurisdictional and choice of law mechanisms which fail to account for power asymmetries, save to the extent that public policy exceptions might provide some *ex-post* safeguards. This, however, reveals a further tension insofar as the response to individual power disparity is viewed through the prism of the state rather than the individual's experience. A state-centric approach to private international law focusing on the state as the relevant unit having an interest in conflicts processes could equally have adverse effects for women insofar as they are subsumed in the state narrative.[117]

A relational feminist approach to private international law therefore provides particularly useful insights in the context of some aspects of private international law in that it seeks to resolve private disparity with reference to private interests, rather than framing those interests exclusively with reference to the community.[118] This is especially illuminating in the context of international surrogacy, for example, insofar as the role of the state tends towards the disempowerment of women in vulnerable and life-altering circumstances.[119] Relational feminism provides tools to focus on the private interests in private relationships, as opposed to the orthodox focus on the interactions of public policies of states.[120] In this construct, courts might look beyond generalised categorisations of vulnerability and focus instead on the extent to which consent in the specific instance is unfettered by asymmetry.[121] Equally, in the context of child abduction, a relational feminist approach would look beyond the mechanistic rigidity of a returns mechanism which favours automaticity over exploration of the circumstances which motivated the removal of a child.

[113] ibid.
[114] For discussion of some of those instruments, see section II above and the references therein.
[115] H Charlesworth, C Chinkin and S Wright, 'Feminist Approached to International Law' (1991) 85 *American Journal of International Law* 613, 625.
[116] Keyes (n 14) 18.
[117] Banu (n 18) 9–14.
[118] ibid, 17–29.
[119] ibid.
[120] ibid, 30–31.
[121] ibid.

The rationale of relational feminism in private international law is especially seductive when viewed on its own terms. It appears, at face value, to resolve both the problem of the paternalistic state and the fallacy of unrestrained autonomy.[122] Judges would be empowered to look to the particularities of each case, as opposed to relying on blunt prescriptions which disregard diversity of experience and outlook. However, it is submitted that disregarding the advantage of predictability in private international law is itself problematic when viewed from the perspective of any party in a weaker economic position.

The role of feminist thought in private international law must therefore be more nuanced than any single prescription. Whereas private international law is often framed as a discipline which facilitates the resolution of transnational disputes, its primary function, as with all law, is to predict outcomes. Predictability reduces costs, thereby enhancing access to justice for the party with lesser financial means. Those predictable outcomes can only be mediated by states. It is in the legal design of those predictable outcomes that feminist perspectives might be especially instructive. Contemporary feminist critiques of international law therefore offer a clearer route to challenging the international system insofar as they recommend more sustained analysis of the effects of interstate relations on women's lived experiences.[123] As with other international instruments, private international law conventions would benefit from clearer focus on the unintended consequences of chosen methods of harmonisation which treat matters of particular interest to women as concerns for national law. Feminist analyses of international law correctly note that this tends to result in a lack of regard for the place of women in the international order. From a private international law perspective, outcomes can be more acute than would be the case if mere disregard were the only concern. International harmonisation which privileges state choices tends to exacerbate the problematic effects of those choices by granting extraterritorial recognition to the harms they may cause.

It follows, in our view, that there is a need for more sustained and structured consideration of the effects of private international law instruments and principles on women. This necessitates the mainstreaming of feminist critiques of the law with a view to ensuring that the discipline is both populated by women and considerate of women's distinct and diverse interests, experiences and vulnerabilities. To this end, feminist legal scholarship, even with its rich, unsettled methodologies and ideologies, serves an essential consciousness raising function which merits a more central role in the continuing evolution of private international scholarship and law-making.[124]

[122] ibid.

[123] See H Charlesworth and C Chinkin, 'Introduction to the 2022 edition' in *The Boundaries of International Law: A Feminist Analysis: With a New Introduction*, 3rd edn (Manchester University Press, 2022).

[124] See, eg, CA MacKinnon, 'Feminism, Marxism, Method, and the State: An Agenda for Theory' (1982) 7 *Journal of Women in Culture and Society* 513.

PART II

Civil and Commercial Matters in Private International Law

6

Damage

ANDREW DICKINSON

I. Introduction

Jonathan Fitchen was a thoughtful and meticulous scholar. As his published writing demonstrates, he immersed himself in the *travaux préparatoires* of the European Union's private international law instruments in order to enlighten readers as to their innate structures and to untangle difficult issues.[1]

Occasionally, key concepts within these instruments are forged not by careful (or not so careful) sculpting in the negotiating chamber, but by the haphazard evolutionary forces emanating from case law. This chapter considers one important example of this phenomenon, which today plays a prominent role in both the Recast Brussels I Regulation[2] and the Rome II Regulation.[3] The chapter's purpose is to examine, as Jonathan might have done, the source and evolution of the concept of 'damage' in these instruments through a series of decisions of the European Court of Justice (ECJ) over the course of almost half a century.

It is difficult to locate something without knowing what it is. Although it now occupies a central position in the European Union's set of private international law rules for non-contractual obligations, the concept of 'damage' is nonetheless remarkably difficult to define. According to Article 2 of the Rome II Regulation, 'damage shall cover <u>any consequence</u> arising out of tort/delict, unjust enrichment, *negotiorum gestio* or *culpa in contrahendo*'.[4] This broad expression is not easily

[1] For a fine example, see Jonathan's analysis of the rules for recognition and enforcement of Member State judgments in A Dickinson and E Lein (eds), *The Brussels I Regulation Recast* (Oxford University Press, 2015) ch 13, Pts IV and V.

[2] Regulation (EU) No 1215/2012 of the European Parliament and of the Council of 12 December 2012 on jurisdiction and the recognition and enforcement of judgments in civil and commercial matters (Recast), [2012] OJ L351/1, esp Art 7(2), which deploys the same connecting factor as Art 5(3) of the 1968 Brussels Convention (see section II below) and the original Brussels I Regulation (Regulation (EC) No 44/2001 of 22 December 2000 on jurisdiction and the recognition and enforcement of judgments in civil and commercial matters, [2001] OJ L12/1).

[3] Regulation (EC) No 864/2007 of the European Parliament and of the Council of 11 July 2007 on the law applicable to non-contractual obligations (Rome II), [2007] OJ L199/40, especially Art 4(1).

[4] Emphasis added.

reconciled with Article 4 of the same Regulation, which distinguishes damage from 'the event giving rise to the damage' and from 'the indirect consequences of that event', and Recitals 16 and 17 which also contrast 'direct damage' with 'indirect consequences'. Those distinctions, in turn, will be familiar to students of the ECJ's case law with respect to the 1968 Brussels Convention and its successor instruments, although the Court has, perhaps wisely, never attempted a comprehensive definition of a term which lacks a secure textual foothold. Instead, the case law has elucidated the concept only gradually, and sometimes imperceptibly, to the point where its contours can now be traced.

The central submission of this chapter is that the concept of 'damage' within EU private international law is an active one which fixes upon the way in which the relevant event brings about its (claimed) effects upon the victim, by adversely affecting a legally protected interest of that person to which the claim relates. This opens up the possibility of classifying different kinds of legally protected interests, with a view to developing autonomous approaches for locating interferences with them.

II. Conception

In the French language version of the 1968 Convention, the word '*dommage*' appears in Article 5(4) of the Convention ('*une action en réparation de dommage*') and adjectivally in Articles 5(3), 9 and 12(3), each of which refers to '*le fait dommegable*'. The German language version similarly refers in Article 5(4) to '*eine Klage auf Schadenersatz*' and in Articles 5(3), 9 and 12(3) to '*das schädigende Ereignis*', and the same pattern can be seen in the Italian[5] and Dutch[6] language versions. The English translation of the Convention,[7] prepared upon the UK's accession to the European Community, but before its accession to the Convention, refers instead, in Article 5(4) to 'a civil claim for damages' and in Articles 5(3), 9 and 12(3) to 'the harmful event', expressions which seem less precise,[8] although the difference in terminology does not seem to have given rise to significant difficulty in practice.[9]

[5] Art 5(4): *un'azione di risarcimento di danni;* Arts 5(3), 9 and 12(3): *l'evento dannoso.*

[6] Art 5(4); *[een] rechtsvordering tot schadevergoeding;* Art 5(3), 9 and 12(3): *het schadebrengende feit.*

[7] 1968 Brussels Convention on jurisdiction and the enforcement of judgments in civil and commercial matters, [1972] OJ L299/32.

[8] Compare the English text of Preliminary Draft Convention on the Law Applicable to Contractual and Non-Contractual Obligations (1972), Art 10(1), referring to 'an event which has resulted in damage or injury'. The French language text, modelled on the 1968 Brussels Convention, also refers to '*un fait dommageable*'.

[9] For the difficulties encountered by the English courts in interpreting the concept of 'damage' in the rule (6B PD3.1(9)) governing service out of the jurisdiction in tort cases, see *Four Seasons Holdings Inc v Brownlie* [2017] UKSC 80, [2018] 1 WLR 192; *FS Cairo (Nile Plaza) LLC v Brownlie* [2021] UKSC 45, [2022] AC 995. Following the Supreme Court's decision in the second *Brownlie* case, the concept has become detached from its counterpart in the (formerly applicable) Brussels I regime (see *FS Cairo (Nile Plaza) LLC v Brownlie*, above, [35]–[44], [52]–[56] (Lord Lloyd-Jones), [179]–[180], [183] (Lord Leggatt)).

With respect to Article 5(3) of the Convention, laying down the rule of special jurisdiction for matters relating to tort etc, the Jenard Report observed:[10]

> Article 5(3) uses the expression 'the place where the harmful event occurred'. The Committee did not think it should specify whether that place is the place where the event which resulted in damage or injury occurred, or whether it is the place where the damage or injury was sustained. The Committee preferred to keep to a formula which has already been adopted by number of legal systems (Germany, France).

This ambiguity was famously explored by the ECJ in *Handelskwekerij GJ Bier BV v Mines de potasse d'Alsace SA*, and resolved in favour of a flexible interpretation, favouring 'both the place where the damage occurred and the place of the event giving rise to it'.[11] As to the former concept, the Court referred in passing to 'damage to [the claimant's] plantations' and to 'expensive measures to limit that damage',[12] but otherwise offered no guidance as to its meaning. The Advocate General, who favoured awarding jurisdiction only to the courts for the place in which the damage for which compensation is claimed occurred, suggested that the 'harmful event' could only be located 'where the act is legally speaking complete, that is where the injury to the legal rights of the person suffering it occurs'.[13]

III. Ontogenesis

A. Separation

As noted, the ECJ's decision in *Bier* had already distinguished between 'the damage' and 'the event in which that damage originates' observing that liability in tort etc can only arise when there is a causal connection between the two.[14] Subsequently, the Court drew a further distinction between 'initial damage'[15] and other consequences of allegedly wrongful conduct. Four cases attest to this development. In *Netherlands v Rüffer*, Advocate General Warner rejected as

[10] 'Report by Mr P Jenard on the Convention of 27 September 1968 on jurisdiction and the enforcement of judgments in civil and commercial matters' [1979] OJ C59/1, 26. A similar ambiguity in the text of Art 10(1) of the Preliminary Draft Convention on the Law Applicable to Contractual and Non-Contractual Obligations (1972) (n 8) was acknowledged by the authors (Giuliano, Lagarde and van Sasse van Ysselt) in their Report on that Draft: see K Siehr in O Lando, B von Hoffmann and K Siehr (eds), *European Private International Law of Obligations* (JCB Mohr, 1975) 48–49. Siehr describes the language of the Draft, modelled on the 1968 Brussels Convention, as 'somewhat delphic'.

[11] Case 21/76 *Handelskwekerij GJ Bier BV v Mines de potasse d'Alsace SA* [1976] ECR 1735, para 24.

[12] ibid, para 3.

[13] ibid, Opinion of AG Capoporti, para 9. This prescient remark foreshadows the evolution of distinct categories of 'protected interest' within the European Court's case law concerning the concept of damage (see section III.B. below).

[14] ibid, [16]. See also Case C-242/20 *HRVATSKE ŠUME doo v BP Europe SE* [2021] ECLI:EU:2021:985, [2022] ILPr 209, [53]–[55].

[15] Terminology first deployed by AG Darmon in his Opinion in Case C-220/88 *Dumez France SA v Hessische Landesbank* [1990] ECR I-49, paras 52–53.

'ill-founded' the suggestion that damage to the Dutch state had occurred either in The Hague, where it had its seat of government, or in Delfzijl, where goods salvaged from the wreck of the defendant's vessel had been sold thereby crystallising the shortfall in the claimant's costs of removing it from another location.[16] The Court held the Convention inapplicable to the facts of the case, and did not address this question.[17] Subsequently, in *Dumez France SA v Hessische Landesbank*, the Court held that 'the place where the damage occurred' referred only to 'the place where the event giving rise to the damage, and entailing tortious [etc] liability, directly produced its harmful effects upon the person who is the immediate victim of that event', and not 'the place where the indirect victims of the damage ascertain the repercussions on their own assets'.[18] In the Court's view, 'the harm alleged by the [claimant] parent companies ... is merely the indirect consequence of the financial losses initially suffered by their subsidiaries following cancellation [by the defendants] of the loans and the subsequent suspension of the works'.[19] In *Marinari v Lloyd's Bank plc*, the Court extended that reasoning to a case involving adverse consequences suffered by a single person to exclude from consideration 'the place where ... the victim claims to have suffered financial damage following upon initial damage arising and suffered by him in another Contracting State'.[20] Finally, in *Kronhofer v Maier*, the Court's reasoning straightforwardly ruled out the possibility of conferring jurisdiction on the courts of the place where the claimant is domiciled and his assets are concentrated by reason of the fact that the claimant had suffered financial damage there resulting from the loss of assets in another Contracting State.[21]

B. Specification

These decisions, focusing on the place of 'initial' (or 'direct') damage, are well known. They define the concept of damage negatively, by excluding the 'follow-on' (or 'indirect') consequences of a harmful event. To a more limited extent, the reasoning applied in these cases also helps to identify the features of the decided cases which were thought to constitute the 'initial' or 'direct' damage to which the Court attached significance. In *Dumez*, the ECJ described the damage in *Bier* – 'to crops in the Netherlands' – as having occurred 'by the direct effect of the causal agent, namely the saline waste which had moved physically from one place to another'.[22] With respect to the case before it, the Court in *Dumez* stated that the 'direct consequences' of the defendants' cancellation of loans to the claimants'

[16] Case 814/79 *Netherlands v Rüffer* [1985] ECR 3807, Opinion of AG Warner, 3835–36.
[17] *Netherlands v Rüffer* (n 16) paras 16–17.
[18] Above (n 15) paras 15–21.
[19] ibid, para 13.
[20] Case C-364/93 *Marinari v Lloyd's Bank plc* [1995] ECR I-2719, para 15.
[21] Case C-168/02 *Kronhofer v Maier* [2004] ECR I-6009, para 21.
[22] Above (n 15) para 12.

subsidiaries were 'produced' in Germany, where the parties to the loan contracts were all established and where the building works that were suspended as a result, leading to financial losses for the subsidiaries, had been undertaken.[23] Later in its judgment, it referred to 'the place where the initial damage manifested itself' as being 'closely related to the other components of the liability'.[24] In *Marinari*, Advocate General Darmon suggested that the 'initial damage' involved sequestration of promissory notes and the claimant's imprisonment in the United Kingdom.[25] He drew a contrast between, 'the place where the damage arises' and 'the place where it is suffered', with only the former being of significance for the purposes of Article 5(3).[26] In *Kronhofer*, although the Court did not need to address the point, in view of the question addressed to it, it identified the damage with the loss of particular assets.[27]

The proceedings before the Court in *Marinari* ran in parallel with those in *Shevill v Presse Alliance SA*. Both cases were initially heard in the first half of 1994, and subsequently reopened for further submissions; in each case, Advocate General Darmon gave an Opinion after the first hearing and Advocate General Léger after it. In *Shevill*, by contrast with the other cases referred to above, the Court chose to grasp the nettle of defining the concept of 'damage' in positive terms, both generally and with respect to the particular class of case with which it was concerned (involving defamation by written word). Having confirmed that the bifurcated approach adopted in *Bier* was not limited to cases involving physical or pecuniary loss,[28] the Court picked up the language that it had used in *Dumez* in stating that:

> [T]he place where the damage occurred is the place where the event giving rise to the damage, entailing tortious, delictual or quasi-delictual liability, produced its harmful effects upon the victim.[29]

It continued:

> In the case of an international libel through the press, the injury caused by a defamatory publication to the honour, reputation and good name of a natural or legal person occurs in the places where the publication is distributed, when the victim is known in those places.[30]

In the latter part of its judgment, the Court emphasised that this autonomous interpretation of 'the place where the damage occurred' did not prevent a court

[23] ibid, para 13.
[24] ibid, para 21.
[25] Above (n 20) Opinion of AG Darmon, para 26.
[26] ibid, paras 28–30.
[27] Above (n 21) para 21. On the facts, funds transferred by the claimant into an investment account in Germany had been used to subscribe for highly speculative opinions on the London Stock Exchange, ibid para 7. Whether the damage occurred in Germany or the UK, it did not occur in Austria, where the claimant was domiciled and from where he had originally transferred the funds.
[28] Case C-68/93 *Shevill v Presse Alliance SA* [1995] ECR I-415, para 23.
[29] ibid, para 28.
[30] ibid, para 29.

from applying its own rules of evidence, including any relevant presumption, in determining whether a publication was harmful to the victim.[31]

Three elements of this reasoning are noteworthy. First, the Court's general conception of 'damage' (and of the 'place of damage') involved (1) the *production* (2) of *harmful effects*, (3) *upon the victim*, (4) by the event giving rise to damage. This conception of damage is, therefore, an active one, fixing upon the way in which the relevant event brings about its (claimed)[32] effects upon the victim rather than simply upon the end result. Secondly, following from the first point, the way in which the relevant harmful effects are defined (in *Shevill*, injury to the victim's reputation)[33] is a derivative of the way in which the event giving rise to damage is characterised (in *Shevill*, libel by circulation of a newspaper article).[34] Thirdly, both the event giving rise to damage and the harmful effects produced by that event are to be interpreted autonomously, without reference to the law applicable to the merits of the claim. This last point is emphasised by the way in which the Court dissected the questions put to it by the House of Lords, giving its own interpretation of the 'place where the damage occurred' before looking at the mode of proof of the harmful effects to which it referred.[35] Later, in *Marinari*, the Court specifically rejected a submission by the German government that the conception of 'damage' should take account of the applicable national law on non-contractual civil liability, and in particular on presence or absence of a requirement of 'an actual adverse effect on goods or rights' as a condition of liability or on the location of assets when the obligation to redress the damage arose.[36]

These elements can be seen at play in the Court's later case law, involving a wide variety of claim types. It is convenient to begin with cases involving damage to, or other interferences with, tangible things.

i. Interference with Tangible Things

In *Réunion européenne SA v Spliethoff's Bevrachtingskantoor BV*, involving damage to goods during transportation by sea and then by land, the Court located the damage with respect to a claim against the maritime carrier in the place where that carrier was to deliver the goods,[37] and not the final place of delivery or the place where the damage was discovered.[38] This confirms that the *production* of *harmful*

[31] ibid, paras 34–41.

[32] Here it is important to recognise that, at the stage of determining jurisdiction or the law applicable to a claim, there has yet been no finalisation of the claim. The use of the word 'victim' must be understood in this light, as referring to the person who claims to have been affected by an event for which another person is claimed to be legally responsible.

[33] Above (n 28) para 30.

[34] ibid, paras 24, 29.

[35] ibid, para 34.

[36] Above (n 20) paras 16–20; *cf Sayn-Wittgenstein-Sayn v HM Juan Carlos* [2023] EWHC 2478 (KB), [62]–[63], [78].

[37] Case C-51/97 *Réunion européenne SA v Spliethoff's Bevrachtingskantoor BV* [1998] ECR I-6511, para 35.

[38] ibid, paras 32–34.

effects is not conditional upon their discovery by the claimant, or indeed by anyone else. It is, however, unclear precisely how the Court came to the conclusion that the event giving rise to damage, which it acknowledged 'may be difficult or impossible to locate',[39] produced its harmful effect on the victim at the place of delivery by the maritime carrier. In *Réunion européenne*, fruit consigned on board the defendant's ship ripened prematurely owing to a breakdown in the ship's cooling.[40] If one were to proceed by analogy with *Bier*, the relevant harmful effect produced by the event giving rise to damage would seem to be deterioration of the cargo. Moreover, applying the reasoning in *Dumez*, it should not matter whether the fruit belonged to the consignee under the bill of lading (whose interest the claimant represented) at the time of that deterioration. The point in time at which property passed to the claimant should not affect the specification of damage.[41] On that view, the location of the damage would, as much as the event giving rise to it, likely be impossible to fix and in many cases the known or discoverable facts would point to a place (the high seas) beyond the territorial sovereignty of any state. At first sight, therefore, the Court's ruling as to the location of the damage may seem a rather unprincipled, albeit pragmatic, one in the interests of certainty and the efficacious conduct of proceedings.[42]

A more principled answer may, however, be gleaned from the Opinion of Advocate General Cosmas. His review of the Court's existing case law led him to conclude, first, that 'in order to determine the "place where the damage occurred", it is essential to define the relevant "damage"';[43] secondly, that '"damage" means any harm to the property or person of the plaintiff, where it relates to the event giving rise to the damage, that is to say to the illegal behaviour attributed to the defendant[,] by a direct and causal link';[44] thirdly, if the place where the property was damaged is known and is located in the European Union, the court having jurisdiction will be easily located;[45] fourthly, it may however be impossible to locate this place (at least within the European Union) in such a way as to identify the court having jurisdiction;[46] fifthly, as a matter of fact in the case at hand, the deterioration of goods due to a failure of refrigeration systems on board the defendant's vessel occurred 'during the course of the transport and, at the latest, at the end of the transport';[47] sixthly, the place where the maritime carrier delivered the goods is the last place where the goods were under the carrier's responsibility and suffered the harmful consequences of its (allegedly) unlawful conduct.[48]

[39] ibid, para 33.
[40] ibid, para 3. The fruit consisted of 5,199 boxes of pears (ibid, Opinion of AG Cosmas, para 3).
[41] *cf*, in English tort law, *The Aliakmon* [1986] AC 785 (HL).
[42] *Réunion européenne* (n 37) [36].
[43] ibid, Opinion of AG Cosmas, para 48.
[44] ibid.
[45] ibid, para 54.
[46] ibid. The qualification with respect to the territory of the EU seems unnecessary here. If tangible property is damaged while in a non-Member State, that fact negates the possible application of Art 7(2) on this basis.
[47] ibid, Opinion of AG Cosmas, para 58.
[48] ibid, para 60.

On this view, the reasoning in *Réunion européenne* involves a particular application (for goods in transit) of the general principle that, where an event for which the defendant is responsible causes physical deterioration of a tangible thing, the damage – consisting of the harmful effect of that event upon the proprietary relationship of one or more persons with the thing – is located in the place where the thing was situated at the relevant time.[49] A more straightforward application of this principle can be seen in *Zuid-Chemie BV v Philippo's Mineralenfabriek NV/SA*, a product liability case. In that case, the Dutch buyer had purchased chemicals ('micromix') from a Belgian manufacturer, collected the consignment from the latter's factory in Belgium and transported it to its own factory in the Netherlands before using the chemicals in the manufacture of fertiliser, which (as a result of a defect in the composition of the micromix) was unusable. The ECJ concluded that

> the place where the damage occurred cannot be any other than [the claimant's] factory in the Netherlands where the micromix, which is the defective product, was processed into fertiliser, causing substantial damage to that fertiliser which was suffered by [the claimant] and which went beyond the damage to the micromix itself.[50]

In reaching this conclusion, the Court identified 'the place where the event which gave rise to the damage produces its harmful effects' with 'the place where the damage caused by the defective product *actually manifests itself*.'[51] The italicised words, appearing in the English language version of the judgment, appear to distort slightly those in the Dutch original ('*zich concreet voordoet*'), which emphasise the need for the causal effect to be definitive, conclusive and material, rather than (as the English verb 'manifests' would suggest) outwardly apparent to the senses.[52] As the facts and reasoning in both *Réunion européenne* and *Zuid-Chemie* demonstrate, damage may occur even though it has not yet been discovered and further enquiries (possibly using specialised equipment) will be needed to discover it.[53]

In this connection, it should be noted that, although the Court has sometimes spoken in terms of 'damage to' a tangible thing[54] to signify the physical effect of the event giving rise to damage, that is to use the word in a different sense from its more specific usage in signifying the harm *produced upon* the (direct) victim of the tort by the event giving rise to damage, through the alteration of that person's

[49] See Rome II Regulation, Recital 17.

[50] Case C-189/08 *Zuid-Chemie BV v Philippo's Mineralenfabriek NV/SA* [2009] ECR I-6917, para 29.

[51] ibid, para 27 (emphasis added).

[52] The same idea is conveyed in later judgments, which (unfortunately) use the same English translation: see Case C-352/13 *Cartel Damage Claims (CDC) Hydrogen Peroxide SA v Evonik Degussa GmbH* [2015] 3 WLR 909, para 52 (German – *konkret*); Case C-304/17 *Löber v Barclays Bank plc* [2019] 4 WLR 5, para 27 (same); Case C-709/19 *Vereniging van Effectenbezitters v BP plc* [2021] ILPr 23, para 31 (Dutch). For further discussion of these cases, see section III.B.iii.b below. See also, *Kwok v UBS AG* [2022] EWHC 245 (Comm), [2022] 2 All ER (Comm) 448 [84], [111] (Cockerill J) and [2023] EWCA Civ 222, [2023] 1 WLR 1984 [27]–[28], [45] (Vos MR).

[53] *Zuid Chemie* (n 50) [9].

[54] See text to nn 12, 22 and 50 above.

proprietary relationship with the thing.[55] In this connection, it should be noted there will be damage in the latter sense even if the thing in question does not undergo any physical change but is interfered with in such a way as to cause someone to lose control of it, temporarily or permanently. *Marinari* neatly illustrates this proposition. As the Advocate General explained, the initial damage suffered by the claimant consisted at least in part of the sequestration of promissory notes[56] following the money laundering report made by the defendant bank's staff and occurred in the United Kingdom where the notes were located at the time of their sequestration.[57]

ii. Interference with Personal Health or Freedom

If the identification and location of damage in cases involving interference with tangible things seems rather straightforward, however instructive those cases may be in developing a general understanding of the concept, one may expect the same to be true for interferences with the claimant's personal health or freedom. Indeed, Recital 17 to the Rome II Regulation treats 'personal injury' alongside 'damage to property' when it states that 'the country in which the damage occurs should be the country where the injury was sustained or the property was damaged'. Although damage falling under this heading may sometimes be difficult to locate, for example where an event such as exposure to a toxic substance has a continuing effect upon a person's health, the relevant initial damage will not normally be difficult to specify in cases where the victim's physical condition deteriorates, by injury or illness.[58] Here, the approach taken by the ECJ in cases involving interference with tangible things would suggest that what is being sought is not the symptom, the manifestation of a condition or disease, but the physical cause of it, that is to say the mechanism by which the event giving rise to damage has the capacity to bring about the injury or illness. Although some input from medical experts may be necessary, a detailed causal enquiry at this stage is undesirable. For example, if the claim is that the claimant has been exposed to asbestos as a result of the defendant's activity or failure to take preventative measures, the ingestion of fibres

[55] For an appreciation of this double usage of the term *damnum* in Roman law, and in particular in texts relating to the *Lex Aquilia*, see D Daube in V Arangio-Ruiz (ed), *Studi in Onore di Siro Solazzi nel Cinquantesimo Anniversario del Suo Insegnamento Universitario*, 1899–1948 (Jovene, 1948) 93 ff, reproduced in D Cohen and D Simon (eds), *David Daube: Collected Studies in Roman Law* (Vittorio Klostermann, 1991) vol I, 279 ff. Daube concludes that the primary meaning of *damnum* in these texts is 'loss suffered by the owner' and that apparent references to damage to a thing (*damnum dare corpore suo*) must be understood as denoting 'that loss which a man causes to the owner of a thing by injuring the [thing] with his own hands'.

[56] Strikingly, the face value of the notes was US$752.5 billion.

[57] Above (n 20) Opinion of AG Darmon para 26. Distinct damage (arising from a different event) was arguably sustained by the claimant on the occasion of the initial refusal by bank staff to return the notes, ibid para 2, resulting in temporary deprivation prior to their sequestration by the UK authorities acting on the money laundering report.

[58] See section III.B.i. above.

as a result of that exposure should be taken to constitute damage even though the specific disease from which the claimant suffers does not develop until much later by a complex aetiology and even though the presence of fibres in the claimant's lungs does not constitute actionable damage under national law.[59] That approach is not only relatively straightforward to apply, in terms of locating the damage, but also specifies an occurrence which is likely to be more closely related to the other components of liability.[60] A similar approach to (non-relational)[61] claims for psychiatric illness would lead to a focus on the sensory perception of a trigger event even if a recognised disorder develops, and is diagnosable, only over time.

The ECJ has only rarely had the opportunity to consider 'damage' falling within this category. Its most significant decision, *Lazar v Allianz SpA*, concerns Article 4(1) of the Rome II Regulation. In that case, involving claims brought by relatives of the victim of a road traffic accident, the ECJ confirmed the need for the concept of 'damage' to be given a uniform definition, irrespective of the characterisation of loss in national law.[62] Having noted Article 2[63] and Recital 17, the Court concluded that:

> [W]here it is possible to identify the occurrence of direct damage, which is usually the case with a road traffic accident, the place where the direct damage occurred is the relevant connecting factor for the determination of the applicable law, regardless of the indirect consequences of that accident. In the present case, the damage is constituted by the injuries which led to the death of Mr Lazar's daughter, which, according to the referring court, occurred in Italy. The damage sustained by the close relatives of the deceased, must be regarded as indirect consequences of the accident at issue in the main proceedings, within the meaning of Article 4(1) of the Rome II Regulation.[64]

This conclusion was reinforced, in the Court's view, by Article 15(f) of the Regulation, referring to 'persons entitled to compensation for damage sustained personally', and by the view expressed by the Commission in its original Proposal for the Regulation that this concept refers to compensation for damage sustained on a 'knock-on' basis, whether 'non-material, as in the pain and suffering caused by a bereavement, or financial, as in the loss sustained by the children or spouse of a deceased person'.[65] By contrast with Advocate General Wahl,[66] the ECJ did not

[59] See, in English tort law, *Rothwell v Chemical & Insulating Co Ltd* [2007] UKHL 39, [2008] 1 AC 281.

[60] See *Dumez* (n 15) para 21.

[61] *cf* Case C-350/14 *Lazar v Allianz SpA* [2016] 1 WLR 835, discussed in the following paragraph.

[62] ibid, paras 17–18, 21.

[63] Rome II Regulation.

[64] Above (n 61) para 25.

[65] ibid, paras 26–27. See Commission, 'Proposal for a Regulation of the European Parliament and Council on the Law Applicable to Non – Contractual Obligations (Rome II)' COM(2003) 427 final, 24. The use of the word 'psychological' in the English language version of the judgment to translate the word '*morale*' in the original Italian seems too narrow.

[66] *Lazar* (n 61) Opinion of AG Wahl, paras 53–66. Subsequently, in Case C-498/20 *ZK v BMA Braunschweigische Maschinenbauanstalt AG* (Court of Justice, 10 March 2022) paras 59–60, the ECJ expressly recognised the desirability, for the sake of consistency, of taking account of the Brussels I case law on this issue, referring to Recital 7 to the Rome II Regulation.

refer directly to its case law concerning the Brussels I regime, although its conclusion is perfectly consistent with that case law.

Finally, *Marinari* provides an example of a case involving interference with the claimant's freedom, without personal injury. In the Advocate General's view, the initial damage to Mr Marinari included his arrest in the United Kingdom.[67]

iii. Interference with Relational Autonomy

By common consensus, the concept of 'damage' becomes more difficult to apply with respect to the financial and other non-material consequences of conduct which is said to be wrongful.[68] The focus in the literature, and in the case law of the ECJ, has been on claims involving financial loss not consequential upon an interference with health, freedom or tangible property. It is submitted, however, that it is useful to treat cases of this type as part of a wider class of cases involving interferences with relational autonomy, that is to say where the event giving rise to damage affects the freedom of the claimant (or another person or class of persons) to deal with others in a particular manner. On this view, following the high-level approach taken with respect to the preceding categories, one seeks to identify and locate the mechanism by which the event giving rise to damage has impaired a person's relational autonomy in a sufficiently 'concrete'[69] way.

This proposed treatment generates a trichotomy involving interferences with the freedom to deal with tangible things (see section III.B.i above), interferences with a person's own wellbeing or freedom (see section III.B.ii above) and interferences with the freedom to deal with other persons. On this view, cases such as *Shevill*,[70] involving reputational injury, or *eDate Advertising GmbH v X*,[71] involving violations of privacy, fall within this class, insofar as the publication (or accessibility) of material to third parties in a particular place impairs (or has the capacity to impair) the respect that those persons have for the reputation or privacy of the victim. Arguably, the position of the relatives in *Lazar* could also be analysed along the same lines, as involving not the indirect consequences of the death of a primary victim but as the loss of relational autonomy due to the extinction of family relationships by death.

The ECJ's case law, principally with respect to financial loss, suggests that a further delineation within this class is helpful: between cases in which the event giving rise to damage distinctly and individually impairs the claimant's (or other victim's) relational autonomy and cases in which that event collectively impairs the

[67] Above (n 20) Opinion of AG Darmon, para 26. See also *Sayn-Wittgenstein-Sayn v HM Juan Carlos* (n 36) (harassment).

[68] Lord Collins of Mapesbury et al (eds), *Dicey, Morris & Collins: The Conflict of Laws*, 16th edn (Sweet & Maxwell, 2022) [35–026]–[35–027].

[69] Text to n 52 above. As noted, this term should be understood to require that the relevant effect upon the victim should be definitive, conclusive and material and seems more likely to be a determinative factor in cases of this kind than those within the preceding categories.

[70] Text to nn 28–35 above. See also, Case C-251/20 *Gtflix Tv v DR* [2022] ILPr 10.

[71] Joined Cases C-509/09 and C-161/10 *eDate Advertising GmbH v X* [2011] ECR I-10269.

relational autonomy of a class of persons whose membership includes the person suffering financial loss.[72] In the former type of case, the enquiry focuses solely on the impairment to the victim's relational autonomy. In the latter type of case, the enquiry focuses first on the impairment of collective relational autonomy before turning, by way of fine-tuning, to consider the position of the victim.

a. Interference with Individual Relational Autonomy

Dumez[73] provides a good example of this type of case. As all relevant facts occurred in Germany, the ECJ did not need to choose between the withdrawal by the defendant banks of project finance from the subsidiaries and the impact of that decision on the implementation of the projects as the occurrence constituting the damage sustained by the subsidiaries, which in turn led to the subsidiaries' insolvency and had an adverse financial impact on the claimant parent companies. The better view is that the withdrawal of the loans, a matter of contractual obligation between the banks and the subsidiaries, resulted in an impairment of the autonomy of the subsidiaries in their relationships with their counterparties in the construction contracts at the moment when (and in the place where) they were unable to perform their obligations to provide building services.

The leading decision of the ECJ within this category is *Universal Music International Holding BV v Schilling*.[74] As a result of the defendant's alleged negligence in drafting a share purchase agreement, the claimant purchaser, a Dutch company, concluded in the Czech Republic a contract containing a term for the fixing of the sale price that was significantly less favourable to it than the parties' original letter of intent had contemplated. A dispute arose with the sellers and was

[72] See *Vereniging van Effectenbezitters v BP plc* (n 52), Opinion of AG Campos Sánchez-Bordona [2020] ECLI:EU:C:2020:1056, [84], distinguishing between 'diffuse', 'collective' and 'individual' interests. The recent decision in *ZK v BMA Braunschweigische Maschinenbauanstalt AG* (n 66) also falls within the latter category (see nn 73 and 94 below). *cf* Case C-27/17 *AB 'flyLAL-Lithunian Airlines' v Starptautiskā lidosta 'Rīga' VAS* [2018] ECLI:EU:C:2018:136, Opinion of AG Bobek, paras 32, 56, focusing on damage to the private interests of individuals (specific damage) to the exclusion of damage to the public interest (general damage).

[73] Text to n 23 above. See also, eg, Case C-18/02 *DFDS Torline A/S v SEKO Sjöfolk Facket för Service och Kommunikation* [2004] ECR I-1417, para 42 (industrial action leading to withdrawal of vessel from its normal route and hire of another vessel to serve the same route). Compare *ZK v BMA Braunschweigische Maschinenbauanstalt AG* (n 66) paras 31–35, 59–61 (parent company's failure to fund subsidiary resulted in its inability to continue as a going concern, resulting in an action by the liquidator on behalf of all creditors). As noted above (n 72), this is perhaps best characterised as an interference with collective relational autonomy (ie, the creditors' freedom to deal with the subsidiary). Recent examples within this class in the English courts include: *AMT Futures Ltd v Marzillier* [2017] UKSC 13, [2018] AC 439, [27] (inducement by third party to contracting parties to breach choice of court agreement by bringing legal proceedings in Germany, which the claimant needed to defend); *Kwok v UBS AG* (n 52) [113]–[115] (Cockerill J) and [50]–[53] (Vos MR) (negligent misrepresentations causing claimants to structure financing arrangements in a particular way, involving the provision and then liquidation of security in London). The judgments in both English +cases contain valuable discussions of the ECJ and other case law.

[74] Case C-12/15 *Universal Music International Holding BV v Schilling* [2016] QB 697.

resolved by a settlement agreement, also concluded in the Czech Republic before an arbitration board, which imposed an obligation on the claimant to pay the sellers a fixed amount. That obligation was discharged by payment from an account held by the claimant in the Netherlands. The Dutch Supreme Court referred a number of questions concerning the identification and location of damage.

The Court's reasoning may be summarised as follows. First, the share purchase agreement, which placed the claimant under an obligation to pay a greater amount than originally provided for, arose in the Czech Republic.[75] Secondly, the damage 'became certain in the course of the settlement agreed between the parties before the arbitration board, in the Czech Republic, on 31 January 2005, the date on which the actual sale price was fixed' and, therefore, placed an 'irreversible burden' on the claimant's assets.[76] Thirdly, 'the loss of some assets happened in the Czech Republic, the damage having occurred there'.[77] Fourthly, this conclusion was not invalidated by the finding that the settlement amount was paid from a bank account in the Netherlands, having regard to the Court's earlier decisions in *Marinari* and *Kronhofer*.[78] As the Court put it: '[p]urely financial damage which occurs directly in the applicant's bank account cannot, in itself, be qualified as a "relevant connecting factor" within *[Art 7(2) of the Recast Brussels I Regulation]*', especially as the claimant may have had the choice to pay from one of several bank accounts.[79] Fifthly, in order to confer jurisdiction on the courts for the place where the 'purely financial damage' (in the Dutch original text of the judgment, *zuiver financiële schade*) occurred, there must be other circumstances specific to the case which contribute to attributing jurisdiction to those courts.[80]

Three aspects of reasoning are puzzling.

(1) The reference to 'purely financial damage' might be taken to suggest that a payment from a bank account qualifies, in principle, as 'damage', according to the ECJ's conception of the term, but is excluded for teleological reasons from operating as a connecting factor within what is now Article 7(2) of the Recast Brussels I Regulation. The better view would seem to be that it did not, at least on the facts of this case, constitute 'damage' at all, as the claimant's autonomy in managing its bank accounts was not constrained. As the Court pointed out,[81] it could have chosen to pay the settlement sum from any bank account.

(2) It is, perhaps, not immediately clear what 'assets'[82] the Court had in mind as having been lost in the Czech Republic. In context, the reference must be

[75] ibid, para 30.
[76] ibid, para 31.
[77] ibid, para 32.
[78] ibid, paras 34–35. See text to nn 20–21 above. The Court distinguished (ibid paras 36–37) its earlier decision in Case C-375/13 *Kolassa v Barclays Bank plc* [2015] ILPr 14 (see text to nn 86–90 below).
[79] *Universal Music* (n 74) para 38.
[80] ibid, para 39.
[81] ibid, para 38.
[82] Text to n 77 above.

understood with reference to the earlier statement that the settlement agreement had placed an 'irreversible burden' on the claimant's assets, ie, the claimant's entire patrimony.[83] It was the imposition of the monetary obligation to pay the settlement sum, constraining the claimant's ability to deal with its body of assets as it thought fit, that constituted a 'loss' of those assets.

(3) Although the Court did not need to choose between the place of the original contract and the place of the settlement agreement, as both were concluded in the Czech Republic, its reasoning might be taken to suggest that it would have favoured the latter on the basis that the price was not 'fixed' or 'irreversible' until that point.[84] This view seems to rest on rather shaky foundations. As cases involving personal injury or damage to property make clear, it is not necessary that the extent of the damage be determined or event determinable as a precondition to the application of Article 7(2). Would the provision have been held inapplicable if the claimant had brought proceedings before settling its dispute with the sellers or if it had, as yet, taken no steps in relation to that dispute? Moreover, the conclusion of a settlement agreement was an act of mitigation, and therefore comparable to the sale of the seized cargo in *Netherlands v Rüffer*.[85] It should have been characterised as an indirect consequence of the initial imposition of an unfavourable contractual obligation.

In light of the above, the more satisfactory rationalisation of the Court's reasoning in *Universal Music* is that damage to the claimant occurred when (and where) it assumed an obligation under the share purchase agreement to pay a sum greater than the amount that it had intended, by reason of having been placed at a disadvantage in its negotiations with the seller due to the defendant's alleged negligence.

b. Interference with Collective Relational Autonomy

In *Universal Music*, the ECJ found it necessary to distinguish its earlier decision in *Kolassa v Barclays Bank plc*, a prospectus liability case, in which it had concluded that jurisdiction could be conferred under Article 5(3) when 'loss occurred itself directly in the applicant's bank account held with a bank established within the area of jurisdiction of those courts'.[86] The Court offered the explanation that the conclusion that it had reached in *Kolassa* was 'made within the specific context of the case which gave rise to that judgment, a distinctive feature of which was the existence of

[83] Text to n 76 above.

[84] *Universal Music* (n 74) para 31. On the use by the ECJ of the language of 'irreversibility' and similar expressions, see *Kwok v UBS AG* (n 52) [116] (Cockerill J).

[85] Text to n 16 above.

[86] Above (n 78) para 55. Unfortunately, the Court did not specify whether the bank account to which it referred was the money account from which payment for the securities was transferred, or the securities account into which the relevant interests in securities were credited before falling in value. See text to nn 121–23 below.

circumstances contributing to attributing jurisdiction to those courts'.[87] The Court referred approvingly to passages from the Opinion of Advocate General Szpunar in which he had described the 'specific' facts of *Kolassa*, as follows: 'The defendant in that case, a British bank, had published a prospectus concerning the financial certificates in question in Austria and it was an Austrian bank that had sold those certificates'.[88] Advocate General Szpunar also referred to the ECJ's earlier decision in *Cartel Damage Claims Hydrogen Peroxide SA v Akzo Nobel NV*, involving alleged restrictions of competition through a cartel. In that case, the Court had concluded that the damage consisted of 'additional costs incurred because of artificially high prices' in the market for hydrogen peroxide and could be located, 'for each alleged victim taken individually … in general, at that victim's registered office'.[89] In the Advocate General's view, that statement did not establish a general rule that damage occurred in the principal place of establishment of the harmed undertaking: it was, instead, 'explained by the particular features of that case, in which a large number of persons had been harmed'.[90]

In both *Kolassa* and *Cartel Damage Claims*, the defendants' alleged wrongful conduct was committed in the 'marketplace' with the potential to harm all participants in that market. In *Kolassa*, the defendant had marketed securities in Austria by distributing its prospectus there.[91] In *Cartel Damage Claims*, the defendants had advertised and sold hydrogen peroxide within the EEA-wide market for that product.[92] The effect of that conduct was to impair the autonomy of all participants in the market in question in their dealings with third-party suppliers. Although it might have been possible to treat that general effect, in itself, as damage for the purposes of assigning jurisdiction (and determining the law applicable),[93] this would have presented two difficulties. First, the connecting factor lacks precision and would locate the 'damage' (and the resulting jurisdiction, or law applicable to a non-contractual obligation) across the entire marketplace.[94] Secondly, it is insufficiently 'concrete' in terms of its relationship to the facts of the case before the court. Accordingly, as the Court made clear in *Cartel Damage Claims*,[95] the damage must be specified individually for each market participant by reference to an appropriate

[87] *Universal Music* (n 74) para 37.

[88] ibid, Opinion of AG Szpunar, para 45.

[89] Above (n 52) para 52.

[90] *Universal Music* (n 74) Szpunar AG Opinion, para 47.

[91] Above (n 78) para 13.

[92] See the Commission's infringement decision at *Akzo* (Case COMP/F/C.38.620) Commission Decision 2006/903/EC, [2006] OJ L353/54.

[93] Rome II Regulation, Art 6(3)(a) refers to 'the law of the country where the market is, or is likely to be, affected'. As Recital 21 emphasises, is a 'clarification' of the general rule in Art 4(1) pointing to the law of the country in which the damage occurs.

[94] See *AB 'flyLAL-Lithuanian Airlines'* (n 72) Bobek AG Opinion paras 31–33. Compare *ZK v BMA Braunschweigische Maschinenbauanstalt AG* (n 66) paras 32–35, 61, where the loss suffered collectively by the general body of creditors could satisfactorily be located in a single place, being the place of establishment of the unfunded, bankrupt subsidiary.

[95] Text to n 89.

secondary connecting factor relating to the circumstances of its own claim. This results in a two-stage process in which the relational disadvantage suffered, collectively, by all market participants and occurring across the marketplace as a whole is focused, or fine-tuned, by reference to the circumstances of the particular case.

This 'alignment of two elements'[96] can be seen most clearly in the Court's later jurisprudence in cases involving restrictions of competition[97] and unfair competition.[98] In *Verein für Konsumenteninformation v Volkswagen AG*, in which the defendant had manipulated data relating to the emission of exhaust gases from its vehicles, the ECJ identified the relevant 'damage' as being 'loss in value of the vehicles in question stemming from the difference between the price paid by the purchaser for such a vehicle and its actual value owing to the installation of software that manipulates data relating to exhaust gas emissions'.[99] This occurred only when the vehicles were purchased by 'the final purchaser who considers himself adversely affected'[100] and cannot be said to constitute 'purely financial damage' as the case 'concerns a defect that affects vehicles, which are tangible assets'.[101] The damage occurs 'when such a vehicle is purchased from a third party'.[102] This conclusion, in the Court's view, was consistent with Article 6(1) of the Rome II Regulation[103] as the defendant's conduct 'being likely to affect the collective interests of consumers as a group, constitutes an act of unfair competition' and 'may affect those interests in any Member State within the territory of which the defective product is purchased by consumers'.[104]

More recently, in *RH v AB Volvo*, involving a cartel in the market for trucks across the European Economic Area, the ECJ specifically referred to the established infringement of Article 101 of the Treaty on the Functioning of the European Union,[105] leading to the conclusion that the damage occurred 'in that market'.[106] That conclusion, being consistent with Article 6(3)(a) of the Rome II

[96] Case C-30/20 *RH v AB Volvo* [2021] 5 CMLR 16, Opinion of AG de la Tour, para 58.

[97] Case C-27/17 *AB 'flyLAL-Lithunian Airlines' v Starptautiskā lidosta 'Rīga' VAS* (Court of Justice, 5 July 2018); Case C-451/18 *Tibor-Trans Fuvarozó és Kereskedelmi Kft v DAF Trucks NV* [2020] 1 WLR 1477; *RH v AB Volvo* (n 96). See also Case C-191/15 *Verein für Konsumenteninformation v Amazon EU Sàrl* [2017] 2 WLR 19, concerning the collective interests of consumers.

[98] Case C-343/19 *Verein für Konsumenteninformation v Volkswagen AG* [2021] 1 WLR 40.

[99] ibid, para 29 (also para 34).

[100] ibid, para 31.

[101] ibid paras 32–33. This last part of the reasoning ('affects vehicles, which are tangible assets') is hard to follow, as the interference with the vehicle as a tangible asset took place upon its manufacture and affected the value of the vehicle at its original point of sale. The essence of the complaint in the present case was not that a defect in the vehicle had caused loss, but that the concealment of a defect to all vehicles of a particular class had caused loss to participants in the market for that product.

[102] ibid, para 35.

[103] See Rome II Regulation, Recital 21 emphasising that Art 6(1), like Art 6(3)(a), is a clarification of the general rule in Art 4(1) (see n 93 above).

[104] *Verein für Konsumenteninformation v Volkswagen AG* (n 98) para 39 (also para 38 emphasising the need for the court to assess market conditions in ruling upon the claim).

[105] See a summary of the Commission's infringement decision at [2017] OJ C216/9.

[106] *RH v AB Volvo* (n 96) para 31.

Regulation,[107] was (obviously) not, however, sufficient to confer jurisdiction on every Member or EEA State court.[108] Additionally, therefore, regard must be had to the circumstances of the individual market participant(s) affected by the restriction of competition by or through whom the claim is brought, through the introduction of a secondary connecting factor. Following the approach in *Verein für Konsumenteninformation v Volkswagen AG*, if the victim of the market manipulation only purchased the goods affected within the jurisdiction of a single court, 'the court having jurisdiction … is that of the place where the goods are purchased',[109] 'irrespective of whether the goods [at] issue were purchased directly or indirectly from the defendants, with immediate transfer of ownership or at the end of a leasing contract'.[110] In the case of purchases made in several places, the Court cited its earlier decision in *Cartel Damages Claims* to support the conclusion that the damage can be located at the victim's registered office, provided that it is within the market affected by the collusive practices.[111]

In *AB 'flyLAL-Lithunian Airlines'*, where the defendants' anti-competitive agreement and predatory pricing had hindered the claimant's ability to compete in the market for flights to and from Vilnius Airport, the Court concluded that the damage consisted of the loss of sales[112] and could be located in the place of the market where the claimant 'conducts the main part of its sales activities relating to such flights'.[113] The Court referred to 'the alignment of … two elements'[114] consisting of 'distortion of competition in that market'[115] and 'losses incurred by an airline on flights operated to and from the capital of the Member State where that company is established'.[116] Although the Court did not state this expressly, this combination was sufficient to confer jurisdiction on the Regional Court of Vilnius, in which the proceedings had been brought.

[107] ibid, para 32.

[108] ibid, para 38. The Court acknowledged the possibility that each Member State within the market affected might coordinate jurisdiction through a specialised court, but that possibility was conditional upon establishing damage within that Member State (ibid, paras 35–37).

[109] ibid, para 39.

[110] ibid, para 40. Unfortunately, the Court did not address the question as to how the relevant transaction was to be located. In his Opinion (n 96) paras 86–88), AG Richard de la Tour favoured an 'economic approach' to the concept of 'purchase' involving identification of the place where the transaction under which the asset became part of the purchaser's assets was 'concluded', being 'in a wide sense as being the place where agreement was reached on the asset and the price, and not that where the price was paid or the asset was made available'. See also, *Verein für Konsumenteninformation v Volkswagen AG* (n 98) Campos Sánchez-Bordona AG Opinion, para 74; Case C-882/19 *Sumal SL v Mercedes Benz Trucks España SL* [2021] Bus LR 1755, para 65. *cf Löber*, Bobek AG Opinion (n 110) paras 77–78, referring to national law.

[111] *RH v AB Volvo* (n 96) paras 41–42.

[112] *AB 'flyLAL-Lithunian Airlines' v Starptautiskā lidosta 'Rīga' VAS* (n 97) para 36.

[113] ibid, paras 39–40.

[114] ibid, para 40.

[115] ibid, para 38.

[116] ibid, para 39.

The same combination of factors can be identified in the ECJ's treatment of claims relating to the marketing of securities.[117] In *Löber v Barclays Bank plc*, the Court effectively affirmed its earlier decision in *Kolassa*. Having noted the discussion of the latter decision in *Universal Music*,[118] the Court pointed out that a variety of specific circumstances justified conferring jurisdiction upon 'the Austrian courts', including the claimant's domicile, the location of bank accounts from which payments were made, and the places of establishment of the participating banks.[119] The Court then stated that:

> [I]t is furthermore apparent from the order for reference that she acquired the certificates on the Austrian secondary market, that the information supplied to her concerning those certificates is that in the prospectus which relates to them as notified to the Österreichische Kontrollbank (Austrian supervisory bank) and that, on the basis of that information, she signed in Austria the contract obliging her to make the investment, which has resulted in a definitive reduction in her assets.

This reasoning, which accords with that adopted by the Court in the competition law cases, combines the elements of collective impairment of relational autonomy within the Austrian market for securities coupled with a circumstance (conclusion of a contract) relevant to the market participant in the case at hand. This, however, leads to a puzzle. Why did the Court then conclude that the damage to the claimant had occurred at 'the place where the bank is established in which the applicant possessed the bank account in which the damage occurred' when the reasoning in the competition law cases would specify the place of the affected transaction or, in the case of multiple transactions, the place of the victim's domicile?[120] A possible answer is provided by the specific circumstances giving rise to the claims in *Kolassa* and *Löber* according to which the actual cause of the claimants' financial losses resulted from the fact that the fund in which they indirectly invested was operated as a pyramid scheme resulting in the subsequent misappropriation of the underlying assets.[121] Accordingly, on this view, no 'concrete'[122] loss occurred at the point of the transaction but only thereafter at a time when the claimants were locked into their investment and vulnerable to the fraud committed against the underling fund. On this view, the nature of the impairment of their investment was, therefore, different from that, for example, in the *Volkswagen* case in which the asset acquired was, from the outset, worth less than the price paid.[123]

Most recently, in *Vereniging van Effectenbezitters v BP plc*, the ECJ distinguished its earlier judgments in *Kolassa* and *Löber* and, in so doing, emphasised

[117] Kolassa (n 78): Löber (n 52); *Vereniging van Effectenbezitters v BP plc* (n 52).
[118] Text to nn 87–88 above.
[119] *Löber* (n 52) para 32. The reference to 'the Austrian courts' is unfortunate, as these connecting factors pointed to different regional jurisdictions within Austria (Graz, Salzburg, Vienna).
[120] Text to nn 96–111 above.
[121] *Kolassa* (n 78) Szpunar AG Opinion, para 19; *Löber* (n 52) para 9.
[122] *Löber* (n 52) para 27. See text to n 52 above.
[123] Text to nn 99–102 above.

the synthesis of two elements that operates in cases of this type. In that case, shareholders represented by the claimant organisation had, in the period before or shortly after the incident on the Deepwater Horizon platform, bought, held or sold shares and depositary receipts in the defendant company (listed on various stock exchanges), which they held through investment accounts in the Netherlands.[124] The basis on which the claim was put was that the defendant had provided its shareholders with inaccurate, incomplete and misleading information leading them to take investment decisions which they would not otherwise have taken, or would have taken on more favourable terms.[125] The claimant relied on *Kolassa* and *Löber* to locate the damage in the Netherlands on the basis that 'the loss in the form of the devaluation of the shares on foot of BP's unlawful conduct, occurred directly in the Netherlands' in the investment accounts held there.[126] The Court, however, contrasted the circumstances of those cases, in which an entity notifying a prospectus in a particular Member States may foresee that persons domiciled in those Member States might invest and suffer damage, with those in the case before it, in which the defendant was only subject to statutory reporting obligations as a result of the listing of its securities. It was only in those places that 'such a company can reasonably foresee the existence of an investment market and incur liability'.[127] Again, the reasoning points to the conclusion that the damage consisted in the effect of the defendant's allegedly wrongful conduct upon the relevant marketplace(s), and supports its classification as a case involving the impairment of collective relational autonomy. As the defendant's securities were not listed upon any stock exchange established in the Netherlands, this excluded the possibility of the Dutch court claiming jurisdiction on this basis, so that it was not necessary for the Court to identify a further (secondary) connecting factor or factors to locate the damage within the area of the market.[128]

These cases share with those involving individual relational autonomy the idea that the event giving rise to damage has resulted in an impairment of freedom of action. In the first category (individual relational autonomy) it is the impact on a specific person that must be examined and located; in the second category (collective relational autonomy) the analysis must logically begin with the impact on a class of persons, although further fine-tuning may be necessary, in particular in cases of market participation, in order to establish a satisfactory mechanism for locating the damage suffered by the individual members of the class.

[124] Vereniging van Effectenbezitters v BP plc (n 52) paras 7–10.

[125] ibid, para 11.

[126] ibid, para 15. The logic of this submission position is questionable. Although the value of the shares fell when the claimant made full disclosure as to the effect of the incident, this was a consequence of its (belated) compliance with its informational duties and not its earlier breach which (as in the *Volkswagen* case) had distorted the market in which the shareholders undertook transactions.

[127] ibid, paras 34–35.

[128] *cf* ibid, Opinion of AG Sánchez-Bordona, paras 47–59 denying the significance of certain factors, including the global dissemination of information regarding the defendant's shares.

C. Infringement of Intellectual Property Rights: A Case Apart

A distinct, non-autonomous approach to the concept of 'damage' in the Brussels I regime has been taken with respect to claims for infringement of intellectual property rights. The explanation for this difference in approach is that intellectual property rights are territorial, and non-uniform, such that the nature and scope of the protected interest (and of the prohibited interferences with that interest) can only be determined by the law of the place for which protection is granted,[129] which for jurisdiction purposes must be the law of the forum Member State.[130] The territorality principle is observed by the requirement that 'the alleged damage may occur within the jurisdiction of the court',[131] although that 'damage' will vary according to the character of the right in question and is a matter left to be determined by the national court.[132] For example, in the case of a right to reproduce, distribute or exhibit photographs, the relevant 'damage' may be the reproduction, distribution or exhibiting of photographs in the forum Member State.[133] As this line of case law does not contribute to the autonomous conception of 'damage' in EU law, it is not necessary to consider it further here.

D. Definition: The Contribution of Advocate General Bobek

Valuable insights on the topic at hand were offered by Advocate General Bobek in his Opinions in *Löber*[134] and, before that, in *AB 'flyLAL-Lithunian Airlines'*.[135] In the *flyLAL* Opinion, he pointed out that:

- Within the Brussels I regime, 'damage' is an aspect of the autonomous, EU law concept of 'harmful event' used to determine jurisdiction by identifying places with a close relationship to the dispute.[136]
- Since the judgment in *Bier*, the Court has analysed this concept in terms of cause ('event giving rise to damage') and consequence ('damage').[137]
- The notion of damage as an aspect of the 'harmful event' differs from the notion of 'damage' which is part of the substantive assessment of a tort and

[129] See Rome II Regulation, Art 8.

[130] Case C-523/10 *Wintersteiger AG v Products 4U Sondermaschinenbau GmbH* [2013] Bus LR 150, paras 25–28 (registered right); Case C-170/12 *Pinckney v KDG Mediatech AG* [2013] Bus LR 1313, paras 32–33, 39–46 (unregistered right).

[131] *Pinckney*, ibid para [43]; *Hi Hotel HCF Sarl v Spoering* [2014] 1 WLR 1912, para 40.

[132] *Pinckney* (n 130) para 46; *Hi Hotel* (n 131) para 39.

[133] *Hi Hotel* (n 131) paras 36–37.

[134] Above (n 110). The case is discussed above, text to nn 117–23.

[135] Above (n 72). The case is discussed above, text to nn 112–16.

[136] *AB 'flyLAL-Lithunian Airlines'*, Bobek AG Opinion (n 72) paras 29, 92. *cf* Rome II Regulation, Art 4.

[137] *AB 'flyLAL-Lithunian Airlines'*, Bobek AG Opinion (n 72) para 29.

which identifies the adverse consequences for a specific claimant that serve as the basis for the calculation of pecuniary damages. The latter, unlike the former, is defined principally by reference to national law.[138]

- The Court's case law has qualified the concept of 'damage' by reference to criteria of specificity (relating to the interests of individuals that are the subject of the claim in question)[139] and 'immediacy' (separating the 'initial damage' from subsequence adverse consequences):[140] as the Advocate General put it, 'what matters is the location of the initial damage to the protected interest of the claimant'.[141]
- In examining concepts of causation for jurisdiction purposes, the court seised takes as established the alleged claims (without investigating their merits) and seeks to identify points of connection that support its claim to jurisdiction.[142]
- The jurisdictional assessment requires 'a review of the basic factual and legal characteristics of the case at an abstract level', both to characterise the subject matter of the claim and to apply the connecting factor.[143]
- Within the category of 'tort, delict or quasi-delict', the type of tort alleged must be identified as a pre-condition to determining the relevant points of contact.[144]

In *Löber*, Advocate General Bobek noted that:

> Events come in chains or bundles. The classical problem of tortious liability, both in its substantive dimension (for deciding on the merits of a claim for damages) as well as the procedural one (for deciding on international jurisdiction) is the singling out of the one event that is both necessary and determinant with regard to the harm that ensued.[145]

Turning to the concept of 'damage' and building on his analysis in *flyLAL*, he suggested that:

> [T]he notion of 'damage' in the phrase 'place where the damage occurred', refers to the harm caused in the sense of direct adverse consequences on the legally protected interests of a specific claimant. That is why … the Court continues to refer to 'initial damage'

[138] ibid, para 30. See text to nn 35–36 above.

[139] ibid, paras 32–36. The statement (para 33) that 'the place where the damage occurred' is 'subject to the condition that such a place is situated within a Member State which actually protects the right allegedly infringed' seems questionable, having been borrowed from the Court's case law on intellectual property rights, for which a distinct, non-autonomous approach has been taken (see section III.C above).

[140] ibid, para 42.

[141] ibid, para 67. See also *Vereniging van Effectenbezitters v BP plc* (n 52) Opinion of AG Sánchez-Bordona, para 83.

[142] *AB 'flyLAL-Lithunian Airlines'*, Bobek AG Opinion (n 72) para 92, with reference to *Universal Music* (n 74) para 44. This section of the Opinion is concerned with the 'event giving rise to damage' but the point is equally pertinent in the present context.

[143] *AB 'flyLAL-Lithunian Airlines'*, Bobek AG Opinion (n 72) para 94. See also, *Kwok v UBS AG* (n 52) [49] (Vos MR).

[144] ibid.

[145] *Löber* (n 52) Opinion of AG Bobek (n 110) para 49 with reference to his Opinion in *flyLAL* (n 72) paras 94–99.

in the sense of 'initial harm', excluding places of (later) 'indirect financial damage' that results and follows from that initial harm.

What specific harm the potential claimant is being protected from and when that type of harm might occur depends on the specific type of tort invoked.[146]

Although one might quibble with some of the detail within these two Opinions,[147] and it must be acknowledged that the Advocate General's specific approach to the location of damage on the facts of the case before him was not followed by the Court in *Löber*, this general account of the concept of 'damage' is persuasive and, it is submitted, consistent with the analysis within this chapter. The analysis in section III.B above represents an attempt to build upon this framework by identifying within the ECJ's case law a classification of different types of harm by reference to an autonomous classification of the legally protected interest at stake. It allows the following conclusions to be drawn.

IV. Conclusion

This chapter has suggested that the concept of 'damage' within EU private international law is an active one which fixes upon the way in which the relevant event brings about its effects upon the victim. 'Damage' occurs when (and where) the event giving rise to damage produces a relevant harmful effect upon a person (the 'victim')[148] by adversely affecting a legally protected interest of that person to which the claim relates.

The ECJ's existing body of case law, examined above, suggests the following classification of legally protected interests:

Interest affected	Defined autonomously?	Harmful effect	Where located
Interference with freedom to deal with a tangible thing	Yes	An occurrence affecting a thing in which the victim has a proprietary interest with the capacity to cause deterioration in or loss of control of the thing	Where the thing was situated at the time of the occurrence
Interference with personal health or freedom	Yes	An occurrence affecting the victim with the capacity to cause deterioration in physical or mental health or loss of liberty	Where the person was situated at the time of the occurrence

(continued)

[146] ibid, paras 69–70. See also *Kwok v UBS AG* (n 52) [49] (Vos MR).
[147] See above, nn 72, 110, 139.
[148] Not necessarily the claimant (see text to n 18 above).

(Continued)

Interest affected	Defined autonomously?	Harmful effect	Where located
Interference with individual relational autonomy	Yes	An occurrence affecting the victim's ability to transact or engage with one or more third parties	Where the affected transaction or engagement took place or would have taken place but for the occurrence
Interference with collective relational autonomy	Yes	An occurrence affecting the victim's ability as a member of a class to deal with others as a member of that class (in particular, as a participant in a market for a product of service)	Where relations with the class are affected In cases involving market participants, where the affected market is located, with further targeting by an appropriate secondary connecting factor
Intellectual property rights	No	Infringement of an intellectual property right	Where the right in question provides the protection claimed by the victim

It is not suggested that this classification is exhaustive or that it is the only possible way of organising the subject matter. It is, of course, open to further development by the ECJ and in national jurisprudence. Nevertheless, if like Jonathan Fitchen's private international law scholarship, it helps to cast light on a concept that has hitherto travelled under the radar, the purpose of this chapter will have been fulfilled.

7

Cryptocurrency Transfers in Distributed Ledger Technology-Based Systems and their Characterisation in Conflict of Laws

BURCU YÜKSEL RIPLEY*

In memory of Professor Jonathan M Fitchen, with the highest regard to his research excellence and vast knowledge – from theory to practice in private international – and with the greatest gratitude to his generosity in his support, encouragement and mentorship.

I. Introduction

In modern payment systems that are used today, non-cash payments – including international ones – are predominantly executed by banks, acting as an intermediary between payers and payees, in the form of bank-to-bank (interbank) funds transfers through bank accounts.[1] The basic structure of this method of making payments finds its origins from the early banking system in the sixteenth century with the emergence of goldsmith banks[2] which made in-house payments by adjusting the ledgers they kept for their customers without any need for a physical exchange of assets.[3] The introduction of a central clearing bank to the system, later on, simplified the process of interbank payments through interbank settlements on the ledgers

* The author would like to thank Professor Matthias Lehmann for his valuable comments and suggestions on an earlier draft of this chapter. The author also benefited from feedback from the readers of the earlier draft published on SSRN and thanks to them all. All errors or omissions are the author's.

[1] B Geva, 'Banking in the Digital Age – Who is Afraid of Payment Disintermediation?' (2018), available at: digitalcommons.osgoode.yorku.ca/all_papers/322, 4; R Ali, J Barrdear, R Clews and J Southgate, 'Innovations in Payment Technologies and the Emerge of Digital Currencies' (2014) 54 *Bank of England Quarterly Bulletin* 262, available at: www.bankofengland.co.uk/-/media/boe/files/quarterly-bulletin/2014/innovations-in-payment-technologies-and-the-emergence-of-digital-currencies.pdf, 263.

[2] On this issue, see eg, K Jongchul, 'How Modern Bank Originated: The London Goldsmith-Bankers' Institutionalization of Trust' (2011) 53 *Business History* 939.

[3] Ali et al, 'Innovations in Payment Technologies' (n 1) 263 and 264.

being held with the central clearing bank.[4] The structure has evolved over time and with technological developments, most notably with the emergence of electronic funds transfer (EFT) in the second part of the twentieth century[5] which replaced paper-based transfers to a large extent by increasing the speed of payments and reducing the risks associated with them.[6] However, the core structure of the system remained the same until 2009 as being centralised and relying on intermediation.[7]

In 2009, a fundamental structural change was introduced to making payments with the emergence of the first cryptocurrency, ie, Bitcoin[8] underpinned by blockchain as a specific way of data structuring based on distributed ledger technology (DLT).[9] This innovation in payments, combined with both new decentralised payment mechanisms and cryptocurrencies, has allowed for non-cash payments to be made outside the banking system directly from payer to payee and secure digital records to be held independently of the usual central trusted authorities such as banks (ie, without intermediation).[10] This has significantly reduced the transaction cost and time in international payments.[11]

This global paradigm shift, starting with the possibilities of cryptocurrencies in payments, has introduced new challenges for private international law as reflected in some of the recent scholarly work in the area[12] as well as the recent work of the Hague Conference on Private International Law (HCCH) on private international law implications of the digital economy.[13] The issue of characterisation of cryptocurrency transfers in DLT-based systems is at the heart of some of the key private international law questions, including the determination of the law applicable to cryptocurrency transfers. In terms of characterisation, the efforts have thus far mainly focused on characterising cryptocurrencies themselves as

[4] ibid.

[5] Geva, 'Banking in the Digital Age' (n 1) 19; Ali et al, 'Innovations in Payment Technologies' (n 1) 263.

[6] The other notable development was the introduction of electronic money, see Geva, 'Banking in the Digital Age' (n 1) 20-21; Ali et al, 'Innovations in Payment Technologies' (n 1) 263.

[7] Geva, 'Banking in the Digital Age' (n 1) 28; Ali et al, 'Innovations in Payment Technologies' (n 1) 263.

[8] Bitcoin was introduced in 2009 by its pseudonymous founder, Satoshi Nakamoto, following the publication of a 9-page White Paper in 2008 establishing the core structure of the system as 'a purely peer-to-peer version of electronic cash allowing online payments to be sent directly from one party to another without going through a financial institution serving as a trusted third party'. See S Nakamoto, "Bitcoin: A Peer-to-Peer Electronic Cash System", available at: bitcoin.org/bitcoin.pdf.

[9] Ali et al, 'Innovations in Payment Technologies' (n 1) 264.

[10] Geva, 'Banking in the Digital Age' (n 1); R Ali, J Barrdear, R Clews and J Southgate, 'The Economics of Digital Currencies' (2014) 54 *Bank of England Quarterly Bulletin* 276, available at: www.bankofengland.co.uk/-/media/boe/files/quarterly-bulletin/2014/the-economics-of-digital-currencies.pdf?la=en&hash=E9E56A61A6D71A97DC8535FEF211CC08C0F59B30, 277.

[11] See generally, Ali et al, ibid, 281.

[12] See eg, D Fox and S Green (eds), *Cryptocurrencies in Public and Private Law* (Oxford University Press, 2019); A Bonomi, M Lehmann and S Lalani (eds), *Blockchain and Private International Law* (Brill, forthcoming).

[13] HCCH, 'Developments with respect to PIL implications of the digital economy, including DLT', Preliminary Document No 4 REV of January 2022, available at: assets.hcch.net/docs/b06c28c5-d183-4d81-a663-f7bdb8f32dac.pdf; Preliminary Document No 4 of November 2020, available at: assets.hcch.net/

money, property or claim and a discussion around the application of the *lex situs* as the predominant law applied to international property and the consideration of the relevant conflict of laws rules regarding the transfer of intangibles (such as Article 14 of the Rome I Regulation[14] in the European Union and as retained by the United Kingdom[15] post Brexit, or Rule 135 in *Dicey, Morris and Collins* at English common law)[16] for cryptocurrency transfers. Both approaches are criticised on different grounds.

Although the underlying idea behind cryptocurrencies is to create a system facilitating payments outside banking systems, this does not necessarily mean that concepts and legal principles relating to banking are of no use in the context of cryptocurrencies.[17] The purpose of this chapter is to offer a new perspective on the characterisation, in conflict of laws, of cryptocurrency transfers taking place within DLT-based cryptocurrency systems by utilising an analogy to EFTs and funds transfer systems. The chapter first considers cryptocurrencies and their transfers in DLT-based systems. Building on that foundation, the chapter then examines legal characterisation of cryptocurrency transfers in DLT-based systems under unitary and segmented approaches and considers the potential effects of both approaches on the law applicable to cryptocurrency transfers. Although this chapter focuses on cryptocurrency transfers, the analysis it offers and the proposals it puts forward are potentially relevant and applicable to the transfer of digital assets in DLT-based systems more broadly.

II. Cryptocurrencies and their Transfers in Distributed Ledger Technology-Based Systems[18]

A. Cryptocurrencies and Cryptocurrency Systems

Cryptoassets can be broadly understood as cryptographically secured digital representations of value which can be transferred, stored, or traded electronically by the

docs/8bdc7071-c324-4660-96bc-86efba6214f2.pdf; and HCCH, 'Proposal for the Allocation of Resources to Follow Private International Law Implications relating to Developments in the Field of Distributed Ledger Technology, in particular in relation to Financial Technology', Preliminary Document 28 of February 2020, available at: assets.hcch.net/docs/f787749d-9512-4a9e-ad4a-cbc585bddd2e.pdf.

[14] Regulation (EC) No 593/2008 of the European Parliament and of the Council of 17 June 2008 on the law applicable to contractual obligations (Rome I), [2008] OJ L177/6 (Rome I Regulation).

[15] The Law Applicable to Contractual Obligations and Non-Contractual Obligations (Amendment etc) (EU Exit) Regulations 2019 (SI 2019/834) as amended by the Jurisdiction, Judgments and Applicable Law (Amendment) (EU Exit) Regulations (SI 2020/1574).

[16] See Lord Collins of Mapesbury et al (eds), *Dicey, Morris & Collins on the Conflict of Laws*, 15th edn (Sweet & Maxwell, 2014) para 24R-050.

[17] See generally, C Hare, 'Cryptocurrencies and Banking Law: Are There Lessons to Learn?' in D Fox and S Green (eds), *Cryptocurrencies in Public and Private Law* (Oxford University Press, 2019).

[18] On this issue, see generally, B Yüksel Ripley and F Heindler, 'The Law Applicable to Crypto Assets: What Policy Choices Are Ahead of Us?' in A Bonomi, M Lehmann and S Lalani (eds) *Blockchain and Private International Law* (Brill, forthcoming).

use of DLT or a similar technology.[19] Cryptocurrencies constitute a sub-category of cryptoassets,[20] which are mainly used as a means of exchange but are not state backed,[21] such as Bitcoin.[22] They are issued privately, not by a central bank or another authorised institution in a given country. Stablecoins, aiming to maintain their value against one or more reference assets like a fiat currency or a commodity (eg, Libra), and Central Bank Digital Currencies (CBDCs), issued by central banks, are usually considered separately from non-state backed cryptocurrencies.

Among their common characteristics, cryptocurrencies exist only electronically and they are underpinned by DLT.[23] In order for a value, such as a cryptocurrency, to function as a means of payment, there is also a need for a payment system to securely transfer that value as well as a ledger within the system to record the values stored.[24] In the case of cryptocurrencies, this is done by the use of a distributed ledger. If the cryptocurrency system is underpinned by blockchain, which is a type of DLT, the leger is updated in groups of validated transactions called blocks and chained to each other by cryptography.[25]

[19] Although there is no universally agreed definition of cryptoassets, definitions given so far in different initiatives are broadly similar. See eg, European Commission, 'Proposal for a Regulation of the European Parliament and of the Council on Markets in Crypto-assets, and amending Directive (EU) 2019/1937' COM (2020) 593 final, Art 3(2); HM Treasury, 'UK regulatory approach to cryptoassets and stablecoins: Consultation and call for evidence' January 2021, available at: assets.publishing.service.gov.uk/government/uploads/system/uploads/attachment_data/file/950206/HM_Treasury_Cryptoasset_and_Stablecoin_consultation.pdf. As the UK Jurisdiction Taskforce pointed out in its legal statement on cryptoassets and smart contracts, formulating a precise definition in this area is difficult and unlikely to be useful given the great diversity of systems and assets in existence and the rapid technological development. See UK Jurisdiction Taskforce, 'Legal statement on cryptoassets and smart contracts' (2019), available at: 35z8e83m1ih83drye280o9d1-wpengine.netdna-ssl.com/wp-content/uploads/2019/11/6.6056_JO_Cryptocurrencies_Statement_FINAL_WEB_111119-1.pdf, para 26.

[20] There is no universally agreed classification of cryptoassets. For an overview of major token classification frameworks, see eg, JG Allen, M Rauchs, A Blandin and K Bea, 'Legal and Regulatory Considerations for Digital Assets' (2020), available at: www.jbs.cam.ac.uk/wp-content/uploads/2020/10/2020-ccaf-legal-regulatory-considerations-report.pdf, 10.

[21] 'Cryptocurrency' is not a term preferred in the UK in relevant policy papers and documents, probably to avoid any confusion with fiat currencies, as cryptocurrencies are not currently considered as money or currency in the UK. See Burcu Yüksel, 'Is the UK heading towards regulation of cryptoassets? Findings from the UK Cryptoassets Taskforce Final Report' (*Aberdeen Law School Blog*, 15 December 2018), available at: www.abdn.ac.uk/law/blog/is-the-uk-heading-towards-regulation-of-cryptoassets-findings-from-the-uk-cryptoassets-taskforce-final-report/. Under the classification of the UK Cryptoassets Taskforce based on the functions of cryptoassets as exchange tokens, security tokens and utility tokens, cryptocurrencies correspond to exchange tokens. See UK Cryptoassets Taskforce, 'Final report' (2018), available at: assets.publishing.service.gov.uk/government/uploads/system/uploads/attachment_data/file/752070/cryptoassets_taskforce_final_report_final_web.pdf, 11–15.

[22] On the current cryptoassets landscape, see eg, Yüksel Ripley and Heindler, 'The Law Applicable to Crypto Assets' (n 18).

[23] See ibid.

[24] Ali et al, 'Innovations in Payment Technologies' (n 1) 264.

[25] For this technical process, see eg, ibid 266 and 268–69; Bank for International Settlements, 'Annual Economic Report' (2018), available at: www.bis.org/publ/arpdf/ar2018e.pdf (BIS 2018 Report) 97.

Although the specific technicalities of each cryptocurrency system may differ, a cryptocurrency system can be 'permissionless' or 'permissioned'[26] depending on how the ledger is accessed and updated and by whom.[27] Permissionless cryptocurrency systems, like Bitcoin, have a public ledger[28] distributed across pseudonymous participants and updated by a consensus of miners who informally work in a peer-to-peer manner as transaction verifiers and bookkeepers around the world with no central coordination.[29] For the use of computing power and resources in this process which involves solving complex algorithmic equations by special purpose-built hardware[30] and the demonstration of their work, known as 'proof-of-work' in Bitcoin,[31] miners receive an allocation of the cryptocurrency and any transaction fees offered by the respective parties to the transaction as a reward.[32] Most cryptocurrency systems are currently permissionless systems.[33] Permissioned cryptocurrency systems, on the other hand, have a private ledger updated by trusted participants, known as trusted nodes, under the permission of an entity which is generally the company that has developed the cryptocurrency in question.[34]

B. Technical Operation of Cryptocurrency Transfers

Transfers of cryptocurrencies in DLT-based systems are sometimes called 'on-chain' transfers as they are executed and recorded on the ledger within the cryptocurrency system. This is in contrast to 'off-chain' transfers which, as per the agreement of the parties, are not executed and recorded on the ledger but take place outside the cryptocurrency system, for instance, by the passing of the private key to the payee by the payer.[35]

In cryptocurrency systems, each participant has a public key (used to encrypt data) paired with a private key (used to decrypt data), and transactions take place

[26] See eg, UK Government Chief Scientific Adviser, 'Distributed Ledger Technology: beyond block chain' (2015), available at: assets.publishing.service.gov.uk/government/uploads/system/uploads/attachment_data/file/492972/gs-16-1-distributed-ledger-technology.pdf. Some systems can be a combination of both. Permissionless systems can sometimes be called 'public systems', while permissioned systems are called 'private systems'.

[27] See generally, Yüksel Ripley and Heindler, 'The Law Applicable to Crypto Assets' (n 18).

[28] All Bitcoin transactions can be viewed in real time by anyone without any need for a Bitcoin account registration or log in at: www.blockchain.com/explorer.

[29] See generally, Ali et al, 'Innovations in Payment Technologies' (n 1) 266 and 268; BIS 2018 Report (n 25).

[30] See Ali et al, 'Innovations in Payment Technologies' (n 1) 273–74.

[31] For the fundamentals of the proof of work scheme as explained by Nakamoto, see (n 8) 2–4. See also, eg, Ali et al, 'Innovations in Payment Technologies' (n 1) 273–74; BIS 2018 Report (n 25) 98.

[32] Ali et al, 'Innovations in Payment Technologies' (n 1) 277–78.

[33] UK Cryptoassets Taskforce, 'Final report' (n 21) 11.

[34] BIS 2018 Report (n 25) 96-97; UK Cryptoassets Taskforce, 'Final report' (n 21) 10.

[35] On on-chain and off-chain transfers, see generally, UK Jurisdiction Taskforce, 'Legal statement' (n 19) paras 45 and 48.

between the digital wallets of participants.[36] This is, to some extent, similar to a bank account which a customer holds with a bank to send and receive funds and accesses it by a username and password. However, the technical operation of a cryptocurrency transfer in DLT-based systems, in certain respects, is very different from that of a typical funds transfer in centralised systems which rely on trusted third parties/intermediaries, like banks, to execute transfers and to record transactions on central ledgers.[37] In cryptocurrency systems, payments are directly made between the respective participants after being verified by other participants in the system. The ledger, which includes the entire history of all the transactions that have ever occurred within the system, is distributed and shared across the system and cannot be modified by a participant secretly.[38] The advantages that DLT-based systems offer, such as traceability and transparency, privacy, integrity, immutability, verification of receipt, high-level security and immunity and direct peer-to-peer real-time transaction, remove the need for a trusted third party/intermediary, such as a bank, to execute transfers and record transactions centrally.[39]

The technical operation of cryptocurrency transfers can be illustrated through the following steps of a Bitcoin transfer.[40] A payer issues a payment message which includes, at least, a reference to the previous transaction through which the cryptocurrency was acquired, the address to pay and the amount to pay. The payer creates a digital signature by encrypting the payment message with his or her private key which can only be decrypted with the corresponding public key. After digitally signing the message, the payer broadcasts the message and the corresponding public key to the system so that the transaction can be verified by miners. The miners gather this new transaction into a candidate block and begin verification which includes validation and achieving consensus by the proof-of-work. When a miner successfully verifies the block, it broadcasts the block containing the payer's transaction to all miners. If all transactions in the block are valid, the miners accept the block by adding the block to the end of their copies of the chain and work on creating the next block by using the hash of the accepted block as the previous hash. The payee receives the payment.

[36] Ali et al, 'Innovations in Payment Technologies' (n 1) 268–70, 273–74.

[37] ibid, 262.

[38] See R de Caria, 'A Digital Revolution in International Trade? The International Legal Framework for Blockchain Technologies, Virtual Currencies and Smart Contracts: Challenges and Opportunities' in UNCITRAL, *Modernizing International Trade Law to Support Innovation and Sustainable Development* (2017), available at: aperto.unito.it/retrieve/handle/2318/1632525/464608/R.%20de%20Caria%2c%20A%20Digital%20Revolution%20%282017%29.pdf, 106.

[39] See eg, Burcu Yüksel and Florian Heindler, 'Use of Blockchain Technology in Cross-Border Legal Cooperation under the Conventions of the Hague Conference on Private International Law (HCCH)' (*Aberdeen Law School Blog*, 15 August 2019), available at: www.abdn.ac.uk/law/blog/use-of-blockchain-technology-in-crossborder-legal-cooperation-under-the-conventions-of-the-hague-conference-on-private-international-law-hcch/. On the other hand, scalability issues linked to the ever-growing ledger has led to the emergence of other third-party intermediaries in the crypto market such as cryptocurrency wallet providers and cryptocurrency exchanges. See generally, BIS 2018 Report (n 25) 99, 105.

[40] For the fundamental steps of the system as explained by Nakamoto, see (n 8). On this process, see generally, Ali et al, 'Innovations in Payment Technologies' (n 1) 268–70 and 273–74.

III. Characterisation of Cryptocurrency Transfers in Distributed Ledger Technology-Based Systems and its Effect on the Applicable Law

There has been an ongoing discussion as to whether cryptocurrencies are to be characterised as money or legal tender, or property, or something else.[41] The responses from jurisdictions which have considered the matter have been varied[42] so far. The debate has gained a new dimension with El Salvador's adoption of Bitcoin as legal tender, the first country to do so in the world, and raised further issues regarding the application of the principle of *lex monetae* in the context of cryptocurrencies.[43] The legal nature of cryptocurrencies and cryptocurrency transfers in DLT-based systems will predominantly depend on the approaches that jurisdictions adopt in their substantive laws, and it may differ from one jurisdiction to another. However, the issue is also linked to conflict of laws through the question of characterisation.

Characterisation (classification or qualification), in general, is an issue arising from differences, which exist among legal systems, in the categorisation of legal matters or in the treatment of legal matters that are in the same or similar categories.[44] In conflict of laws, characterisation is the first step in a conflict of laws analysis following the identification of a foreign element that a matter involves. It refers to a process or technique which is used to assign a matter[45] to the

[41] On the characterisation of cryptocurrencies, see Yüksel Ripley and Heindler, 'The Law Applicable to Crypto Assets' (n 18); F Krysa, 'Taxonomy and Characterisation of Crypto Assets' in A Bonomi, M Lehmann and S Lalani (eds), *Blockchain and Private International Law* (Brill, forthcoming); A Dickinson, 'Cryptocurrencies and the Conflict of Laws' in D Fox and S Green (eds) *Cryptocurrencies in Public and Private Law* (Oxford University Press, 2019) 118–37; C Proctor, 'Cryptocurrencies in International and Public Law Conceptions of Money' in D Fox and S Green (eds) *Cryptocurrencies in Public and Private Law* (Oxford University Press, 2019) 33–55.

[42] For a comparative study on this matter relating to Bitcoin, see Law Library of Congress, US Global Legal Research Directorate, 'Regulation of Bitcoin in selected jurisdictions' (2014), available at: www.loc.gov/item/2014427360/. See also, Yüksel Ripley and Heindler, 'The Law Applicable to Crypto Assets' (n 18); RM Lastra and JG Allen, 'Virtual currencies in the Eurosystem: challenges ahead' (European Parliament, Policy Department for Economic, Scientific and Quality of Life Policies, 2018), available at: www.europarl.europa.eu/cmsdata/150541/DIW_FINAL%20publication.pdf, 18–21; UK Cryptoassets Taskforce 'Final report' (n 21) para 2.13; B Geva and D Geva, 'Non-State Community Virtual Currencies' in D Fox and S Green (eds) *Cryptocurrencies in Public and Private Law* (Oxford University Press, 2019) 301–03; Allen et al (n 20) 21–22.

[43] For the argument that there seems to be no room for the application of the principle of *lex monetae* to cryptocurrencies which are not state-backed on the ground that there is no issuing state whose law could be applied to them, see Yüksel Ripley and Heindler, 'The Law Applicable to Crypto Assets' (n 18). On the *lex monetae* in relation to obligations denominated in Bitcoin or analogous cryptocurrencies, see also Dickinson (n 41) paras 5.76–5.80. Regarding El Salvador's adoption of Bitcoin as legal tender, see eg, FE Alvarez, D Argente and D van Patten, 'Are Cryptocurrencies Currencies? Bitcoin as Legal Tender in El Salvador' (2022) National Bureau of Economic Research (NBER) Working Paper Series, Working Paper 29968, available at: www.nber.org/system/files/working_papers/w29968/w29968.pdf.

[44] See O Kahn-Freund, 'General Problems of Private International Law' (1974) 143 *Recueil des Cours* 139, 369.

[45] For different views on what it is that is characterised, see eg, FM Wilke, *A Conceptual Analysis of European Private International Law: The General Issues in the EU and its Member States* (Intersentia, 2019) 113–14.

appropriate category of conflict of laws rules of a given forum in a given case and which initiates the determination of the applicable law.[46] Various methods have been put forward to address the issue of characterisation in conflict of laws, with many of them being considered rather theoretical.[47] There are, however, four main methods suggesting that characterisation should be made according to the *lex fori* (which still remains the predominant method), *lex causae*, autonomous concepts, or categories of the *lex fori* as a starting point followed by an examination of the relevant foreign rules in their own context.[48] A court, unless there is a binding rule on the method to adopt on characterisation in its private international law,[49] is at liberty to apply one of these methods or take a different approach to solve the issue of characterisation in a given case.

In conflict of laws, characterisation of cryptocurrencies largely affects the law applicable to their transfers. Characterisation of cryptocurrencies as a thing/property suggests the potential application of the *lex situs* to cryptocurrency transfers, which is the predominant law for international property referring to the law of the country where the thing/property is located.[50] On the other hand, their characterisation as a claim, which can be transferred by way of assignment, suggests the potential application of conflict of laws rules on assignment of claims (such as Article 14 of the Rome I Regulation) to cryptocurrency transfers.[51]

However, neither of those suggestions seem to offer a satisfactory solution for cryptocurrency transfers and are criticised on different grounds.[52] The application of the *lex situs* to cryptocurrency transfers is deemed rather unsuitable as, when it comes to cryptocurrencies transferred in DLT-based systems, there is no *situs* as such in its traditional understanding due to the difficulties in geographical localisation in these systems deriving from their decentralised and distributed nature.[53] Conflict of laws rules on assignment of claims, such as Article 14 of Rome I or Rule 135 in *Dicey, Morris and Collins* at English common law governing various issues regarding the transfer of intangibles, are considered to be of no or little relevance

[46] See TC Schmidt, 'The Incidental Question in Private International Law' (1992) 233 *Recueil des Cours* 305, 333.

[47] See generally, Collins et al (n 16) para 2-008.

[48] See generally, ibid, para 2-010–2-014; P Beaumont and PE McEleavy, *Anton's Private International Law*, 3rd edn (W Green, 2011) para 4.11–4.20; Kahn-Freund (n 44) 371–73; Schmidt (n 46) 333–34.

[49] For some rare examples of provisions on characterisation found in the laws of EU Member States, see Wilke (n 45) 117–18. It has been argued that such provisions tend to have limited effect on judges '[b]ecause abstract methods are often too crude for specific problem', see C Goetzke and R Michaels, 'Characterisation' in P Beaumont and J Holliday (eds), *A Guide to Global Private International Law* (Hart Publishing, 2022) 36.

[50] Krysa (n 41).

[51] ibid.

[52] See generally, ibid.

[53] See Yüksel Ripley and Heindler, 'The Law Applicable to Crypto Assets' (n 18); Krysa (n 41); A Held, 'Cryptoassets and Decentralised Ledgers: Does Situs Actually Matter?' in A Bonomi, M Lehmann and S Lalani (eds), *Blockchain and Private International Law* (Brill, forthcoming); Financial Markets Law Committee (FMLC), 'Distributed Ledger Technology and Governing Law: Issues of Legal Uncertainty' (2018), available at: fmlc.org/wp-content/uploads/2018/05/dlt_paper.pdf, para 4.4–4.8.

in cryptocurrency transfers on the ground that they frequently do not involve a claim in the sense of a legally enforceable right arising under the law applicable to the relationship between participants in the system.[54] This leads to the result that there may be, strictly speaking, neither a law governing the assigned claim nor an assigned debtor within the meaning of Article 14 of Rome I or Rule 135 in *Dicey, Morris and Collins*.[55]

Notwithstanding the debate on the characterisation of cryptocurrencies, this chapter proposes an alternative solution for the characterisation of cryptocurrency transfers that focuses on the characteristics of cryptocurrency systems as a whole within which transfers are taking place (ie, unitary approach) and, in cases where this is not feasible, on the characteristics of individual cryptocurrency transfers (ie, segmented approach).[56]

A. Unitary Approach

Under the unitary approach, the focus is on cryptocurrency systems as a whole within which transfers are taking place by giving consideration to similarities as well as differences between cryptocurrency systems and funds transfer systems.

Funds transfer systems are electronic systems which are established, owned and operated in a given country or region by a central bank or by a private company.[57]

[54] For this argument regarding Art 14 of the Rome I Regulation, see Dickinson (n 41) paras 5.101 and 5.106.

[55] Held (n 53), Krysa (n 41); A Held, A Macpherson and B Yüksel Ripley, 'United Kingdom (UK) Report for Questionnaire in View of the General Report on Cryptocurrencies: The Impossible Domestic Law Regime?', International Academy of Comparative Law (Intersentia, forthcoming). See also, FMLC (n 53) para 6.12–6.15 and 6.25–6.27.

[56] B Yüksel Ripley, 'The Law Applicable to (Digital) Transfer of Digital Assets: The Transfer of Cryptocurrencies via Blockchains', European Association of Private International Law (EAPIL) Founding Conference, Denmark, June 2022 ('Transfer of Digital Assets'). This terminology on the approaches is used in the context of EFTs by Geva (see B Geva, *Bank Collections and Payment Transactions* (Oxford University Press, 2001) 211) and others. Although this chapter adopts the same terminology on the approaches, it uses them in a rather different meaning for cryptocurrency transfers from EFTs. In the context of EFTs, the unitary and segmented approaches respectively refer to an understanding that an EFT can be seen as a single transaction (as, from the perspectives of the payer and payee, there is one single transaction which credits and debits their respective bank accounts) or as a series of successive bilateral/multilateral operations (as, from the perspective of banks involved in the transfer, there is a series of individual payment orders). See 'International Credit Transfers: Comments on the draft Model Law on International Credit Transfers', A/CN.9/WG.IV/WP.49 (1991) XXII Yearbook of UNCITRAL 214, available at: www.uncitral.org/pdf/english/yearbooks/yb-1991-e/yb_1991_e.pdf, Comment 4, 259. On the characterisation of EFT, see generally, B Yüksel, *Uluslararası Elektronik Fon Transferine Uygulanacak Hukuk* (XII Levha, 2018) (*EFT*) 52–59.

[57] See eg, the Clearing House Automated Payment System (CHAPS) in the UK; the Federal Reserve Wire Network (Fedwire) and the Clearing House Interbank Payments System (CHIPS) in the US; the Trans-European Automated Real-time Gross Settlement Express Transfer System (TARGET2) in the EU; the Bank of Japan Financial Network System (BOJ-NET) in Japan; and the EFT System in Turkey.

Transfers of funds are processed through clearing[58] and settlement[59] via accounts of participating banks being held with the central bank or company within the system on a multilateral basis. Funds transfer systems are typically governed by multilateral contacts[60] and involve direct relationships between participants (which are usually banks or sometimes financial institutions) themselves and with the system itself. These relationships are subject to the rules and regulations of the funds transfer system which a bank is to unconditionally agree to in order to be able to participate in the system, and comply with, once it participates in the system. The relationships between participating banks and the system, and between the participating banks themselves are therefore contractual in nature.[61] The former is based on existing provisions of the contract.[62] For the latter, although there is no explicit contract concluded between each participating bank, the contractual nature of the relationship can be presumed to be established by implication based on participation of a bank in the system.[63]

In cryptocurrency systems, the system rules and regulations are replaced by consensus rules or consensus protocols.[64] Consensus rules are a key feature of many systems as cryptocurrency transactions are accepted by system participants as valid only on the basis of these consensus rules.[65] The consensus rules can therefore be regarded as self-enforcing in practice, irrespective of their enforceability in law.[66] By analogy to the relationships between participants of funds transfer systems, it can be argued that there are relationships between

[58] The process of exchanging payment orders between the banks is known as clearing which can be bilateral between the two respective banks or multilateral through a centralised clearing house; see eg, EP Ellinger, E Lomnicka and CVM Hare, *Modern Banking Law*, 5th edn (Oxford University Press, 2011) 564. In a broader sense, by encompassing the settlement of obligations, clearing is defined by Geva as 'the interbank exchange and processing of payment instructions, which may be in execution of customers' instructions, with the view of calculating and establishing respective bank debit and credit positions available for settlement', see Geva, *Bank Collections and Payment Transactions* (n 56) 4; B Geva, 'The Clearing House Arrangement' (1991) 19 *Canada Business Law Journal* 138, 138.

[59] Settlement is defined as 'payment of the interbank obligations arising from the respective debit and credit positions resulting from the clearing', see Geva, *Bank Collections and Payment Transactions* (n 56) 4.

[60] R Cranston, 'Law of International Funds Transfers in England' in W Hadding and UH Schneider (eds), *Legal Issues in International Credit Transfers* (Duncker & Humblot, 1993) 225.

[61] Yüksel, *EFT* (n 56) 95.

[62] Cranston (n 60) 225.

[63] For this view in Swiss law, see J Bischoff, 'The Factual Significance and Legal Regulation of International Funds Transfers in Switzerland' in W Hadding and UH Schneider (eds), *Legal Issues in International Credit Transfers* (Duncker & Humblot, 1993); and in Turkish law, see AB Kocaman, 'Banka Havalesi-Kavram ve İşlemin Köşeleri Arasındaki İlişkiler' in M Ünal, V Başpınar and S Yılmaz (eds), *Prof Dr Fikret Eren'e Armağan* (Yetkin, 2006) 712; AB Kocaman, 'Banka Havalesinde Ciro Sözleşmesi Çerçevesinde Verilen Ödeme Talimatının Hukukî Niteliği' (2000) 20(3) *Banka ve Ticaret Hukuku Dergisi* 17, 21. On the issue, see generally, Yüksel, *EFT* (n 56) 95–96.

[64] eg, for the consensus protocol that the XPR ledger uses, see: xrpl.org/intro-to-consensus.html#:~:text=The%20XRP%20Ledger%20uses%20a,have%20occurred%20in%20which%20order.

[65] UK Jurisdiction Taskforce, 'Legal statement' (n 19) para 30.

[66] ibid.

participants of cryptocurrency systems and that these relationships are contractual in nature established by implication based on participation in a given system.[67]

Given that the underlying idea of Bitcoin and other cryptocurrency systems based on, or inspired by Bitcoin, was to create a system outside law and governed by code,[68] one might question this argument on the ground that participants of cryptocurrency systems might not contemplate the creation of legal relationships between them at all. At a theoretical level, that view might be appealing to some but, in practice, when a dispute arises from a cryptocurrency transfer, the view has little practical value as disputes are resolved within the legal framework and not in a legal vacuum.

In addition, the proposed characterisation focusing on cryptocurrency systems under the unitary approach offers a workable starting point for determining the law applicable to cryptocurrency transfers taking place within these systems. It also leads to the result that all transfers taking place within a cryptocurrency system can be, in principle, subject to the same law which is the law that governs the cryptocurrency system.[69] That would offer an ideal solution for the law applicable to cryptocurrency transfers as the ledger would not split in terms of its applicable law. The application of a single law to a system facilitating various transactions among different participants has several advantages and this idea of 'one system-one law' has been accepted and reflected in determination of the applicable law in some other similar contexts. Examples include Article 4(1)(h) of the Rome I Regulation, concerning contracts concluded within a multilateral system which brings together or facilitates the bringing together of multiple third-parties buying and selling interests in financial instruments, and the use of escape clauses for transactions consisting of linked contracts, such as guarantee, reinsurance, letter of credit and EFT.[70] Some cryptocurrency transfers taking place within cryptocurrency systems may be consumer transactions. In such cases, the application of a single law to a given cryptocurrency system would mean that the protection of consumers will be left to the relevant substantive law rules, rather than conflict of laws rules, in order to prevent the application of different laws to different transactions taking place in a given system.[71]

[67] Yüksel Ripley, 'Transfer of Digital Assets' (n 56). See Dickinson (n 41) para 5.31 who reached a similar conclusion but on a different ground based on the recognition that the relationships between participants in cryptocurrency systems are sufficiently akin to those between parties in a contractual relationship to justify applying a common set of rules to identify a competent court for their disputes and rules of law applicable to their obligations towards one another. *cf* Krysa (n 41).

[68] For the origins of the famous quote of 'code is law', see L Lessig, *Code: And Other Laws Of Cyberspace* (Basic Books, 1999); and L Lessig, 'Code is Law' (2000) *Harvard Magazine*, available at: www.harvardmagazine.com/2000/01/code-is-law-html, who actually raised the opposite argument.

[69] Yüksel Ripley, 'Transfer of Digital Assets' (n 56).

[70] See Yüksel Ripley and Heindler, 'The Law Applicable to Crypto Assets' (n 18).

[71] The same rationale is reflected in Art 6(4)(e) of the Rome I Regulation which removes protection provided to consumers under the conflict of laws rules in Arts 6(1) and 6(2) for contracts concluded within the type of system falling within the scope of Art 4(1)(h).

The proposed characterisation would work particularly well in determining the applicable law in permissioned DLT-based systems having a system owner or operator and participants who are known to each other. Choice of law will be considered effective in permissioned systems under the unitary approach before forums which accept the principle of party autonomy in contractual conflicts under either a general provision, such as Article 3 of the Rome I Regulation, or a special provision.[72] The law selected by the system rules (or consensus rules or protocols depending on system technicalities) can therefore be binding on all system participants as the participants have unconditionally agreed to these system rules, which include the choice of law, in order to be able to participate in the system and to comply with the rules once they have participated in the system.[73] In funds transfer systems, there is usually a choice of law clause in system rules that provide for the general principles of the given system and regulate the rights and obligations of the system owner and participants. The law governing the system, in principle, also governs the rights and obligations of the participants. For example, the CHAPS in the United Kingdom has selected English law as the governing law[74] whereas the CHIPS in the United States has selected the law of the state of New York.[75] In the United States, a special provision is explicitly provided in the Uniform Commercial Code (UCC), which has been widely adopted by states in relation to funds transfer systems, in §4A-507(c). The provision gives funds transfer systems the freedom of selecting the law of a particular jurisdiction to govern the rights and obligations of all parties to a funds transfer, including the originator[76] and the beneficiary,[77] and provides that this choice of law is binding on them if they have notice that the funds-transfer system might be used in the funds transfer and notice of the choice of law by the system.[78] In the absence of a choice of law, although such an absence

[72] Party autonomy in applicable law allows parties to agree on the law applicable to their relationship and this principle, in particular in relation to contractual relationships, is widely accepted worldwide by a large number of states subject to certain limits. For a comprehensive analysis on party autonomy in private international law and its operation from a comparative perspective, see A Mills, *Party Autonomy in Private International Law* (Cambridge University Press, 2018); and SC Symeonides, *Codifying Choice of Law Around the World: An International Comparative Analysis* (Oxford University Press, 2014).

[73] One issue which may arise in this context is the interplay between a choice of law by the system rules and a choice of law between parties to a given transfer taking place within the system, in cases where they are different laws.

[74] See s 15(1) of the CHAPS Reference Manual, version 1 July 2022, available at: www.bankofengland.co.uk/-/media/boe/files/payments/chaps/chaps-reference-manual.pdf.

[75] See Rule 3 of the CHIPS Rules and Administrative Procedures, effective 21 March 2022, available at: www.theclearinghouse.org/-/media/new/tch/documents/payment-systems/chips_rules_and_administrative_procedures_03-21-2022.pdf.

[76] Under UCC § 4A-104(c), '"originator" means the sender of the first payment order in a funds transfer'. The term can be understood, for the purposes of this chapter, as the payer.

[77] Under UCC § 4A-103(3), '"beneficiary" means the person to be paid by the beneficiary's bank'. The term can be understood, for the purposes of this chapter, as the payee.

[78] UCC § 4A-507(c): 'A funds-transfer system rule may select the law of a particular jurisdiction to govern (i) rights and obligations between participating banks with respect to payment orders transmitted or processed through the system, or (ii) the rights and obligations of some or all parties to a funds transfer any part of which is carried out by means of the system. A choice of law made pursuant to

would probably be rare in permissioned DLT-based systems, the determination of the applicable law can still be reasonably straightforward depending on the forum's objective conflict of laws rules on contractual relationships. The contemporary private international law framework, which makes the contractual relationships subject to the law that they are most closely connected with, usually provides for presumptions based on characteristic performance,[79] or a special catalogue for some types of contracts along with presumptions[80] or special conflict of laws rules for certain contracts and a general conflict of laws rule for others.[81] They would most likely result in the applicable law, in the absence of a choice of law, being the law of the company that owns or operates the system as the law of the service provider or of the characteristic performer, or as the law with which the system is most closely connected.

For permissionless DLT-based systems, however, the proposed characterisation would not be feasible for determining the applicable law. There are more differences than similarities between funds transfer systems and permissionless systems. Funds transfer systems are centralised systems typically operating in a localised manner in a given country or region in the currency of that country or region and with a system owner or operator and participants that are known to each other. Permissionless systems are, on the other hand, decentralised and distributed systems typically operating cross-border with no obvious system owner or operator and among pseudonymous participants that are unknown to each other. In terms of choice of law, it does not seem very possible under such a system structure for all system participants, who are pseudonymous and located all over the world, to agree upon an applicable law and also upon the same applicable law. This would lead to the applicable law almost always being determined according to the forum's objective conflict of laws rules on contractual relationships. Given that there is no obvious service provider or characteristic performer in permissionless systems whose law could be applied and that the closest connection test may indicate in the circumstances a rather tenuous connection to a law (or the law of a country) as the

clause (i) is binding on participating banks. A choice of law made pursuant to clause (ii) is binding on the originator, other sender, or a receiving bank having notice that the funds-transfer system might be used in the funds transfer and of the choice of law by the system when the originator, other sender, or receiving bank issued or accepted a payment order. The beneficiary of a funds transfer is bound by the choice of law if, when the funds transfer is initiated, the beneficiary has notice that the funds-transfer system might be used in the funds transfer and of the choice of law by the system. The law of a jurisdiction selected pursuant to this subsection may govern, whether or not that law bears a reasonable relation to the matter in issue'.

[79] See eg, Art 24(4) of the Turkish Code on Private International Law and Procedural Law (*Milletlerarası Özel Hukuk ve Usul Hukuku Hakkında Kanun*) Law No 5718, 27 November 2007, published in the *Turkish Gazette* dated 12 December 2007 and numbered 26728.

[80] See eg, Art 117 of the Swiss IPRG (*Schweizerisches Bundesgesetz über das Internationale Privatrecht IPRG*) 18 December 1987, available in English at: www.fedlex.admin.ch/eli/cc/1988/1776_1776_1776/en, as amended by the Federal Act of 25 September 2020 on the Adaptation of Federal Law to Developments in Distributed Ledger Technology, in force since 1 February 2021 (AS 2021 33; BBl 2020 233).

[81] See eg, Art 4 of Rome I Regulation.

governing law of decentralised and distributed systems, the determination of the law applicable to cryptocurrency transfers under the unitary approach would not be feasible for permissionless systems. In the absence of an internationally agreed conflict of laws rule on the issue, it would be very likely that different courts in different jurisdictions may reach different conclusions on the law governing these systems. This would undermine legal certainty and predictability and give room for forum shopping.

B. Segmented Approach

Given the shortcomings of applying the unitary approach to characterisation for cryptocurrency transfers taking place in permissionless DLT-based systems, this chapter proposes a different approach, ie, the segmented approach, to be applied to these systems, which focuses on individual transfers rather than the system as a whole and gives consideration to the similarities, as well as the differences, between cryptocurrency transfers and EFTs.

An EFT is the movement of funds between different bank accounts by electronic means.[82] It enables the transfer of value by adjusting the balances of the relevant bank accounts without the need for the physical transfer of money.[83] An EFT is a chain transaction initiated by a payment order given by a payer to his bank, following from authentication and verification carried out by a series of interbank operations, and technically completed when the payee's bank credits the payee's account.[84] This, on certain aspects, resembles a cryptocurrency transfer. Based on the technical operation of cryptocurrency transfers as explained in section II.B of this chapter and in an analogy to EFT, a cryptocurrency transfer can be characterised as a transaction contractual in nature[85] with different stages but with one single economic purpose to realise which is the transfer of value from the payer to the payee.

The proposed characterisation focusing on individual cryptocurrency transfers in a given system under the segmented approach offers a workable starting point

[82] For different definitions of EFT having this similar core, see eg, B Geva, *The Law of Electronic Funds Transfers* (Matthew Bender, 1994) 1--6; S Karageorgiou, 'Electronic Funds Transfers: Technical & Legal Overview' (Thesis, University of London Queen Mary and Westfield College, 1990) 33; C Proctor, *The Law and Practice of International Banking*, 2nd edn (Oxford University Press, 2015) para 19.05; United Nations Commission on International Trade Law, *UNCITRAL Legal Guide on Electronic Funds Transfers* (1987), available at: www.uncitral.org/pdf/english/texts/payments/transfers/LG_E-fundstransfer-e.pdf.

[83] R Cox and J Taylor, 'Funds Transfer' in M Brindle and R Cox (eds), *Law of Bank Payments* (Sweet & Maxwell, 2017) para 3-002; Ellinger, Lomnicka and Hare (n 58) 559.

[84] This explanation is relevant to the technical operation of credit transfers as most international funds transfers are credit transfers not debit, see Cox and Taylor, ibid, para 3-014; Geva, *Bank Collections and Payment Transactions* (n 56) 86; A Malek and J Odgers, *Paget's Law of Banking*, 14th edn (Lexis Nexis, 2014) para 25.55.

[85] See section III.A for the argument on the contractual nature of the relationships between system participants.

for determining the law applicable to cryptocurrency transfers taking place within permissionless DLT-based systems. Each transfer can therefore be subject to its own applicable law. Parties' freedom to choose the applicable law would depend on the interpretation of 'parties' whose agreement is needed for a choice of law agreement.[86] If it is only the payer and the payee whose agreement is needed on the applicable law, choice of law can function effectively and the given transfer can be governed by the law chosen by the payer and the payee. In cases where the payer and the payee know each other, such an agreement can exist before the transfer takes place. In other cases, it would still be possible for them to agree on a choice of law after a dispute arises and such a choice could be given effect depending on the forum's conflict of laws rules.[87] In consumer transactions, party autonomy in applicable law would be subject to the approach that the given forum takes on the protection of consumers by the application of conflict of laws rules.[88] On the other hand, in addition to the payer and the payee, if miners involved in a given transfer would be considered as parties to the transfer whose agreement is also needed for a choice of law, it would be highly unlikely for all these parties to agree upon an applicable law not only before a transfer takes place, due to the structure of permissionless DLT-based systems as explained above and the element of pseudonymity, but also after a dispute arises given the unlikeliness of all of these parties being present before the same court.

In the absence of a choice of law, the determination of the applicable law of cryptocurrency transfers can still pose certain challenges depending on the forum's objective conflict of laws rules on contractual relationships. This is rather in contrast to the determination of the applicable law of EFTs because of certain differences that exist between cryptocurrency transfers and EFTs. In a typical EFT, there are separate bank accounts and the amount is transferred from one to another by adjusting the balances of the relevant bank accounts via debiting the amount from one account and crediting it to another.[89] When it is a domestic EFT, it includes the banks of the payer and payee and usually also a central bank. When it is an international EFT, in most cases it also includes one or more correspondent banks. The interbank payments are processed through clearing and settlement either on a bilateral basis between the two respective banks that

[86] On the limitations of party autonomy in the context of international EFTs, see Yüksel, *EFT* (n 56) 166–68.

[87] This would, however, probably be a rare situation. In cases where the parties are able to come to an agreement on the applicable law, there is a strong argument that it would be more likely that they could come to an agreement on the merits of the dispute and resolve it. See C Şanlı, E Esen and İ Ataman-Figanmeşe, *Milletlerarası Özel Hukuk*, 4th edn (Vedat, 2015).

[88] In the context of the Rome I Regulation, it seems that in most cases Art 6 will not apply as a mere participation in a cryptocurrency system is not sufficient, on its own, to indicate that the trader 'pursues his commercial or professional activities in the country where the consumer has his habitual residence', or 'by any means, directs such activities to that country or to several countries including that country' within the meaning of Art 6. However, particular circumstances of a given case may suggest otherwise. For this argument, see Dickinson (n 41) para 5.69–5.70.

[89] Cox and Taylor (n 83) para 3-002; Ellinger, Lomnicka and Hare (n 58) 559.

are correspondents holding an account with the other,[90] or on a multilateral basis on the books of a common correspondent bank or of a central bank in a funds transfer system.[91] At the very heart of the system, there is a central ledger and intermediation. This makes it easier to determine the objectively applicable law based on the criteria such as the location of the service provider or characteristic performer, which is the bank in EFTs.[92] In a cryptocurrency transfer, on the other hand, there is in general terms an electronic (or digital) record documenting who has transferred what to whom in the cryptocurrency system and the wallet software figures from that record how much is attributed to each identity.[93] At the very heart of the systems, there is a distributed ledger and disintermediation.

Despite these differences between cryptocurrency transfers and EFTs, the proposed characterisation under the segmented approach could nevertheless offer a workable solution for the determination of the law applicable to cryptocurrency transfers taking place within permissionless systems based on the closets connection of a given transaction. Appropriate weight can be given to factors relating to the parties to the transaction (eg, the location of the payer or the payee if this is known) or, through the application of the technique of the 'accessory connection', the transfer can be made subject to the law that governs the underlying relationship between the parties as the main connection.[94] Consumer transactions would require an analysis in light of the approach that the given forum takes on the protection of consumers by the application of conflict of laws rules.[95]

However, under the segmented approach, the ledger will split in its applicable law as each transfer will be subject to its own applicable law. Splitting the applicable law is not desirable for systems facilitating various transactions among their participants as it would, in many cases, lead to the application of different laws to transactions taking place withing these systems. This is criticised also in the context of DLT-based systems on different grounds.[96] However, identifying a single law which is appropriate to apply to all cryptocurrency transactions taking place within a given permissionless DLT-based system is extremely difficult, if not impossible, in the absence of widely accepted and internationally agreed conflict of laws rules. This is particularly because there is no obvious service provider or characteristic performer in these systems whose law could be applied as a single

[90] Geva, *The Law of Electronic Funds Transfers* (n 82) 1–28; Ellinger, Lomnicka and Hare (n 58) 564; Malek and Odgers (n 84) para 22.32.

[91] Geva, *The Law of Electronic Funds Transfers* (n 82) 1–28; Ellinger, Lomnicka and Hare (n 58) 564; Malek and Odgers (n 84) para 22.32.

[92] In EFTs involving correspondent banks as well as the banks of the payer and payee, further questions might arise as to which of these banks will be considered the service provider or characteristic performer for the purposes of determining the applicable law. See Yüksel, *EFT* (n 56) 168–73.

[93] In cryptocurrency systems working on a pseudonymous basis, such as Bitcoin, true identities of participants are not disclosed. The ledger records the amount attributed to public addresses, rather than a person.

[94] Yüksel Ripley, 'Transfer of Digital Assets' (n 56).

[95] See above (n 88).

[96] See generally, FMLC (n 53).

law and the decentralised and distributed nature of the systems may indicate only a tenuous connection under the closest connection test to a law (or the law of a country) to govern all cryptocurrency transactions taking place within these systems. Rather than trying to find a single law for permissionless DLT-based systems, it would be more feasible to adopt the segmented approach, identify the law applicable to each cryptocurrency transfer, and deal with any unsatisfactory result arising from the potential application of that law on a case-by-case basis by using the devices that exist in conflict of laws for that kind of situation, such as escape clauses, as appropriate.

As explained in the technical operation of cryptocurrency transfers in section II.B of this chapter, there are different stages in cryptocurrency transfers. Further to the segmentation of cryptocurrency systems into transactions under the segmented approach for the purposes of characterisation and determination of the applicable law, one might raise – in an analogy to EFT – the possibility of the segmentation of each transfer into the transfer's stages. Where there is a problem or contingency in a cryptocurrency transfer in a given system, it seems technically possible to be able to see how and at which stage of the transfer it arose if the given system is a well-engineered one and the underlying cryptography is correct. Such a segmentation may therefore be technically possible for the determination of the applicable law of each stage of the transfer. However, in contrast to EFTs, cryptocurrency transfers are typically executed among pseudonymous participants who are unknown to each other and with the involvement of miners informally working in a peer-to-peer manner around the world with no central coordination in a given system. Tracking down all participants involved in different stages of a cryptocurrency transfer would be difficult, costly, time-consuming and probably unnecessary. Such a segmentation in a transfer for the purpose of determining the law applicable to each stage of the transfer, which is applied to EFTs,[97] would be therefore neither feasible nor desirable for cryptocurrency transfers.

IV. Conclusion

Cryptocurrency transfers in DLT-based systems challenge, as a new phenomenon, the traditional concepts and techniques of conflict of laws. One of them is characterisation, which is the first step in a conflict of laws analysis following the identification of a foreign element that a given matter involves and which initiates and affects the determination of the applicable law.

In relation to the issue of characterisation of cryptocurrency transfers in DLT-based systems, the suggestions that have been put forward thus far have mainly attempted to characterise cryptocurrencies as a thing/property, leading to the application of the *lex situs* as the predominant law applied to international

[97] See generally, Yüksel, *EFT* (n 56) 124–65.

property, or as a claim transferable by way of assignment, leading to the potential application of conflict of laws rules on assignment of claims (such as Article 14 of the Rome I Regulation or Rule 135 in *Dicey, Morris and Collins* at common law governing various issues regarding the transfer of intangibles) to cryptocurrency transfers. However, neither of these suggestions is considered satisfactory for cryptocurrency transfers in DLT-based systems. This is because of the difficulties in geographical localisation in these systems, which makes the *lex situs* rather unsuitable in this context, and because of the lack of a claim, in most cases, to assign as a legally enforceable right arising under the law applicable to the relationship between system participants as well as the lack of an assigned debtor.

This chapter takes a new perspective on characterisation of cryptocurrency transfers in DLT-based systems by utilising an analogy to EFTs and funds transfer systems. Cryptocurrency transfers taking place within DLT-based systems resemble, in some aspects, EFTs taking place within funds transfer systems. EFTs, as transfers of value by adjusting the balances of the relevant bank accounts without any need of physical transfer of money, are processed in the funds transfer systems via accounts of participating banks being held with the system owner or operator according to system rules to which each participating bank unconditionally agrees in order to be able to participate in the system and to comply with once it participates in the system. The relationships between participating banks and the funds transfer system, and between the participating banks themselves are therefore contractual in nature. By analogy to funds transfer systems, it can be argued that there are contractual relationships between participants of cryptocurrency systems established by implication based on participation in a given system. Similar to EFTs, cryptocurrency transfers taking place within cryptocurrency systems are also contractual in nature with different stages but with one single economic purpose to realise, which is the transfer of value from the payer to the payee.

This chapter proposes a characterisation under the unitary approach by focusing on the characteristics of cryptocurrency systems as a whole and in an analogy to funds transfer systems. Accordingly, all transfers taking place within a cryptocurrency system among different system participants can, in principle, be subject to the same law which is the law that governs the cryptocurrency system. The proposed characterisation would work well in determining the applicable law in DLT-based systems having a system owner or operator. The applicable law would be determined according to the choice of law, depending on the subjective conflict of laws rules on contractual relationships in a given forum, if there is a choice as such in the system rules (or consensus rules or protocols). In the absence of such a choice, the applicable law would be determined according to the objective conflict of laws rules on contractual relationships in a given forum which would most likely be the law of the company that owns or operates the system as the law of the service provider or of the characteristic performer, or as the law with which the system is most closely connected, depending on the criterion that the forum adopts.

The characterisation under the unitary approach, however, may not be feasible for systems which facilitate transfers, with no obvious system owner or operator, among pseudonymous participants. As fallback for such cases, this chapter accordingly proposes a characterisation under the segmented approach by focusing on individual transfers rather than the system as a whole and in an analogy to EFTs. This proposal offers a workable starting point for determining the law applicable to cryptocurrency transfers taking place within these systems by making each transfer subject to its own applicable law. This law can be the chosen law by the payer and payee in a given transfer if they are considered in a given forum the only 'parties' whose agreement is needed for choice of law (excluding miners). In the absence of a choice of law, although the determination of the law applicable to cryptocurrency transfers can still pose certain challenges, these can be overcome by giving appropriate weight to factors relating to the payer and the payee of the cryptocurrency transfer in question (including the underlying relationship between them) in determining the applicable law of the transfer. Although this would result in the ledger being split in its applicable law, any unsatisfactory result arising from that can be dealt with on a case-by-case basis by using the devices of conflict of laws available for that kind of situation, such as escape clauses, as appropriate.

Under the current cryptocurrency landscape, it can be anticipated that the unitary approach would find a scope of application mainly for permissioned systems whereas the segmented approach would typically be relevant to permissionless systems. However, it is important that these approaches should be agile and future-proof in their application and interpretation. Given that cryptocurrency systems are self-contained systems, what matters for the application of the proposed approaches for characterisation and determination of the applicable law is therefore how a cryptocurrency system is designed and internally operated, not how it is externally labelled or categorised in a given time at a given place.

8

Environmental Litigation in the European Union: All Quiet on the Western Front?

LAURA CARBALLO PIÑEIRO*

I. Introduction

Although the political agendas across the world seek to align themselves with the United Nations (UN) Sustainable Development Goals (SDGs), their shortcomings are fuelling legal mobilisation to address pressing environmental concerns, for example, through climate change litigation. In addition to cases targeting states and measures undertaken to reduce greenhouse gas emissions,[1] others have been brought against private companies.[2] They follow other high-profile cases dealing with gross violations of human rights such as the one brought against the Shell group as a result of extensive pollution allegedly caused by oil perforation in the Niger Delta (Nigeria) and its impact on the people living in the region, with judgments in the United States,[3] the Netherlands[4] and the

* PaxNature Project (PID2022-142484NB-C22).

[1] *Urgenda Foundation v The Netherlands* [2015] HAZA C/09/00456689 (24 June 2015); aff'd (9 October 2018) (District Court of the Hague, and The Hague Court of Appeal (on appeal)) (affirmed by the Supreme Court, 20 December 2019); *Notre Affaire à Tous and Others v France*, Nos 1904967, 1904968, 1904972, 1904976/4-1 (Paris Administrative Court) (3 February 2021).

[2] *Milieudefensie et al v Royal Dutch Shell* (26 May 2021) (District Court of the Hague) (ECLI:NL:RBDHA:2021:5337); *Notre Affaire à Tous and Others v Total* (filed 29 January 2020).

[3] *Kiobel v Royal Dutch Petroleum Co*, 569 US 108, 133 S CT 1659 (2013). See, among others, MC Marrullo and FJZ Cabot, 'Transnational Human Rights Litigation. Kiobel's Touch and Concern: A Test under Construction' (2016) 1 *Papeles el tiempo de los derechos*, available at: redtiempodelos-derechos.com/publicaciones-2/papeles-el-tiempo-de-los-derechos/; CA Whytock, DE Childress III and MD Ramsey, 'Forward: After Kiobel – International Human Rights Litigation in State Courts and Under State Law' (2013) 3 *UC Irvine Law Review* 1.

[4] See *Rechtbank*' s-*Gravenhage*, 24 February 2010, ECLI:NL:RBSGR:2010:BM1470 (*Barizaa Manson Tete Dooh and Vereniging Milieudefensie v Royal Dutch Shell Plc and Shell Petroleum Development Company Ltd*). The Hague District Court concluded in its final judgment that Royal Dutch Shell Netherlands was not responsible for oil spills in Nigeria, but the Nigerian subsidiary was. See judgment of 30 January 2013, ECLI:NL:RBDHA:2013:BY9845, and comments by N Jägers, KD Jesse and J Vershuuren, 'The Future of Corporate Liability for Extraterritorial Human Rights Abuses: The Dutch Case Against Shell' [2014] *American Journal of International Law* 36. In June 2017 and after the class action initiated in the US had been finally dismissed, Ester Kiobel and the other widowers of the

United Kingdom.[5] In all these cases, the claimants did not bring their case before the courts of the country where the damage occurred, but to courts in countries from which defendants operate, shopping for a jurisdiction able to deal with complex litigation and hoping for the application of law with stricter environmental standards than the country of damage.[6]

These cases are the crystallisation of a long journey with some remarkable milestones such as the 1972 UN Conference on the Human Environment in Stockholm and the 1992 Río de Janeiro Conference on Environment and Development, which did not only give content to the environmental protection principle but opened the door to their operationalisation by requesting the involvement of members of the public in their protection. The Convention on Access to Information, Public Participation in Decision-Making and Access to Justice in Environmental Matters, signed in Aarhus on 25 June 1998 (Aarhus Convention),[7] has been instrumental to this end. However, and despite these achievements, access to justice in environmental matters appears to be restricted in a majority of jurisdictions as the above-mentioned cases illustrate.[8] They have been conducted in a selected number of jurisdictions not only because of the defendant's seat, but because of the procedural mechanisms therein available that are rarely found elsewhere.

activists killed by the Nigerian government in 1995 in a case related to their demonstrations against oil pollution brought a lawsuit against Shell in the Netherlands. The case was dismissed on 23 March 2022. See Business & Human Rights Resource Center, 'Shell lawsuit (re executions in Nigeria, Kiobel v Shell, filed in the Netherlands)' (2022), available at: www.business-humanrights.org/en/latest-news/shell-lawsuit-re-executions-in-nigeria-kiobel-v-shell-filed-in-the-netherlands/.

[5] See *Bodo Community v Shell Petroleum Development Company (Nigeria) Ltd ('SPDC')* brought before the High Court in London, but this Court did not pronounce judgment because a non-judicial settlement was reached first. See John Vidal, 'Shell announces £55m payout for Nigeria oil spills' *Guardian* (7 January 2015), available at: www.theguardian.com/environment/2015/jan/07/shell-announces-55m-payout-for-nigeria-oil-spills. More recently, the High Court in London decided on *Okpabi and others v Royal Dutch Shell* [2017] EWHC 89, [2017] Bus LR 1335, concluding that it did not have international jurisdiction on the case.

[6] Another remarkable case is *Aguinda v Texaco, Inc*, 142 F Supp 2d 534 (SDNY 2001), the unfortunate judgment from which the Chevron/Ecuador saga arises. Following very serious oil pollution allegedly committed by Aguinda in the Oriente region in Ecuador, Ecuadorians and Peruvians affected initiated a putative class action in the US dismissed by the cited judgment on grounds of *forum non conveniens*. While Peruvians did not find access to justice in their country, Ecuadorians did because of the issuance of *Ley de Gestión Medioambiental* (1999), Law 99/37 by which a collective action mechanism was established in Ecuador. Likewise, Ecuador adhered to ILO Convention No 169 concerning indigenous and tribal peoples in independent countries (1989). On this legal basis, litigation was initiated at the Lago Agrio Court against Chevron, the company which took over Aguinda in the US.

[7] Aarhus Convention, 2161 UNTS 447, entered into force on 30 October 2001 and has been ratified by 47 states that made up the region UNECE, including countries of Europe, Asia, United States and Canada. As none of the Latin America countries are a party to this Convention, the Declaration on the application of Principle 10 of the Rio Declaration on Environment and Development in Latin America and the Caribbean, signed at the UN Conference on Sustainable Development (Río+20), done in Rio de Janeiro in June 2012, is to be welcomed and celebrated that it has finally concluded with the Regional Agreement on Access to Information, Public Participation and Justice in Environmental Matters in Latin America and the Caribbean, adopted on 4 March 2018 (Escazú Agreement).

[8] However, the fight for environmental justice is reaching more and more countries as can be learnt, eg, from the report provided by Environmental Law Alliance Worldwide (ELAW), *Holding*

Some of those jurisdictions are within the European Union where the Aarhus Convention has been implemented. This chapter addresses, first, the steps taken by the European Union to ensure the Aarhus Convention's application, and second, its shortcomings, in particular when it comes to private enforcement. Despite the encouragement of the Aarhus Convention Compliance Committee (ACCC), making collective redress mechanisms available for environmental protection is still a pending subject at EU level. Directive (EU) 2020/1828,[9] was supposed to fill this gap, but environmental protection has been left out of its scope unless consumers are involved, as the *Dieselgate* case illustrates.[10] Hence, we are still waiting for a common approach to private enforcement of environment protection at EU level.

The European Commission's Proposal for a Directive of the European Parliament and of the Council on Corporate Sustainability Due Diligence[11] might also add to reinforcing transnational environmental protection by enlarging the situations in which corporations might be held accountable for their participation in the global supply chain.[12] The following section of this chapter focuses on the steps taken at EU level to address transnational environmental damage and the manner in which this Proposal might enhance the current scenario. The chapter concludes that all has been too quiet at the EU legislative level as regards enhancing environmental protection. Although judicial activism has shown the way forward, private international law is compelled to support sustainable development by providing mechanisms capable of ensuring transnational corporate accountability and the application of the polluter-pays principle. In this respect, further harmonisation of the procedural aspects operationalising such accountability is needed as Jonathan Fitchen suggested in one of his brilliant works, although addressing the issue from a general perspective.[13] I hope that this conversation would have had him engaged as he was not only an outstanding professor of private international law, but also a man of many interests and passions, including leaving behind a better world for future generations. Thank you, dear Jon, for your many inspirational achievements.

Corporations Accountable for Damaging the Climate (2014), available at: www.elaw.org/system/files/elaw.climate.litigation.report.pdf, addressing the cases of Brazil, Colombia, Ecuador, India, Kenya and Mexico.

[9] Directive (EU) 2020/1828 of the European Parliament and of the Council of 25 November 2020 on representative actions for the protection of the collective interests of consumers and repealing Directive 2009/22/EU, [2020] OJ L409/1.

[10] See an excellent overview of this Directive's limitations in these matters by L García Álvarez, 'La aplicación en materia ambiental de las acciones de representación para la protección de los intereses colectivos de los consumidores. A propósito de la Directiva (UE) 2020/1828' (2021) 3 *Revista Ítalo-española De Derecho Procesal* 59.

[11] Commission, 'Proposal for a Directive of the European Parliament and of the Council on Corporate Sustainability Due Diligence and amending Directive (EU) 2019/1937' COM(2022) 71 final.

[12] See the case law brought before EU courts to pursue this type liability in A Marx, C Bright, N Pineau and J Wouters, 'Corporate Accountability Mechanisms in EU Member States for Human Rights Abuses in Third Countries' Working Paper No 212 (March 2019) Leuven Centre for Global Governance Studies, including many involving environmental damage.

[13] J Fitchen, 'Unharmonised Procedural Rules: Is there a Case for Further Harmonisation at EU Level?' in P Beaumont, M Danov, K Trimmings and B Yüksel (eds), *Cross-Border Litigation in Europe* (Hart Publishing, 2017).

II. Access to Justice in Environmental Matters

A. Origins: Principle 10 of the 1992 Río de Janeiro Declaration on Environment and Development

Environmental protection has become a critical issue placed high on most political and economic agendas for many reasons that have already been put forward at the UN Conference on Environment and Development, held in Rio de Janeiro in 1992. From that moment on, access to justice in these matters has also received a boost on account of one of the Conference's principles, ie, sustainable development relies on the public's access to decision-making processes and also to justice.[14] Along these lines, transparency has found its way into trade negotiations, in particular those involving public procurement.

Against this backdrop, international instruments such as the Aarhus Convention are essential to implement Principle 10 of the Rio Declaration. The European Union has signed the latter and implemented it by different instruments including the Directive on Public Access to Environmental Information,[15] the Directive on Public Participation in Decision-Making[16] –both addressed to the Member States – and a Regulation on the application of the provisions of the Aarhus Convention to Community institutions and bodies.[17] It has, nevertheless, failed to release a Directive on access to justice in environmental matters. While the European Commission issued a Proposal for a Directive in 2003,[18] no further action has been taken to date.[19] In fact, the EU's adherence to the Convention was

[14] 'Environmental issues are best handled with the participation of all concerned citizens, at the relevant level. At the national level, each individual shall have appropriate access to information concerning the environment that is held by public authorities, including information on hazardous materials and activities in their communities, and the opportunity to participate in decision-making processes. States shall facilitate and encourage public awareness and participation by making information widely available. Effective access to judicial and administrative proceedings, including redress and remedy, shall be provided'. See Principle 10, *Report of the United Nations Conference on Environment and Development, Rio Declaration on Environment and Development* (UN Document, 3–14 June 1992), available at: www.un.org/documents/ga/conf151/aconf15126-1annex1.htm (hereafter Rio Declaration).

[15] Directive 2003/4/EC of the European Parliament and of the Council of 28 January 2003 on public access to environmental information and repealing Council Directive 90/313/EEC, [2003] OJ L41/26.

[16] Directive 2003/35/EC of the European Parliament and of the Council of 26 May 2003 providing for public participation in respect of the drawing up of certain plans and programmes relating to the environment and amending with regard to public participation and access to justice Council Directives 85/337/EEC and 96/61/EC, [2003] OJ L156/17.

[17] Regulation (EC) No 1367/2006 of the European Parliament and of the Council of 6 September 2006 on the application of the provisions of the Aarhus Convention on Access to Information, Public Participation in Decision-making and Access to Justice in Environmental Matters to Community institutions and bodies, [2006] OJ L264/13.

[18] See Commission, 'Proposal for a Directive on access to justice on environmental matters' COM(2003) 624 final.

[19] The matter is further discussed in Communication from the Commission of 28 April 2017: Commission, 'Notice on Access to Justice in Environmental Matters' C(2017) 2616 final, para 10, but discarded due to lack of consensus.

accompanied by a declaration which pointed out that it was impossible to reach a consensus about the implementation of Article 9(3) of the Aarhus Convention.[20]

This provision deals with access to justice in environmental protection matters highlighting the obligation to create private enforcement mechanisms against public and private polluters. The main hurdle seems to be reconciling the different perspectives of Member States as regards *locus standi*, in particular when it comes to granting non-governmental organisations (NGOs) legal standing. Legal divergence as to this issue is particularly acute across the European Union and this seems to be the main reason why a Directive on access to justice in environmental matters has not been issued yet.[21] While some Member States accept the principle of *actio popularis*, others restrict access to court through different procedural requirements.

Even the European Union has been accused of restricting access to the courts in environmental matters.[22] In accordance with the 2006 Regulation on the application to the provisions of the Aarhus Convention to the Community institutions and bodies, only NGOs, and only in some restricted cases, were entitled to challenge decisions taken by these bodies. The ACCC delivered an opinion in 2017,[23] condemning these restrictions and finally the 2006 Regulation has been amended to entitle members of the public to challenge EU institutions and bodies' decisions.[24]

[20] The Community adherence to the Convention was approved on 17 February 2005 ([2005] OJ L124/1) and the declaration states as follows: 'the legal instruments in force do not cover fully the implementation of the obligations resulting from art 9(3) of the Convention as they relate to administrative and judicial procedures to challenge acts and omissions by private persons and public authorities other than the institutions of the European Community … Consequently, its Member States are responsible for the performance of these obligations at the time of approval of the Convention by the European Community and will remain so unless the Community, in the exercise of its powers under the EC Treaty, adopts provisions of Community law covering the implementation of those obligations'.

[21] The 2003 Proposal for a Directive on access to justice on environmental matters (n 18) only contained a reminder, that Art 9(3) of the Aarhus Convention also applies to private persons, meaning that access to justice in these matters is also to be made available for these persons and not only states. Art 4(1) of this Proposal entitles NGOs to sue states such as Art 12(1) of Directive 2004/35/EC now does.

[22] See Case C-321/95 *Stichting Greenpeace Council (Greenpeace International) and Others v Commission of the European Communities* [1998] ECR I-01651 in which Greenpeace was not entitled to appeal the financial decision of funding with ERDF two power stations. See also a critique by JH Jans, 'The Rule of Law and European Environmental Policy'; H Somsen, 'Current Issues of Implementation, Compliance and Enforcement of EC Environmental Law', both in L Krämer (ed), *Recht und Um-Welt. Essays in Honour of Prof Dr Gerd Winter* (Europa Law Publishing, 2003).

[23] See Case ACCC/C/2008/32 *European Union*, Findings (Part II), adopted on 17 March 2017.

[24] Regulation (EU) 2021/1767 of the European Parliament and of the Council of 6 October 2021 amending Regulation (EC) No 1367/2006 on the application of the provisions of the Aarhus Convention on Access to Information, Public Participation in Decision-making and Access to Justice in Environmental Matters to Community institutions and bodies, [2021] OJ L356/1. However, this amendment still blocks access to justice in those cases in which state aid is involved despite the ACCC Findings and recommendations with regard to Communication ACCC/C/2015/128 concerning compliance by the European Union Adopted by the Compliance Committee on 17 March 2021. Despite these shortcomings, legal claims against EU decisions have already started to be initiated. See Arthur Neslen, 'ClientEarth launches legal action against EU over unsustainable fishing quotas' *Guardian* (25 March 2022), available at: www.theguardian.com/environment/2022/mar/25/clientearth-legal-action-eu-unsustainable-fishing-quotas.

B. Environmental Damage in Context

The role of tort law in environmental protection is often questioned in favour of public environmental law. This tension can be traced to the Aarhus Convention to the extent that it takes for granted the complementary, although limited, role that tort law plays in ensuring environmental protection alongside public environmental law. Its usefulness is attested, though, by the fact that it is being resorted to in most judicial systems.[25] However, in order to improve the efficiency of environmental protection claims in the courts, collective actions appear to be key to the extent that they seem to be the only proceedings able to deal efficiently with environmental damage and, therefore, properly enforce the polluter-pays principle.

Damage caused by pollution has special characteristics which make it difficult to be brought to justice. These features include its long period of latency, which makes it difficult to identify possible victims. Often, the damage done to the individual may be less than the expected recovery in the courts. This creates a disincentive for private persons to litigate because, even when it is worth litigating, proof of causation can be too difficult to justify legal action. All of these problems could be better handled in a group action, because grouping individual damage rights into a single proceeding overcomes the economic hurdle, at least better than an individual action does.[26] While litigation costs may still be daunting in a group action, collective actions make claiming more feasible.[27] Despite these positive aspects, group actions request specific regulation because of the constitutional problems they pose.[28] These constitutional issues are very interesting, but deal with traditional damages and as such, fall outside the scope of this chapter.

A further hurdle that private law encounters with regard to protecting the environment is that its intervention is generally limited to those cases where a property has been affected or there is personal injury. In other words, it is still limited in many jurisdictions to those cases where a right to compensation exists because

[25] The topic has been addressed by the Hague Conference while considering a Convention on civil liability for environmental damage. See C Bernasconi, 'Civil Liability Resulting from Transfrontier Environmental Damage: A Case for the Hague Conference?' (5–6 Preliminary Doc 8, HCCH), available at: www.hcch.net/upload/wop/gen_pd8e.pdf, 55.

[26] See M Cappelletti, 'Vindicating the Public Interest through the Courts: A Comparativist's Contribution' in M Cappelletti and B Garth (eds), *Access to Justice: Emerging Issues and Perspectives*, vol III (Sijthoff, 1979).

[27] Compensation for environmental damage would be better achieved by collective justice and group actions, which could claim for damages suffered by volunteers either while preventing further environmental damage or undertaking conservation work. Courts and legislators have acknowledged the costs incurred by environmental organisations while undertaking such activities, but have overlooked individual volunteers. For further analysis of this issue, see M Carballo Fidalgo, 'Los daños a voluntarios del caso *Prestige*' in MPG Rubio and SA González (eds), *La responsabilidad por los daños causados por el hundimiento del Prestige* (Iustel, 2007).

[28] Group actions can undermine the due process rights of class members, because individual rights are decided in proceedings not attended by the individual. In order to assure individual due process rights, group actions provide specific guarantees such as opt-in/opt-out rights, increased judicial monitoring, and/or the right to appeal to third parties. See a detailed discussion in CI Nagy, *Collective Actions in Europe: A Comparative, Economic and Transsystemic Analysis* (Springer, 2019).

personal injury or property damage is involved, but not to those in which damage has been caused to the environment, in 'no man's land'. However, this is an obsolete limitation today as it is now necessary to come up with a solution that provides access to justice for environmental damage.[29] Against this backdrop, the recognition of environmental damage as a cause of action, known as pure ecological damage if compensation is sought, is to be saluted as a victory in itself.

The release of Directive 2004/35/EC of the European Parliament and of the Council of 21 April 2004 on environmental liability with regard to the prevention and remedying of environmental damage,[30] reflects this recognition. However, the Directive only grants legal standing to states in order to act/claim against operators.[31] Environmental associations and NGOs can claim against a state's (in)activity, but not directly against private operators in accordance with this Directive which, nevertheless, can be implemented by national law-makers including such a legal standing, ie, providing for actions that can be brought by either members of the public or NGOs against private operators either claiming for their right to a healthy environment or for pure ecological damage.

C. Legal Standing to Make a Claim for Environmental Damage

The establishment of environmental damage as a source of tort law raises the question as to who has the legal standing to claim it. If it causes harm to a person or private property, legal standing is not an issue. However, should the damage be purely ecological or impairing the right to a healthy environment, the establishment of who is entitled to sue for it is more complicated. The first answer is to grant legal standing to states and public entities. The second answer, which is more in accordance with Principle 10 of the Rio de Janeiro Declaration, also entitles private persons and NGOs. As mentioned above, the European Union has not gone as far as that, and all the attempts made in that direction have failed.

The paralysis concerning the interpretation of Article 9(3) led the ACCC to issue a declaration highlighting the difference between Article 9(2) and its reference to 'members of the public concerned', and Article 9(3) which refers to

[29] See EHP Brans, *Liability for Damage to Public Natural Resources* (Erasmus University, 2001); AR González, *El daño ecológico puro* (Thomson-Aranzadi, 2008).

[30] Art 2 of Directive 2004/35/EC defines environmental damages as 'a) damage to protected species and natural habitats, which is any damage that has significant adverse effects on reaching or maintaining the favourable conservation status of such habitats or species … b) water damage, which is any damage that significantly adversely affects the ecological, chemical and/or quantitative status and/or ecological potential … c) land damage, which is any land contamination that creates a significant risk of human health being adversely affected as a result of the direct or indirect introduction, in, on or under land, of substances, preparations, organisms or micro-organisms'.

[31] See Art 12 of Directive 2004/35/EC restricting NGOs' legal standing to those cases in which states have not taken measures to prevent or restore environmental damage. Moreover, only NGOs complying with the Directive's requirements are entitled to sue.

'members of the public'. In this vein, the Committee suggests a broad interpretation of Article 9(3) so as to include environmental organisations. Although the Aarhus Convention does not require the establishment of an *actio popularis* and Article 9(3) indicates that *locus standi* is granted to those meeting 'the criteria, if any, laid down in national law', the Committee also indicates that 'the Parties may not take the clause … as an excuse for introducing or maintaining so strict criteria that they effectively bar all or almost all environmental organisations from challenging acts or omissions that contravene national law relating to the environment'.[32]

In view of these findings, the Commission launched a study aimed at a comprehensive overview of the different measures adopted in the Member States to implement Article 9(3) of the Aarhus Convention and related provisions.[33] The study concluded in a very similar way to the suggestions made by the Committee, even proposing the introduction of an actio popularis, since it has not been possible to identify noteworthy abuses in those Member States which have adopted that system. Regrettably, this study has not triggered any further binding action within the European Union despite the recommendation in this direction included in the Commission Recommendation of 11 June 2013 on common principles for injunctive and compensatory collective redress mechanisms in the Member States concerning violations of rights granted under Union Law,[34] and in the Communication, 'Towards a European Horizontal Framework for Collective Redress',[35] as well as in the European Parliament Resolution of 12 February 2012, 'Towards a coherence European approach to collective redress'.[36]

Collective interests concern members of the public in general. This is a proposition which should lead to the establishment of an actio popularis, making it possible for NGOs and individuals to claim against public and private polluters, and thus enhancing environmental protection.[37] This approach sounds, though,

[32] ACCC, 'Report of the meeting. Findings and Recommendations adopted by the Compliance Committee on the Aarhus Convention on 16 June 2006' (ECE/MP.PP/C.1/2006/4/Add.2, 26 June 2006), available at: unece.org/fileadmin/DAM/env/documents/2006/pp/ECE_MP.PP_C.1_2006_4_Add.2_e.pdf, para 35.

[33] Commission, 'Summary Report on the inventory of EU Member States' measures on access to justice in environmental matters, commissioned by the EU and the individual country reports', available at: ec.europa.eu/environment/aarhus/study_access.htm.

[34] [2013], OJ L201/60. See Recital 7 thereof which reads as follows: 'Amongst those areas where the supplementary private enforcement of rights granted under Union law in the form of collective redress is of value, are consumer protection, competition, environment protection, protection of personal data, financial services legislation and investor protection. The principles set out in this Recommendation should be applied horizontally and equally in those areas but also in any other areas where collective claims for injunctions or damages in respect of violations of the rights granted under Union law would be relevant'.

[35] Commission, 'Communication from the Commission to the European Parliament, the Council, the European Economic and Social Committee and the Committee of the Regions "Towards a European Horizontal Framework for Collective Redress"' COM(2013) 401 final.

[36] European Parliament Resolution of 2 February 2012 on 'Towards a Coherent European Approach to Collective Redress' (2011/2089(INI)) [2013] OJ C239E/32.

[37] See, on citizen suits in the US, JC Dernbach, 'Citizen Suits and Sustainability' (2004) 10 *Widener Law Review* 503.

too liberal to states which are adamant about preserving the *point d'intérêt, point d'action* principle.[38] The legal situation has, nevertheless, evolved over the years as have the pressing challenges posed by pollution and climate change on local economies. The acknowledgement of the environmental damage concept and that of environmental protection as a collective interest have significantly contributed to this evolution. At the very least, it has ended up granting legal standing to NGOs to claim for this type of damage, although only in restricted terms on grounds of avoiding a potentially paralysing avalanche of lawsuits. With the excuse of procedural abuse,[39] law-makers have restricted access to court by imposing procedural requirements that require the plaintiff to be representative.[40] There are, however, powerful reasons for advocating otherwise.

First, the opposite of a proliferation of collective actions is more likely to happen even if legal standing is open to members of the public and not only to NGOs. The above-mentioned study promoted by the European Commission has already made it clear that the number of lawsuits is low in countries such as Portugal – where an actio popularis in environmental matters is allowed,[41] or Sweden – which has also interpreted legal standing broadly.[42] This is due to a lack of incentives to litigate and because it is very difficult to find an altruistic Don Quixote willing to claim. Although NGOs fill the void somewhat, they also have to fight against a lack of funding and resources.[43] Second, moving forward to a common approach at the EU level could avoid unfair competition and forum shopping if attention is paid to the fact that litigants can only bring their claims to countries that favour a broad

[38] See, eg, art 41 of the Spanish Law 26/2007 of 23 October on Environmental Liability.

[39] An example frequently used to illustrate procedural abuse is that of an association set up by lawyers and their employees and wives. However, H Koch, 'Group and Representative Actions in West German Procedure' in E Jayme (ed), *German National Reports in Civil Law Matters for the XIIIth Congress of Comparative Law in Montréal 1990* (CF Müller, 1990) 35, points out: 'if an association is only established for fee collection purposes by an attorney, this might be a problem of professional ethics but should not be controlled by rules of standing'.

[40] This approach can be found in the public consultation 'Towards a Coherent European Approach to Collective Redress' (n 36) para 25. The representativeness concept used in the US class actions has inspired this approach although its meaning has been altered to further restrict access to justice. See L Carballo Piñeiro, *Las acciones colectivas y su eficacia extraterritorial* (Santiago de Compostela University Publishing House, 2009).

[41] Law No 83/95, of 31 August, on the right to take part in administrative proceedings and the right to popular action states: 'Everyone shall be granted the right of popular action, either personally or via associations that purport to defend the interests in question, including the right of an aggrieved party or parties to apply for the corresponding compensation, in such cases and under such terms as the law may determine, in particular to: a) promote the prevention, cessation or judicial prosecution of offences against public health, consumer rights, the quality of life or the preservation of the environment and the cultural heritage; b) safeguard the property of the State, the Autonomous Regions and local authorities'. These provisions are supplemented by Law No 19/2014 of 14 April, on Environment Policy.

[42] See L Ervo, 'The impact of the Directive on Representative Actions for the Protection of the Collective Interests of Consumers on the East-Nordic countries' legislation' (2020) 3 *Revista Italo-Española de Derecho Procesal* 143.

[43] Unlike other class actions, citizen suits do not allow *quota litis* because judgment recovery goes to the State. NGOs find resources because most of the time they settle the case with the defendant, the

approach to this issue, and regulate transversal collective actions such as France,[44] Hungary,[45] the Netherlands, Slovenia[46] and now also Italy.[47]

Accordingly, a broad approach to the issue of legal standing ought to be promoted across the European Union,[48] as suggested by the European Parliament Resolution of 26 October 2017 on the application of Directive 2004/35/EC.[49] The latter concludes by reiterating that this Directive entitles persons adversely affected by environmental damage to ask the competent authorities to take action, but 'also notes that Union law stipulates that European citizens should be guaranteed effective and timely access to justice' as laid down in Article 9(3) of the Aarhus Convention, Article 6 of the Treaty on European Union and the relevant provisions of the European Convention for the Protection of Human Rights. It also notes that Article 191 of the Treaty of Functioning of the European Union enshrines that the costs of the environmental harm should be borne by the polluter, and 'calls therefore on the Commission to come up with a legislative proposal on minimum standards for implementing the Aarhus Convention's access to justice pillar'.[50] More specifically, the European Parliament 'asks the Commission to assess the possibility of introducing collective redress mechanisms for breaches of the Union's environmental law'.[51]

This recommendation is behind the discussion that preceded the update in consumer collective redress. However, although taking into account the Aarhus Convention,[52] the 2020 Directive on representative actions for the protection of the collective interests of consumers fails to address these concerns in a direct manner. In particular, and despite acknowledging that legal divergence as regards these mechanisms across the European Union might lead to the distortion of fair competition between infringing and compliant operators,[53] Directive 2020/1828 only covers cases seeking cessation of, and/or compensation for, infringements of EU law against the collective interests of consumers.

proceeds are employed either to go on litigating, or to implement environmental projects when it is not possible to restore the environment. See MS Greve, 'Private Enforcement of Environmental Law' (1990) 65 *Tulane Law Review* 339, 351.

[44] ss 826-2 to 826-24 of the French Code of Civil Procedure make collective actions available to discuss discrimination, environmental and personal data and healthcare matters.

[45] See ss 580–91 of the 2018 Hungarian Code of Civil Procedure.

[46] Art 2 of the Slovenian Law on Collective Actions.

[47] See Law No 31 of 12 April 2019 (*Gazetta Ufficiale*, 18 April 2019); and A Giussani, 'La nuova azione di classe in Italia' (2020) 3 *Revista Italo-Española de Derecho Procesal* 5.

[48] eg, this approach can be found in the case law of the Court of Justice, such as Case 137/14 *European Commission v Federal Republic of Germany* (Court of Justice, 15 October 2015).

[49] European Parliament Resolution of 26 October 2017 on the application of Directive 2004/35/EC of the European Parliament and of the Council of 21 April 2004 on environmental liability with regard to the prevention and remedying of environmental damage (ELD) (2016/2251(INI)), [2018] OJ C346/184.

[50] ibid, para 48.

[51] ibid, para 46.

[52] See Directive 2020/1828, Recital 75.

[53] See ibid, Recital 2.

In addressing environmental law infringements, two restrictions stand out from Directive 2020/1828. The first concerns the personal scope of the Directive which only focuses on consumers but does not take into consideration concerned individuals in general. By the same token, only qualified entities acting as consumer representatives can bring this type of cases before EU courts.[54] And the second stems from only covering EU law as listed in Annex 1. Hence, it is up to the Member States to decide whether to extend these actions beyond listed EU consumer law or not, thereby not putting an end to the legal divergence across the European Union in these matters. For our purposes, and although some listed EU instruments deal with environmental matters,[55] claims related to them cannot be brought to protect the environment as such, but only if a consumer-trade relationship has taken place in relation to them.[56] Accordingly, it can be concluded that this Directive does not address environmental protection as such, but only as a side-effect of protecting the collective interests of consumers.

III. Environmental Damage and EU Private International Law

A. Is Environmental Damage Covered by EU Private International Law?

The inclusion of environmental damage in the scope of EU private international law[57] has been controversial on account of it being a matter in the hands of a state, and thus of public interest.[58] As said, the approach has changed since Directive 2004/35/EC which specifically refers to the Brussels I Regulation[59] to determine

[54] If they are in compliance with Art 4 of Directive 2020/1828.

[55] Regulation (EC) No 1272/2008 of the European Parliament and of the Council of 16 December 2008 on classification, labelling and packaging of substances and mixtures, amending and repealing Directives 67/548/EEC and 1999/45/EC, and amending Regulation (EC) No 1907/2006, [2008] OJ L353/1, Arts 1–35; Regulation (EC) No 66/2010 of the European Parliament and of the Council of 25 November 2009 on the EU Ecolabel, [2010] OJ L27/1, Arts 9–10.

[56] See further, García Álvarez, 'La aplicación en materia ambiental de las acciones de representación para la protección de los intereses colectivos de los consumidores' (n 10) 67.

[57] This chapter does not address specific cases of transnational environmental liability such as the one caused by oil pollution at sea or nuclear energy. Literature is extensive on these matters, but see, in particular, L García Álvarez, *Competencia judicial internacional, daños ambientales y grupos transnacionales de empresas* (Comares, 2016).

[58] On this debate, see K Fach Gómez, 'Environmental Damage' (2017) *European Encyclopedia of Private International Law* 657, 661; L García Álvarez, *Daños ambientales transnacionales y acceso a la justicia* (Dyckinson, 2016). On the significance of the notion 'environmental damage' to establish the connecting points, see O Boskovic, 'The law applicable to violations of the environment – regulatory strategies' in F Cafaggi and H Muir-Watt (eds), *The Regulatory Function of European Private Law* (Edward Elgar, 2009) 192.

[59] Council Regulation (EC) No 44/2001 of 22 December 2000 on Jurisdiction and the Recognition and Enforcement of Judgments in Civil and Commercial Matters, [2001] OJ L12/1.

international jurisdiction in environmental matters.[60] At the time this Directive was released, an EU regulation on the law applicable to non-contractual obligations had not yet been provided, for which reason there is no specific reference to one. However, the Directive remarks that it does not contain conflict rules applicable to environmental damage, and sets out that

> where a Member State identifies damage within its borders which has not been caused within them … it may seek, in accordance with this Directive, to recover the costs it has incurred in relation to the adoption of preventive or remedial measures.[61]

Such costs would typically be recovered from operators who have caused the damage from abroad, or who have their domicile in a foreign country.

Accordingly, Directive 2004/35/EC includes in its scope cases of transnational environmental damage taking the precaution to make it clear that, while it does not prescribe either international jurisdiction or conflict rules, it is compatible with the Brussels I Regulation,[62] implying that environmental damage cases are 'civil and commercial matters' and submitted to the latter. The fact that some countries also entitle NGOs to recover the costs incurred while preventing or restoring environmental damage reinforces this conclusion insofar as it weakens the exclusive role granted to the state by the Directive, an exclusivity which could give rise to the idea that legal standing is a public law power.[63]

Regulation (EC) No 864/2007 of the European Parliament and of the Council of 11 July 2007 on the law applicable to non-contractual obligations (Rome II)[64] confirms this interpretation by laying down a conflict rule whose scope covers 'environmental damage or damage sustained by persons or property as a result of such damage',[65] and defines environmental damage 'as meaning adverse change in a natural resource, such as water, land or air, impairment of a function performed by that resource for the benefit of another natural resource or the public, or impairment of the variability among living organisms',[66] in line with Directive 2004/35/EC. As a result, it does not matter that states are the only ones entitled to bring actions against operators according to the Directive; such claims are 'civil and commercial matters' within the scope of the Brussels I (Recast) and Rome II Regulations.

One further issue could be raised on account of the close relationship between collective and public interests and whether collective actions fall within the

[60] See Directive 2004/35/EC, Recital 10.

[61] Art 15(3) Directive 2004/35/EC.

[62] The Brussels I Regulation has been replaced by Regulation (EU) No 1215/2012 of the European Parliament and of the Council of 12 December 2012 on jurisdiction and the recognition and enforcement of judgments in civil and commercial matters (recast), [2012] OJ L351/1.

[63] Art 3(3) of Directive 2004/35/CE makes it clear that private parties have no rights under its scope of application, although the phrase, 'without prejudice of national legislation' means that those rights can potentially be granted.

[64] [2007] OJ L199/1.

[65] See ibid, Art 7.

[66] See ibid, Recital 24.

European Regulations' scope of application or not. The Court of Justice has already addressed the matter in a positive way in the *Henkel* case.[67] In this vein, Article 7(2) of Brussels I Recast settles the issue by laying down that the claim may be brought before 'the courts for the place where the harmful event … may occur'. Moreover, the Rome II Regulation sets out a general rule to clarify that it applies 'also to non-contractual obligations that are likely to arise [Article 2(2)], and to damage that is likely to occur [Article 2(3)(a) and (b)]'. Therefore, it does not matter if the claim seeks compensation or an injunction, the applicable law is delivered by Article 7 thereof.[68]

However, the challenge of getting access to a jurisdiction to claim for environmental damage remains in those EU Member States which do not provide for collective actions. As to the others, the defendant's domicile, in particular after the Owusu case,[69] has provided the key head of jurisdiction for this type of litigation with the benefit that *forum* non conveniens cannot be resorted to,[70] thereby opening up jurisdictions to bring parent companies to court as well as their subsidiaries as co-defendants.[71] The question mark is whether the conflict rule provided by Article 7 of the Rome II Regulation is sufficient to protect the environment. The next section focuses on this provision and whether it will be affected by the Proposal for a Directive of the European Parliament and of the Council on Corporate Sustainability Due Diligence presented by the European Commission. It is to note that the European Parliament made its own proposal which did contain a new conflict rule to be included in the Rome II Regulation. However, in order to not overlap with Article 7,[72] it did not pass onto the final proposal or the one provided by the European Commission, which have both opted for classifying

[67] See Case C-167/00 *Verein für Konsumenteninformation* y *Karl Heinz Henkel* [2002] ECR I-08111, para 50.

[68] Regarding the characterisation of injunction relief when it comes to environmental damage originating from immovable property, see TK Graziano, 'The Law Applicable to Cross-Border Damage to the Environment' (2007) 9 *Yearbook of Private International Law* 80.

[69] Case C-281/02 *Owusu v Jackson* [2005] ECR I-01383.

[70] A paramount example of the problems raised by this device in this type of case can be found in the *Texaco/Chevron v Ecuador* saga. See, among many others, DP Fernández Arroyoand and L Carballo Piñeiro, 'Parallel proceedings: Texaco/Chevron lawsuits (re Ecuador)' in H Muir-Watt et al (eds) *Global Private International Law: Adjudication without Frontiers* (Edward Elgar, 2019) 58. The UK withdrawal from the EU has raised issues as to whether this forum will still be open for this type of case once the Brussels I Recast Regulation is no longer the *forum non conveniens*. Hence, European Coalition for Corporate Justice, 'NGOs and legal experts call on the EU to allow UK accession to the Lugano Convention on access to justice grounds' (ECCJ, 2021), available at: corporatejustice.org/news/ngos-and-legal-experts-call-on-eu-to-allow-uk-accession-to-lugano-convention/. These matters were one of the worries of Jonathan Fitchen: J Fitchen, 'The PIL consequences of Brexit' (2017) 3 *Nedelands Internationaal Privaatrecht* 411.

[71] However, see, discussing the need to introduce a *forum necessitatis*, GEDIP, 'Proposal concerning the private international law aspects of the future European instrument on corporate due diligence and corporate accountability' (October 2021); O Boscovic, 'Update on PIL Aspects of Environmental Damage and Human Rights Violations in Supply Chains' (EAPIL, 2021), available at: eapil.org/2021/12/21/update-on-pil-aspects-of-environmental-damage-and-human-rights-violations-in-supply-chains/.

[72] According to European Parliament, Legal Affairs Committee, *Draft report with recommendations to the Commission on corporate due diligence and corporate accountability* (2020/2129(INL)) 35, this

their rules if finally approved as overriding mandatory provisions. Remarkably, no further private international law issues have been discussed.

B. The Impact of Regulating Sustainable Corporate Governance on the Conflict Rule on Environmental Damage

Articles 14, 7 and 4(1) of the Rome II Regulation establish the conflict rule on environmental damage. First, party autonomy is allowed subject to restrictions in order to protect the victim.[73] Second, and in default of agreement, environmental damage is submitted to the law of the place where damage occurs unless the victim chooses the law of the place where the event originated. Hence, environmental protection is reached by empowering the victim to choose the most favourable law not just between the *lex loci damni* and the *lex delicti commissi*,[74] but also by agreeing on an even more protective law than the latter.

In case Article 14 does not apply or no law is chosen, applying the *lex loci damni* as the law governing environmental damage aims at putting all victims and polluters on an equal footing. While victims are compensated according to the law where their interests have been damaged, polluters are also dealt with equally, no matter where they were acting from. As a rule, the indirect consequences of the defendant's actions cannot be taken into account for reasons of predictability. However, a wide interpretation is given to this principle when it comes to environmental matters and the actionable consequences of the actions leading to damage do not depend on them being foreseeable by the defendant. This is essential in environmental protection because, as the Chernobyl accident has shown, airborne particles and emissions can have very far-reaching damaging effects on the environment.[75] Nevertheless, the application of the *lex loci damni* is not always the most environmentally friendly, as the string of litigation against Shell illustrates. Although Dutch courts exercised jurisdiction against both the Dutch parent company and the Nigerian subsidiary, they applied Nigerian law in accordance with the conflict rule herein examined. In the final judgment, the claim against the Nigerian company was partially upheld, but the claim against Royal Dutch Shell

proposed conflict rule provides victims with a choice between the legislation of the country in which the damage occurred (*lex loci damni*), that of the country in which the event that gave rise to damage took place (*lex loci delicti commissi*) and that of the place where the defendant company is domiciled or, if it has no domicile in an EU country, that of the Member State where it operates. See, pointing out the legal uncertainty that such rule could trigger if approved, G Rühl, 'Human Rights in Global Supply Chains: Do We Need to Amend the Rome II Regulation?' (EAPIL, 2021), available at: eapil.org/2020/10/09/human-rights-in-global-supply-chains-do-we-need-to-amend-the-rome-ii-regulation.

[73] Art 14 Rome II.

[74] See Graziano (n 68) 74, who also quotes German jurisprudence where this option has already been applied and, because of its effectiveness, has been followed by the European legislator.

[75] See Graziano (n 68) 73; SC Symeonides, 'Tort Conflicts and Rome II: A View from Across' in HP Mansel et al (eds), *Festschrift für Erik Jayme*, vol 1 (Sellier, 2004) 951.

was dismissed on grounds of it not being accountable for its subsidiary's actions according to Nigerian law.[76]

The location of the place where the event giving rise to the damage occurred has been subjected to interpretation when the defendant is a corporate company because it could be located in two different countries: where the decision was taken and where it was implemented and gave rise to environmental damage. There is a full array of arguments to let the plaintiff choose between those laws as well,[77] but one stands out – the environmental protection. In particular, the place from where the parent company makes decisions, transfers know-how and provides financial and human resources to the country which suffers environmental damage, should be considered the location where the harmful event occurred as well.[78] This has been accepted by some courts and in some cases.[79] However, it cannot be said that this interpretation has been widely accepted.[80]

The problem with not upholding this line of reasoning is that it is not in line any more with current developments in corporate social and environmental responsibility, especially after the OECD Guidelines for Multinational Enterprises and the UN Guiding Principles on Business and Human Rights which seek to foster a corporate culture based on human rights compliance, including during their interaction, direct or indirect, with other businesses across the supply chain, by putting in place all the necessary mechanisms to avoid infringement.[81] Since corporate environmental responsibility is an answer to the globalisation processes and their regulatory gaps, it cannot be ignored while determining the applicable law

[76] See the three judgments pronounced by the Hague District Court (Rechtbank's-Gravenhage) 30 January 2013, ECLI:NL:RBDHA:2013:BY9845; ECLI:NL:RBDHA:2013:BY9850 (dismissing the claims) and ECLI:NL:RBDHA:2013:BY9854 (granting compensation to be paid by the Nigerian subsidiary). On these judgments, see L Enneking, 'The Future of Foreign Direct Liability? Exploring the International Relevance of the Dutch Shell Nigeria Case' (2014) 10 *Utrecht Law Review* 1, 44.

[77] See further, G Betlem and C Bernasconi, 'European Private International Law, the Environment and Obstacles for Public Authorities' (2006) 122 *Law Quarterly Review* 128.

[78] See P Muchlinski, 'The Bhopal Case: Controlling ultrahazardous industrial activities undertaken by foreign investors' (1987) 50 *Modern Law Review* 545; AC Seward III, 'After Bhopal: Implications for parent company liability' (1987) 21 *International Lawyer* 695; J Westbrook, 'Theories of parent company liability and the prospects for an international settlement' (1985) 20 *Texas International Law Journal* 321.

[79] A leading case is *Dow Chemical Co v Castro Alfaro*, 786 S W 2d 674, 679 (Tex 1990). For further analysis of environmental liability and *forum non conveniens*, see FK Juenger, 'Environmental Damage' in C McLachlan and P Nygh (eds), *Transnational Tort Litigation: Jurisdictional Principles* (Clarendon Press, 1996).

[80] See *Okpabi* (n 5) where the High Court in London examined whether Royal Dutch Shell could be held responsible for the pollution in Ogoniland on grounds of the qualified relationship between the parent company and the Nigerian subsidiary, and whether the parent company could have influenced the decisions of the Nigerian company. This approach was taken at the admission of jurisdiction stage in order to ensure whether the plaintiffs were bringing truly related actions or not. As this was not sufficiently established, the High Court dismissed the claim against the parent company, and thus, that against the Nigerian company as it could not appreciate such a connection.

[81] UN Human Rights Office, 'Guiding Principles on Business and Human Rights' (UN, 2011), available at: www.ohchr.org/sites/default/files/documents/publications/guidingprinciplesbusinesshr_en.pdf, in particular, principles 10, 13, 19, 23 and 26.

to injunctions and compensation for environmental damage,[82] ie, due diligence has to inform the determination of the harmful event's place. More specifically, the due diligence concept may significantly broaden the civil liability of companies in respect of environmental damage by constructing a corporate obligation to prevent and properly address environmentally adverse impacts 'with respect to their own operations, the operations of their subsidiaries, and the value chain operations carried out by entities with whom the company has an established business relationship'.[83]

If finally approved, the European Commission's Proposal on Sustainable Corporate Governance would thus inform the application of Article 7 of the Rome II Regulation and the meaning of the place of the event giving rise to damage, at least when it comes to environmental damage.[84] However, the ongoing legislative process is very shy on private international law provisions with only a reference to the overriding mandatory character of the rules therein envisaged. In line with the underlying goals, the Proposal should be assertive as regards the *locus delicti* being also the place where decisions leading to environmental adverse impacts have been taken.[85] In jurisdictions where environmental litigation is feasible, this type of approach has already been followed as the Swedish *Arika v Boliden* case[86] and the Dutch *Milieudefense v Shell* case,[87] both illustrate. Moreover, the strong recommendation of not using Article 17 of the Rome II Regulation on rules of conduct and safety of the place of injury to hamper the application of the law of the event giving rise to damage has already been put forward,[88] and should be included in the final instrument. This ongoing legislative work is an opportunity that cannot be missed to ensure transnational corporate accountability.

[82] Principle 25 of the UN Guiding Principles, ibid, sets out that efficient and adequate non-judicial remedies should be established. Such an approach could avoid costly litigation as illustrated by the settlement reached by Shell in the *Bodo Community* case (n 5).

[83] See Art 1 of European Commission Proposal for a Directive on Sustainable Corporate Governance, COM/2022/71 final.

[84] Although closely related, human rights infringements across the value chain is a concept different from environmental damage and would thus be subject to the general rules of the Rome II Regulation, in particular Art 4 and the *lex loci damni* which might not be best placed to judge the defendant's conduct. For this reason, and while this has been regretted, the proposal for a specific conflict rule in the Rome II Regulation as proposed by the European Parliament Draft Report, a specific approach is still missing, and thus broadening the scope of Art 7 to cover these cases has been put on the table. See GEDIP (n 71).

[85] eg, O Boskovic, 'La loi applicable aux actions pour violations des droits de l'homme en matière commerciale' (11 February 2021) *Recueil Dalloz* 252, suggests using a Recital in the Rome II Regulation to confirm this interpretation.

[86] See *Arica Victims KB v Boliden Mineral AB* (2019) 27 March, decided by the Court of Appeals of Upper Norrland, which indicates as regards to the *lex loci delicti commissi* that: 'This center may be established with regard to where the qualitatively important elements have their focus rather than according to quantitative criteria'.

[87] Above (n 2).

[88] See GEDIP (n 71). The European Parliament Committee of Legal Affairs has issued a Report on this proposal on 8 May 2023 [A9-0184/2023] which does not address any of these matters.

IV. Final Remarks

Against the backdrop of increasing environmental adverse impacts as a result of human-induced climate change,[89] the European Union has levelled up its efforts to address them with different measures that, for example, include a Proposal for a Directive on Sustainable Corporate Governance. The latter might have a positive impact on the interpretation of the current conflict rules on environmental damage by expanding private operators' civil liability. However, these potential advancements have not been accompanied by a clear stance on access to justice by members of the public in these matters. While some high-profile cases have not only been celebrated as critical to achieving the UN SDGs, but also proven the essential role that private enforcement is meant to play in ensuring environmental protection, the European Union is far away from ensuring that private operators can be brought to court by individuals and NGOs across the European area of justice.

Courts have an important say in environmental matters and have significantly contributed to evolving traditional private international law rules to better protect global interests and values such as the environment and human rights.[90] In this vein, some authors have reminded us of the role that international courts may play in environmental protection,[91] as the European Court of Human Rights case law illustrates.[92] Either on the side of international courts or domestic courts, judicial and arbitral[93] activism remains critical in addressing the complex conflicts of interests arising out of environmental matters. However, while imagination has helped to address problems that go well beyond the narrow limits of national legislation,[94] it has important limitations which certainly require the EU law-maker to catch up with the revolution running only in the courts of some Member States while others cannot but report that it is all quiet on the Western Front.[95]

[89] See the Intergovernmental Panel on Climate Change (IPCC), *Climate Change 2022. Impacts, Adaptation and Vulnerability* (IPCC, 2022), available at: www.ipcc.ch/report/ar6/wg2/.

[90] See, on these movements from the private international law angle, L Carballo Piñeiro and X Kramer, 'The Role of Private International Law in Contemporary Society: Global Governance as a Challenge' (2014) 7 *Erasmus Law Review* 109.

[91] The establishment of an ad hoc international court on environmental matters has been proposed. See J Spier, 'The Urgent Need of Judicial Cooperation to Map Solutions to Come to Grips with the Major Global Challenges' in P Mankowski and W Wurmnest, *Festchrift für Ulrich Magnus zum 70. Geburtstag* (Sellier, 2014), citing Ulrich Magnus. The author rejects an ad hoc tribunal, but supports judicial activism. Also, a special section had already been established within the International Court of Justice, but ended up closing because the states did not bring any cases in.

[92] As in *Öneryildiz v Turkey* (2004) 39 EHRR 12 and in particular *Tatar v Romania*, Application no 67021/01 (ECtHR, 27 January 2009) specifically mentioning the right to a healthy and protected environment in connection with Art 8 of the European Convention for the Protection of Human Rights and Fundamental Freedoms.

[93] See, on these reasons, P Sands, 'Litigating environmental disputes: courts, tribunals and progressive development of international law' (2007) 37 *Environmental Policy and Law* 66.

[94] B de Sousa Santos, 'Law: A Map of Misreading. Toward a Postmodern Conception of Law' (1987) 14 *Journal of Law and Society* 279, 281, pointing out that law is not only positivism but 'imagination, representation and description of reality'.

[95] EM Remarque, *All Quiet on the Western Front* (trans AW Wheen) (first published 1929; Penguin 1987).

9

International Trade Agreements and Private International Law: Narrowing Mutual Links

CARMEN OTERO GARCÍA-CASTRILLÓN*

I. Introduction

As a result of the 'fourth industrial revolution', the digital economic and social age that we live in gives rise to the 'globalisation' era,[1] which finds its deepest roots in the economic sphere. Leaving aside the debates about economic liberalisation, 'post-capitalism', 'neo-feudalism and 'techno-feudalism' theories,[2] and despite the nationalism and autarchy waves,[3] the worldwide connections and the spread of supply and logistic chains is an undeniable fact. Hence, trade, finance and investment are vital components of international economic, political and security orders. A myriad of complex issues are involved in these economic affairs. In this regard, it is sufficient to note that the United Nations 2030 quest for a general sustainable development sets a number of 'Sustainable Development Goals' (SDGs)[4] for

* Spanish Research Project, 'El Derecho del Comercio internacional en la era de la economía digital y las guerras comerciales' (PID2020-113968RB-I00).

[1] This phenomenon implies the idea of approximation, or even integration, and can be perceived in different ways depending on the academic field. As to PrIL, see H Muir Watt, 'Globalization and Private International Law' in *Encyclopedia of Private International Law*, vol II (Edward Elgar, 2017).

[2] Neo-feudalist theories rebirth policies of governance, economy and public life reminiscent of those pertaining to feudal societies: unequal rights and legal protections for common people and for powerful elitist groups that dominate societies and generate relations of lordship and serfdom between the rich and the poor. As in the medieval feudal model, assets are owned by the few techno-feudal lords. Ellen Brown, 'How America Went From Mom-and-Pop Capitalism to Techno-Feudalism' (18 May 2021), available at: scheerpost.com/2021/05/18/how-america-went-from-mom-and-pop-capitalism-to-techno-feudalism/.

[3] R Eatwell and M Goodwin, *National Populism: The Revolt Against Liberal Democracy* (Penguin, 2018).

[4] United Nations, 'Sustainable Development Goals', available at: www.undp.org/sustainable-development-goals?utm_source=EN&utm_medium=GSR&utm_content=US_UNDP_PaidSearch_Brand_English&utm_campaign=CENTRAL&c_src=CENTRAL&c_src2=GSR&gclid=CjwKCAiAqIKNBhAIEiwAu_ZLDq94bMiKPwDWaWOi54-StF3KqhewonbmtwX77G-wuwhZhcHSv5u_JRoCdC8QAvD_BwE. Along its lines, the World Economic Forum adopted the Great Reseat initiative in 2020, available at: www.weforum.org/great-reset.

which transnational economic transactions play an essential role. In particular, beyond ensuring that the international system becomes more inclusive and enables an increasing number of women to play an active role (SDG 5: Gender Equality); economic transactions are vital for economic growth (SDG 8); the reduction of inequalities between and within countries (SDG 10); and for peace and justice (SDG 16); all of these goals requiring appropriate public–private partnerships (SDG 17).

Together with states, private parties and companies are the essential transnational actors. As Basedow puts it:

> [I]t is in the first instance a matter for the private actors to implement their intentions and to find or conceive of the framework of legal rules facilitating that implementation … But this does not make the role of States superfluous. They supplement and correct private initiative in numerous contexts.[5]

In other words, though the inherent ecumenical nature of human beings explains the expansion of our activities beyond any legal community at any time in history,[6] private parties would not have reached that far without an appropriate liberalising regulatory regime. Merchants have always looked for ways to overcome the hardships created by frontiers to the point that, in Pillet's words, 'le commerce international est un pur fait, mais un fait qui a donné naissance au droit international tout entier' ['International trade is a mere fact, but a fact that has given birth to international law as a whole'].[7]

Since the globalisation phenomenon gained a starring role in the second half of last century, two of its dimensions can be highlighted. On the one hand, states' economies are intricately linked; hence, under this interdependence it is not possible to talk about 'national economies' without taking into consideration the international situation (macro). On the other hand, economic transactions take place in a global – transnational – economic space; in other words, within an 'international commercial society' (micro). These approaches can be confirmed by looking at the recent goods shortages after Brexit[8] and those following the Covid-19 pandemic[9] leading, among others, to hardship and *force majeure* cases.

[5] J Basedow, *The Law of Open Societies: Private Ordering and Public Regulation in the Conflict of Laws* (Brill, 2015) 348. As for public regulation, he focuses on commercial embargos and countermeasures.

[6] K Siehr, 'Private International Law, History of' in *Encyclopedia of Private International Law*, vol II (Edward Elgar, 2017).

[7] A Pillet, 'Sur les droits fondamentaux des États, dans l'ordre des raports internationaux et sur la solution des conflits qu'ils font naitre', *Revue General de Droit International Privé*, vol. V, 1898, 72.

[8] Brexit and tax changes contributed to a lack of heavy goods qualified drivers in the UK, also leading to petrol shortages; Grace Pocock, 'Heavy goods vehicle driver shortage' (House of Lords, 20 October 2021), available at: lordslibrary.parliament.uk/heavy-goods-vehicle-driver-shortage/ accessed November 2021. This is also the case in other professions in need of foreign workers, like farmers, food manufacturers and social care.

[9] The global supply chains have been seriously affected both by global shipping issues as well as shortages of raw materials and semiconductors. See Allianz Trade, 'Global Trade Report-Battling off Supply Chains Disruption' (Allianz Trade, 9 December 2021), available at: www.eulerhermes.com/en_global/news-insights/economic-insights/Global-Trade-Report-Battling-out-of-supply-chain-disruptions.html.

The double dimension marries well with the classic academic public and private international law divide (PIL–PrIL) and has traditionally left international trade regulation out of the scenario of the latter despite it constituting the basic framework for trans-border transactions.

This piece pays tribute to Professor Jonathan Fitchen by elaborating on a reasoning that aims to leave behind strict understandings of PrIL and to open up approaches closer to real practice in international trade agreements. Beyond globalisation, nowadays the digital economy keeps on challenging legal academics and practitioners, particularly PrIL ones,[10] to adapt and/or reformulate the understanding of trans-border economic operations. This attempt conforms to the holistic and interdisciplinary tendencies in academia[11] but, nonetheless, does not lose perspective of what is needed in classrooms. To this end, this contribution endeavours to present how PrIL and international trade agreements interrelate, and how PrIL theory has overshadowed or limited its practical needed role in international trade law.

II. The Private–Public International Law Divide and International Trade Agreements in Perspective: From Theory to Practice

The dividing line between PIL and PrIL as academic autonomous disciplines has been widely discussed. In Struyken's words, this subject has 'fascinated and divided the spirits'.[12] Far from being outdated, the topic is still an issue in practice and theory.[13] In particular (though not exclusively), in international economic transactions for which, relying on PIL and/or PrIL, there are also academic 'sub-disciplines' under titles such as international economic law, international trade and investment law, global administrative law and international business or

[10] Nevertheless, as H Muir-Watt, above (n 1), puts it, this has only superficially affected PrIL theory and practice since its basis and reasoning models remain unaltered.

[11] eg, RB Zoellick, 'Making International Relations Research on Trade More Relevant to Policy Officials' in D Maliniak, S Peterson, R Powers and MJ Tierney (eds), *Bridging the Theory–Practice Divide in International Relations* (Georgetown University Press, 2020) 125, suggest further studying (1) the effects of private, transnational links fostered by trade, relationships between open markets, open societies and common values; (2) trade facilitation, institutional development and links to multinational enterprises and supply chains; (3) connection between international economic regimes with regimes to address other topics such as human rights and the environment; and (4) the role of trade regimes in developing the rule of law and win–win exchange.

[12] AVM Struycken, 'La contribution de l'Académie au développement de la science et de la pratique du Droit International Privé' (1998) 271 *Hague Collected Courses* 33.

[13] Among others, R Michaels, 'Public and Private International Law: German Views on Global Issues' (2008) 4 *Journal of Private International Law* 121; A Mills, 'Public and Private International Law' in *Encyclopedia of Private International Law*, vol II (Edward Elgar, 2017); V Ruiz-Abou-Nigm, K McCall-Smith and D French, *Linkages and Boundaries in Private and Public International Law* (Hart Publishing, 2018).

commercial law.[14] Simplifying the debate and departing from the social function of the law, it is possible to affirm that the societal object that each of these legal disciplines serve, alongside providing them with their academic scientific autonomy, is what helps to draw their respective theoretical boundaries.

The approximation to PrIL's object is necessarily descriptive: departing from a juridically fragmented world, it entails the presence of a foreign element in the legal situations in which private subjects, and public law ones when not acting on the basis of their *imperium* (reserved for PIL), are involved.[15] Historically, the foreign element is a clear perpetual constituent[16] which, in Siehr's words, makes 'modern' PrIL as 'any addressing of problems involving different sets of laws for different types of person'.[17] In this way, Siehr is already pointing to the function of PrIL that, as Lalive noted, has always been the same.[18] More precisely, PrIL's function consists in determining the legal regime that will be applied, including pointing out the norms as much as their application and adaptation to the particular case. Equally, the exercise of this function is always faced in accordance with a series of evolving values[19] (justice, human rights) and social aspirations (legal predictability and certainty) that take into consideration the various interests at stake (those of private subjects and states' policy objectives).[20] To this end, whilst jurisdiction,[21] relying on sovereignty, is the point of departure, territoriality,[22] together with comity,[23] reasonableness[24] is an essential legal principle and cooperation is

[14] A Mills, 'Connecting Public and Private International Law' in V Ruiz-Abou-Nigm, K McCall-Smith and D French, *Linkages and Boundaries in Private and Public International Law* (Hart Publishing, 2018) 29, perceives them as 'regimes' resulting of the development of PIL. In this realm, it is interesting to note the project on 'Global Administrative Law' headed by B Kingsbury and RB Steward, available at: www.iilj.org/gal/project/.

[15] Naturally, the evolution of the academic discipline and of the understanding of the foreign element concept can be historically analysed. See Siehr (n 6).

[16] ibid.

[17] ibid, 1390.

[18] P Lalive, 'Nouveaux regards sur le droit international privé, aujourd'hui et demain' (1994) 1–2 *Revue suisse de droit international et de droit européen* 3, 26: '(S)i le contenú du droit international privé, ses règles et ses méthodes évoluent, la finalité ne change pas, puisque,à toutes les époques, ils s'agi du mémme problème' ['Though the content, norms and methods in PrIL evolve, its goals do not change, and that is because, at all times, it faces the same problem'].

[19] LM Friedmann, 'Is there a Modern Legal Culture?' (1994) 7(2) *Ratio Juris* 117, 118–19, uses the expression 'legal culture': people's ideas, values, attitudes and opinions on the law and the legal system.

[20] J Maury, 'Rêgles générales des conflits de lois' (1936-III) 57 *Hague Collected Courses* 415.

[21] R Michaels, 'Jurisdiction: Foundations' in *Encyclopedia of Private International Law*, vol II (Edward Elgar, 2017).

[22] For a detailed analysis on the territoriality concept, see F Rigaux, *Derecho Internacional Privado. Parte General* (Civitas, 1986) 64–71. T Kono, 'Territoriality' in *Encyclopedia of Private International Law*, vol II (Edward Elgar, 2017).

[23] TW Dornis, 'Comity' in *Encyclopedia of Private International Law*, vol II (Edward Elgar, 2017).

[24] A Lowenfeld, *International Litigation and the Quest for Reasonableness: Essays in Private International Law* (Clarendon Press, 1996) 229–31. Along this line, FA Mann, 'The doctrine of international jurisdiction revisited after twenty years' (1984-III) 186 *Hague Collected Courses* 28–29, states that: 'principle of reasonableness … appears unobjectionable, so long as it is understood that mere political, economic, commercial or social interests are to be disregarded when it comes to weighting which every test of reasonableness implies … for arbitrariness is substantially the same as unreasonableness'.

a desirable working tool. In addition, since legal fragmentation is the cause of PrIL situations, normative harmonisation, or even, unification,[25] be it substantive, procedural or both, clearly eases the way towards resolving their difficulties.

Following the nineteenth-century bilateral Friendship, Commerce and Navigation treaties, multilateral and regional international trade agreements gained relevance in the second half of the twentieth century, leading to the creation of the World Trade Organization (WTO) and a large number of regional integration processes entailing both customs unions and free trade areas (FTAs).[26] In principle, these treaties essentially dealt with the conditions for the import and export of goods between the Contracting States. However, as the Friendship, Commerce and Navigation treaties did, they turned to encompass other subject matters such as services, intellectual property, investments, etc. Beyond the functioning of the international organisations (eg, the WTO, European Union) and the international nature of treaties as a legal source, these issues were automatically classified as part of PIL content. This was because the object of this legal discipline essentially comprises the ordering of relationships between states and the regulatory function of these instruments dealt with the entry/exit commercial operations – governed by public-administrative norms – from the parties' territories. PrIL seemed to have no role in this area. However, it is argued this can be considered an overly radical approach resulting from the PIL–PrIL distancing after the nineteenth-century consolidation of PrIL autonomy.[27]

Relying on the different jurisdictional dimensions (jurisdiction to prescribe, to adjudicate – including judicial and administrative authorities – and to enforce),[28]

[25] Normative harmonisation implies establishing common minimum standards that can be further implemented in different ways. Unification entails common and identical norms for a number of different legal communities (states). Whilst harmonisation is characterised as 'law that has not been created with the intention of getting rid of the existing differences, but rather with the goal of merely reducing those differences', Uniform law is defined as 'a set of identically worded legal rules that are binding on a general level in more than one jurisdiction where they are also supposed to be interpreted and applied in the same manner'. F Ferrari, 'Uniform Substantive Law and Private International Law' in *Encyclopedia of Private International Law*, vol II (Edward Elgar, 2017).

[26] See General Agreement on Tariffs and Trade (Geneva, 30 October 1947) 55 UNTS 187 (GATT), Art XIV and General Agreement on Trade in Services (Marrakesh, Morocco, 15 April 1994) 1869 UNTS 183 (GATS), Art V.

[27] F Rigaux, 'Le pluralisme en Droit International Privé' in M Pérez González (ed), *Hacia un nuevo orden internacional y europeo. Libro homenaje al profesor M Díaz de Velasco* (Civitas, 1993) 1424. In particular, he points to the following excesses of positivism, that overly narrowed the discipline coverage by ignoring the considerable contribution of public law to the regulation of private relationships.

[28] FA Mann, 'The Doctrine of International Jurisdiction Revisited After Twenty Years' (1984) 186 *Hague Collected Courses* 67, states that 'the international jurisdiction to adjudicate is not a separate type of jurisdiction, but merely an emanation of the international jurisdiction to legislate … a state's right of regulation is exercised by legislative jurisdiction which includes adjudication'. On the distinction, KM Meesen, 'Drafting Rules on Extraterritorial Jurisdiction' in KM Meesen (ed), *Extraterritorial Jurisdiction in Theory and Practice* (Kluwer, 1996) 226, states 'whether it has more than a descriptive value and actually contributes to settling and defining the law from an international perspective, I do not know. At least, there is no reason for us to single out just the one or other aspect'. Nevertheless, he adds 'no one really cares before the law is implemented at which point there is still occasion to call for restraint. Only enforcement and adjudication bring matters to ahead'.

PrIL establishes the applicable legal regime on the basis of the territoriality principle. Looking at regulatory jurisdiction, Ehrenzweig referred to the different normative techniques stating that direct norms are analysed to establish their scope of application and indirect norms are studied to determine the possibilities for the application of foreign laws.[29] As Ago, put it, direct norms have a 'virtually universal' character.[30] It is basically this way, always with due respect to states' international obligations,[31] that the territorial/extraterritorial[32] application of domestic legal rules is unilaterally decided. Although it is generally accepted that public laws are not to be applied extraterritorially (coincidence *forum-ius*),[33] this is no longer obviously straightforward. Neither is it the case that PrIL situations cannot be addressed by administrative authorities.

Competition law shows a clear case of extraterritorial application both in public/administrative proceedings – where the public interest defence has a dominant role – and in antitrust damages claims before national courts.[34] Similarly, in other transnational proceedings where public interests or public law norms are prominent, such as environmental, workers or personal data protection, norms can be applied extraterritorially.[35] Moreover, in adopting such decisions, it is not strange that foreign norms are somehow taken into consideration, both in their public-administrative instance and, eventually, in the subsequent judicial claim before the courts. This is particularly the case when an FTA applies. Despite territoriality (on the basis of sovereignty) not being questioned in FTAs, even when regulatory[36] or adjudicatory[37] criteria are expressly included, the calls for cooperation[38] open up this possibility. Along this line, it

[29] AA Ehrenzweig, 'Specific Principles of Private International Law' (1964-II) 124 *Hague Collected Courses* 180.

[30] R Ago, 'Regles générales des conflits de lois' (1936-IV) 57 *Hague Collected Courses* 26.

[31] Derived, mostly, from international treaties and human rights commitments (in particular as to the jurisdiction to adjudicate). The last ones apply to individuals and do not generally extend to legal persons.

[32] See above (n 22).

[33] JD González Campos, 'Les liens entre la compétence judiciaire et la competence legislative en droit international privé' (1977-III) 156 *Hague Collected Courses* 331. The existence of an imperative/policy rule has an immediate positive impact on international jurisdiction to adjudicate.

[34] M Danov and C Otero García-Castrillón, 'Competition Law Enforcement: Private International Law and Access to Effective Legal Remedies in Cross-Border Cases' in P Beaumont and J Holliday (eds), *A Guide to Global Private International Law* (Hart Publishing, 2022).

[35] See references to data protection in section III and section IV.

[36] eg, Arts 135–36 and 128–29 of the Trade and Cooperation Agreement between the EU and the European Economic Community for Atomic Energy, on the one side, and the United Kingdom of Great Britain and Northern Ireland, on the other (EU–UK TCA), [2021] OJ L149/10, expressly refers to the law of the provision of services.

[37] eg, Art 360 EU–UK TCA; and Art 29.1 of its Protocol on Administrative Cooperation and Combating Fraud in the field of Value Added Tax and on Mutual Assistance for the recovery of claims related to taxes and duties.

[38] eg, EU–UK TCA, along with the general transparency and good regulatory practices (Arts 350–51), incorporates it in areas such as Technical Barriers to Trade (TBT) (Arts 96–97) and Sanitary and Phitosanitary (SPS) (Arts 79–80, 84–85), and Energy (Arts 317–18; technical cooperation; Arts 319–24, renewables and efficiency and, in a separate agreement, nuclear energy).

should not be outweighed that, in different areas, trade liberalisation is subject to decisions on the equivalence of normative and supervisory standards of the trade partner[39] or even to the maintenance of a 'level playing field'.[40]

A state's unilateral decisions on the extraterritorial application of its own norms on private parties' operations respond to economic and/or political interests. As it happened in an eminent case in the competition field that reached the WTO,[41] these situations can eventually entail a 'manipulation' of the extraterritorial application of national rules, implying what Bahgwati called 'aggressive unilateralism'.[42] Private parties are then used as a means to force ('convince' or 'sanction') other states' behaviour in a way that resembles economic coercion measures.[43] It is well established that economic coercion measures use private parties' situations and interests with political and economic ends. In such cases, although unilateralism has been criticised for reflecting a chauvinist behaviour provoking conflicts between states, it has also been defended as a useful means to reach multilateral effects through forcing other countries to change their actions.[44] From this perspective, together with countermeasures (ie, blocking statutes adopted to safeguard private parties' situations before economic coercion measures) they are traditionally left to PIL despite their consequences possibly being of great significance in private transactions.[45]

[39] eg, as to financial services (Arts 182–89) EU–UK TCA; as to sanitary and phytosanitary measures (Art 6.14) EU–Japan Economic Partnership Agreement (EU–Japan Economic Partnership), available at: trade.ec.europa.eu/doclib/docs/2018/august/tradoc_157228.pdf.

[40] The EU–UK TCA is built on the respect for individuals' fundamental rights and the compromise with the protection of equivalent standards in the labour and social (Art 386) as much as in the environmental (Art 390) fields.

[41] *Japan – Measures Affecting Consumer Photographic Film and Paper*, Panel Report (adopted 31 March 1998) WT/DS44/R, known as the *Kodak* case.

[42] J Bhaghwati, 'Aggressive Unilateralism. An Overview' in J Bhawghati and HT Patrick (eds), *Aggressive Unilateralism: America's 301 Trade Policy and the World Trading System* (Harvester Wheatsheaft 1991); AD Smith, 'Bringing Down Private Trade Barriers; An Assessment of US Unilateral Options: Section 301 of the 1974 Trade Act and Extraterritorial Application of US Antitrust Law' (1994–95) 16 *Michigan Journal of International Law* 241, 245. 'When antitrust statutes are deployed to promote export opportunities, the line between aggressive trade policy and the goal of preserving a healthy, competitive environment for the sake of US firms and consumers begins to blur'.

[43] As Basedow, *The Law of Open Societies* (n 5) 509 puts it, 'by orders directed to individuals and companies they (States) use these private actors as hostages or levers to put pressure in other States'.

[44] C Dordi, 'From West to East: Trade, IP and Investment after the Crisis' in *Global Digital Encounters*, 28 May 2020, 14–15 refers to the US measures adopted against China's illegal trans-shipments of goods with US destinations through Vietnam and other countries aiming to avoid US tariffs. They are said to explain China's leaving behind that practice and holding customs negotiations with those countries, available at: thinkfide.com/global-digital-encounters/gde-2-from-west-to-east-trade-ip-and-investment-after-the-crisis/.

[45] They do not necessarily entail a PIL breach and Basedow, 'Blocking Statutes' in *Encyclopedia of Private International Law*, vol II (Edward Elgar, 2017), recognised that this issue has not been sufficiently dealt with by PrIL. As to the COVID-19 exports bans, see B Yüksel Ripley and Ü Halatçı Ulusoy, 'COVID-19 Related Export Bans and Restrictions Under WTO Law and the Determination of their Legal Effects on International Sale of Goods Contracts Between Parties Located in WTO Member States: Interplay Between Public and Private International Law' in P Sooksripaisarnkit and D Prasad (eds), *Blurry Boundaries of Public and Private International Law*.

The PrIL academy has shown a natural preference for the study of conflict of laws and domestic courts' international competence, leaving behind somewhat the study of the scope and interactions of direct substantive regulations, particularly those more closely connected with public law, notwithstanding their impact in international transactions. In recent times, however, it is recognised that the new areas and the reinforcement of their public-unilateral (and extraterritorial) regulations (ie, data protection, environment, labour) are calling strongly for PrIL attention. Working on 'constructions which try to draw private and public international law closer together is (are) now more justified than ever'.[46]

III. WTO and Free Trade Agreements

The WTO and FTAs have been progressively incorporating new subject matters ranging from manufacturing and provision of services safety to human rights, passing through environmental and data protection and gender equality, all closely related to the SDGs. For each of them, substantive minimum standards are incorporated. It seems evident that, whilst sitting on a WTO basis, FTAs are often more comprehensive than WTO Agreements. They cover cutting-edge topics that WTO members cannot all address at the same time or stage of development. However, the expansive repercussions of FTAs – the so-called 'collective unilateralism'[47] or 'the Brussels effect'[48] – cannot be disregarded as it seems to have a stronger impact than the feared 'race to the bottom'.[49] Furthermore, admitting different (multilateral) speeds, liberalisers are often willing to work among themselves to push for freer trade bilaterally, regionally and globally.[50] Most trade negotiations are joint problem-solving exercises (reconciling differences, making trade-offs, gaming arguments, assembling coalitions and matching interests). Participants bring different political and negotiating cultures to the table and manage 'offensive' and 'defensive' interests so that they can both achieve a good result and sell it back home.[51]

[46] DP Fernández Arroyo, 'Foreword' in *Linkages and Boundaries in Private and Public International Law* (Hart Publishing, 2018).

[47] P-M Dupuy, 'The Place and Role of Unilateralism in Contemporary International Law' (2000) 11 *European Journal of International law* 19, 20.

[48] A Bradford, 'The Brussels Effect' (2012) 107 *Northwestern University Law Review* 1. Pointing to the use of power to encourage positive changes, see B Cooreman and G van Calster, 'Trade and Sustainable Development Post-Lisbon' in M Hahn and G Van der Loo (eds), *Law and Practice of the Common Commercial Policy* (Brill 2020).

[49] AA Berle and GC Means, *The Modern Corporation and Private Property* (Macmillan, 1932), pointing to the overall standards reduction as a result of regulatory competition.

[50] Along this line, Zoellick (n 11) 126–27, sees negotiations in the WTO based on coalitions of the willing that share extensive and exclusive rights and responsibilities (their precedents could be Tokyo Round codes).

[51] In Zoellick's words (n 11) 124, 'Good negotiators seek to understand their counterparts' sensitivities and help to solve their problems in a win–win fashion. Negotiators help others provide explanations to use domestically. Even trade negotiators who recognize the economic benefits of reducing their own country's barriers of subsidies often need to manage the politics of such concessions'.

In this scenario, different domestic standards can become the most common international trade obstacle. Therefore, the search for common multilateral or regional standards opens up as the necessary means to challenge existing and future trade barriers. Beyond setting their basic canons (regarding substantive as much as procedural issues), WTO and FTA agreements often refer this task, expressly or impliedly, to international organisations[52] as well as to the work of specialised committees.[53] It is also important to acknowledge the regulatory work achieved by international private institutions in this field.[54] At the end of the day, with (compulsory or recommended) or without this international harmonisation, states adopt domestic unilateral imperative norms (in principle, territorial) for private parties involved in cross-border operations.

It is clear that the ultimate beneficiaries of the WTO and FTA systems are the economic actors.[55] For obvious reasons, they are the group first interested in the existence and compliance with agreed standards as well as in the working of the whole system. With this in mind, it cannot be a surprise that these agreements regularly compel states to have administrative and judicial procedures (without entering into the determination of international jurisdiction to adjudicate) available for private parties' defence of their own interests.[56] The achievement of this goal could be reinforced when international (or institutional) norms are recognised as self-executive in character. Though this can be the case when international norms are sufficiently clear and unconditional, the tendency in trade agreements is precisely the opposite. The ordinary approach in FTAs is to expressly state that their norms do not create rights for private parties that they can directly claim.[57] It must be admitted that accepting the self-executive character of certain international treaty norms could ease and promote their application through private parties' actions before national authorities. Moreover, in this way they could further contribute to the surveillance of states' compliance with their international obligations. But this is not yet the case.

[52] eg, Codex Alimentarius, dependent on the UN World Health Organization (WHO) and Food and Agriculture Organization (FAO), available at: www.fao.org/fao-who-codexalimentarius/about-codex/members/es/. The OECD does also work on establishing evidence-based international standards and finding solutions to a range of social, economic and environmental challenges.

[53] eg, in the Technical Barriers area, the WTO Committee adopted in 2000 a Decision on Principles for the development or international standards, guides and recommendations, available at: www.wto.org/english/tratop_e/tbt_e/principles_standards_tbt_e.htm, which are also relevant in the work of the specialised committees established in FTAs.

[54] eg, the International Organisation for Standardisation (ISO), available at: www.iso.org/about-us.html; and the Internet Corporation for Assigned Names and Numbers (ICANN), available at: www.icann.org/resources/pages/welcome-2012-02-25-en.

[55] eg, the EU–UK TCA refers to the service providers (Arts 135–36) and investors (Arts 128–29).

[56] eg, Arts 31(i) and 31(j), 32 and 41.4 of the Agreement on Trade-Related Aspects of Intellectual Property Rights (Marrakesh, Morocco, 15 April 1994) (TRIPS), Art VI.2(a) GATS, Art X.3(b) GATT.

[57] eg, Art 5 EU–UK TCA. See, among others, Case C–280/93 *Germany v Council* [1994] ECR I-04973, paras 109–10.

As has been noted, whilst insisting on the availability of procedures to review administrative decisions,[58] neither the WTO nor FTAs enter into judicial adjudication or cooperation aspects. On the contrary, for example, the General Agreement on Trade and Services (GATS) and the Agreement on Trade-Related Aspects of Intellectual Property Rights (TRIPs) specify that their general most favoured nation treatment (MFNT)[59] – and even national treatment (NT)[60] – do not extend to judicial benefits. Leaving aside this exclusion, and the effects that trade norms can have in traditional PrIL conflict of laws and jurisdiction,[61] some PrIL doctrine in the European Union has regretted the missed opportunity to introduce judicial cooperation standards in FTAs.[62]

For the time being, the active role of private parties in international trade surveillance is essentially stimulated through instruments such as EU Regulation 654/2014 on the exercise of the Union's rights for the application and enforcement of international trade rules.[63] This Regulation provides a procedure for direct complaints before EU authorities from community industry, community enterprise and providers of services[64] looking for a reaction before third states (arguably) infringing their trade liberalising commitments (bilateral or multilateral).[65] This entails that the instrument is meant to defend private parties' interests in open international trade. Under the procedure, they acquire a protagonist role as 'police' and 'claimants' of third states' non-compliance with international trade compromises. Nevertheless, final decisions on how to proceed are exclusively adopted by EU institutions on the basis of the Union's policy and economic interests. It is true that the mere threat of acting on this basis can contribute to 'motivate' a change on a third state's allegedly infringing measure. Nonetheless, the EU final decisions can be appealed before the Court of Justice of the European Union (CJEU).[66] From the opposite perspective, private parties can always claim before the CJEU against

[58] eg, See above (n 56) and Art 62 TRIPS.

[59] eg, Art 4(a) TRIPS.

[60] eg, Art 2.3 TRIPS.

[61] See above, section IV.

[62] M Weller, 'Judicial Cooperation of the EU in Civil Matters in its Relations with Non-EU States – A Blind Spot?' (2018), available at: papers.ssrn.com/sol3/papers.cfm?abstract_id=3134324.

[63] Regulation (EU) 654/2014 of 15 May 2014 concerning the exercise of the Union's rights for the application and enforcement of international trade rules, [2014] OJ L189/50, amended by Regulation 2021/167 of 10 February 2021, [2021] OJ L 49/1.

[64] For definitions, see Art 2 and, on the procedures, see Arts 3 and 4 of Regulation 3286/94 of 31 March 1994 laying down Community procedures in the field of the common commercial policy in order to ensure the exercise of the Community's rights under international trade rules, in particular those established under the auspices of the WTO, [1994] OJ L349/71.

[65] Recital 10 of the Regulation states that it is meant to 'ensure the coherent application of the enforcement mechanism in trade disputes relating to international trade agreements, including regional or bilateral agreements' and their trade and sustainable development chapters.

[66] Consolidated Version of the Treaty on the Functioning of the European Union, [2008] OJ C115/50 (TFEU) Art 263: 'The Court of Justice of the European Union shall review the legality of legislative acts, of acts of the Council, of the Commission … other than recommendations and opinions, and of acts of the European Parliament and of the European Council intended to produce legal effects vis-à-vis third parties'.

alleged EU violations of its trade commitments as long as they are directly affected by the measure.[67]

Moreover, the EU Commission statement on this Regulation expressly states that '(W)hen preparing draft implementing acts, the Commission will undertake extensive consultations ... expects to receive input from private stakeholders affected by third country measures or by possible commercial policy measures to be adopted by the Union'.[68] Along this line, it is important to note that the participation of the civil society is progressively gaining traction in trade events and negotiations[69] as well as in trade agreements themselves.[70] This clearly contributes to the pervasive transparency commitments of trade agreements, therefore assisting surveillance and, moreover, helping in the surrounding regulatory legitimisation debates.

Together with standardisation, cooperation is a major tool in the WTO and FTAs. In addition to the cooperation with other international organisations,[71] technical and even financial cooperation between states is previewed.[72] It is meaningful to single out the promotion of cooperation in the competition law field.[73] There is no multilateral mechanism to facilitate international cooperation in this area but some bilateral agreements facilitate cooperation between national competition authorities within[74] or outside trade agreements[75] and recently, the EU–UK Trade and Cooperation Agreement (TCA) incorporated some substantive law principles and provisions.[76] However, the definition of 'enforcement activities'[77] provided in these agreements indicates that international cooperation is limited to collaborations between public-administrative competition

[67] ibid. 'Any natural or legal person may, under the conditions laid down in the first and second paragraphs, institute proceedings against an act addressed to that person or which is of direct and individual concern to them, and against a regulatory act which is of direct concern to them and does not entail implementing measures'.

[68] Commission Statement on Regulation (EU) 654/2014 of 15 May 2014, [2014] OJ L189/50, 'Similarly, the Commission expects to receive input from public authorities that may be involved in the implementation of possible commercial policy measures to be adopted by the Union'.

[69] eg, as to the WTO, Civil Society Organizations (CSO) working on trade-related issues attended the Director General's briefing on possible deliverables at MC12, concerning how the WTO is going to ensure inclusive participation of all members at the conference and how CSOs can contribute to efforts to reach a positive outcome at the 12th Ministerial Conference; see: www.wto.org/english/news_e/news21_e/ngo_24nov21_e.htm.

[70] eg, Arts 12, 13 and 14 EU–UK TCA.

[71] Art XXVI GATS and Arts 68–69 TRIPS.

[72] Art XXV GATS and Art 67 TRIPS.

[73] Art IX.2 GATS and Art 40.3 TRIPS.

[74] eg, Chapter 11 of the EU–Japan Economic Partnership.

[75] eg, Agreement between the Government of the United States of America (US) and the Commission of the European Communities regarding the application of their competition laws, [1995] OJ L95/47 (US–EC Agreement). See others in: ec.europa.eu/competition-policy/international/bilateral-relations_en.

[76] Arts 358 and 359 EU–UK TCA.

[77] eg, Art I.2(c) US–EC Agreement.

authorities in different jurisdictions.[78] In antitrust matters, as in other international trade areas, there are no mechanisms for judicial cooperation.[79]

Finally, the cohabitation of the WTO regime with international investment agreements (IAs), particularly their respective dispute settlement mechanisms, cannot be disregarded. It entails the risks for private operators that the same international legal standards be interpreted differently.[80] In this line, it is interesting to briefly note the increasing formal link between FTAs and IAs[81] reinforcing the need for legal coherence between the systems.

As has been noted, there is a '[M]ultiplication of regimes and institutions giving rise to a rather uncoordinated, fragmented and rather deformalized regulatory landscape'[82] which, obviously, has a particularly relevant impact in transboundary economic transactions and calls for a thoughtful analysis. PrIL, focused on the legal fragmentation with implications for private parties' transactions, should not be disparate from this reality.

IV. Narrowing Links: From Practice to Theory

In an internationally open world, it is essential for private parties, firstly, to be aware of the legal system that can be applied in their transboundary economic operations (scope of regulatory jurisdiction), which initially depends on the states' unilaterally or multilaterally decided norms on the determination of the applicable law (be they conflict of law or substantive rules). In this context, the states' regulatory jurisdiction is being limited/conditioned by the WTO, FTAs and IAs. In addition, it seems clear that the existence of some degree of cooperation between the states linked to the transactions can have a positive impact when facing conflictive situations.

Recently, PrIL scholarly works have started to approach the international trade regime. An express entry on the WTO has been included in the Encyclopaedia of PrIL.[83] This entry points out that, when deciding on the applicable law, the conflict of laws rule (presiding the entry orientation) also decides on the horizontal assignment

[78] Art 361.2 EU–UK TCA refers to 'the European Commission or the competition authorities of the Member States, on the one side, and the United Kingdom's competition authority or authorities, on the other side'.

[79] The EU–UK TCA refers to Law Enforcement and Judicial Cooperation in Criminal Matters (Part III).

[80] Fortunately, this did not happen in the investment arbitration dispute parallel to the one maintained within the WTO regarding the respect for trademark rights substantive content; *Philip Morris Brands Sàrl, Philip Morris Products SA and Abal Hermanos SA v Uruguay Occidental Republic* ICSID No ARB/10/7, on the one hand and, on the other, *Australia – Certain Measures Concerning Trademarks, Geographical Indications and Other Plain Packaging Requirements Applicable to Tobacco Products and Packaging*, Panel Report (adopted 28 August 2018) WTO/DS435 and DS467.

[81] eg, EU–UK TCA (Part II; first rubric –trade, transport and other dispositions; third title – services and investment).

[82] Ruiz-Abou Nigm, McCall-Smith and French (n 13) 5.

[83] TW Dornis, 'WTO and Private International Law' in *Encyclopedia of Private International Law*, vol II (Edward Elgar 2017).

of the normative power and, as a consequence, the PrIL 'regulatory function' can conflict with the state's international obligations. This could occur when the application of the *lex causae* entails the violation of WTO agreements; particularly the non-discrimination commitments (NT or MFNT). In other words, even if the determination of the applicable law does not restrict trade by itself, the application of the intended law can eventually cause discrimination (legal of factual) in goods or service imports. Hence, this international trade obligation reaches both substantive and conflict of laws provisions.[84] Recognising the obvious difference in the vertical integration level between the WTO and the European Union (multilateral versus regional liberalisation), it is concluded that the WTO does not have a 'direct impact' in PrIL.[85] Therefore, even from a 'traditional' conflict of laws approach, an indirect impact of international trade regulation in the resolution of foreign legal situations cannot be excluded and thus there is need, at least, to take it into consideration.

In this persistent PrIL approach the analysis seems to be limited to the law applicable to a contractual or non-contractual case, basically through conflict of laws rules. Following this line, reference could also be made to the use of the public policy concept/exception.[86] But, moreover, it is through the adoption of imperative rules that states maintain a certain degree of intervention in order to preserve the standards/protection level that they consider adequate in international commercial transactions. Beyond the confluence of territorial norms in these transactions, the standard-setting goal (harmonisation) – conditioned by international trade regulation – brings another connecting point between PrIL and international trade agreements that calls for their paths be narrowed.

For example, in the area of personal data protection, though a formulation through conflict of laws norms is possible (and even desirable), the tendency is to regulate through unilateral norms, turning back to the statutory school and its extension of policy rules. In other words, the tendency is to regulate by establishing the extraterritorial reach of national substantive standard-setting rules. This resort to unilateralism has been explained considering the 'public law' character of these data protection legal instruments.[87] Of course, states are aware of the consequent operational difficulties for transnational operations which, in addition to regulatory overlaps or gaps,[88] can entail trade obstacles.[89]

[84] Basedow, *The Law of Open Societies* (n 5) 217–18, states that, however, where the unequal treatment results from the agreement of private parties, the rule will not be infringed since it does not result from a state's measure.

[85] Dornis, 'WTO and Private International Law' (n 83) 1846.

[86] P Lagarde, 'Public Policy' in *International Encyclopedia of International Law*, vol III (1994); I Thoma, 'Public Policy' in *Encyclopedia of Private International Law*, vol II (Edward Elgar 2017).

[87] Analysing the EU Data Protection Regulation, E Rodríguez Pineau and E Torralba Mendiola, 'La protección de las transmisiones internacionales de datos transfronterizas; una tarea por completar' in E Rodríguez Pineau and E Torralba Mendiola (eds), *La protección de las transmisiones de datos transfronterizas* (Tirant lo Blanch 2021) 209.

[88] ibid, 146.

[89] C Otero García-Castrillón, 'Protección de datos en la economía digital. Una aproximación desde la regulación del comercio internacional' in E Rodríguez Pineau and E Torralba Mendiola (eds), *La protección de las transmisiones de datos transfronterizas* (Tirant lo Blanch 2021).

Technology and global communications expansion is unstoppable in the present digital economy. Therefore, it is vital to look for pragmatic ways to guarantee, on the one hand, personal data protection as much as, on the other hand, legal certainty and efficiency for economic operators, for which adapting to different legal regimes has a tremendous economic cost. In this area as in others, such as human rights and the SDG connected topics, in addition to more international rapprochement (mutual concessions), coordination and cooperation (for which stakeholders' contributions seem a necessity), together with self-limitation/comity attitudes (such as the position of the CJEU in the case of the right to be forgotten)[90] states are required to pursue the most efficient protection possible.[91] Hence, whilst more stringent standards or more efficient enforcement mechanisms may be desirable, it is not clear that the situations can be tackled solely from a PrIL perspective focused on conflict of laws rules, overriding mandatory provisions and public policy. There is a need for a more collaborative, sharing, multilateral world to overcome these difficult situations affecting both private parties and states.

In this realm, e-commerce (including data transfers and personal data protection), is presently part of WTO negotiations[92] and has special chapters in FTAs.[93] On a different scale, it is interesting to note the recently created EU and US (who are not yet linked by an FTA) bilateral Trade and Technology Council (TTC) to coordinate approaches to key global trade, economic and technology issues steering mutual cooperation through different working groups. Looking to enhance mutual trust both between states and private parties, the importance of and commitment to consulting closely with diverse stakeholders is expressly highlighted.[94]

It must be admitted that trade agreements have not as yet been expressly combined with concrete judicial cooperation measures; and probably will not be, at least in the short run. In the case of EU FTAs, it has been considered unfortunate to not even try to incorporate commitments of accession to the Hague Conference PrIL instruments. Therefore, there is support for some explicit connection between the EU's civil cooperation and its common commercial policy[95] through the incorporation of rules in trade agreements. This trend is possibly building on

[90] Case C-507/17 *Google Inc v Commission nationale de l'informatique et des libertés* (CNIL) [2020] 1 WLR 1993, para 62.

[91] C Kuner, 'Reality and Illusion in EU Data Transfer Regulation Post *Schrems*' (2017) 18 *German Law Journal* 881, 917.

[92] WTO, 'Joint Initiative On E-commerce', available at: www.wto.org/english/tratop_e/ecom_e/joint_statement_e.htm#:~:text=A%20group%20of%2071%20WTO,intention%20to%20commence%20these%20negotiations.

[93] eg, Comprehensive and Progressive Agreement for Trans-Pacific Partnership (CPTPP or TPP-11), available at: www.sice.oas.org/Trade/TPP/CPTPP/Spanish/CPTPP_Index_s.asp; US, Mexico and Canada Free Trade Agreement (USMCA), available at: ustr.gov/trade-agreements/free-trade-agreements/united-states-mexico-canada-agreement/agreement-between, EU–UK TCA, EU–Japan Economic Partnership.

[94] Launched in June 2021, available at: ec.europa.eu/commission/presscorner/detail/en/IP_21_2990, the TTC initiated its works in September 2021. The Commission has set up a one-stop-shop on its online 'Futurium' platform, to collect input from all interested parties; see: futurium.ec.europa.eu/en/EU-US-TTC.

[95] Weller (n 62), the EU's competence would be based on Arts 207 and 81 TFEU.

the success of FTAs in fostering cooperation and approximation of its members in the variety of areas – with public and private interests closely related to SDGs – that are being progressively incorporated. Nonetheless, after all that has been said, it does not seem necessary to reach that point in order to perceive the practical and theoretical narrowing links between PrIL and international trade law. The general isolation of PrIL theory from the WTO and FTAs is not a response to the apparent reality.

V. Conclusions

Globalisation continues to be the socio-economic phenomenon that dictates the evolution of PrIL academic tendencies. In PrIL, a primary dimension of globalisation can be said to reside in the generalised claim of the 'private' aspects of relationships and of the individualism, particularly around the defence of human rights (without losing sight of multiculturalism) and sustainability. There is a 'global' assumption of the values associated with the respect for the individual's dignity and freedom in an open world. In this scenario, the self-regulation initiatives add up to the public intervention tendencies in line with UN SDGs and the 'Great Reset' initiative.

As a natural consequence, it is possible to perceive the development of attitudes and instruments providing for the individual's defence against the state's actions (a 'proceduralisation' phenomenon) as well as the 'materialisation' (or substantive direction) of PrIL techniques.[96] The substantive trend of PrIL is perceived in sectors covered by private law as much as in those governed by public law, where the classic regulatory interventionism takes place. Together, proceduralisation and materialisation – with open legal criteria and margin for evaluating the legal interests at stake in a certain case (reasonableness)[97] – contribute to raising the relevance of the adjudicatory body (judicial and administrative) in the development of PrIL.

In this context, the need to deal 'globally' with the difficulties of international transactions requires permeable frontiers between PIL and PrIL. Beyond their historical links, Van Loon concedes that they are forced, together with national law, to grow and develop inter-connectedly.[98] Lowenfeld expressly recognised their reciprocal influence and stated that the frontiers between those two disciplines

[96] With a different origin – international, institutional, national, private, and with a different nature – treaty, model laws, guides, and regulatory methods – direct and indirect.

[97] As Lagarde (n 86) 15, puts it, justice requires that each State considers the potentially applicable legal system merits not just on the parties' expectations but also on the stability of transnational socio-economic transactions and the materialisation of foreign states' legitimate interests.

[98] JHA Van Loon, 'The Increasing Significance of International Co-operation for the Unification of Private International Law' in Universiteit van Amsterdam (eds), *Forty Years On: The Evolution of Post War Private International Law in Europe* (Kluwer, 1990) 117.

are unavoidably diluted[99] and, from the European Economic Community experience, Mengozzi expressly pointed to international trade law and PrIL interactions by analysing the impact of WTO law on the judicial protection of the rights and interests of traders as well as to the administrative means they can use to face trade barriers.[100] For his part, Petersmann sees the need to assist both states and individuals in reacting against public and private abuses (government and market failures), whilst contributing to the improvement of public goods, including human rights (which are at the core of the matter and have a functional relation with it), such as the fight against global warming. His approach not only transcends the international public–private divide as much as the national–transnational one, but also resorts to social sciences, especially international and development economy and the economic analysis of law.[101]

Jonathan Fitchen's work provides an exemplary model on how PrIL research does not just live in an ivory tower, but builds bridges between theory and practice fostering collaboration between the legal actors, the academy and the policy communities. He cared about the pressing real-world problems and ventured outside the university walls offering useful insights to help develop policy solutions. In an attempt to follow this approach, it is argued that PrIL could better integrate (and be integrated) into the study of international trade agreements with a pragmatic view in line with present holistic academic tendencies, and, henceforth, promote international cooperation towards the attainment of SDGs.

[99] A Lowenfeld, *International Economic Law* (Oxford University Press, 2008) v and vii, states that 'everything is related to everything else – trade to investment to monetary affairs, dispute settlement to sanctions and to unilateral vs collective action, economic law to public international law and to private international law'. R Bismuth, D Carreau, A Hamann and P Juillard, *Droit international économique*, 6th edn (Dalloz, 2017): 'trois piliers du droit international économique que sont le commerce international, l'investissement étranger et les relations monétaires et financières internationals … ces différentes disciplines ne sont pas pour autant analysées de manière cloisonnée tant les interactions entre les trois branches sont nombreuses' ['the three pillars of international economic law are international trade, foreign investment and international monetary and financial relations … therefore, these different disciplines are not analysed in a compartmentalised manner as the interactions between the three branches are numerous'].

[100] P Mengozzi, 'Private international law and the WTO law' (2001) 292 *Hague Collected Courses* 253. Along these lines, B Hess, 'Private Public Divide in International Dispute Resolution' (2017) 388 *Hague Collected Courses* 49, argues that it would be misleading to qualify parts of the current dispute resolution system as purely 'commercial' and other parts as purely 'public or administrative'. There are revolving doors between the systems and the same procedures are often applied; what really matters is the proper delineation of different remedies which functionally protect the same interests and rights.

[101] EU Petersmann, *International Economic Law in the 21st Century: Constitutional Pluralism and Multilevel Governance of Interdependent Public Goods* (Hart Publishing, 2012) 11, 14 and 57. From a cosmopolitan citizen perspective, he conceptualises and justifies international economic law as a system of legal norms and practices aimed at the promotion of the economic efficiency and sustainable development, but also the compliance with human rights and democratic self-governance.

10

Cross-Border Protection of Human Rights: The 2021 German Supply Chain Due Diligence Act

GIESELA RÜHL

I. Introduction

In the summer of 2021, after long and heated debates, the German legislature adopted the Act on Corporate Due Diligence Obligations for the Prevention of Human Rights Violations in Global Supply Chains, also known as the Supply Chain Due Diligence Act (Lieferkettensorgfaltspflichtengesetz – LkSG).[1] Following in the footsteps of other European countries, notably France, the new law establishes mandatory human rights due diligence obligations and, hence, requires German

[1] Gesetz über die unternehmerischen Sorgfaltspflichten zur Vermeidung von Menschenrechtsverletzungen in Lieferketten (Lieferkettensorgfaltspflichtengesetz, hereafter, LkSG), BGBl. I, 2959 ff. A (semi-official) English translation is available at the website of the Federal Ministry of Labor and Social Affairs (*Bundesministerium für Arbeit und Soziales – BMAS*, available at: www.bmas.de/SharedDocs/Downloads/DE/Internationales/act-corporate-due-diligence-obligations-supply-chains.pdf%3bjsessionid=CD0566A73AB32BD8B75B2154D5F226AF.delivery1-replication?__blob=publicationFile&v=2. See for first evaluations: E Ehmann, 'Das Lieferkettensorgfaltspflichtengesetz (LkSG) kommt!' (2021) 4 *Zeitschrift für Vertriebsrecht* 205; E Ehmann and D Berg, 'Das Lieferkettensorgfaltspflichtengesetz (LkSG): ein erster Überblick' (2021) 15 *Gesellschafts- und Wirtschaftsrecht* 287; T Helck, 'Gesetz über die unternehmerischen Sorgfaltspflichten in Lieferketten: Worauf sich Unternehmen zukünftig vorbereiten müssen' (2021) 27 *Betriebs-Berater* 1603; H-G Kamann and P Irmscher, 'Das Sorgfaltspflichtengesetz – Ein neues Sanktionsrecht für Menschenrechts- und Umweltverstöße in Lieferketten' (2021) 7 *Neue Zeitschrift für Wirtschafts-, Steuer- und Unternehmensstrafrecht* 249; D Leuering and D Rubner, 'Lieferkettensorgfaltspflichtengesetz' (2021) 13 *Neue Juristische Wochenschrift Spezial* 399; A Schmidt-Räntsch, 'Sorgfaltspflichten der Unternehmen – Von der Idee über den politischen Prozess bis zum Regelwerk' (2021) 7–8 *Zeitschrift für Umweltrecht* 387; E Wagner and M Ruttloff, 'Das Lieferkettensorgfaltspflichtengesetz – Eine erste Einordnung' (2021) 30 *Neue Juristische Wochenschrift* 2145; G Wagner, 'Das Lieferkettengesetz: Viele Pflichten, keine Haftung' in A Tölle, J Benedict, H Koch, S Klawitter, C Paulus and F Preetz (eds), *Selbstbestimmung: Freiheit und Grenzen: Festschrift für Reinhard Singer zum 70. Geburtstag* (Berliner Wissenschafts-Verlag, 2021).

companies – for the first time – to protect human rights in their supply chains.[2] The Act has, therefore, rightly been described as a 'milestone'.[3]

However, in addition to praise the new law has also attracted a lot of criticism and not only from opponents of mandatory human rights due diligence obligations, but also from supporters:[4] while they welcome the establishment of a legally binding framework to better protect human rights in global supply chains, they argue that the reach of the Act is too limited. In particular, they bemoan that the Act relies on public enforcement mechanisms only and refrains from imposing any civil liability on companies for violations of the newly established due diligence obligations.

The following chapter takes this criticism – and the adoption of the German Supply Chain Act more broadly – as an occasion to take a closer look at the newly created obligations to better protect human rights in global supply chains. In particular, it sheds light on the effects of the Act under private law and discusses whether private international law may (or may not) help to effectuate the new provisions in a cross-border context. Since Jonathan Fitchen was not only a preeminent scholar of private international law, but also deeply interested in – and open to – developments in other countries, it is my hope that the following contribution would have appealed to him.

II. From the 'Ruggie Principles' to the German Supply Chain Act

The German Supply Chain Act – like other national legislation in the field – goes back to the UN Guiding Principles for Business and Human Rights, the so-called 'Ruggie Principles'.[5] Adopted in 2011, the Guiding Principles set out in great detail what measures companies should take to identify, prevent and mitigate human rights violations and how they should react if human rights violations

[2] Note that the Act also serves to better protect the environment (*cf* s 2(2) and 2(4) and s 3 LkSG). However, for reasons of space, the following chapter focuses on the protection of human rights.

[3] Statement of Gerd Müller, the Federal Minister for Economic Cooperation and Development, available at: www.bmz.de/de/entwicklungspolitik/lieferketten. In a similar vein, G Wagner, 'Haftung für Menschenrechtsverletzungen in der Lieferkette' (2021) 21 *Zeitschrift für Wirtschaftsrecht* 1095; Wagner, 'Das Lieferkettengesetz: Viele Pflichten, keine Haftung' (n 1) 693.

[4] See, eg, 'Initiative Lieferkettengesetz, Noch nicht am Ziel, aber endlich am Start', available at: lieferkettengesetz.de; European Center for Constitutional and Human Rights, 'Bundestag verabschiedet Lieferkettengesetz, press release of 11 June 2021', available at: www.ecchr.eu/pressemitteilung/bundestag-verabschiedet-lieferkettengesetz/.

[5] UN Human Rights Office, 'Guiding Principles on Business and Human Rights' (UN, 2011), available at: www.ohchr.org/sites/default/files/documents/publications/guidingprinciplesbusinesshr_en.pdf.

occur.[6] However, since the Guiding Principles do not create new international law obligations,[7] states are not required to transpose them into domestic law.[8] Many countries have nonetheless taken the Ruggie Principles as an opportunity to create legally binding due diligence obligations to advance the protection of human rights in global supply chains. Examples include the 2015 UK Modern Slavery Act,[9] the 2017 French law on the supervisory obligations of parent companies and contracting companies,[10] the so-called Loi de vigilance, and the 2019 Dutch Child Labour Due Diligence Act.[11]

Germany, in contrast, initially refrained from adopting any legally binding human rights due diligence regime. Instead, the 2016 German National Action Plan (NAP) called on companies to voluntarily comply with the Ruggie Principles.[12] However, any hopes that companies would follow this call were largely disappointed: two surveys conducted in 2019 and 2020 by the German government concluded that only 13–17 per cent of all German companies could be considered compliant with the NAP.[13] Gerd Müller, the Federal Minister for Economic Cooperation and Development at the time, and Hubertus Heil, the Federal Minister of Labour and Social Affairs, took this sobering result as an opportunity to move forward with the implementation of a legally binding framework for the protection of human rights, a step which had already been announced in the NAP in case a majority of companies failed to comply voluntarily.[14] The rest is history: shortly before the end of the legislation period, the German Due Diligence Supply Chain Act (LkSG) was adopted.

[6] ibid, 13 ff, Principles 11–24.

[7] ibid, 1 ('Nothing in these Guiding Principles should be read as creating new international law obligations').

[8] ibid, 2.

[9] Modern Slavery Act 2015, ch 30.

[10] Loi No 399/2017 du 23 mars 2017 relative au devoir de vigilance des sociétés mères et des entreprises donneuses d'ordre, JO du 28 mars 2017. See for a detailed discussion with further references G Rühl, 'Die Haftung von Unternehmen für Menschenrechtsverletzungen. Die französische Loi de vigilance als Vorbild für ein deutsches Wertschöpfungskettengesetz?' in G Bachmann, S Grundmann, K Krolop and A Mengel (eds), *Festschrift für Christine Windbichler zum 70. Geburtstag am 8. Dezember 2020* (De Gruyter, 2020).

[11] Wet van 24 oktober 2019 houdende de invoering van een zorgplicht ter voorkoming van de levering van goederen en diensten die met behulp van kinderarbeid tot stand zijn gekomen (Wet zorgpflicht kinderarbeid), Staatsblad 2019, 401.

[12] National Action Plan for Business and Human Rights of 21 December 2016, Implementation of the UN Guiding Principles on Business and Human Rights 2016–2020 (Federal Foreign Office, 2016), available at: www.auswaertiges-amt.de/blob/610714/fb740510e8c2fa83dc507afad0b2d7ad/nap-wirtschaft-menschenrechte-engl-data.pdf.

[13] Final Report: Monitoring the National Action Plan for Business and Human Rights 2016–2020 (Federal Foreign Office, 2021), available at: www.auswaertiges-amt.de/blob/2417212/9c8158fe4c7374 26fa4d7217436accc7/201013-nap-monitoring-abschlussbericht-data.pdf, 5.

[14] National Action Plan (n 12) 10.

III. Human Rights-Related Due Diligence Obligations

According to section 3(1) sentence 1 LkSG, the new German Supply Chain Act pursues two aims: first, to minimise human rights-related risks, and second, to end violations of human rights-related obligations.[15] In order to achieve these two aims, the Act establishes an impressive number of legally binding due diligence obligations that are modelled on the Ruggie Principles.[16] According to sections 4, 5, 6 and 7 LkSG companies covered by the Supply Chain Act must establish a risk management system, perform regular risk analyses, take appropriate measures to prevent human rights violations and – if a violation of human rights occurs – take appropriate measures to end or minimise the extent of the violation. According to sections 8, 9 and 10 LkSG, companies must also establish an internal complaints procedure, document compliance with the due diligence obligations and report to the competent authority, the Federal Office for Economic Affairs and Export Control.

However, the due diligence obligations established by the Supply Chain Act do not only impress because they are so numerous. They are also impressive because they are very broad: under section 2(5) sentence 1 LkSG, they refer to all products and services of the companies covered by the Act as well as all steps in Germany and abroad necessary to produce their products and provide their services, ranging from the extraction of raw materials to the delivery to the end customer. Moreover, according to section 2(5) sentence 2 LkSG, the due diligence obligations do not only extend to actions in the company's own business area, but also to the actions of all its direct and indirect suppliers. For the first time in German history, the Supply Chain Act, thus, introduces due diligence obligations that require companies to watch out for what other, legally independent companies are doing.[17]

However, what looks big and impressive at first sight, starts to shrink when taking a closer look. In fact, the Supply Chain Act contains several limitations that substantially decrease the reach of the new law. According to section 3(1) LkSG, for instance, companies only have to fulfil the above-mentioned due diligence obligations within their 'supply chains' as defined by section 2(5) sentence 1 LkSG. Companies, therefore, only have to follow section 3 ff LkSG with regard to the manufacturing of products and the provision of services, while other business relationships are excluded.[18] In addition to that, the intensity of the due diligence obligations decreases along the

[15] Note that the Act also aims to minimise environment-related risks and to end violations of environment-related obligations (*cf* s 3(1) LkSG). However, as set out at the beginning (n 2), the following chapter ignores that aspect of the Act and focuses on the protection of human rights.

[16] See Ehmann, 'Das Lieferkettensorgfaltspflichtengesetz (LkSG) kommt!' (n 1) 206; Ehmann and Berg (n 1) 288 ff; Helck (n 1) 1604 ff; Kamann and Irrmscher (n 1) 251; Leuering and Rubner (n 1) 399 f; Wagner and Ruttloff (n 1) 2147 ff; Wagner, 'Das Lieferkettengesetz: Viele Pflichten, keine Haftung' (n 1) 699 ff.

[17] See, for a detailed discussion, G Wagner, 'Haftung für Menschenrechtsverletzungen' (2016) 80 *Rabels Zeitschrift für ausländisches und internationales Privatrecht* 717, 757 ff.

[18] See, with regard to the insofar identical draft of the German Supply Chain Act of March 2021, below (n 30); E-M Kieninger, 'Englisches Deliktsrecht, internationale Unternehmensverantwortung

supply chain. In fact, they are only fully applicable with regard to the company's own business area (as defined by section 2(6) LkSG) and the company's relations with its direct suppliers (as defined by section 2(7) LkSG).[19] With regard to indirect suppliers, in contrast, companies only have to set up the complaint mechanism required by section 9 LkSG meaning, in particular, that there is no obligation to establish a human rights risk management system or to conduct regular risk analyses concerning the more distant links of the supply chain.[20]

Further limitations relate to the substantive and the personal scope of the due diligence obligations. When it comes to the substantive scope, Section 2(1) LkSG makes clear that the Supply Chain Act does not protect human rights as such. Rather, it offers protection only insofar as human rights are covered by the eleven Conventions listed in the Annex to the Supply Chain Act. And even with regard to these Conventions, protection is only afforded in relation to the prohibitions specifically listed in Section 2(2) LkSG.[21] In terms of the personal scope, the reach of the due diligence obligations is further limited because the Supply Chain Act does not apply to all companies incorporated or active in Germany. Rather, under Section 1(1) LkSG, the Act only applies to companies that have, first, their central administration, their principal place of business, their administrative headquarters or their statutory seat in Germany and, second, 3.000 or more employees.[22] Even though the scope of application will be extended to companies with at least 1.000 employees as of 1 January 2024, only a small fraction of companies based in Germany will have to comply with the already limited requirements of the Supply Chain Act.[23]

und deutsches Sorgfaltspflichtengesetz' (2021) 6 *Recht der Internationalen Wirtschaft* 331, 336 as well as D Krebs, 'Menschenrechtliche und umweltbezogene Sorgfaltspflicht: Der Wettlauf zwischen europäischer und deutscher Rechtssetzung' (2021) 7–8 *Zeitschrift für Umweltrecht* 394, 396.

[19] See Kamann and Irrmscher (n 1) 251.

[20] See Ehmann and Berg (n 1) 290; Helck (n 1) 1606. See also the relevant considerations regarding the draft of the Supply Chain Act of 2021 below (n 30) of Kieninger, 'Englisches Deliktsrecht, internationale Unternehmensverantwortung und deutsches Sorgfaltspflichtengesetz' (n 18) 336; and Krebs (n 18) 397 f.

[21] See Ehmann and Berg (n 1); Kamann and Irrmscher (n 1) 251; Wagner, 'Das Lieferkettengesetz: Viele Pflichten, keine Haftung' (n 1) 700. See also, with regard to the draft of the Supply Chain Act published in March 2021, below (n 30) Krebs (n 18) 398 ff.

[22] See Leuering and Rubner (n 1) 399; Wagner and Ruttloff (n 1) 2145 as well as, with regard to the draft of the Supply Chain Act published in March 2021, below (n 30) Krebs (n 18) 395. For a critical evaluation of the limitation to companies located in Germany, see Wagner, 'Haftung für Menschenrechtsverletzungen in der Lieferkette' (n 3) 1098; Wagner, 'Das Lieferkettengesetz: Viele Pflichten, keine Haftung' (n 1) 698 f. In a similar vein, G Rühl, 'Unternehmensverantwortung und (Internationales) Privatrecht' in E-M Kieninger, A Reinisch and A Peters (eds), *Unternehmensverantwortung und Internationales Recht* (CF Müller, 2020) 125 f; Rühl, 'Die Haftung von Unternehmen für Menschenrechtsverletzungen' (n 10) 1432 f; G Rühl, 'Towards a German Supply Chain Act? Comments from a Choice of Law and a Comparative Perspective' (2020) 11 *European Yearbook of International Economic Law* 55, 58; Wagner, 'Haftung für Menschenrechtsverletzungen' (n 17) 781; J Schmidt, 'Lieferkettengesetzgebung: Sorgfalt!' (2021) 7 *Europäische Zeitschrift für Wirtschaftsrecht* 273, 274.

[23] According to E-M Kieninger, 'Miniatur: Lieferkettengesetz – dem deutschen Papiertiger fehlen die Zähne' (2021) 2 *Zeitschrift für die gesamte Privatrechtswissenschaft* 252, 253, approximately 2,900 companies will be covered by the Act as of 2024 (equalling 0.1% of all German companies).

IV. Public versus Private Enforcement

The fact that the human rights-related due diligence obligations established by the Supply Chain Act are limited in many ways, has attracted a lot of criticism from supporters of a legally binding regime for the protection of human rights.[24] However, the harshest reactions have been directed against the legislature's decision to dispense with any private enforcement of the Act. In fact, according to section 12 ff LkSG, the obligations created by section 3 ff LkSG will only be publicly enforced by the Federal Office of Economics and Export Control. Section 3(3) LkSG, in contrast, expressly rejects any civil liability for violations of section 3 ff LkSG even though such liability – in contrast to the public enforcement mechanism heavily regulated by the Act – would not require a large, centrally and hierarchically organised administration.[25]

The final version of the Supply Chain Act, thus, takes a clear stance in the heated debate about the enforcement of human rights due diligence obligations. And it does so in a way that deviates greatly from what was originally planned: an (unofficial) draft of the Federal Ministry for Economic Cooperation and Development of February 2019 had explicitly provided that the due diligence obligations of the Act should be considered as obligations under private law, thus giving rise to damages in case of violations.[26] By the same token, a White Paper presented in March 2020 noted – under the heading 'enforcement' – that a violation of the Act would constitute a legal basis for damages claims.[27] Finally, in the summer of 2020, the two responsible federal ministers, Gerd Müller and Hubertus Heil, also emphasised their intention to allow victims to sue for damages should human rights due diligence obligations be violated.[28]

However, all these drafts and announcements met with fierce resistance, particularly from the German business community.[29] And also the then

[24] See the references above (n 4).

[25] For a discussion of the advantages and disadvantages of private enforcement, see G Wagner, 'Tort Law and Human Rights' in M Saage-Maaß, P Zumbansen, M Bader and P Shahab (eds), *Transnational Legal Activism in Global Value Chains* (Springer, 2021) 227 ff.

[26] Federal Ministry for Economic Cooperation and Development, 'Gestaltungsmöglichkeiten eines Mantelgesetzes zur nachhaltigen Gestaltung globaler Wertschöpfungsketten und zur Änderung wirtschaftsrechtlicher Vorschriften (Nachhaltige Wertschöpfungskettengesetz – NaWKG) einschließlich eines Stammgesetzes zur Regelung menschenrechtlicher und umweltbezogener Sorgfaltspflichten in globalen Wertschöpfungsketten (Sorgfaltspflichtengesetz – SorgfaltspflichtenG)'.

[27] Federal Ministry of Labour and Social Affairs and Federal Ministry for Economic Cooperation and Development, 'Entwurf für Eckpunkte eines Bundesgesetzes über die Stärkung der unternehmerischen Sorgfaltspflichten zur Vermeidung von Menschenrechtsverletzungen in globalen Wertschöpfungsketten (Sorgfaltspflichtengesetz)', 10 March 2020.

[28] See the joint press release of 14 July 2020, available at: www.bmz.de/de/aktuelles/heil-mueller-lieferkettengesetz-30764.

[29] For a detailed evaluation of the business sector's influence on the legislative process, see A Paasch and K Seitz, 'Lieferkettengesetz: Aufstand der Lobbyisten', April 2021, available at: www.misereor.de/fileadmin/publikationen/briefing-lieferkettengesetz-aufstand-der-lobbyisten-2021.pdf.

German Federal Minister for Energy and Economic Affairs, Peter Altmaier, signalled early on that a Supply Chain Act should not place too great a burden on German companies. The first official draft of the Act of March 2021,[30] therefore, omitted any positive or negative reference to civil liability, which created uncertainty as to the significance of the Act under private law.[31] To resolve this uncertainty, the Committee on Employment and Social Affairs of the German Parliament recommended the inclusion of a new section 3(3) LkSG, which was ultimately adopted.[32] The paragraph consists of two sentences, each with a very different thrust.

A. Section 3(3) Sentence 1 LkSG: Exclusion of Any Civil Liability

According to section 3(3) sentence 1 LkSG, any 'violation of the obligations under this Act does not give rise to any liability under civil law'. The provision, thus, makes clear that the Supply Chain Act itself does not provide a basis for damages claims. Of course, this already follows from the fact that the Act itself does not contain any liability provisions. It is, therefore, more important that section 3(3) sentence 1 LkSG also clarifies that damages claims for violations of the Act cannot be based on other provisions of German law either. In particular, the provision excludes liability under German tort law, notably under section 823(1) and 823(2) of the German Civil Code (Bürgerliches Gesetzgebuch – BGB).[33]

[30] Draft legislation of the Federal Government of Germany, Gesetz über die unternehmerischen Sorgfaltspflichten in Lieferketten, March 2021. See, for an evaluation of this draft, E Ehmann, 'Der Regierungsentwurf für das Lieferkettengesetz: Erläuterung und erste Hinweise zur Anwendung' (2021) 3 *Zeitschrift für Vertriebsrecht* 141; A Keilmann and F Schmidt, 'Der Entwurf des Sorgfaltspflichtengesetzes – Warum es richtig ist, auf eine zivilrechtliche Haftung zu verzichten' (2021) 15 *Zeitschrift für Wirtschafts- und Bankrecht* 717; Kieninger, 'Miniatur: Lieferkettengesetz' (n 23); S Lutz-Bachmann, K Vorbeck and L Wengenroth, 'Menschenrechte und Umweltschutz in Lieferketten – der Regierungsentwurf eines Sorgfaltspflichtengesetzes' (2021) 16 *Betriebs-Berater* 906; M Nietsch and M Wiedmann, 'Der Regierungsentwurf eines Gesetzes über die unternehmerischen Sorgfaltspflichten in der Lieferkette' (2021) 3 *Corporate Compliance Zeitschrift* 101; Schmidt, 'Lieferkettengesetzgebung: Sorgfalt!' (n 22); Wagner, 'Haftung für Menschenrechtsverletzungen in der Lieferkette' (n 3); F von Westphalen, 'Es kreißten die Berge' (2021) 9 *Zeitschrift für Wirtschaftsrecht* 435.

[31] See Ehmann, 'Der Regierungsentwurf für das Lieferkettengesetz' (n 30) 149 f; Kieninger, 'Englisches Deliktsrecht, internationale Unternehmensverantwortung und deutsches Sorgfaltspflichtengesetz' (n 18) 336; Kieninger, 'Miniatur: Lieferkettengesetz' (n 23) 254; German Bar Association (Deutscher Anwaltverein – DAV), Position Statement No 27/2021, 23 ff, para 49 ff; Wagner, 'Haftung für Menschenrechtsverletzungen in der Lieferkette' (n 3) 1100 ff.

[32] Official Record of the German Parliament (*Bundestagsdrucksache*) 19/30505.

[33] Ehmann, 'Das Lieferkettensorgfaltspflichtengesetz (LkSG) kommt!' (n 1) 206; Ehmann and Berg (n 1) 291; Schmidt-Räntsch (n 1) 393; Wagner, 'Das Lieferkettengesetz: Viele Pflichten, keine Haftung' in *Festschrift für* (n 1) 707; Wagner and Ruttloff (n 1) 2149.

i. No Liability under Section 823(2) BGB

According to section 823(2) BGB, a victim may claim damages if the tortfeasor violates a statute that is intended to protect another person (so-called 'protective statute' – *Schutzgesetz*). The provision enables damages claims for the breach of obligations established outside civil law[34] and is commonly understood to function as a 'transmission belt' that transfers values from other areas of law, notably from public law, into tort law.[35] Had the legislature not included section 3(3) sentence 1 LkSG, it would, therefore, have been obvious to classify the Supply Chain Act as a protective statute within the meaning of section 823(2) BGB – and to allow damages claims for violation of the Act's human rights due diligence obligations on the basis of this provision.[36]

However, as section 3(3) sentence 1 LkSG makes abundantly clear, it was the legislature's explicit intention to exclude this very possibility. In fact, according to the explanatory memorandum accompanying the Act, due diligence obligations established by the Supply Chain Act are to be enforced and sanctioned (only) 'in administrative proceedings and by means of administrative law', which has to be emphasised 'in particular with regard to Section 823(2) BGB'.[37]

ii. No Liability under Section 823(1) BGB

Section 3(3) sentence 1 LkSG, however, does not only exclude civil liability under section 823(2) BGB.[38] It also excludes liability based on section 823(1) BGB, the general clause of German tort law which allows victims to claim damages if the tortfeasor, intentionally or negligently, unlawfully injures the life, body, health, freedom, property or another right of another person. Certainly, neither the Supply Chain Act itself nor the explanatory memorandum expressly exclude liability under section 823(1) BGB. However, section 3(1) sentence 1 LkSG leaves no room for doubt that violations of the due diligence obligations established by the Supply Chain Act shall not result in any civil liability. And this includes any liability for culpable and unlawful violation of one of the rights mentioned in section 823(1) BGB.[39]

[34] G Wagner in *Münchener Kommentar zum Bürgerlichen Gesetzbuch*, vol 7, 8th edn (CH Beck, 2020) § 823 BGB, para 532 (with further references).

[35] s 823(2) BGB reads: 'The same duty is held by a person who commits a breach of a statute that is intended to protect another person.' (Official English translation, available at: www.gesetze-im-internet.de/englisch_bgb/englisch_bgb.html#p3489.).

[36] For a detailed evaluation, see Wagner, 'Haftung für Menschenrechtsverletzungen in der Lieferkette' (n 3) 1102 ff.

[37] Official Record of the German Parliament *(Bundestagsdrucksache – BT-Drs)* 19/30505, 38.

[38] s 823(1) BGB reads: 'A person who, intentionally or negligently, unlawfully injures the life, body, health, freedom, property or another right of another person is liable to make compensation to the other party for the damage arising from this.' (Official English translation, available at: www.gesetze-im-internet.de/englisch_bgb/englisch_bgb.html#p3489.).

[39] In the same vein, Wagner, 'Das Lieferkettengesetz: Viele Pflichten, keine Haftung' (n 1) 707 ff.

B. Section 3(3) Sentence 2 LkSG: Civil Liability According to Other Legal Provisions

Section 3(3) sentence 1 LkSG is accompanied and complemented by section 3(3) sentence 2 LkSG, which stipulates that 'any liability under civil law arising independently of this Act remains unaffected'. The provision, hence, makes clear that the exclusion of liability for violations of the Supply Chain Act's due diligence obligations by virtue of section 3(3) sentence 1 LkSG does not exclude civil liability based on the violation of human rights due diligence obligations that follow from other provisions of German law. Section 3(3) sentence 2 LkSG, thus, suggests that such liability does, in fact, exist. But is this actually the case? Are companies liable for harm done in their supply chains?

The prevailing view in the literature answers this question in the negative.[40] By the same token, courts have been reluctant to establish human rights due diligence obligations that might be the basis for damages claims. However, over the past years, a number of voices in the literature have tried to argue that civil liability for human rights violations may in fact be based on German tort law, contract law or company law.[41] Furthermore, trends in other countries show that courts are, in fact, inclined to turn to the general rules of civil law, especially tort law, to further the protection of human rights and the environment in global supply chains. For instance, the UK Supreme Court held in *Vedanta* in 2019[42] and in

[40] For a detailed discussion of the state of the discussion with further references, see Rühl, 'Unternehmensverantwortung und (Internationales) Privatrecht' (n 22) 114 f.

[41] See, eg, H Fleischer and S Korch, 'Zur deliktsrechtlichen Verantwortlichkeit von Auftraggebern in der Lieferkette' (2019) 42 *Zeitschrift für Wirtschaftsrecht* 2181, 2189 f; M Saage-Maaß and M Leifker, 'Haftungsrisiken deutscher Unternehmen und ihres Managements für Menschenrechtsverletzungen im Ausland' (2015) 42 *Betriebs-Berater* 2499, 2503 ff; C Thomale, 'Zur Versicherung der Kapitalgesellschaft durch ihre Gläubiger' in C Behme, M Fries and J Stark (eds), *Versicherungsmechanismen im Recht*, (Mohr Siebeck, 2016) 131; C Thomale and L Hübner, 'Zivilrechtliche Durchsetzung völkerrechtlicher Unternehmensverantwortung' (2017) 8 *JuristenZeitung* 385, 391 f; C Thomale and M Murko, 'Unternehmerische Haftung für Menschenrechtsverletzungen in transnationalen Lieferketten' (2021) 1 *Europäische Zeitschrift für Arbeitsrecht* 40, 48 ff; M-P Weller, L Kaller and A Schulz, 'Haftung deutscher Unternehmen für Menschenrechtsverletzungen im Ausland' (2016) 216 *Archiv für die civilistische Praxis* 387, 413 ff. For an overview with further references, see Rühl, 'Unternehmensverantwortung und (Internationales) Privatrecht' (n 22) 106 ff; L Rudkowski, 'Nachhaltigkeit in den internationalen Lieferketten als Haftungsrisiko für deutsche Unternehmen' (2020) 6 *Corporate Compliance Zeitschrift* 352, 354 ff.

[42] *Lungowe v Vedanta* [2019] UKSC 20, [2020] AC 1045. S Asmussen and G Wagner, 'Menschenrechtsklagen vor englischen Gerichten: Von Yachten zu Konzernen' (2020) 4 *Zeitschrift für Europäisches Privatrecht* 979, 985; Fleischer and Korch, 'Zur deliktsrechtlichen Verantwortlichkeit von Auftraggebern in der Lieferkette' (n 41) 2186 f; E-M Kieninger, 'Vedanta v Lungowe: Ein Meilenstein für Klagen gegen europäische Konzernmütter für Umweltschäden und Menschenrechtsverletzungen durch drittstaatliche Tochtergesellschaften' (2020) 1 *Praxis des Internationalen Privat- und Verfahrensrechts* 60 ff; Kieninger, 'Englisches Deliktsrecht, internationale Unternehmensverantwortung und deutsches Sorgfaltspflichtengesetz' (n 18) 333 ff; Kieninger, 'Miniatur: Lieferkettengesetz' (n 23) 255; Rühl, 'Unternehmensverantwortung und (Internationales) Privatrecht' (n 22) 121 ff; A Schall, 'Die erhöhten Haftungsrisiken für Menschenrechtsverletzungen nach King Okpabi v Royal Dutch Shell – und die

Okpabi in 2021[43] that, under certain circumstances, parent companies may be liable for violation of the general common law duty of care if third parties suffer injuries as a result of the activities of their foreign subsidiaries. And in *Hamida Begum*, the Court of Appeal confirmed in 2021 that a company may be liable when foreign contractors cause human rights violations.[44] Innovative ways to protect human rights and the environment under private law have also recently been pursued in the Netherlands where the District Court of Den Haag invoked the general clause of Dutch tort law in a sensational decision to order the oil company Shell to reduce its CO2 emissions.[45]

In light of these and other developments, including the recent decision of the German Federal Constitutional Court on the unconstitutionality of the German Federal Climate Act,[46] it cannot be ruled out that German civil courts will accept the invitation of section 3(3) sentence 2 LkSG to hold German companies liable based on other provisions of German private law.[47] That this may even have been the legislature's intention follows from section 11 LkSG. According to this provision, persons claiming to have been violated in a legal position pursuant to section 2(1) LkSG may authorise a domestic trade union or non-governmental organisation to bring proceedings to enforce their rights before (German) civil courts in its own capacity.[48] However, since the Supply Chain Act itself does not establish any rights that could potentially be enforced in civil proceedings, section 11 LkSG only gains relevance if courts find other ways to hold German companies liable for the violation of human rights in their supply chains.[49]

überraschende Enthaftungswirkung des Lieferkettengesetzes' (2021) 24 *Zeitschrift für Wirtschaftsrecht* 1242, 1246 f.

[43] *Okpabi v Royal Dutch Shell* [2021] UKSC 3, [2021] 1 WLR 1294. See H Fleischer and S Korch, 'Okpabi v Royal Dutch Shell und das deutsche Deliktsrecht in Konzernlagen' (2021) 14 *Zeitschrift für Wirtschaftsrecht* 709; Kieninger, 'Englisches Deliktsrecht, internationale Unternehmensverantwortung und deutsches Sorgfaltspflichtengesetz' (n 18) 333; Kieninger, 'Miniatur: Lieferkettengesetz' (n 23) 255; Schall (n 42) 1246.

[44] *Hamida Begum v Maran* (UK) [2021] EWCA Civ 326. See Kieninger, 'Englisches Deliktsrecht, internationale Unternehmensverantwortung und deutsches Sorgfaltspflichtengesetz' (n 18) 334.

[45] Rechtbank Den Haag, judgement of 26 May 2021, ECLI:NL:RBDHA:2021:5339.

[46] BVerfG, Resolution of 24 March 2021, ECLI:DE:BVerfG:2021:rs20210324.1bvr265618. See, for a first appraisal, C Möllers and N Weinberg, 'Die Klimaschutzentscheidung des Bundesverfassungsgerichts' (2021) 22 *JuristenZeitung* 1069.

[47] In a similar vein, Ehmann, 'Das Lieferkettensorgfaltspflichtengesetz (LkSG) kommt!' (n 1) 206; Wagner, 'Das Lieferkettengesetz: Viele Pflichten, keine Haftung' (n 1) 708.

[48] See Wagner, 'Das Lieferkettengesetz: Viele Pflichten, keine Haftung' (n 1) 705 f; Wagner and Ruttloff (n 1) 2150.

[49] s 11 LkSG gains further relevance in light of private international law, specifically if a case is brought under the law of a foreign state. For details, see below, section V.

V. Private Enforcement via Private International Law?

In light of the foregoing, it becomes clear that the Supply Chain Act in its current state has no significance under private law, and in particular does not provide a basis for civil liability. This finding may be regretted.[50] However, one may also take the position that the lack of civil liability is not a big deal – because the rules of private international law do not lead to the application of German law anyway.[51] In fact, according to the relevant provision of the Rome II Regulation,[52] that is Article 4(1), liability for human rights violations is governed by the law of the country in which the damage occurs (ie, the law of the 'place of injury'). In the typical supply chain case – where the actual injury happens abroad – it is, thus, foreign law that will be applicable.[53] Undoubtedly, there are voices in literature who argue that the law at the seat of the company claimed to be liable may be applied by virtue of Article 4(3) of the Rome II Regulation.[54] These proposals, however, come with severe (methodological and substantive) problems and are, therefore, rightly rejected by the majority in the literature.[55] Consequently, even if the Supply Chain Act or other provisions of German (tort) law were to establish civil liability for the violation of human rights-related due diligence obligations, the rules of (European) private international law would prevent these liability provisions from taking effect.

A second glance, however, suggests that this analysis might be too shortsighted. In fact, it could be possible to classify the human rights due diligence obligations established by section 3 ff LkSG as overriding mandatory provisions in the meaning of Article 16 of the Rome II Regulation or as rules of safety and conduct in the meaning of Article 17 of the Rome II Regulation. Section 3 ff LkSG

[50] See references above (n 4).

[51] The situation might be different with regard to environmental damages as in such cases, according to Art 7 Rome II Regulation, the victim may choose between the law of the place of injury and the law of the place of action. See, for an evaluation with further references, Rühl, 'Unternehmensverantwortung und (Internationales) Privatrecht' (n 22) 98 ff.

[52] Regulation (EC) No 864/2007 of the European Parliament and of the Council of 11 July 2007 on the law applicable to non-contractual obligations (Rome II), [2007] OJ L199/40.

[53] For a detailed evaluation of the law applicable to human rights violations with further references, see H-P Mansel, 'Internationales Privatrecht de lege lata wie de lege ferenda und Menschenrechtsverantwortlichkeit deutscher Unternehmen' (2018) 2–3 *Zeitschrift für Unternehmens- und Gesellschaftsrecht* 439, 453 f; A-C Mittwoch, 'Die Notwendigkeit eines Lieferkettengesetzes aus der Sicht des Internationalen Privatrechts' (2020) 7 *Recht der Internationalen Wirtschaft* 397, 399 ff; Rühl, 'Unternehmensverantwortung und (Internationales) Privatrecht' (n 22) 95 ff; Wagner, 'Haftung für Menschenrechtsverletzungen' (n 17) 739 ff.

[54] For a detailed discussion, see Rühl, 'Unternehmensverantwortung und (Internationales) Privatrecht' (n 22) 101 ff, as well as Mittwoch (n 53) 399 ff.

[55] Rühl, 'Unternehmensverantwortung und (Internationales) Privatrecht' (n 22) 101 ff. In a similar vein, Mansel (n 53) 473; Wagner, 'Haftung für Menschenrechtsverletzungen' (n 17) 749 f.

would then supersede the due diligence obligations of foreign law, and thus could potentially give rise to liability under foreign law. Through the 'backdoor' of private international law, the Supply Chain Act could, therefore, still gain private law effect.

A. Due Diligence Obligations as Overriding Mandatory Provisions?

According to Article 16 of the Rome II Regulation 'nothing in this Regulation shall restrict the application of the provisions of the law of the forum in a situation where they are mandatory irrespective of the law otherwise applicable to the non-contractual obligation'. The provision, thus helps to enforce certain norms, namely the so-called overriding mandatory provisions of the forum, against the otherwise applicable law. But which provisions qualify as 'overriding mandatory provisions'?

Unfortunately, the term is not defined in Article 16 of the Rome II Regulation. However, there is broad consensus[56] that it is to be interpreted in accordance with Article 9 of the Rome I Regulation[57] which defines overriding mandatory provisions as provisions 'the respect for which is regarded as crucial by a country for safeguarding its public interests, such as its political, social or economic organisation, to such an extent that they are applicable to any situation falling within their scope'. It is, therefore, essentially up to the national legislature to classify provisions of domestic law as overriding mandatory in nature. And according to the case law of the Court of Justice of the European Union (CJEU) national legislatures have broad discretion to do so.[58] With regard to section 3 ff LkSG, the question, therefore, is whether the German legislature considered them as being so decisive for safeguarding Germany's public interests, notably its political, social or economic organisation, that they should supersede the otherwise applicable law.

Unlike the question of whether the Supply Chain Act establishes civil liability, this question is not answered by the Act itself. Instructive, however, is a look into the drafting history. It reveals quite clearly, that the German legislature did not want to turn the due diligence obligations of the Supply Chain Act into overriding mandatory

[56] A Junker in *Münchener Kommentar zum Bürgerlichen Gesetzbuch*, vol 13, 9th edn (CH Beck, 2021), Article 16 Rome II Regulation, para 12; F Maultzsch in *BeckOnline GrossKommentar*, 1 June 2021, Article 16 Rome II Regulation, paras 14 ff, available at: beck-online.beck.de/?vpath=bibdata/komm/BeckOGK/cont/BeckOGK.htm (all with further references).

[57] Regulation (EC) No 593/2008 of the European Parliament and of the Council of 17 June 2008 on the law applicable to contractual obligations (Rome I), [2008] OJ L177/6.

[58] Case C-184/12 *Unamar* (17 October 2003) para 41 ff; Case C-149/18 *Da Silva Martins* (31 January 2019) para 30 ff. See also, Maultzsch (n 56), Article 16 Rome II Regulation, para 24 f; Rühl, 'Towards a German Supply Chain Act?' (n 22) 65. See also, E-M Kieninger, M Krajewski and F Wohltmann, 'Rechtsgutachten und Entwurf für ein Gesetz zur Umsetzung menschenrechtlicher und umweltbezogener Sorgfaltspflichten', 9 June 2021, available at: papers.ssrn.com/sol3/papers.cfm?abstract_id=3863292, 53 f.

provisions. In fact, section 15 of the 2019 (unofficial) draft,[59] which aimed to characterise the Act's due diligence obligations as 'mandatory … irrespective of the law otherwise applicable to the non-contractual obligation', neither found its way into the (official) draft of the Act published in March 2021 nor into the final version of the Supply Chain Act. In addition, a last-minute motion in the Committee of Labour and Social Affairs to reinstate the provision was explicitly dismissed by the majority in the Committee.[60] It is, hence, not possible to classify section 3 ff LkSG as overriding mandatory provisions in the meaning of Article 16 of the Rome II Regulation and to apply them against the otherwise applicable law.[61] As a result, the only way to lend the new provisions private law effect is Article 17 of the Rome II Regulation.

B. Due Diligence Obligations as Rules of Safety and Conduct?

Article 17 of the Rome II Regulation addresses cases in which the tortfeasor acts in one country whereas the harm occurs in another. It provides that 'in assessing the conduct of the person claimed to be liable, account shall be taken, as a matter of fact and in so far as is appropriate, of the rules of safety and conduct which were in force at the place and time of the event giving rise to the liability'. If section 3 ff LkSG can be classified as 'rules of safety and conduct' they may, hence, become relevant even though the claim for damages itself is subject to foreign law in accordance with Article 4(1) of the Rome II Regulation. But can they?

In the literature on the German Supply Chain Act, this question is occasionally answered in the affirmative.[62] However, the better arguments speak against the application of Article 17 of the Rome II Regulation. To begin with, there is, again, the drafting history. While it is true that the application of Article 17 of the Rome II Regulation – unlike the application of Article 16 of the Regulation – was never expressly rejected, Article 17 of the Rome II Regulation was at least briefly discussed in a hearing of the Committee on Human Rights and Humanitarian Aid in October 2020.[63] In the further course of the legislative proceedings, however,

[59] See above (n 26).

[60] Official Record of the German Parliament (*Bundestagsdrucksache*) 19/30505, 28.

[61] In a similar vein, Ehmann, 'Das Lieferkettensorgfaltspflichtengesetz (LkSG) kommt!' (n 1) 206 as well as Ehmann and Berg (n 1) 291. However, in support of their conclusion, they do not rely on the (insofar unambiguous) drafting history of the Supply Chain Act, but rather on s 3(3) LkSG.

[62] Ehmann, 'Das Lieferkettensorgfaltspflichtengesetz (LkSG) kommt!' (n 1) 206; Ehmann and Berg (n 1) 291; Schmidt-Räntsch (n 1) 394. See also – with regard to the draft of the Supply Chain Act published in March 2021 (n 31) – Ehmann, 'Der Regierungsentwurf für das Lieferkettengesetz' (n 30) 150 f. The enforcement of national due diligence obligations under Art 17 Rome II Regulation is further supported by Rudkowski (n 41) 354; Saage-Maaß and Leifker (n 41) 2502. Mansel (n 53) 467 considers such a solution at least to be 'possible'.

[63] M Saage-Maaß, 'Schriftliche Stellungnahme zur Anhörung des Ausschusses für Menschenrechte und humanitäre Hilfe des Deutschen Bundestages zum Thema "Menschenrechte und Wirtschaft"' (Bundestag, 28 October 2020), available at: www.bundestag.de/resource/blob/802074/478a02bc71adfcf2e4f25f489e886fd2/stellungnahme_dr-saage-maass-data.pdf, 11.

Article 17 of the Regulation was never mentioned again. Discussions rather focused on Article 16 of the Regulation. It follows, that the German legislature did not consider the provisions of the Supply Chain Act to be 'rules of safety and conduct' in the meaning of Article 17 of the Rome II Regulation. In any event, application of Article 17 of the Regulation would contravene the legislature's intention to exclude any civil liability based on violations of section 3 ff LkSG as well as its decision not to give the Supply Chain Act precedence over the otherwise applicable foreign law via Article 16 of the Rome II Regulation.

In addition, it is also unclear whether Article 17 of the Rome II Regulation – having regard to its intent and purpose – can be applied to cases such as the ones at issue here: Article 17 attempts to compensate for the fact that Article 4(1) of the Rome II Regulation calls for application of the law of the place of injury rather than the law of the place of action. In cases where these places are in different countries it may, therefore, happen that the tortfeasor is liable under a law that might be hard for him (or her) to predict.[64] To ensure that tortfeasors may trust that an action that is permitted at the place of action will not give rise to liability under the otherwise applicable law, Article 17 of the Rome II Regulation establishes that 'account shall be taken,[65] as a matter of fact and in so far as is appropriate' of the rules of safety and conduct of the place of action.[66] The provision, thus, primarily intends to benefit and protect the tortfeasor. In contrast, it is unclear – and subject to debate – whether the provision can also be applied where this would disadvantage the tortfeasor because the rules of safety and conduct at the place of action happen to be stricter than the rules of safety and conduct of the otherwise applicable law.[67] The final word in this matter rests, of course, with the CJEU. However, broad application of Article 17 of

[64] J von Hein, 'Die Behandlung von Sicherheits- und Verhaltensregeln nach Art 17 der Rom II-Verordnung' in H Kronke and K Thorn (eds), *Grenzen überwinden – Prinzipien bewahren: Festschrift für Bernd von Hoffmann* (Gieseking Verlag, 2011) 140; J von Hein in G-P Calliess and M Renner (eds), *Rome Regulations: Commentary*, 3rd edn (Wolters Kluwer, 2020), Article 17 Rome II Regulation, para 1; Junker (n 56), Article 17 Rome II Regulation, para 1; M Lehmann in *Nomos Kommentar BGB*, vol 6, 3rd edn (CH Beck, 2019), Article 17 Rome II Regulation, paras 2 and 3.

[65] For an analysis on how to interpret the term 'account shall be taken', see von Hein, 'Die Behandlung von Sicherheits- und Verhaltensregeln nach Art 17 der Rom II-Verordnung' (n 64) 153; von Hein in *Rome Regulations* (n 64), Article 17 Rome II Regulation, para 30; Junker (n 56), Article 17 Rome II Regulation, para 22 ff; Lehmann (n 64), Article 17 Rome II Regulation, para 59 ff.

[66] Note that Art 17 Rome II Regulation does not use the term 'place of action' but speaks of 'the place of the event giving rise to the liability'. However, it is generally accepted that the latter term must be understood to mean the place of action. See von Hein, 'Die Behandlung von Sicherheits- und Verhaltensregeln nach Art 17 der Rom II-Verordnung' (n 64) 147 f; von Hein in *Rome Regulations* (n 64), Article 17 Rome II, para 21; Junker (n 56), Article 17 Rome II Regulation, para 18; Lehmann (n 64), Article 17 Rome II Regulation, para 1; Maultzsch (n 56), Article 17 Rome II Regulation, para 43 f; W Wurmnest in *Juris PraxisKommentar BGB*, vol 6, 1 March 2020, Article 7 Rome II Regulation, para 51.

[67] The view that Art 17 Rome II Regulation can be applied is held, eg, by von Hein, 'Die Behandlung von Sicherheits- und Verhaltensregeln nach Art 17 der Rom II-Verordnung' (n 64) 152; Lehmann (n 64), Article 17 Rome II Regulation, para 37a; P Mankowski, *Internationales Privatrecht*, vol II (CH Beck, 2020); Maultzsch (n 56), Article 17 Rome II Regulation, para 75. The opposite view is supported by LFH Enneking, 'Judicial Remedies: The Issue of Applicable Law' in JJA Rubio and K Yiannibas (eds), *Human Rights in Business* (Routledge, 2017) 59; A Halfmeier, 'Zur Rolle des Kollisionsrechts bei der

the Rome II Regulation – to the benefit and the disadvantage of the tortfeasor – would mean that the law of the place of injury, applicable by virtue of Article 4(1) of the Rome II Regulation, would *de facto* always be modified and superseded by the law of the place of action. This result, however, would contravene the European legislature's decision that the applicable law shall be the law of the place of injury – and not the law of the place of action.[68]

However, even if one disregards these concerns, the application of Article 17 of the Rome II Regulation comes with problems. And this is because it is unclear whether section 3 ff LkSG can be classified as rules of safety and conduct of the (relevant) place of action. Certainly, there can be little doubt that Germany, with regard to section 3 ff LkSG, is the place of action, as the obligations imposed by these provisions are to be fulfilled by companies at the place of their seat which will always be Germany.[69] However, with regard to Article 17 of the Rome II Regulation, this matters only if violation of the obligations established by section 3 ff LkSG can, in fact, be characterised as relevant action. Doubts that this can actually be done arise for two reasons.

To begin with, an act or omission can only be considered as an event giving rise to liability in the meaning of Article 17 of the Rome II Regulation and, hence, as relevant action, if there is a causal link between the act or omission and the damage suffered.[70] With regard to section 3 ff LkSG and the damage in question – that is, for example, the death of a person as a result of the collapse of a factory building at the end (or the beginning) of the supply chain – it is doubtful whether such a causal link exists because the obligations imposed under the Supply Chain Act are not conceived as obligations to achieve a specific aim, but as (mere) obligations to use reasonable efforts.[71] They are mere '*Bemühenspflichten*' (*obligations de moyen*) as opposed to '*Erfolgspflichten*' (*obligation de résultat*).

zivilrechtlichen Haftung für Menschenrechtsverletzungen' in M Krajewski, F Oehm and M Saage-Maaß (eds), *Zivil- und strafrechtliche Unternehmensverantwortung für Menschenrechtsverletzungen* (Springer, 2018) 42 f; Rühl, 'Unternehmensverantwortung und (Internationales) Privatrecht' (n 22) 103; Rühl, 'Towards a German Supply Chain Act?' (n 22) 61; Wagner, 'Haftung für Menschenrechtsverletzungen' (n 17) 742; A van Hoek, 'Transnational Corporate Social Responsibility' in F Pennings, Y Konijn and A Veldman (eds), *Social Responsibility in Labour Relations: European and Comparative Perspectives* (Wolters Kluwer, 2008) 166; C Wendelstein, '"Menschenrechtliche" Verhaltenspflichten im System des Internationalen Privatrechts' (2019) 1 *Rabels Zeitschrift für ausländisches und internationales Privatrecht* 111, 143 f.

[68] See Wagner, 'Haftung für Menschenrechtsverletzungen' (n 17) 742 f.

[69] Maultzsch (n 56), Article 17 Rome II Regulation, paras 45 and 45.1. See, however, von Hein in *Rome Regulations* (n 64), Article 7 Rome II Regulation, para 18, who advocates locating the place of action in the event of a violation of a supervisory duty regarding sources of danger at the location of the source of danger. In a similar vein with regard to the supervisory duty of parent companies regarding their subsidiaries, von Hein in *Rome Regulations* (n 64), Article 17 Rome II Regulation, para 21.

[70] See von Hein in *Rome Regulations* (n 64), Article 7 Rome II Regulation, para 18; Junker (n 56), Article 7 Rome II Regulation, para 22; Wurmnest (n 66), Article 7 Rome II Regulation, para 52.

[71] See Official Record of the German Parliament *(Bundestagsdrucksache)* 19/30505, 2 as well as Ehmann and Berg (n 1) 288; Leuering and Rubner (n 1) 399 f; Wagner, 'Das Lieferkettengesetz: Viele Pflichten, keine Haftung' (n 1) 700; Wagner and Ruttloff (n 1) 2145 f.

However, even if one assumes – or finds – that there is (some form of) a causal link between the violation of section 3 ff LkSG and the damage in question, this is not enough to trigger the application of Article 17 of the Rome II Regulation. In addition, the violation must also be a *relevant* cause.[72] In the case of cross-border environmental damage, where Article 7 of the Rome II Regulation allows victims to choose between the law of the place of injury and the law of the place of action, it is, therefore, disputed whether the relevant place of action can be located at the seat of the parent or buyer company. A number of voices in the literature assume this to be the case if relevant decisions are made at the seat or if the parent or buyer company violates environmental organisation, monitoring or control obligations that it has to fulfil at its seat.[73] Others, in contrast, argue that actions or omissions at the seat should always be excluded as irrelevant preparatory acts.[74] They claim that the place of action is only at the place where the actual cause of the environmental damage – for example, the emitting plant – is to be located.[75] Applied to human rights violations this view would argue that the relevant cause for the damage in question is where the final decisions that caused the human rights violations – such as the decision to not comply with local fire safety regulations – are made. It is, therefore, unclear whether a violation of the obligations imposed by section 3 ff LkSG can actually be considered as relevant action in the meaning of Article 17 of the Rome II Regulation. The final word rests, again, with the CJEU.

VI. Conclusion and Outlook

In light of the above, it is fair to conclude that the new German Supply Chain Act does not have much – or even anything – to offer in terms of private law.[76] While

[72] Junker (n 56), Article 7 Rome II Regulation, para 22. See also, P Huber in *BeckOnline GrossKommentar* (n 56), Article 7 Rome II Regulation, para 36 ff.

[73] S Demeyere, 'Liability of a Mother Company for its Subsidiary in French, Belgian, and English Law' (2015) 23 *European Review of Private Law* 385, 388 f; Enneking (n 67) 53; M Habersack and M Ehrl, 'Verantwortlichkeit inländischer Unternehmen für Menschenrechtsverletzungen durch ausländische Zulieferer – de lege lata und de lege ferenda' (2019) 219 *Archiv für die civilistische Praxis* 155, 188 f; Mansel (n 53) 462 f; CO Carcá-Castrillón, 'International Litigation Trends in Environmental Liability: A European Union–United States Comparative Perspective' (2011) 3 *Journal of Private International Law* 551, 571 f. In this vein, Rechtbank Den Haag in the earlier mentioned Shell judgment (n 43) (arguing that the relevant place of action was at the company's seat in the Netherlands). See, for a more detailed (and critical) discussion, G te Winkel and X van Heesch, 'The Shell judgment – a bombShell in private international law?' (2021) 3 *Nederlands internationaal privaatrecht* 532.

[74] von Hein in *Rome Regulations* (n 64), Article 7 Rome II Regulation, para 18; Halfmeier (n 67) 41; Huber (n 72), Article 7 Rome II Regulation, para 38; M Lehmann and F Eichel, 'Globaler Klimawandel und Internationales Privatrecht' (2019) 83 *Rabels Zeitschrift für ausländisches und internationales Privatrecht* 77, 96; Wagner, 'Haftung für Menschenrechtsverletzungen' (n 17) 744. According to von Hein in *Rome Regulations* (n 64), Article 7 Rome II Regulation, para 18, this also applies if the event giving rise to the damage constitutes a violation of a supervisory duty regarding a source of danger.

[75] In this vein, the English Court of Appeal in *Begum* (n 44) para 90 (arguing that a 'mere paper transaction' with no direct effect on the environment at all cannot amount to an event giving rise to damage).

[76] In a similar vein, Wagner, 'Das Lieferkettengesetz: Viele Pflichten, keine' (n 1) 710 f.

it is true that (a few) large companies based in Germany will soon have to fulfil a large number of due diligence obligations to protect human rights in their supply chains, the Act neither provides a basis for victims to sue for damages, nor can the newly created human rights due diligence obligations be considered as overriding mandatory provisions or as rules of safety and conduct in the meaning of Articles 16 or 17 of the Rome II Regulation. According to Article 4(1) of the Rome II Regulation liability for human rights violations will, therefore, continue to be governed (completely) by foreign law which is a disappointment for all those who would have preferred a stricter and more rigorous legal framework for the protection of human rights in the global supply chain.

However, 'the opera ain't over "til the fat lady sings"' – or so the saying goes. With regard to the protection of human rights, this means that the adoption of the German Supply Chain Act is not necessarily the end of the matter. In fact, further legislation is already being discussed, namely on the European level. The current reference point of this discussion is a Proposal for a Directive on Corporate Sustainability Due Diligence published by the European Commission in February 2022.[77] The Proposal follows a draft Directive adopted by the European Parliament in March 2021 as part of a legislative resolution[78] and contains far-reaching due diligence obligations as well as a provision on civil liability.[79] In addition, the draft makes clear that the liability provision shall be overriding mandatory provision in nature within the meaning of Article 16 of the Rome II Regulation.[80] Should the proposed Directive actually be adopted, the national provisions implementing the Directive will, thus, have to be applied by all courts located in a Member State of the European Union irrespective of the otherwise applicable (foreign) law. The next steps of the European legislative are, thus, eagerly awaited. This holds true all the more as actions of international companies can be more effectively and more purposefully regulated on an international level than on a national level.[81]

[77] 'Proposal for a Directive of the European Parliament and of the Council on Corporate Sustainability Due Diligence and amending Directive (EU) 2019/1937', COM(2022) 71 final.

[78] European Parliament resolution of 10 March 2021 with recommendations to the Commission on corporate due diligence and corporate accountability (2020/2129(INL)). See Kamann and Irrmscher (n 1) 255 ff; Krebs (n 18); J Schmidt, 'Unternehmensrecht: Supply chain due diligence – EP-Entwurf' (2021) 11 *Neue Zeitschrift für Gesellschaftsrecht* 435.

[79] See Art 22(1) of the Proposal (n 77).

[80] See Art 22(5) of the Proposal (n 77).

[81] Rühl, 'Unternehmensverantwortung und (Internationales) Privatrecht' (n 22) 125 f; Rühl, 'Die Haftung von Unternehmen für Menschenrechtsverletzungen' (n 10) 1432 ff; Rühl, 'Towards a German Supply Chain Act?' (n 22) 74 ff. In the same vein, Krebs (n 18) 396; Wagner, 'Haftung für Menschenrechtsverletzungen' (n 17) 781; Schmidt, 'Unternehmensrecht: Supply chain due diligence – EP-Entwurf' (n 78); Schmidt, 'Lieferkettengesetzgebung: Sorgfalt!' (n 22) 274.

11

International Commercial Arbitration: Law Applicable to Merits and 'Creeping' Judicial Substantive Review

PATRICIA ŽIVKOVIĆ*

I. Introduction

The landscape for the choice of substantive law in international commercial arbitration differs from the framework designed for national courts in international litigation. This distinction is often not sufficiently acknowledged, both in university curricula and in dispute resolution practice. It is a gap that the late Professor Jonathan Fitchen and I often discussed and were ready to cover in our complementary teaching. For that reason, I considered it appropriate to write on this topic in his memory and to provide a contribution to some of the pending issues in this area.

The foundations for the discussion are described in section II, where the technical distinctions between the choice of substantive law in international commercial arbitration and the choice of substantive law in national courts are explained. Section III will deal with the phenomenon of 'creeping' substantive review in international commercial arbitration. One of the most commonly mentioned advantages of arbitration over litigation is the absence of appeals, but there will be no attempt to discuss the truth of this oft-cited statement. Instead, the focus will be on the developments in national courts' practice that constitute 'creeping' substantive review, ie, the international practices that allow a limited review of merits in arbitral awards. These practices can be classified in the following manner:

* I would like to thank my research assistants Ms Konstantina Kalaitsoglou and Mr Raiyan Chowdhury, whose help with this chapter was invaluable, and the Centre for Private International Law, which granted funding for their professional assistance. Finally, I am grateful to my friends and colleagues Dr Alisdair MacPherson and Dr Euan West for reading an earlier draft of this chapter.

A. (Broad) interpretation of public policy by national courts under the law of the seat and the law of the place of enforcement to cover substantive public policy, in particular overriding mandatory rules, *or* taking a 'second look' when it comes to the arbitrators' application of law in matters of *domestic* public interest; and
B. Review of the choice of law and/or application of the law by national courts based on the parties' argument to the effect of having been 'taken by surprise' by the arbitrator's determination of the applicable law and/or its application to the case.

It is important to note that the practices examined in this chapter belong to jurisdictions that do not provide for an appeal in international arbitration. Unlike some jurisdictions in which the applicable arbitration laws allow an appeal of an arbitration award on points of law (although only in a limited number of cases), the jurisdictions addressed in this chapter (except for England and Wales) lack such provisions for international arbitral awards. They accept the general principle in international arbitration under which no substantive review of arbitrators' decisions is to be conducted by national courts.

To see how these practices developed and to understand the full complexity of the issues they involve, we need first to look at the process of the determination of the law applicable to merits and the principles behind its application by arbitral tribunals. We must also look at the associated intricacies of such decision-making processes stemming from the differing legal nature of arbitral tribunals and national courts.

II. The Determination and Application of the Law Applicable to Merits in International Commercial Arbitration

The determination of the law applicable to merits and its application by arbitral tribunals, as well as the legal issues related to it, are tightly connected to the source of arbitrators' decision-making power as perceived through the lenses of delocalised arbitration theory:[1] namely, as will be discussed below, arbitrators are more detached from private international laws of the seat than national courts and they rely heavily on procedural rules chosen by the parties and/or their discretion in the process of the determination of the law (section II.A). Due to the delocalisation of arbitral tribunals in that respect from the seat and other jurisdictions, and the lack of substantive review as a principle in international arbitration, the intricacies of reintroducing such a review by national courts are particularly interesting when it

[1] E Gaillard, *Legal Theory of International Arbitration* (Brill, 2012).

comes to the application of overriding mandatory rules and the legal principle *iura novit arbiter* (section II.B).

A. Determination of the Law Applicable to Merits in International Commercial Arbitration

International commercial arbitration does not exist in a legal vacuum. However, it functions in a different legal environment from that of national courts. Unlike national courts, arbitral tribunals do not have a forum, ie, jurisdiction. This means that they are not automatically subject (at least not to the full extent) to the legal system of the jurisdiction in which the arbitration is seated. The procedural law governing arbitration proceedings stems from the law of the seat (unless chosen by the parties); however, the work of arbitrators and their procedural decisions can be (and sometimes it is highly desirable for them to be) framed with the law of the potential place of enforcement in mind. On top of this legal baseline, the procedure is governed by the procedural rules chosen by the parties or, in the absence of such a choice, is determined by the arbitral tribunal. These rules can be provided by an arbitration institution; drafted by the parties; or determined by arbitrators.

Beyond the legal-procedural setting, a myriad of legal issues of a procedural and a substantive nature might arise in international commercial arbitration, for which the tribunal will need to determine the applicable law. However, unlike national courts, arbitral tribunals will not have a coherent set of private international law provisions to consult before making their decisions. A different law may govern each issue, thus creating a 'concoction' of potentially relevant laws:

- The law governing the arbitration agreement.
- The law, or the relevant legal rules, governing merits, ie, the substantive issues in dispute.
- The law governing recognition and enforcement of the award.
- The law governing the effects of bankruptcy of one of the parties to ongoing arbitration.
- The law governing the allocation of costs in arbitration, etc.

When it comes to the determination of the law applicable to merits in arbitration, two aspects need to be observed:

1. who determines the applicable law, and
2. the potential range of the rules that might be determined applicable.

Concerning who determines the applicable law, party autonomy is recognised as the cornerstone of this matter in international arbitral practice, ie, the parties' choice of the law applicable to the merits is the primary source for determining the governing law of the dispute.[2] In the absence of such a choice, the usual practice recognised in laws and rules is that the arbitral tribunal will determine the governing law.[3]

When it comes to the arbitrators' determination, this is where the first main difference between national courts' and arbitral tribunals' stances regarding private international law is visible and it stems from the tribunals' lack of a forum. Since arbitral tribunals are not embedded fully in the legal system of any jurisdiction, private international laws of the country of the seat are not directly applicable in international arbitration taking place within the relevant jurisdiction.[4] Hence, when determining the governing law, arbitral tribunals are to follow the guidance provided by the applicable arbitration rules or the arbitration law of the seat, in the absence of the former. The methods for determination of the governing law can have a looser or tighter connection to private international law, as designed for application by national courts. These methods can roughly be systematised as follows:

1. An arbitral tribunal determines the governing law by the private international law rules which it considers applicable.[5]
2. An arbitral tribunal determines the governing law without any reference to private international law rules, but instead it *directly* determines the applicable law that it deems appropriate.[6]

In other words, the relevant arbitration rules or arbitration laws will determine to what extent arbitrators are bound to justify their decisions on the governing law, but even in cases where the rules or the law require them to refer to private international law, they do not usually specify a jurisdiction. This is a natural consequence of the lack of a forum for arbitrators as decision-makers.

The first of the above-mentioned methods is, to an extent, a reflection of the localised theory of arbitration and will usually find its place in national arbitration

[2] s 46(1) of the English Arbitration Act 1996; Art 1511 of the French Arbitration Act 2011; Art 28(1) of the UNCITRAL Model Law on International Commercial Arbitration (UN, 2008), available at: uncitral.un.org/sites/uncitral.un.org/files/media-documents/uncitral/en/19-09955_e_ebook.pdf; Art 21(1) of the 2021 International Chamber of Commerce (ICC) Rules (ICC, 2021), available at: iccwbo.org/dispute-resolution-services/arbitration/rules-of-arbitration/; Art 22.3 of the 2020 London Court of International Arbitration (LCIA) Rules (LCIA, 2020), available at: www.lcia.org/Dispute_Resolution_Services/lcia-arbitration-rules-2020.aspx; Art 35(1) of the UNCITRAL Arbitration Rules (UN, 2021), available at: uncitral.un.org/sites/uncitral.un.org/files/media-documents/uncitral/en/21-07996_expedited-arbitration-e-ebook.pdf.

[3] s 46(3) of the English Arbitration Act 1996; Art 1511 of the French Arbitration Act 2011; Art 28(2) of the UNCITRAL Model Law; Art 21(1) of the 2021 ICC Rules; Art 22.3 of the 2020 LCIA Rules; Art 35(1) of the UNCITRAL Arbitration Rules.

[4] M Petsche, 'The Application of Mandatory Rules by Arbitral Tribunals – Three Salient Issues' (2020) 1 *ELTE Law Journal* 69, 72.

[5] s 46(3) of the English Arbitration Act 1996; Art 1511 of the French Arbitration Act 2011; Art 28(2) of the UNCITRAL Model Law.

[6] Art 1511 of the French Arbitration Act 2011; Art 21(1) of the 2021 ICC Rules; Art 22.3 of the 2020 LCIA Rules; Art 35(1) of the UNCITRAL Arbitration Rules.

laws, rather than in institutional arbitration rules, given that national legislators are more interested in anchoring arbitral tribunals to the jurisdiction than are independent arbitral institutions. This theory echoes the stance that the legitimacy of the arbitration process stems from the seat, as it is the national courts that have the ultimate power to decide whether an arbitral award is or is not to be set aside.[7] As a counterweight to this theory stands the transnational theory or the theory of arbitral order, which claims that 'the juridicity of arbitration is rooted in a distinct, transnational order … and not in a national legal system'.[8] This is a more acceptable approach for independent arbitral institutions, which in principle allow arbitral tribunals to determine the governing law without indicating any specific private international law rule, but by simply finding such a law 'appropriate' in the circumstances.

Further scope for deviation from usual practice in determining the governing law in court proceedings is available to arbitrators thanks to the range of laws and legal rules that can be chosen as applicable law. In that sense, the parties to arbitration in principle enjoy a broader expression of party autonomy than in court proceedings when it comes to exercising their right to choose the governing law. It can be said that such a choice includes for the party in arbitration the following options:

1. State (national) law.
2. Combination of state (national) laws, ie, *dépecage*.
3. Non-state laws or rules or guidelines, including transnational law/*lex mercatoria*.
4. Equity and good conscience.[9]

Whereas the first two options are available before national courts, the last two are thus far available only in arbitration.[10] The availability of a choice of non-state law for both the parties and the arbitral tribunal will again depend on the provisions of applicable arbitration rules or arbitration laws, and it is determined by the use of different terminology. The expression 'rules of law' includes non-state legal rules such as *lex mercatoria*, general principles, trade usages, and transnational public policy.[11] The notion 'law', on the other hand, encompasses only state-issued legal rules. For example, the UNCITRAL Model Law on International Commercial Arbitration makes a clear difference between the scope of potentially governing laws at the disposal of the parties and arbitral tribunals. Whereas the parties may choose '*rules of law* … applicable to the substance of the dispute' (emphasis added), the tribunals can decide only to apply 'the law'.[12] The same approach is

[7] Gaillard (n 1) 15–24.
[8] ibid, 35.
[9] See, eg, ch 3 in D Bentolila, *Arbitrators as Lawmakers* (Kluwer Law International, 2017).
[10] ibid, 111, 123.
[11] ibid, 137.
[12] Art 28(1) and 28(2) of the UNCITRAL Model Law.

adopted by the UNCITRAL Arbitration Rules, while the 2021 ICC Rules allow both the parties *and* the arbitral tribunals to choose the non-state law options.[13] As with the 2021 ICC Rules, the 2020 LCIA Rules and the French Arbitration Act reserve the same range of applicable rules for both the parties and the arbitrators.[14] The most restrictive approach is contained, for example, in the English Arbitration Act 1996 which narrows the choice to only a state-issued law for both the parties and the arbitrators.[15] Finally, there is an option for arbitral tribunals to decide the dispute *ex aequo et bono* (in accordance with equity and good conscience) or as amiable compositeur, and this option can only be exercised with the parties' express authorisation.[16]

This short overview of the methods and scope of the determination of the governing law by the parties and arbitrators in arbitration lays down the fundamentals for understanding the main intricacies regarding the application of the law applicable to merits by arbitral tribunals. The lack of a forum (which encompasses the lack of concrete private international law rules), the broader range of potentially governing laws (which include non-state law options), and also the possibility of rendering a decision based on equity not only give arbitration users more flexibility and control over the decision-making procedure, but cause certain intricacies that have not arisen before national courts. These are discussed in the next section.

B. The Intricacies of the Application of the Governing Law by an Arbitral Tribunal

It is generally accepted, as one of the most important principles in international commercial arbitration, that arbitral awards are not subject to an appeal on a point of law. The judicial review of international arbitral awards is limited under most national laws and the Convention on Recognition and Enforcement of Foreign Arbitral Awards (New York Convention) to procedural issues, and it excludes *de novo* review by a national court. Furthermore, as shown above, there is no need for any connection between the governing law and the underlying dispute in international arbitration, unlike the traditional approach in domestic courts. Moreover, when choosing the applicable law, arbitral tribunals are not bound by private international law rules and can apply non-state law under certain circumstances.

This raises, however, several issues, two of which are discussed below. One of them is the application of overriding mandatory rules in arbitration, which are

[13] Art 35(1) of the UNCITRAL Arbitration Rules; Art 21(1) of the 2021 ICC Rules.

[14] Art 22.3 of the 2020 LCIA Rules; Art 1511 of the French Arbitration Act 2011.

[15] s 46(1) and 46(3) of the English Arbitration Act 1996.

[16] Art 28(3) of the UNCITRAL Model Law; Art 1512 of the French Arbitration Act 2011; Art 21(3) of the 2021 ICC Rules; Art 22.4 of the 2020 LCIA Rules; Art 35(2) of the UNCITRAL Arbitration Rules.

an inherent part of private international law and applicable as a matter of comity by national courts.[17] There is, however, no such duty of comity for international arbitrators.[18] However, by not applying the mandatory rules they might jeopardise the enforceability of their arbitral award, so a proper understanding of the issue is needed.

The second issue involves the parties' expectations for the arbitrators to know the governing law and the extent to which the transmission of the principle *iura novit curia* is possible in arbitration based on the arbitrators' decision-making role. It is quite reasonable for the parties to rely on the judge's knowledge of the applicable law; however, in international arbitration, where there is no appeal, and the principle of party autonomy leads to broadened conceptions of applicable laws, it becomes a question of whether there is any way for the parties to challenge the application of a certain rule of law or law. The practice has shown that there is, and such an argument can be formulated in procedural terms as an expression of a party's right to be heard, as shall be shown in this section.

These two issues will be further discussed in turn.

i. *Overriding Mandatory Rules in International Arbitration*

Overriding mandatory rules are the rules passed to protect the public interest of a state.[19] To give a few examples, these rules usually deal with legal situations concerning consumer protection, currency control, environmental protection, trade sanctions, competition law matters, and similar issues involving strong public interests.[20] The most oft-cited definition of overriding mandatory rules (at least for European countries) is the one contained in Article 9 of the Rome I Regulation:

> Overriding mandatory provisions are provisions the respect for which is regarded as crucial by a country for safeguarding its public interests, such as its political, social or economic organisation, to such an extent that they are applicable to any situation falling within their scope, irrespective of the law otherwise applicable to the contract under this Regulation.[21]

When the dispute is resolved by national courts, these norms, at least in principle, are meant to replace a substantive law that is applicable and override party autonomy or the law determined by the forum court in that matter.[22] The national courts' perspective on the application of these rules in arbitration will be addressed in section III, which will discuss the broad interpretation of public policy as these

[17] Petsche (n 4) 81.

[18] ibid.

[19] H Fazilatfar, *Overriding Mandatory Rules in International Commercial Arbitration* (Edward Elgar Publishing, 2019) 1.

[20] Petsche (n 4) 70; Fazilatfar (n 19) 1.

[21] Regulation (EC) No 593/2008 of the European Parliament and of the Council of 17 June 2008 on the law applicable to contractual obligations, [2008] OJ L177/6 (Rome I).

[22] Fazilatfar (n 19) 1.

rules can often be seen as a reflection of the substantive public policy of a state. In this section, the arbitral tribunals' perspective will be summarised.

At the moment, there is no uniform stance in international arbitration as to whether overriding mandatory rules are to be taken into account by arbitrators. The approaches often differ depending on whether the overriding mandatory rules belong to the legal system of the law applicable to the merits (*lex causae*), or to the legal system of a third country, including the law of the seat (*lex loci arbitri*), and the law of potential enforcement (ie, the law foreign to *lex causae*).[23] However, what is interesting is that the practice seems to be equally divided on the applicability of either of these sets of rules. Namely, arbitral tribunals have concluded both in favour of the application of such mandatory norms in arbitration when they form part of *lex causae*, but also against it.[24] When the overriding mandatory norms form part of the law of a third country, the results are again the same – arbitral tribunals have decided both in favour of and against such an observation of *foreign* overriding mandatory rules.[25]

It can be concluded then that the observation and application of overriding mandatory rules by international arbitrators are still very much decided on a case-by-case basis, and that they have the discretion to choose whether to apply them or not. Unlike national courts, international arbitrators are not bound by legislation providing for the application of overriding mandatory norms and the principle of comity. Hence, international arbitrators have the freedom to design and express their legal thinking on the matter. As an example, one arbitral tribunal noted the following:

> In the case of the mandatory law of a particular state, the thrust of the conditions for its extraterritorial application is that such state must have a strong and legitimate interest to justify the application of such a law in international arbitration. Furthermore, if the respective law contains both public and civil (private) law rules, and if the extraterritorial application of only the latter rules is at stake, it must be shown that such state has a strong and legitimate interest in justifying the application of these civil (private) law rules in international arbitration.[26]

Whether an arbitral tribunal will find such a strong and legitimate interest to apply a mandatory rule either of *lex causae* or of a third country, is entirely up to them. This is not to say that there are no discernible factors that any party involved in international arbitration may find important in arbitrators' decision-making on

[23] Similarly in ibid, 72.

[24] See more in Petsche (n 4); IMN Shehata, 'Application of Overriding Mandatory Rules in International Commercial Arbitration: An Empirical Analysis' (2017) 11 *World Arbitration and Mediation Review* 36.

[25] See more in Petsche (n 4); Shehata (n 24).

[26] ICC Case No 6320 (1992) *XX Yearbook Commercial Arbitration* 1995, 62.

this issue. For example, when discussing the interrelation between party autonomy and mandatory rules, one arbitral tribunal noted as follows:

> In assessing the facts and circumstances and the relative merits of party autonomy versus mandatory, unwaivable law, the determination of what constitutes unwaivable public policy and morals is paramount. On the one hand, there clearly is a type of public policy that overrides contrary party autonomy. If choice of law is made for a fraudulent purpose such as to avoid tax or currency regulations or application of competition laws where there is a clear and unmistakable national or international purpose, such a public policy is doubtless unwaivable. In such a case an arbitral award which contravenes such a clearly mandatory national policy is unlikely to be enforceable under the New York Convention.[27]

It can be seen then that international arbitrators are aware they are not operating in a legal vacuum, and they need to consult the legal systems that may threaten the legitimacy of their award. This is the law of the potential place of enforcement in the example above. The expansion of the interpretation of public policy in a way such as to encompass *substantive* public policy, as will be shown below, might nudge arbitral tribunals into the application of such mandatory rules to avoid rendering an award unenforceable, and also to prevent the annulment of their award at the seat, as will be addressed in section III.

ii. Iura Novit Arbiter

Another complexity connected to the application of the governing law by arbitral tribunals is the extent to which the arbitrators are bound by the parties' choice of governing law. While the parties' agreement remains a cornerstone of arbitration, the role of the arbitrators is not one-dimensional. The nature of their role is adjudicatory as they are, simply put, private judges. One of the main legal maxims under which the national judges decide is '*iura novit curia*' (the judge knows the law). This legal maxim, when roughly translated into arbitration language as '*iura novit arbiter*', gives arbitrators the power to apply the law even when the law has not been referred to by the parties. Due to the theoretical origins of the principle *iura novit curia*, which stem mainly from civil law countries, and the lack of a forum for international arbitrators, commentators are sceptical regarding its observation in international arbitration.[28]

At the same time, one will easily conclude that it is inherent in the arbitrators' mandate to know the law and to ensure that the choice of law provisions are duly

[27] *AdvanSix Inc v Brasilfert Comercio e Representacao, LTDA* (Final Award) [2017] Arbitrator Intelligence Materials.

[28] J Jemielniak and S Pfisterer, 'Iura Novit Arbiter Revisited: Towards a Harmonized Approach?' (2015) 20 *Uniform Law Review* 56, 67.

recognised and enforced in arbitration. For example, the German Arbitration Law 1998 provides in section 1051(1) that '[t]he arbitral tribunal shall decide the dispute *in accordance with such rules of law as are chosen by the parties as applicable* to the substance of the dispute' (emphasis added).[29] The question is how much discretion in the application of the chosen rules of law arbitrators can exercise under such provisions in light of the principle '*iura novit arbiter*'. This is especially important to consider given that when a national court makes an error in law, the parties have relief against such a decision through an appeal before the higher courts. In most jurisdictions, arbitral awards are final and binding decisions, against which the appeal is not allowed, and they are subject to *limited* review in proceedings for setting aside or enforcement proceedings. More importantly, the review of merits, including an error in law, is not allowed in either of these proceedings.

National courts have confirmed that the application of the substantive law beyond the submissions made by the parties does not directly open the door to any of the remedies within the arbitration realm. At the same time, in extreme circumstances, manifest disregard of the rules of law can be a legitimate ground for each of the parties either to challenge an arbitrator during the proceedings, or to challenge an award once the proceedings are finalised, as will be discussed in the next section.

III. 'Creeping' Substantive Review in International Commercial Arbitration

Based on the intricacies regarding the application of the governing law by arbitral tribunals explained in section II, the principle of the *limited* judicial review of international arbitral awards is not always duly followed. In fact, quite the opposite is the case, as two established court practices have accepted a contrary approach in this matter by allowing a substantive review of international arbitral awards in specific circumstances:

A. (Broad) interpretation of public policy by national courts under the law of the seat and the law of the place of enforcement to cover substantive public policy, in particular overriding mandatory rules, *or* taking a 'second look' when it comes to the arbitrators' application of law in matters of *domestic* public interest; and
B. Review of the choice of law and/or application of the law by national courts based on the parties' argument to the effect of having been 'taken by surprise' by the arbitrator's determination of the applicable law and/or its application to the case.

These two practices will now be addressed in turn in this part of the chapter.

[29] L Bosman (ed), 'German Arbitration Act 1998 (Book 10 ZPO)' Supplement No 98 *ICCA International Handbook on Commercial Arbitration.*

A. The Substantive Review of Arbitral Awards under the Broad Interpretation of Public Policy

The *Mitsubishi v Soler* case from 1985 signalled a change in policy in terms of arbitrability of antitrust (competition law) matters in the international context, but also in the application of overriding mandatory rules by international arbitrators.[30] The US Supreme Court decided that the mere appearance of antitrust disputes does not touch upon the validity of the selected forum (in this case, arbitration) and gave the green light to the arbitrators to decide on such matters. Moreover, the Supreme Court in this case also left a legal loophole that was thoroughly discussed in the next few decades – and that loophole is called the 'second look' doctrine. The 'second look' doctrine stands for the national courts' opportunity to check the arbitrator's application of the law involving public interest at a later stage, or in the words of the Supreme Court:

> Having permitted the arbitration to go forward, the national courts of the United States will have the opportunity at the award-enforcement stage to ensure that the legitimate interest in the enforcement of the antitrust laws has been addressed. The Convention reserves to each signatory country the right to refuse enforcement of an award where the 'recognition or enforcement of the award would be contrary to the public policy of that country' ... While the efficacy of the arbitral process requires that substantive review at the award-enforcement stage remain minimal, it would not require intrusive inquiry to ascertain that the tribunal took cognizance of the antitrust claims and actually decided them.[31]

The scope of the 'second look' by national courts is still debated by commentators,[32] but the policy change was clear – with the confirmed stance on promoting the enforceability of international arbitral awards dealing with certain substantive issues, the Supreme Court also indicated that the courts could supervise such an application at the enforcement stage via the notion of public policy.

Such a notion of public policy that includes the possibility to look at the substantive issues decided by an arbitral tribunal goes beyond the initial procedural nature of public policy and is called 'substantive public policy'. Overriding mandatory rules, as the norms that are introduced specifically to protect a state's public interests, reflect public policy.[33] Whether they will be encompassed by the definition of substantive public policy under arbitration-related laws is another matter that will be discussed here.

[30] *Mitsubishi Motors Corp v Soler Chrysler-Plymouth, Inc*, 105 S Ct 3346 (1985); Bentolila (n 9) 120.

[31] *Mitsubishi Motors Corp* (n 29).

[32] G Born, *International Commercial Arbitration*, 2nd edn (Kluwer Law International, 2014) 981.

[33] The relationship between overriding mandatory norms and public policy is a significant issue comprehensive discussion of which is not possible in the space of a single chapter. For those who are interested in learning more about the historical development of mandatory rules and their differences from and similarities to public policy, see Fazilatfar (n 19) 26–29.

The relationship between overriding mandatory rules and substantive public policy is, *inter alia*, determined by the different stages at which the arguments in that regard may be raised. The application of overriding mandatory rules is invoked during the arbitral proceedings, either by the parties or *ex officio* by arbitral tribunals, whereas substantive public policy is considered at the stage of enforcement or setting aside of the arbitral award. Since substantive public policy can be invoked only at a later stage, it is necessary to look at the limitations of its territorial/jurisdictional application: national laws (based on the UNCITRAL Model Law) and the New York Convention invite national courts of the seat or the place of enforcement respectively to assess whether the arbitral award was against the public policy 'of that country'.[34] In practical terms, this means that the decisions regarding the application (or non-application) of a specific overriding mandatory rule or application of substantive law in general by an arbitral tribunal will be observed within the substantive public policy of the *country of the seat* or *place of enforcement*. This is an important consideration for arbitral tribunals at the stage of the application of overriding mandatory rules and the law applicable to merits in general. This also opens a discussion regarding domestically and internationally applicable public policy, and their influence on overriding mandatory rules.

Authors and arbitral tribunals generally tend to agree that internationally (or transnationally) applicable overriding mandatory rules, ie the rules that do not protect *purely* domestic public interests of the state in question, are to be applied in international arbitration by arbitral tribunals or at least considered by arbitrators.[35] On the other hand, the rules that are designed to protect *only* the domestic public interests of a state are less likely to be observed in international arbitration. National courts that are deciding on the challenges against arbitral awards will observe the public policy of their state. There is a stance that such public policy needs to be internationally recognised public policy, although some jurisdictions still support the view that domestic public policy should be equally applicable and protected.

The wide definition of public policy under national laws and the New York Convention which includes not only *internationally* recognised substantive public policy but also *domestic* public policy, may be a limitation on the validity and enforceability of an arbitral award not only when it comes to the application of overriding mandatory rules: it may also provide a hidden legal obstacle for the parties when it comes to the application of domestic mandatory rules by arbitral tribunals.

One of the jurisdictions that adopts the narrow notion of public policy when reviewing international arbitration awards is France, which defines it as a set of

[34] Art 34(2)(b)(ii) of the UNCITRAL Model Law; Art V(2)(b) of the Convention on the Recognition and Enforcement of Foreign Arbitral Awards (adopted 10 June 1958, entered into force 7 June 1959) 330 UNTS 3 (New York Convention).

[35] For more discussion on this, see Petsche (n 4) 87.

fundamental rules and principles that are to be respected even in international matters.[36] Some other jurisdictions that adopt the narrow notion of public policy, and favour limiting it solely to internationally recognised fundamental principles, with some acknowledged nuances when it comes to the proceedings for annulment and international enforcement, are Germany and Switzerland.[37] By extension, this applies to substantive public policy as well, which in these jurisdictions includes, inter alia, fundamental principles such as the principle of good faith, the principle *pacta sunt servanda*, the prohibition of abuse of right, and the principle that contracts with an illegal purpose are unenforceable.[38] The popularity of such narrower concepts of public policy has also prompted the naming of this approach as 'pro-arbitration bias'.[39]

On the other side of the spectrum lie jurisdictions that have shown a tendency to apply the broader notion of public policy, which encompasses not only *substantive* matters under public policy but also values of *domestically* recognised public interest. One of those jurisdictions is Poland, where national courts are criticised for expanding the ground of public policy too broadly.[40] National courts in Poland, when deciding on the annulment or enforcement of arbitral awards, have gone beyond all three narrow dimensions of reviewing the awards, as shown below in Figure 1. They have reviewed the substantive issues; observed the principles of domestic public interests; and have gone so far as to review the factual findings and proper application of law in some instances.[41]

Figure 1 Three dimensions of potential expansion of the public policy ground for challenging international arbitral awards

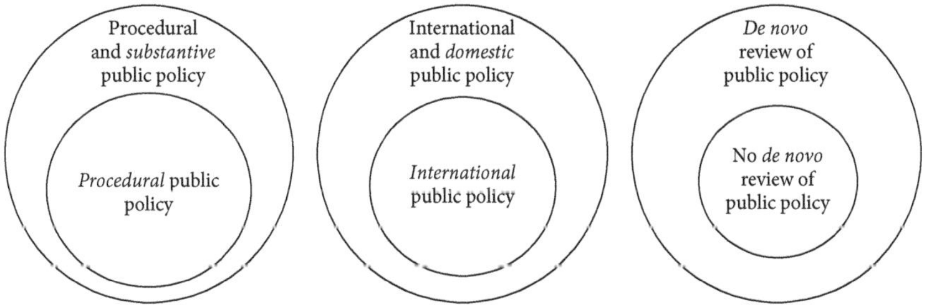

Hence, it is important to note the complexity that the expansion of the public policy ground for challenging arbitral awards brings to the table. The matter is

[36] J Koepp and A Ason, 'An Anti-Enforcement Bias? The Application of the Substantive Public Policy Exception in Polish Annulment Proceedings' (2018) 35 *Journal of International Arbitration* 157, 162.
[37] ibid, 162–63.
[38] ibid, 162, 163.
[39] ibid, 161.
[40] ibid, 168–69.
[41] ibid.

firstly decided by international arbitrators who apply the substantive law. They will be given a task to apply (and sometimes to choose) the law applicable to the merits; research the potentially applicable overriding mandatory rules; and question their nature and coverage by the public policy challenge and parties' expectations. To do that successfully, international arbitrators should be aware of the law of the seat and the law of potential places of enforcement and the relevant court practice in all three dimensions of potential expansion of public policy as shown above.

Another court practice that has served as a ground for 'creeping' substantive review touches upon parties' expectations as well and allows the parties to challenge an arbitral award based on an argument that they were taken by surprise, even when no public substantive public policy violation can be found. This practice is explained in the next section.

B. Substantive Review of Arbitral Awards Based on a Party's Argument of having been 'Taken by Surprise'

'Manifest disregard of the law' as a separate ground for a challenge of an award is still a topic of discussion – both in jurisprudence and in the doctrine.[42] The main controversy that surrounds it is its infringement of the finality of an award, and the inherent ambiguity which opens the possibility for the national courts to review the merits of a case.[43] However, this chapter focuses on jurisdictions which do not provide for such an explicit ground in their legislation. In these jurisdictions, the jurisprudence has so far crystallised a possibility that the manifest disregard of the law presents a violation of a right to be heard, or to put it more broadly, a violation of due process. The national courts' decisions are not, however, uniform in their approaches.

For example, the Swiss Federal Supreme Court confirmed its approach that a right to be heard in a case of manifest disregard of the law should be interpreted restrictively.[44] Prominent commentators in this jurisdiction state that:

> This stems from the principle of *jura novit curia* ('the court knows the law'), according to which an arbitral tribunal seated in Switzerland can determine the legal provisions (even under foreign law) applicable to the dispute and can thus rely on other legal provisions than those submitted by the parties. This has important practical implications as a party cannot, in the course of the proceedings, rely on the right to be heard to comment on new legal theories introduced by one party as it could do with regard to new facts.[45]

[42] FT Schwarz and H Ortner, 'The Arbitration Procedure – Procedural Ordre Public and the Internationalization of Public Policy in Arbitration' 2008 *Austrian Arbitration Yearbook* 133, 204.

[43] ibid.

[44] E Leimbacher and G von Segesser, 'BGer 4A_554/2014, Federal Supreme Court of Switzerland, 1st Civil Law Chamber, 15 April 2015' A contribution by the ITA Board of Reports.

[45] Georg von Segesser and Katherine Bell, 'Arbitration in Switzerland: Non-Swiss Parties Should Be Aware of the Arbitrator's Powers under the Swiss Principle of Jura Novit Curia' (*Kluwer Arbitration Blog*, 15 September 2015), available at: arbitrationblog.kluwerarbitration.com/2015/09/15/

However, the Court left the option for the parties to make an argument, but only if they proved that they were 'taken by surprise', or that the so-called element of 'unpredictability' was present.[46] In other words, the parties should not be surprised by an arbitrator or a tribunal which based its decision on a legal rule that they could not have anticipated. The Court found no such 'surprise' in this case.

In 2009, the Swiss Federal Supreme Court also held that the tribunal should have at least invited the parties to present their arguments under this 'unexpected' law and regarding its *applicability*.[47] The latter raises an interesting question: why should the parties be invited to comment on the applicability of the law? Is this not a decision inherent in the mandate of a tribunal? If not, is such a procedural error to be considered severe enough to lead to a violation of due process? Perhaps the answer lies somewhere in the distinction between the legal systems which treat the *foreign* law as a fact, subject to the argumentation of the parties, and those which treat it as a law, and put it entirely in the hands of a decision-maker.

The latter approach was adopted by the Finnish Supreme Court which concluded that by awarding damages based on a legal doctrine that neither party invoked nor had an opportunity to comment on, the arbitral tribunal did not exceed its authority or fail to provide the parties with a sufficient opportunity to present their cases.[48] On the other hand, the Svea Court of Appeal would allow the parties to instruct the tribunal on which law to apply, and if the tribunal disregarded such joint instructions, this would constitute a procedural error based on which the parties may challenge an award.[49] Therefore, one can see that even civil law countries do not have the same approach to this issue and that its resolution will depend largely on the jurisdiction in which the award is challenged or in which the recognition and enforcement are sought. Commentators also agree that a complete switch to a law-as-a-fact approach, as customarily used in common law jurisdictions, would not be the best way forward in these matters, and that the answer lies somewhere in between.[50]

The situation calls for the attention of legislators who might want to address this issue in the next round of reforms of their arbitration laws. Until then, there are several options available which might provide better solutions than the non-uniform system of setting aside or non-enforcement of awards.

The first solution is provided in some arbitration rules via the procedure of the *revocation and challenge* of arbitrators who manifestly disregard the rules of

arbitration-in-switzerland-non-swiss-parties-should-be-aware-of-the-arbitrators-powers-under-the-swiss-principle-of-jura-novit-curia.

[46] ibid.

[47] Laurent Lévy, 'Jura Novit Curia? The Arbitrator's Discretion in the Application of the Governing Law' (*Kluwer Arbitration Blog*, 20 March 2009), available at: arbitrationblog.kluwerarbitration.com/2009/03/20/jura-novit-curia-the-arbitrators-discretion-in-the-application-of-the-governing-law/.

[48] T Meinander and J Waselius, 'Werfen Austria GmbH v Polar Electro Europe BV, Zug Branch, Supreme Court, 2008:77, 2 July 2008' A contribution by the ITA Board of Reports.

[49] *MHH AS v Axel's Konsult och Förvaltning AB* [2014] T 2610-13.

[50] Jemielniak and Pfisterer (n 28) 67.

law chosen by the parties. An example of institutional rules under which such a challenge would be possible is the 2020 LCIA Rules which provide in Article 10.2 that '[t]he LCIA Court may determine that an arbitrator is unfit to act … if that arbitrator … acts in deliberate violation of the Arbitration Agreement'. Even if the arbitration rules which are applicable in a particular case do not provide for such an explicit ground for a challenge in this regard, such a ground should be presumed. The manifest disregard of the rules of law chosen by the parties would be a violation of the parties' agreement, but it remains to be seen what extent of this disregard needs to be in order not to be considered to fall within the scope of the arbitrator's mandate. Also, the manifest disregard of the rules of law chosen by the parties might not be known to the parties until the award is rendered. Therefore, the jurisprudence on the setting aside or enforcement of awards in which arbitrators disregarded the rules of law chosen by the parties can be a useful lesson.

The second solution is the remitting of the award. Instead of setting aside the award, national courts should have the option to remit such an award to the tribunal for reconsideration. This would reduce the efforts and funds invested in arbitration proceedings. For example, the remitting of the award is available under section 68(3)(a) of the English Arbitration Act 1996. In the same way, the national courts which decide on the enforcement of such an award should consider partial enforcement. They should explore whether there are parts of an award that are not influenced by the relevant procedural error and preserve the parts of the award which are enforceable.

Finally, the parties who wish to avoid these situations should not consent to *limited* judicial review of an award. They can either choose a seat of arbitration in the jurisdiction which provides for an appeal on arbitral awards, or they can opt for the appellate rules of one of the institutions that provide them.

These options, however, do not resolve the dilemma for national courts which are eventually confronted with a party's argument that they were surprised by arbitrators' application of the law, but can prevent these situations.

IV. Conclusion

International commercial arbitration has been experiencing a policy change over the last 35 years. The pro-arbitration approach sometimes seems to bite its own tail. In the past, limited court review was praised and welcomed by the arbitration community, while today it does not equally serve the interests of all the parties involved in arbitration. One should not, therefore, reject everything that does not meet the 'traditional' concept of international arbitration, but instead learn from the market and foster legal developments when needed.

This chapter addressed two phenomena that are contrary to the traditional view that there is no judicial review of the merits in international commercial arbitration. One of them is the broad interpretation of public policy by national courts, whereas the other is the possibility recognised by national courts for the parties to claim a 'surprise' by arbitrators' application of law as a violation of due process. The extent of these new practices will differ from jurisdiction to jurisdiction, but they will inevitably invoke a discussion of the relationship between three important principles and policies in international arbitration: party autonomy, *iura novit arbiter* and the definition of a state's public policy.

It is important to recognise that these developments are not unequivocal when it comes to their effect on the pro-arbitration approach. For example, the expansion of the public policy ground to encompass substantive public policy was a consequence in some jurisdictions of the expansion of matters considered arbitrable, and which involved strong public interests. In other jurisdictions, it is a reflection of the localised approach to arbitration.

Also, while it seems inherently unfair when arbitrators render an award that 'surprises' in terms of the law of the parties who nominated them, with parties' expectations on one side and the adjudicative nature of the arbitration process on the other, it was not an easy task for national courts to resolve these matters. International arbitration aspires to transnational solutions, but this is one of those questions where all stakeholders in the arbitration will be influenced by their jurisdictional background as to whether the law is to be treated as a fact or not. The answer is not an easy one given the global arena for the enforcement of arbitral awards. However, it is a problem that requires an internationally acceptable legislative proposal.

12

Authentic Instruments in Chinese Private International Law

ZHENG TANG AND XU HUANG

I. Introduction

One significant contribution of Professor Jonathan Fitchen to the private international law scholarship is his comprehensive and in-depth study of authentic instruments in private international law, an important, practical matter largely ignored in private international law literature. While Professor Fitchen's research focuses more on European Union (EU) practice, in particular the practice in France and Germany, we attempt to enrich the literature in this field by contributing our analysis of authentic instruments in Chinese private international law, an area remaining missing from the academic writings.

Professor Fitchen defines an authentic instrument as

> a public document that allows the public official who registers or draws it up to record evidence concerning matters of fact concerning a judicial act that persons may (or must) have formally recorded in such a fashion as to raise a very strong evidential presumption that the factual matters so registered or recorded are, to the extent allowed by the legal system in which the authentic instrument is created, henceforward to be presumed accurate and 'proven'.[1]

In the country where authentic instruments are issued by the authorised entities, they automatically receive legal effects to prove the recorded fact. The overseas effects of authentic instruments, however, are unclear. Since international judicial cooperation on authentic instruments does not exist, the procedural requirements and effects given to foreign authentic instruments largely depend on the domestic law of each country. The cross-border probative and executory effect of authentic instruments is a significant part of private international law, but is overlooked by Chinese private international law scholars and lawyers.

[1] J Fitchen, *The Private International Law of Authentic Instruments* (Hart Publishing, 2020) 1.

II. The Concept of Authentic Instrument in the People's Republic of China (PRC)

There are no international uniform rules regulating authentic instruments. Even in the European Union, where regional harmonisation and cooperation in law and judicial practice in civil and commercial matters are largely achieved, the requirements of authentic instruments differ between Member States. The concept of authentic instruments in China is relevant in private international law in that when the applicant seeks probative or executory effect of Chinese authentic instruments abroad, the foreign country would assess the legality and validity of these instruments pursuant to Chinese law.

In China, an authentic instrument refers to the certificate produced as the result of notarisation. The PRC Notarisation Law defines 'notarisation' as

> the act performed by a notarial institute, upon the application of a natural person, legal person or other organisation and following statutory procedures, to certify the authenticity and legality of a civil juristic act or a fact or document of legal significance.[2]

This definition demonstrates four matters in relation to authentic instruments, namely notarial institute, notarisation procedure, notarised matters and the effects of notarisation.[3] When a Chinese notarial document attempts to obtain probative or executory effects abroad, the foreign court needs to first of all satisfy that the Chinese authentic instrument meets those requirements and is thus valid in Chinese law.

A. Notarial Institutes

Notarial institutes in China were formerly divided into three types, administrative institutes, public institutes and cooperative institutes. By the end of 2017, all 889 administrative notarial institutes, controlled by the government, had completed the transformation into public institutes.[4] Consequently, current notarial institutes in China only include public institutes and cooperative institutes. Public institutes are a unique type of organisation in the Chinese socialist system, fully or partly funded by the government but having independent legal personality.[5] They are

[2] Notary Law of the People's Republic of China (NL), art 2.

[3] Council of the Notariats of the European Union, Comparative Study on Authentic Instruments National Provisions of Private Law, Circulation, Mutual Recognition and Enforcement, Possible Legislative Initiative by the European Union, PE 408.329, available at: www.europarl.europa.eu/RegData/etudes/STUD/2008/408329/IPOL-JURI_ET(2008)408329_EN.pdf.

[4] Circular of the General Office of the Ministry of Justice on the Supervision over the Progress of Notarisation Reform in November (司法部办公厅关于11月份公证改革进展督察情况的通报，2017年12月18日).

[5] W Fan, 'Public Institute Reform in China from the Perspective of Fiscal Logic' (2019) 7 *International Journal of Economic Behavior and Organisation* 28.

non-profit, public-sector organisations, providing public and quasi-governmental services and regulated by the Notary Law.[6] Cooperative notarial institutes are pilot institutes and are encouraged to explore new models of governance.[7]

The threshold to establish a notarial institute in China is low. A notarial institute must have its own name, a fixed office, two or more notaries and the funds necessary for carrying out notarial work.[8] The fixed office provides a platform for the daily administration of the notarial work and for citizens to communicate. Notarial activities *per se* do not need to happen in the 'fixed office'. The reason for requiring two or more notaries is because the law requires at least two notaries to carry out the on-site verification.[9] Any Chinese citizen between the ages of 25 and 65, with good moral, professional knowledge and experience can qualify as a notary.[10]

B. Notarised Matters

Notarised matters are divided into two categories in the Chinese legal system, namely compulsory notarised matters and voluntary notarised matters. Compulsory notarised matters must be verified by notarisation before having legal effects. These include adoption,[11] the power of attorney for an alien,[12] underwriters selling stocks by means of drawing lots,[13] claims for marine pollution damage,[14] criminal evidence in foreign states.[15] Voluntary notarised matters do not need notarisation to be legally effective. These include contract,[16] succession,[17] the power of attorney, statement, gift and will,[18] division of property,[19]

[6] The Notary Law only applies to public notarial institutes. See NL, art 6.

[7] Art 13 of the Opinions on Promoting the Reform and Mechanism Innovation of Notarisation System, Si Fa [2017] No 8 (关于推进公证体制改革机制创新工作的意见, 司发[2017]8号).

[8] NL, art 8.

[9] 'The Rule for Notarisation Procedures' (RNP), Order of the Ministry of Justice of People's Republic of China, 2020, No 145, art 28.

[10] NL, art 18.

[11] Chinese Civil Code, Art 1105(4); for foreign adopters, 'Measures on the Registration of Adoption of Children by Foreigners in the People's Republic of China', Order of the Ministry of Civil Affairs, 1999, No 15, art 12.

[12] 'Regulation on Marriage Registration', Order of the State Council of the People's Republic of China, 2003, No 387, art 5(2).

[13] 'Interim Provisions on the Management of the Issuing and Trading of Stocks', Order of the State Council of the People's Republic of China, 1993, No 112, art 25(2).

[14] 'Regulations of the People's Republic of China on the Dumping of Wastes at Sea', Order of the State Council of the People's Republic of China, 2017, No 676, art 18.

[15] Supreme People's Court, 'Interpretation by the Supreme People's Court Regarding the Application of the Criminal Procedure Law of the People's Republic of China' (2021), art 77 (最高人民法院关于适用中华人民共和国刑事诉讼法的解释，法释 [2021] 1号).

[16] NL, art 11(1).

[17] ibid, art 11(2).

[18] ibid, art 11(3).

[19] ibid, art 11(4).

bid invitation, tendering and auction,[20] marital status, kindred relationship and adoption relationship,[21] birth, existence, death, identity, experiences, educational background, degree, job title, professional title, and having or not having illegal or criminal record,[22] articles of association of a company,[23] preservation of evidence,[24] signature, seal and date as indicated in a document, and duplicate or photocopy of a document conforming with the original document.[25] This is a non-exhaustive list. In principle, a notary could accept the application to certify any matters.

C. Effects of Notarisation

Authentic instruments produced by Chinese notarial institutes have two effects, probative or evidentiary effects, and executory or enforcement effect.[26] The probative or evidentiary effect indicates a notarised action, fact or document of legal significance which shall be presumed genuine and valid, unless rebutted by evidence strong enough to reverse the notarisation.[27] It does not mean the validity of a notarised document cannot be challenged, but that the court has limited room for discretion.[28]

Some notarised documents may certify the creditor's right to receive payment and the commitment of the debtor to accept compulsory execution. If the debtor fails to fulfil his commitment, the creditor may apply for court enforcement.[29] This executory or enforcement effect of notarised documents is also recognised in Chinese law.

D. Notary Procedure

Notary procedure is the basis for an authentic instrument to gain credibility. It is mainly comprised of three steps, application, examination and issuance of certificates. If errors or irregularities occur in the notary procedure, the credibility of the authentic instrument is likely to be questioned and deprived of probative and executory effects.

[20] ibid, art 11(5).
[21] ibid, art 11(6).
[22] ibid, art 11(7).
[23] ibid, art 11(8).
[24] ibid, art 11(9).
[25] ibid, art 11(10).
[26] ibid, arts 36, 37 and 38. Title of chapter V of the NL is effect of notarisation, from art 36 to art 40.
[27] NL, art 36.
[28] In contrast, the authenticity and validity of documentary evidence in the absence of notarisation has more limited non-contentious probative effects which can be more easily challenged. See, Chinese Civil Procedure Law (CCPL), art 67(2).
[29] NL, art 37(1).

Notary procedure is initiated by application. The applicant must provide supporting and other application materials.[30] Supporting materials are fundamental to convince the notary that the underlying content of the authentic instrument is truthful and lawful. Other application materials include the application form and entrustment documents. Notarial institutes will accept application if they are satisfied that applicants have an interest in the matter requesting notarisation and there is no dispute over the matter between the applicants.[31] The notarial institute shall, after accepting an application for notarisation, appoint a notary public,[32] charge the admission fee[33] and inform the party concerned of the legal significance and the possible legal consequences of notarisation.[34]

After acceptance, the notary must make sure the requested matter is genuine and legitimate. Various methods of examination may be adopted, including questioning the party concerned, the witness and any other interested party. In contrast, authenticity and validity of documentary evidence in the absence of notarisation has more limited non-contentious probative effects which can be more easily challenged, such as obtaining the information from relevant entities or individuals; collecting relevant evidentiary materials like documentary evidence, physical evidence and audio-visual materials; conducting on-site investigations; and entrusting professional institutes or personnel to appraise, inspect and test and translate the materials.[35]

E. Challenging Authentic Instruments

A party to an authentic instrument, or a related party, can challenge the authentic instrument before the notary institute,[36] in court,[37] or use it as a defence when the other party applies for compulsory execution of the notarial document in court.[38] The opposing party can apply for the notarial institute to review the notarised authentic instrument.[39] If the content of the instrument is illegal or not genuine, the notarial institute should revoke the instrument. If it contains other 'technical' errors, like the wrong name, the wrong date, etc, the notarial institute should correct the document. The parties having disputes on the content of the notarial document can also bring the dispute to court.[40] But revocation can only be made

[30] RNP, arts 17 and 18.
[31] ibid, art 19.
[32] ibid, art 20.
[33] ibid, art 22.
[34] ibid, art 21.
[35] ibid, art 27.
[36] NL, art 39.
[37] ibid, art 40.
[38] ibid, art 37.
[39] ibid, art 39.
[40] ibid, art 40.

by a notarial institute, instead of court, and revocation will make the notarised instrument void *ab initio*. In other words, where a party challenges a notarised authentic instrument in a court and succeeds, the court would refuse to enforce the instrument or admit it as evidence, but the court has no power to correct or revoke the notarised authentic instrument.[41]

Challenges can be raised as to form or substance. Authentic instruments' validity can be challenged if the authentic institute or notary public is not qualified, if the procedure does not follow the law, if the instrument contains errors, or if the underlying juristic act is illegal, such as the contract notarised being invalid. Challenging formal validity of authentic instrument (*instrumentum*) focuses on serious defects in formalities required to issue the authentic instrument. It does not accurately certify the genuine fact. The incomplete supporting material attached in the notarised authentic instrument may be deficient in some courts, but not others.[42] If the notarised matter requires professional knowledge or expertise to certify it, the court may not trust the qualification of the notarial institute, and may reject the authentic instrument.[43] When a court finds an authentic instrument questionable, it may summon the notary public to give evidence and treat the authentic instrument as unreal if he fails to appear.[44]

Challenging material validity (*negotium*) questions the legality of the underlying content forming the juristic act aimed to be proven by the authentic instrument. A notarial instrument may be challenged if the person performing the juristic act does not have the corresponding capacity;[45] the party's consent to the underlying contract is not genuine;[46] the act violates mandatory rules, or offends public order or good morals.[47]

[41] L Zhang, 'Research on the Problems of Our Country's Notarial Remedy System' (2012) 4 *Justice of China* 54, 56 (张靓：《我国公证救济制度有关问题研究，载《中国司法》2012 第4期，第56页).

[42] *CUI Haisheng and Others v Youzhen Business Consulting Co Ltd and Others*, Beijing No 3 IPC, [2020] Jing 03 Min Zhong No 14299 (崔海生等与优臻商务咨询有限公司等买卖合同纠纷案，[2020]京03民终14299号)(screenshot of webpage is incomplete, not accepted); *COFCO v Huohong General Supermarket*, Inner Mongolia HPC, [2019] Nei Zhi Min Zhong No 72 (中粮集团有限公司与东胜区火红综合超市侵害商标权纠纷案，[2019]内知民终72号)(inconsistent records of preservation of evidence, accepted).

[43] *Heibei Liurenbake Beverage Co Ltd and Others v Hebei Yangyuan Zhihui Beverage Co Ltd*, [2017] Zui Gao Fa Min Shen No 3918 (河北六仁烤饮品有限公司等诉河北养元智汇饮品股份有限公司擅自使用知名商品特有包装、装潢纠纷案，[2017]最高法民申3918号).

[44] *Qingyu Office of Yubei District v Kingston Technology Co Ltd*, Chongqing No 1 IPC, [2020] Yu 01 Min Zhong No 5897 (渝北区晴雨办公用品经营部与金士顿科技有限公司侵害商标权纠纷案，[2020]渝01民终5897号).

[45] *JIANG v Notary Public Office*, available at: www.pkulaw.cn, CLI.C.61009838 (蒋某与公证处公证损害赔偿纠纷案，北大法宝引证码CLI.C.61009838) (performers acted as the parties who deceased years ago).

[46] *YANG v YANG*, Guangdong Province Foshan IPC, [2003] Fo Zhong Fa Min Yi Zhong Zi No 169 (杨某与杨某等继承纠纷上诉案，[2003]佛中法民一终字第169号) (the medical treatment records showed that the person had a serious illness, his mind was unclear and he could not speak, the signature was therefore not an expression of his true intention).

[47] Chinese Civil Code, art 143.

Enforcement of authentic instruments can be challenged, too. If there is an error in the document recording a creditor's right, the people's court shall decide not to execute it.[48] In other words, only the obligation document could be regarded as an enforceable authentic instrument. In the meantime, since the enforceable authentic instrument is part of a general authentic instrument, the obligation document could be treated as a general authentic instrument. Enforcement challenges apply the principle of comprehensive review of both *instrumentum* and *negotium*.[49]

If an authentic instrument is produced abroad, the Chinese court cannot assess if the notarial instrument is genuine and must rely on the Chinese embassy or consular in the country of origin to certify the stamp, seal or signature for the foreign notarial instrument to be genuine, which is called legalisation or authentication. However, legalisation does not prove the authenticity and legality of the content of the foreign notarial document.[50] Even if a foreign notarial document is authenticated, its validity still can be challenged in Chinese courts. China treats authentic instruments as public documents and the law applicable to challenge their validity should be the law of the country where the instruments are produced.

III. Legalisation of Foreign Notarised Documents

China is not a Member State of the Hague Apostille Convention.[51] Under Chinese law, unless otherwise provided for by bilateral treaties, foreign notarised documents cannot be directly admitted in China. They only acquire probative or executory effects after they are certified through legalisation. The same legalisation procedure also applies to Chinese notarised documents attempting to be recognised abroad. Some bilateral treaties have provisions of dispensation of authentication. For example, documents and translations drawn up or certified by courts or other competent authorities in either China or Singapore shall not be subject to authentication in any form provided they are officially sealed.[52]

According to Article 31 of the Measures for Consular Authentication, consular legalisation is an activity in which a consular legalisation agency confirms a document in the name of the state, the purpose of which is to ensure that the document issued by one state can be recognised within the territory of another state, and the foreign legal effect of the document will not be affected due to doubts over

[48] NL, art 37(2).

[49] *Zhongrong International Trust Co Ltd v Dayin Coal Mine Co Ltd and Others*, [2017] Zui Gao Fa Zhi Fu No 7 (镇雄县大银煤矿有限责任公司、郭泽民、郭亚蒙中融国际信托有限公司申请执行其公证债权文书案，[2017]最高法执复7号).

[50] See section III below for more details.

[51] Convention of 5 October 1961 Abolishing the Requirement of Legalisation for Foreign Public Documents (Hague Apostille Convention).

[52] Art 21 of the Treaty on Judicial Assistance in Civil and Commercial Matters Between the People's Republic of China and the Republic of Singapore.

the authenticity of the seal or signature on the document. Consular legalisation procedure is complicated. The applicant should acquire a valid notarised document in the country of origin. This document needs to be certified by the Ministry of Foreign Affairs or other competent authority in the country of origin.[53] This certified document then should be legalised by the Chinese embassy, consular or other authorised agency located in the country of origin. The final legalised document would be admitted in China. Where the creating state has not established diplomatic relations with China, such evidence and notarised documents shall be submitted to the embassy or consulate of a third state that has established diplomatic relations with China for legalisation and then be forwarded to the Chinese embassy or consulate in the third state.[54]

Consular legalisation does not verify the matters certified by the foreign notarial instrument or any other certification document, nor is it responsible for the authenticity and legality of the contents of the document. The document issuing agency shall be responsible for the contents of the document.[55] To put it another way, consular legalisation is only a certification of the seal and signature affixed to an authentic instrument, to avoid legal effect being affected due to doubts about the authenticity of the seal or signature, and does not involve the substantive contents of the document, validity of notarial institute or notary procedure.[56]

Consular legalisation is an indirect, isolated and extremely limited confirmation of the authenticity of authentic instruments. Given that the seal and signature may prove the notarial institute trustworthy, the court may refer to authentication as a reinforcement of authenticity. The Ministry of Foreign Affairs or other competent authority in the state of origin may only verify and confirm the signature or seal of the notarial institute under its registration or knowledge. If this notarial institute is not registered or not known by the competent authority, the legalisation office is not in the proper position to legalise it. However, notarisation in many

[53] Art 20 of the Measures for Consular Authentication require notarisation and authentication by relevant agencies of the country where the document is issued. The relevant agencies are generally Foreign Departments, eg, for Canada, see: ca.china-embassy.org/chn/lsyw/hzqz/bzxz/gzrz12/rz123/. The competent authority may be a federal administration department, eg, for Germany, see: www.mfa.gov.cn/ce/cede//chn/lsfw/gz/t1350564.htm.

[54] Art 40 of the Minutes of the Second National Meeting on Foreign-related Commercial and Maritime Trial (MSNM), Fa Fa [2005] No 26 (第二次全国涉外商事海事审判工作会议纪要，法发[2005] 26号).

[55] 'Measures for Consular Authentication', Order of the Ministry of Foreign Affairs, 2016, No 2, Art 31.

[56] The Chinese concept is similar to conventional concept. According to Art 2 of the Hague Apostille Convention, legalisation means only the formality by which the diplomatic or consular agents of the country in which the document has to be produced certify the authenticity of the signature, the capacity in which the person signing the document has acted and, where appropriate, the identity of the seal or stamp which it bears.

countries does not need to be done by a public office. Many private institutes, such as law firms, are competent to issue a notarised document. It is practically difficult for a legalisation office to obtain and compare the seals and signatures of all private notaries. This makes legalisation lose substantive authentication value.

Authentic instruments issued by a notarial institute or notary in Hong Kong (HK), Macau and Taiwan cannot be legalised by consular authentication because those are separate legal regions in one country.[57] Hong Kong and Macau, as special legal regions in China, do not have a Chinese embassy or consular in their jurisdiction, but have liaison offices of the Central People's government in HK/Macau Special Administrative Regions. However, the separate legal districts and different laws regulating notarisation also make it difficult for China to treat notarised documents from Hong Kong and Macau the same as those created in Mainland China. In Hong Kong and Macau, the notarised instruments shall be examined and sealed by the China Legal Service (HK) and the China Legal Service (Macau).[58] In Taiwan, the notarised matters are limited to 14 categories,[59] and the party should get a notarised authentic instrument in Taiwan and send the copy to the Straits Exchange Foundation in Taiwan, which transfers it to the relevant association of notaries above the level of province in Mainland China then to the people's court. If the people's court finds it necessary to check notarised authentic instruments, they shall send the copy to the association of notaries then to the Straits Exchange Foundation, the examination results will then retrace the steps back to the people's court.[60] The perplexing procedures are far from satisfactory, leading to extra cost, delay and waste of resources. This problem may hardly be improved until the comprehensive simplification of the relevant certification procedure. For example, cancelling the examination and seal by the China Legal Service and retrenching the long delivery journey between Mainland China and Taiwan may be better approaches.

[57] CHKND; Official Reply to the Mutual Recognition of Certification Documents and Notarisation Documents on Civil Registration between the Mainland and Macau, [94] Gang Ban San Zi, No 598 (关于内地与澳门相互承认民事登记证明文件及公证文书事的复函，[94]港办三字第598号); MTNC.

[58] Circular of the Supreme People's Court and the Ministry of Justice on the Validity of Hong Kong-related Notarised Documents (CHKND), Si Fa Tong [1996], No 26 (最高人民法院、司法部关于涉港公证文书效力问题的通知，司发通[1996]026号); Mainland and Macau, available at: www.moj.gov.cn/organisation/content/2017-08/31/flfwgsjj_4132.html. eg, Decision of the Ministry of Justice on Entrusting 12 Macau Lawyers Including Kuang Yuqiu as China's Entrusted Notaries (Macau), Si Fa Tong [2018], No 10 (司法部关于委托邝玉球等12名澳门律师为中国委托公证人(澳门)的决定，司发通[2018]10号).

[59] Succession, adoption, marriage, birth, death, power of attorney, academic qualification, residence, maintenance of relatives, property rights and interests, medical records, taxes, experience and professional certificates.

[60] Implementing Measures for the Agreement between the Mainland and Taiwan on Use and Verification of Notarial Certificates (MTNC), Si Fa [1993], No 6 (海峡两岸公证书使用查证协议实施办法，司发 [1993] 006号).

IV. Effect of Foreign Authentic Instruments in China

A. Probative or Evidential Effect

China recognises the probative effect of foreign authentic instruments through the double legalisation procedure described above. The very recent reform does not alter the procedural difficulty for legalisation, but reduces the need for compulsory authentic instruments to prove facts occurring abroad. Authentic instruments are not mandatorily required for all foreign evidence to acquire domestic probative effect in Chinese courts.[61] The Chinese courts would admit evidence formed abroad without notarisation and authentication if there are reliable means to prove its authenticity, including evidence recognised and approved by effective judgments of Chinese courts or arbitral awards, evidence affirmed by official publications, etc.[62] But foreign authentic instruments are mandatory to prove five matters: (1) the identity of a foreign organisation and the standing of its legal representative;[63] (2) the power of attorney for litigants not domiciled in China;[64] (3) that public documents produced abroad are genuine; (4) evidence concerning personal relationships; and (5) evidence originating from Hong Kong, Macau and Taiwan.[65] The last three issues need more analysis.

i. Foreign Public Documents

First, the definition of public document is not provided in Chinese laws and regulations. Pursuant to Article 114 of the Judicial Interpretation of the Civil Procedure Law,[66] public documents refer to documents made by state authorities, social organisations,[67] or other organisations with social administrative functions under authorities. State authorities are departments engaged in state administrative affairs, including various organs with full state administrative functions, such as the legislature, judiciary, administrative agency, military agency, etc. Social organisations are organisations established and authorised by state authorities

[61] SPC, 'Several Provisions of the Supreme People's Court on Evidence in Civil Proceedings' (PECP), art 10 (最高人民法院关于民事诉讼证据的若干规定，法释 [2019] 19号).

[62] ibid.

[63] SPC, 'Interpretation of the Supreme People's Court on the Application of the Civil Procedure Law of the People's Republic of China' (CCPL Interpretation) (2020), art 523 (最高人民法院关于适用中华人民共和国民事诉讼法的解释，法释 [2020] 20号).

[64] CCPL, art 264.

[65] PECP, art 16.

[66] CCPL Interpretation, art 114. Part of this article provides that matters recorded in instruments produced by state authorities, or other organisations with social administrative functions under authorities shall be presumed to be true, unless it can be overturned by evidence to the contrary.

[67] art 77 of the PECP 2008 provides that evidential weight of public documents made by state authorities and social organisations under authority is more powerful than other documentary evidence. Regardless of the removal in the PECP 2019, it is still reasonable to assume the producers include social organisations.

to conduct social management, such as community health service centres offering vaccine shots and vaccination certificates. Other organisations with social administrative functions are mass organisations voluntarily established by the people, authorised by state authorities to engage in social administrative affairs, such as a women's auxiliary to protect women from domestic violence and provide mediation records. Some organisations are deemed public in China, such as stock exchanges, education and research institutes and arbitration institutes, but they are private in other countries. If these foreign organisations produce a document, could it be treated as a public document in Chinese law? It is likely that the nature of the document should be determined according to the law of the place where the document is produced.

Chinese courts adopt the authentic presumption for public documents. The Supreme People's Court in 'Several Provisions of the Supreme People's Court on Evidence in Civil Proceedings' (PECP) provides that the producer of the public document can produce a duplication containing all or part of the content in the original public document, and the duplication has the same probative effect as the original one. The copy, duplication, excerpt of a document archived by the state agency, after being certified by the archive department or the producer of the original document, has the same probative effect as the original.[68] Since public documents have a very strong probative effect in China, it is important to verify if a public document is genuine. Where a public document is issued by a foreign authority, it is difficult for Chinese courts to verify its authenticity. Unlike the loose connection between ordinary people and sovereignty, public employees bear strict responsibility to protect sovereignty. Public information or acts by public officials are deemed to be closely related to sovereignty. The line between public and private information or acts by public officers, such as acting as witnesses in foreign courts, is unclear. Chinese officials are keen to avoid any issue that may raise questions of harming sovereignty. Under the influence of Chinese attitudes about sovereignty, it is unlikely to require a foreign public officer or official to act as a witness in Chinese courts. It is thus necessary to rely on the notarial institute to produce the authentic instrument. In contrast, the authenticity of private documents, such as contracts, documents produced by private organisations, private mail and message, can be assessed by cross-examination. Therefore, Chinese law does not include compulsory requirements for such foreign evidence to be certified by authentic instruments.

ii. Personal Relationships

A personal relationship in Chinese law is similar to the concept of kinship, which refers to a relationship based on ties of blood, marriage, adoption, or other personal connections. Evidence proving personal relationships includes

[68] PECP, art 91(1).

marriage certificates, guardianship certificates and birth certificates. A personal relationship is defined narrowly so that it excludes relationships created under a business environment, such as the relationship between shareholders or directors and a company.[69] Article 464 of the Chinese Civil Code provides that, for an agreement on establishing a marriage, adoption, guardianship, or the like, personal relationships shall be governed by the laws creating such personal relationships.[70]

Facts about personal relationships shall be ascertained by the courts *ex officio*.[71] In cross-border situations, the courts are generally not allowed to enter other states to perform this duty. On the other hand, personal relationships in China involve the basic ethical values and order of the society. The effect of the judgment made upon evidence involving personal relationships may affect the interests of a third party. The strong evidential value of authentic instruments is therefore necessary to prove personal relationships created abroad.

iii. Evidence Formed in Hong Kong, Macau or Taiwan

Evidence formed in Hong Kong, Macau or Taiwan requires the 'relevant certification procedure'.[72] The law does not specify what the relevant certification procedure is. The literal interpretation seems to suggest that all evidence from separate legal districts in China, including evidence not classified as public documents or involving personal relationships, need authentic instruments to prove their authenticity.

China has four separate territorial units, with different laws and regulations. The same difficulties in relation to public documents and evidence involving personal relationships created in foreign states would not automatically disappear if they were created in different legal regions in China. However, most foreign evidence without notarisation would not be completely declined by Chinese courts. Its authenticity would be verified by cross-examination.[73] It is unclear and irrational to require a higher threshold for inter-regional evidence to prove authenticity than foreign evidence. It is likely that this requirement is caused by the negligence in the law reform, as the PECP narrows down the scope of evidence abroad to be notarised, but the old law concerning inter-regional evidence remains untouched.

[69] *ZHAO Xiaosong v CHOI Chunggwang*, Beijing HPC, [2020] Jing Min Zhong, No 300 (赵小松民间借贷纠纷案，[2020]京民终300号).
[70] Chinese Civil Code, art 464.
[71] CCPL Interpretation, art 92.
[72] PECP, art 16.
[73] MSNM, art 39.

B. Executory Effect of Foreign Authentic Instruments

Chinese law recognises the executory effect of domestic notarial instruments on debts and the debtor's consent to compulsory enforcement.[74] The creditor can apply for the court to enforce the notarial instrument on default. However, Chinese law does not provide clear rules on execution of foreign authentic instruments. There are two approaches concerning the executory effect of foreign authentic instruments.

i. Treating Authentic Instruments as Foreign Judgments

The first approach analogises foreign authentic instruments with foreign judgments. The Chinese Civil Procedure Law and its interpretation have expressly limited the scope of their recognition and enforcement rules to 'judgments and rulings of foreign courts'.[75] Could rules concerning enforcing foreign judgments be relevant to enforcement of foreign authentic instruments?

Authentic instruments and judgments are obviously different. First, authentic instruments can only certify the existence of a fact without verifying that such a fact is valid or legal. In other words, the notary public does not make any decision on the question of law. Secondly, the verification of a fact is based exclusively on original materials provided by one party without the need to consult the opinion of other related persons. The fact, therefore, should be easily verifiable by assessing the authenticity of the original documents. However, when creating an authentic instrument, there is usually no sufficient protection of the other party's due process rights or the right to be heard. Thirdly, once a matter has been litigated and a final judgment is rendered, this judgment would create finality to the disputed matter.[76] The parties therefore have been excluded from the right to re-litigate the matter. An authentic instrument has no *res judicata* effect.[77] The other parties may contest the authenticity of the verified fact by providing evidence proving the contrary. The compulsory executory effect of an authentic instrument is thus not final. It may be revoked by the notarial institute or refused execution by courts after proving substantive errors.[78]

Nevertheless, an authentic instrument is still analogous to judgment. First, an authentic instrument's main function is to verify the authenticity of a fact, such as the existence of a debt. A judgment also needs to ascertain the fact and the

[74] NL, art 37.
[75] CCPL, art 282.
[76] JM Rosenberg, 'Res Judicata: New Standards for Evaluating the Effect of a Change in Law after Judgment' (1978) 30 *Hastings Law Journal* 191, 191.
[77] Fitchen (n 1) 89.
[78] eg, arts 37 and 39 of the NL.

personal liability between the parties. Secondly, an authentic instrument certifies the debtor's admission of debt. The executory effect makes the debtor perform according to its promise. In the judgment, the court orders the debtor to perform. Its enforcement leads to the same consequence. Therefore, enforcing foreign authentic instruments, in principle, has equivalent functioning as enforcing foreign judgments. The executory force makes an authentic instrument a quasi-judicial document.

If one can apply the law concerning foreign judgments to foreign authentic instruments, the foreign authentic instrument at least needs to satisfy all the conditions and requirements applying to enforce foreign judgments. Nevertheless, recognition and enforcement of foreign judgments (FJR) is difficult in China. FJR is only possible either through judicial cooperation treaties, or through reciprocity.[79] China has entered into judicial cooperation treaties with 36 countries, and all limit 'court judgments' to exclude authentic instruments. The establishment of reciprocity is more relaxed nowadays than before, but difficulties continue to exist.[80] Since seeking executory effect of Chinese authentic instruments in foreign courts is very rare and many countries, like China, do not include clear rules making such enforcement possible, it is very likely that China would not enforce foreign authentic instruments based on reciprocity. Therefore, equalising foreign authentic instruments with judgments cannot produce executory effect in China.

ii. Foreign Authentic Instruments as Foreign Administrative Decisions

The second approach treats foreign authentic instruments that have executory effects as foreign administrative decisions. Until recently, most notarial institutes in China were government agencies and notary publics acquired the status of government officials. Errors made by notary publics may have made the state responsible for compensation. Although the 2017 reform changes the nature of notarial institutes into public sector institutes, these institutes are still funded by state finance and the authentic instruments are given authenticity by state authorities. This makes notarisation akin to the exercise of administrative power under public law.[81]

However, this analogy is also problematic. First, it should be the law of the country of origin, instead of the country of destination, to classify the nature of

[79] CCPL, art 281.

[80] eg, *TAN Junping and Others v LIU Zuosheng and CHEN Zhengliang*, Hunan Province Chenzhou IPC, (2020) Xiang 10 Xie Wai Ren, No 1 (谭军平、刘旭坤申请承认和执行外国法院民事判决、裁定案，[2020]湘10协外认1号) (application was dismissed on the ground that the applicants failed to submit the original or a certified copy of the effective judgment); Wenliang Zhang and Guangjian Tu, 'The Hague Judgments Convention and Mainland China–Hong Kong SAR Judgments Arrangement: Comparison and Prospects for Implementation' (2021) 20 *Chinese Journal of International Law* 101, 124 (the likelihood of successful recognition and enforcement of foreign judgments in Chinese people's courts is lower than the success rate of Chinese judgments in other countries).

[81] Fitchen (n 1).

authentic instruments. If the country of origin has made notarisation a regulated, private act, which does not exercise state power, and the notary public personally has professional liability for errors made, China cannot treat this country's notarised documents administrative orders. Secondly, even in China, the main purpose of the reform is to untie notarisation from government acts. To transform notarial institutes into public institutes, previous notaries need to choose to remain as a government official and change their position, or continue to work as a non-official, professional notary public. China also adopts a marketisation approach, to encourage private, cooperative entities to be formed, to provide more competitive and professional notarisation services. Thirdly, even if foreign authentic instruments are treated as administrative decisions, it may be even more difficult for them to receive executory effects in other states than court judgments. Administrative decisions made by public officials are not enforceable in other countries, either by courts or by administrative authorities, due to the doctrine of 'public law taboo'. A country would feel uncomfortable acting as the 'agent' of another country to enforce the latter's administrative decisions. A country would also find that it is inappropriate to review the act of the other state due to comity and sovereign equality.

iii. Enforcement of Foreign Authentic Instruments

In the absence of international or bilateral cooperation mutually recognising executory effects of authentic instruments, enforcement of foreign authentic instruments is difficult, if not impossible, in China. In this current situation, the party who wants to enforce foreign authentic instruments has to file a suit concerning the underlying content contained in an authentic instrument before the Chinese court. The foreign authentic instruments can only be used as evidence in Chinese courts.

V. Improving Chinese Law and Practice

The current Chinese law dealing with foreign authentic instruments has obvious shortfalls. First, foreign authentic instruments need to go through a complicated legalisation process before acquiring legal effects in China. This seriously hampers the efficiency of cross-border business transactions and other transnational interactions with China. The Chinese Foreign Department also finds that the legalisation procedure is impeding cross-border civil and commercial activities of companies and individuals. China is now working on becoming a contracting party of the Hague Apostille Convention,[82] which facilitates the cross-border

[82] Certification Office of Consul Department of Ministry of Foreign Affairs, 'New Model to Facilitate the Flow of Documents Across Borders' 2021(4) *China Notary* 49, 51 (外交部领事司认证处：《便利文书跨国流转的新模式》，载《中国公证》2021年第4期，第51页).

use of public documents through abolishing the requirement of legalisation for foreign public documents including authentic instruments.[83] In the meantime, China should enter more bilateral arrangements with its big trade partners, such as the United States and Japan, to remove the legalisation requirements.

Secondly, China adopts a more stringent approach for Hong Kong and Macau than for foreign authentic instruments, which causes more difficulties for parties seeking recognition of authentic instruments created in Hong Kong and Macau. Given that the current national strategy is to improve integration of Hong Kong and Macau with Mainland China, and to build the Guangdong–HK–Macau Great Bay Area, this is obviously incompatible with the goal.

Thirdly, Chinese law is unclear about the executory effect of foreign authentic instruments. Analysis and current practice suggest that foreign authentic instruments may not have executory effect in China.[84] It seems that China does not mind this status quo. First, the market need to execute foreign authentic instruments is not as big as enforcing foreign judgments. Secondly, refusing to enforce foreign authentic instruments may nevertheless protect Chinese citizens. However, since the executory effect of authentic instruments may prove an efficient way to settle commercial disputes, it may be in China's interests to reconsider its position. There is, so far, no international treaty to facilitate mutual enforcement of authentic instruments and this matter is not a top priority or urgent matter that many countries and international organisations want to address.[85] A unilateral approach may enable China to enforce foreign authentic instruments in China, while the executory effects of Chinese authentic instruments continues to be denied in some countries, which may not be in China's favour. China may consider bilateral agreements with close trade partners to establish reciprocity and create efficiency.

[83] Hague Conference on Private International Law, 'Apostille Handbook: A Handbook on the Practical Operation of the Apostille Convention' (HCCH, 2013), available at: assets.hcch.net/docs/ff5ad106-3573-495b-be94-7d66b7da7721.pdf, 6.

[84] Some states, such as France and Romania, allow the enforcement of foreign authentic instruments to facilitate judicial cooperation and civil and commercial collaboration with these countries.

[85] Only the EU has advanced regional regulations about the enforcement of foreign authentic instruments.

PART III

Family Matters in Private International Law

13

Judicial Subjectivism in Determining the Habitual Residence of Newborns: Wrong Questions and Questionable Answers in *Pope v Lunday*

AUDE FIORINI*

I. Introduction

In the words of Lord McCluskey,

> the law, as laid down in a code, or a statute or in a thousand eloquently reasoned opinions, is no more capable of providing all the answers than a piano is capable of providing music. The piano needs the pianist, and any two pianists, even with the same score, may produce very different music.[1]

The potential for variation in interpretation will understandably be greater in music than in law where the judge does not benefit from artistic licence. Nonetheless, it is now widely acknowledged that a range of non-legal factors can influence judicial decision making[2] including personal values[3] and even cognitive illusions such

* The author acted as adviser to the lawyers for the applicant father.

[1] Lord McCluskey, *Law, Justice and Democracy (The Reith Lectures)* (Sweet & Maxwell, 1987) 7. 'It is difficult to escape the conclusion that the choices which the system leaves the judge free to make are influenced by the judge's personality, his instincts and preferences, his accumulated social and philosophical make-up and his sense of the public mood'. '[A judge] is a person whose experiences, vanities, prejudices, certainties and doubts, however disciplined by training, cannot be wholly suppressed', ibid, 8.

[2] JN Frank, *Courts on Trial: Myth and Reality in American Justice* (Atheneum, 1963); GC Sisk, M Heise and AP Morriss, 'Charting the influences on the judicial mind: an empirical study of judicial reasoning' (1998) 73 *New York University Law Review* 1377; JL Gibson, 'Judges' Role Orientations, Attitudes, and Decisions: An Interactive Model' (1978) 72 *American Political Science Review* 911.

[3] RJ Cahill-O'Callaghan, 'The Influence of Personal Values on Legal Judgments' (2013) 40 *Journal of Law and Society* 596; RJ Cahill-O'Callaghan and BJ Richards, 'Policy, Principle, or Values: An Exploration of Judicial Decision-Making' (2018) 79 *Louisiana Law Review* 397.

as anchoring, hindsight bias and egocentric bias.[4] This is the case even though 'most judges attempt to reach their decisions utilizing facts, evidence, and highly constrained legal criteria, while putting aside personal biases, attitudes, emotions and other individuating factors'.[5]

The potential for the modelling of the decision-making process through subconscious elements is, of course, particularly high in instances where trial courts are afforded a wide degree of discretion and even more so in situations, such as the determination of habitual residence in child abduction cases, where challenging factual situations are commonplace. Rarely though are examples of such shaping as transparent as in *Pope v Lunday*,[6] a dispute involving the alleged wrongful retention of infant twins. Although the Pope twins had been born and had lived in the United States throughout their short lives, the father had petitioned for their return to Brazil, the country in which the parents were established and which he claimed was the twins' habitual residence under the 1980 Hague Convention on the Civil Aspects of International Child Abduction.[7]

The question whether newborns may be habitually resident in a country they have never visited is arising with increased frequency.[8] Return petitions in such cases have had conflicting outcomes internationally[9] as well as domestically.[10]

[4] C Guthrie, JJ Rachlinski and AJ Wistrich, 'Inside the Judicial Mind' (2001) 86 *Cornell Law Review* 777, 829 show that judges like any other humans rely on heuristics that can lead to poor judgments.

[5] ibid, and references.

[6] *Pope v Lunday*, 2019 US Dist LEXIS 220406 (WD Okla, 23 December 2019) aff'd by 835 Fed Appx 968 (10th Cir, 20 November 2020).

Pope v Lunday, 2019 US DIST LEXIS 220406 (WD Okla, 23 December 2019).

[7] Convention on the Civil Aspects of International Child Abduction (adopted 25 October 1980, in force 1 December 1983) 343 UNTS 89 (1980 Hague Convention).

[8] According to global statistics maintained by the HCCH, the number of allegedly abducted infants aged less than 12 months appears to be decreasing in recent years: in 2015, 1% of abducted children were aged 1 or less: Hague Conference, 'Prel Doc No 11 A of September 2017 – Part I – A statistical analysis of applications made in 2015 under the Hague Convention of 25 October 1980 on the Civil Aspects of International Child Abduction – Global report' (HCCH, 2017), available at: assets.hcch.net/docs/d0b285f1-5f59-41a6-ad83-8b5cf7a784ce.pdf, 10; in 2008, 2% were aged 1 or less: Hague Conference, 'Prel Doc No 8 A of May 2011 – A statistical analysis of applications made in 2008 under the Hague Convention of 25 October 1980 on the Civil Aspects of International Child Abduction. Part I – Global Report' (HCCH, 2011), available at: assets.hcch.net/docs/55284570-18df-41ee-a254-418da5108688.pdf, 18. However, the number of published cases involving the question whether newborns may be habitually resident in a country they have never visited appears on the rise eg: *W and B v H (Child Abduction: Surrogacy)* [2002] 1 FLR 1008; *Re F (Abduction: Unborn Child)* [2006] EWHC 2199 (Fam) [2007] 1 FLR 627; *Cass Civ 1ère 26 Oct 2011*, N° de pourvoi 10-19.905, 1015; *5A_346/2012*, IIe Cour de droit civil, TF du 12 juin 2012; *A v A and another (Children: Habitual Residence) (Reunite International Child Abduction Centre intervening)* [2013] UKSC 60, [2013] 3 WLR 761; Case C-111/17 PPU *OL v PQ* (CJ, 8 June 2017); *In re ALC*, 607 F App'x 658 (9th Cir, 2015); *Diagne v DeMartino*, 2018 US Dist LEXIS 156912; *Schwartz v Hinnendael*, 2020 US Dist LEXIS 191923 (ED Wis, 16 October 2020).

[9] In *Cass Civ 1ère 26 Oct 2011* (n 8) (France) the French Cassation court dismissed an appeal against a decision ordering the return to the United States of a newborn who had never been present there; by contrast, in *5A_346/2012* (n 8) (Switzerland), the Swiss Federal Tribunal dismissed an appeal against a decision refusing to order the return of a newborn to Greece, as she had never been present there.

[10] In the US, two appellate court decisions decided four days apart are illustrative of similarly contrasting outcomes: in *Pope v Lunday*, 835 Fed Appx 968 (10th Cir, 20 November 2020) the 10th

The lack of decisional harmony may be explained both by the very diverse factual situations surrounding the underlying parental conflict and by the divergent interpretations afforded to habitual residence. In the United States, until 2020 and the Supreme Court decision in *Monasky v Taglieri*,[11] the habitual residence test varied between different Federal Circuits of Appeals between two extremes: a child-centred approach focusing on a child's acclimatisation to a particular jurisdiction,[12] and a parental intentions test looking at the 'last shared, settled intent of the parents in an attempt to determine which country is the locus of the children's family and social developments'.[13]

Pope v Lunday involved twin boys born in Oklahoma in November 2019. The parents, both American, had been in a long-term (and initially long-distance) relationship since 2014. The father, who had permanent residence status in Brazil, was joined there by the mother in July 2018. The following summer, when she was five months' pregnant, the mother travelled to the United States. She never returned to Brazil. The father petitioned for the return of the neonates within days of their birth. The District Court for the Western District of Oklahoma dismissed the return petition, finding that the father had failed to establish that the twins had their habitual residence in Brazil.[14] The father appealed. While the appeal was pending, the US Supreme Court handed down judgment in *Monasky*, its fourth case under the 1980 Hague Convention. *Monasky* had the potential to reshuffle the cards in the *Pope* case as it first established a new habitual residence test, the 'totality of the circumstances' standard,[15] and in addition clarified that a habitual residence finding was primarily a question of fact and as such could only be overruled for clear error. In November 2020, the trial court judgment in *Pope* was considered consistent with the *Monasky* approach and affirmed by the Court of Appeals for the Tenth Circuit.[16]

The outcome of the case was not unexpected. Statistically the return rate of children who have been abducted to the United States is comparatively low.[17] In

Circuit Court of Appeals affirmed a trial court ruling which had dismissed a return petition concerning twins born in the US who had never been to Brazil on the basis that they did not have a habitual residence there while in *De Carvalho v Pereira*, 308 So 3d 1078, the Court of Appeal of Florida affirmed a trial court's order granting the return of a newborn to Brazil even though the child had been born and lived in the US until the retention started when the child was one month old.

[11] *Monasky v Taglieri*, 140 S Ct 719 (2020).

[12] *Robert v Tesson*, 507 F 3d 981 (6th Cir, 2007).

[13] *Mozes v Mozes*, 239 F 3d 1067, 1084 (9th Cir, 2001).

[14] *Pope v Lunday*, 2019 US DIST LEXIS 220406 (WD Okla, 23 December 2019).

[15] *Monasky* (n 11) 723 and 730.

[16] *Pope* CA (n 10).

[17] Less than a third of children reportedly abducted to the US are returned: according to data published by the US Department of State on reported abductions and returns between 2010 and 2020, the average return rate of children allegedly abducted to the US is 29%, which is noticeably lower than the return rate of children allegedly abducted from the US (44%); see travel.state.gov/content/dam/NEWIPCAAssets/Reported%20Abductions%20and%20Returns%202010-2020%20(002)fv.pdf. This is to be put in the context of the latest worldwide statistics maintained by the HCCH. The global return rate in 2015 was around 45%, see 'Prel Doc No 11 A' (n 8) 3.

addition, few courts have ever found children to be habitually resident in a country that they have never visited.[18] In this context, it was from the outset perhaps unlikely that a return order would be made in favour of the father. What may be questioned, however, are the steps the District Court took to reach this conclusion. Having first expressed a strong personal doubt that newborns are even capable of having a habitual residence, the District Court decided that

> even if a newborn can – or must – be assigned a place of habitual residence, there is no sense in which these children could be considered habitual residents of Brazil. It is undisputed that they were born in the United States to parents who are United States citizens, that they are themselves United States citizens, and that they have not spent a moment of their lives in Brazil, much less enough time that Brazil could be considered the place where they usually reside.[19]

Might a different outcome have been reached in *Pope v Lunday* (including on appeal) if the trial court had approached the problem more rigorously when determining the return petition under the Hague Convention?

This chapter first identifies the questions that need to be addressed in cases of alleged wrongful retention of newborns under the 1980 Hague Convention, and then contrasts this with the approach actually taken by the District Court in *Pope*. It establishes that, given the now limited power of review afforded to US federal appellate courts where habitual residence questions arise as well as the nature of the post *Monasky* habitual residence test, the potential instances of judicial subjectivism cannot readily be corrected. In this *Pope* may, beyond its singular shortcomings, also be illustrative of a risk that the now prevailing understanding of, and approach to, habitual residence in child abduction cases may lead to varying treatment in similar situations depending upon individual judicial predilections.

II. The Application of the 1980 Hague Convention to Cases of Alleged Wrongful Retention: Necessary Questions

The 1980 Hague Convention was established with the dual aim 'to secure the prompt return of children wrongfully removed to or retained in any Contracting State, and to ensure that rights of custody and of access under the law of one Contracting State are effectively respected in the other Contracting States'.[20] Based on the premise of the natural competence of a child's place of habitual residence

[18] The French Supreme Court decision *Cass Civ 1ère 26 Oct 2011* (n 8), is rather isolated: see A Fiorini, 'Habitual residence and the newborn – a French perspective' (2012) 61 *International & Comparative Law Quarterly* 530. In the US, see also, *Uzoh v Uzoh*, 2012 US Dist LEXIS 61112, 12 (NDIII, 2 May 2012).

[19] *Pope* DC (n 14) 9.

[20] 1980 Hague Convention, Art 1.

to deal with custody issues affecting the child, the Hague Abduction Convention uses the key notion of habitual residence in two ways. Under Articles 1–4, the Convention restricts its application to the removal or retention of children from their country of habitual residence in a Contracting State to another Contracting State. If the Convention applies, the court seised then determines the wrongfulness of the removal or retention under Article 3 by analysing the rights which exist in respect of the child under the law of the child's State of habitual residence immediately before the removal or retention. Having confirmed that the matter fell within the scope of the 1980 Convention, the trial court in the *Pope* case would thus have had to decide whether to order the return of the twins under Article 12 by assessing if the father had managed to prove, by preponderance of the evidence, that the case indeed involved a retention of the children, when such retention had actually started what was the children's country of habitual residence at that particular time, that he had custody rights as defined by Article 5 under the law of that country, and that these were being exercised at that time and had been breached, making the retention wrongful under Article 3.

A. Applicability of the 1980 Hague Convention to the *Pope* Case

Both the United States and Brazil were Contracting States of the 1980 Hague Convention at the time of the alleged wrongful retention in 2019. The Convention entered into force in the United States in 1988, and in Brazil in 2000. The United States accepted Brazil's accession in 2003, so that between these two countries, the Convention has been applicable since 1 December 2003.[21] The alleged victims of the retention were neonates, thus children who were well below the age limit of 16 years in accordance with Article 4.

B. Nature and Timing of the Alleged Abduction

The combination of Articles 3 and 4 means that for the Convention to apply, the court must first ascertain when the alleged breach of the custody rights happened (date of removal or retention) before identifying whether the child in question was 'at home at [that] time'[22] in a Contracting State. The first difficult question for the District Court would thus have been whether the case involved a retention of the children, as opposed to a removal. The Convention does not define these terms and the Pérez-Vera Report acknowledges that the 'variety of different circumstances which can combine in a particular case makes it impossible to

[21] See: www.hcch.net/en/instruments/conventions/status-table/acceptances/?mid=606.
[22] *Monasky* (n 11) 726.

arrive at a … precise definition',[23] but stresses that the Convention aims to respond to attempts to establish 'artificial jurisdictional links on an international level, with a view to obtaining custody of a child'.[24] The father argued that this was 'not a case of wrongful removal of the children *in utero*'[25] but one of wrongful retention at birth. Leaving aside the fact that the children were not yet born when the mother travelled to the United States and the (probable) inapplicability of the 1980 Hague Convention to unborn children,[26] the father had not opposed the then pregnant mother's visit to the United States in the summer of 2019,[27] so that there could not have been a *wrongful* removal in this case. The issue was therefore understandably presented as one of retention, whereby the child remains with the abductor beyond the time that had been agreed. But was the father right in referring to a wrongful retention *at birth*? This raised the complicated issue of when to time the start of an alleged retention:[28]

> In a case of wrongful retention, the time begins to run either from the date the child remains with the abducting parent despite the clearly communicated desire of the left behind parent to have the child returned or when the acts of the abducting parent are so unequivocal that the left behind parent knows or should know, that the child will not be returned.[29]

'[S]pecifically courts look to the date when the non-abducting parent was truly on notice that the abducting parent was not going to return the child'.[30] Faced with a fait accompli that the trip of the pregnant mother was to last longer than the few weeks anticipated, several scenarios were possible. The father might well have accepted the idea that the mother would not return until some time after the birth and agreed to the children spending their first days/weeks/months in the United States. Or the parents' relationship might actually have broken down irretrievably upon the discovery of the mother's deception before the birth. Alleging a wrongful

[23] E Pérez-Vera, 'Explanatory Report on the 1980 Hague Child Abduction Convention' (HCCH, April 1981), available at: assets.hcch.net/docs/a5fb103c-2ceb-4d17-87e3-a7528a0d368c.pdf, para 11.

[24] ibid.

[25] *Pope* (n15) 3.

[26] Unlike the 1996 Hague Child Protection Convention (Convention on Jurisdiction, Applicable Law, Recognition, Enforcement and Co-operation in Respect of Parental Responsibility and Measures for the Protection of Children, adopted 19 October 1996, entered into force 1 January 2002), the 1980 Hague Abduction Convention does not specify that it 'applies to children from the moment of their birth' but it is difficult to see how a breach of custody rights (Art 4) could arise in respect of an unborn child devoid of legal personality.

[27] The District Court stressed that the father referred to the mother's alleged deception at the time. This was irrelevant. The subsequent discovery of the abducting parent's misrepresentation would not void the initial consent to the removal, rendering it retrospectively unlawful. Comp, eg, *Flores-Aldape v Kamash*, 202 F Supp 3d 793, 801; *Roche v Hartz*, 783 F Supp 3d 995, 1002 (ND Ohio, 2011); *McKie v Jude*, 2011 US Dist LEXIS 1834, 6 (ED Ky, 2011).

[28] PR Beaumont and PE McEleavy, *The Hague Convention on International Child Abduction* (Oxford University Press, 1999) 40–42; R Schuz, *The Hague Child Abduction Convention: A Critical Analysis* (Hart Publishing, 2013) 142–45.

[29] *Capalungan v Lee*, 2019 US Dist LEXIS 117321, (SD Ohio 2019) 11.

[30] *Blanc v Morgan*, 721 F Supp 2d 749, 762 (WD Tenn, 2010).

retention at birth, the father would thus have to establish that it is only at that point that he understood 'unequivocally', and that he was 'truly on notice', that the mother would not return to Brazil with the children. A similar finding had been made in the case of *Diagne*, where a court found that the day of the child's birth marked the start of his retention, as 'by then it was clear that the mother was not returning'.[31]

Had the Court considered that the facts showed the alleged retention had started *before* the birth,[32] it should have concluded that this rendered the Convention inapplicable without further discussion as to habitual residence. Were the Court instead satisfied that the start of the alleged retention was moments after the birth, the next step would consist in assessing whether the petitioner had satisfactorily established that the children were habitually resident in Brazil at that point.

C. Habitual Residence at Birth

Unlike most retention cases, which revolve around the question of a change of habitual residence,[33] the *Pope* case raised the less frequent issue of how the first habitual residence of a child is established. In line with the factual nature of habitual residence,[34] there is no special rule applicable to the establishment of a first habitual residence. When asked to establish the first habitual residence of a newborn child, courts in the United States have consistently held that 'a newborn's place of birth does not automatically bestow upon that child a habitual residence',[35] and that a newborn's habitual residence is not automatically that of the mother.[36] In the absence of special rules, resort would have had to be had to the standard tests applicable to the determination of habitual residence.

At the time of the ruling, there was no uniform approach to the interpretation of habitual residence in child abduction cases in the United States, and there were only limited precedents in the Tenth Circuit. However, the District Court should have noted an important factor likely to frame its enquiry: on the day of their birth the twins could aptly be described as 'especially young children'. Although 'every Circuit to have determined whether a country constituted a habitual residence consider[ed] both the acclimatization and the shared parental intent standard', 'all but the Fourth and Eighth Circuits prioritize[d] the shared parental standard in

[31] *Diagne* (n 8) 31.

[32] A retention is an 'event occurring on a specific occasion' and 'not a continuing state of affairs', *Re H and Re S (Abduction: Custody Rights)* [1991] 2 AC 476, 500.

[33] Where a change of habitual residence is in issue, subjective factors – parental intentions – and objective factors – showing integration of the child in the country of refuge – may have to be balanced.

[34] Pérez-Vera (n 23) para 66.

[35] *McKie* (n 27); *Cunningham v Cunningham*, 237 F Supp 3d 1246, 1265; *Delvoye v Lee*, 329 F 3d 330, 334 (3rd Cir, 2003); *Uzoh* (n 18); *Kijowska v Haines*, 463 F 3d 583, 587 (7th Cir, 2006); *Holder v Holder*, 392 F 3d 1009, 1020 (9th Cir, 2004).

[36] *Delvoye* (n 35) 333; *Nunez-Escudero v Tice-Menley*, 58 F 3d 374, 379 (8th Cir, 1995).

cases concerning especially young children'.[37] Indeed, in cases such as *Pope*, the goal to ensure that the child is not kept from their family and social environment (which explains the importance attached by some courts to the acclimatisation standard) 'ceases to be of concern … if a child never forms such ties or is incapable of doing so'.[38] Unsurprisingly, the few US courts that had engaged with the issue of how a newborn acquires a habitual residence around the time of birth had concluded that shared parental intent prior to the wrongful removal or retention was 'central to the determination',[39] or 'should be prioritised'.[40]

Having identified that the applicable standard was the parental intention test, the trial court should then have considered whether the father had established that the last shared parental intention (before the retention) was that the children were to live in Brazil. It was uncontested that the parents agreed at 19–20 weeks *in utero* that the children would live in Brazil. The court would thus have had to ascertain whether this was the *last* shared parental intention regarding the children that existed at the relevant time, ie, at birth. Given the circumstances of the case, this may have involved discussing *in limine* whether a child's habitual residence determination may be based on pre-birth parental intentions. When assessing whether there was ever a meeting of minds (as to where to raise the child) other courts in the United States have considered periods of time preceding the child's birth, including the mother's pregnancy or sometimes even pre-conception.[41] Since *Monasky*, courts have continued, within the 'totality of the circumstances' standard, to consider parental intentions established prior to the child's birth in the context of the determination of a very young child's habitual residence.[42] On that basis, the District Court in *Pope* should have assessed on the facts whether the uncontested *in utero* agreement had been replaced by any subsequent agreement[43] or was indeed jointly broken[44] prior to the start of the twins' retention. If, following the breakdown of the parental relationship, for example, the parents had shared the intent that the twins should live in the United States for a while once born, or indeed if the parties were still 'renegotiating' where the twins/ or the family should live, then the Court would have had to dismiss the father's petition as the children could not be habitually resident in Brazil. If, however, the *in utero* agreement had not been replaced by new shared intentions before the retention started, then the court's next step would have been to assess whether

[37] *Ahmed v Ahmed*, 867 F 3d 682, 689–90 (6th Cir, 2017).

[38] ibid. See also, *Redmond v Redmond*, 724 F 3d 729, 746 (7th Cir, 2013); *Karkkainen v Kovalchuk*, 445 F 3d 280, 287 (3rd Cir, 2006); *Whiting v Krassner*, 391 F 3d 540, 550 (3rd Cir, 2004); *Neergaard-Colon v Neergaard*, 752 F 3d 526, 533 (1st Cir, 2014).

[39] *McKie* (n 27).

[40] *Diagne* (n 8) 19. Also, *Nicolson v Pappalardo*, 605 F 3d 100, 104 (1st Cir 2010).

[41] *Flores-Aldape* (n 27); *Ahmed* (n 37); *Nicolson* (n 40); *Diagne* (n 8).

[42] *Douglas v Douglas*, 2021 US App LEXIS 28909 (6th Cir); *Dumitrascu v Dumitrascu*, 2021 US Dist LEXIS 175189 (D Colo, 19 October 2021).

[43] *Cunningham* (n 35).

[44] *Diagne* (n 8) (after a crisis point, the parents had tried, but failed, to agree anew on where to raise the child).

the father had proved that he had custody rights at the relevant time, under the law of Brazil, the law of the children's habitual residence (Article 3).

III. The Courts' Approach in *Pope v Lunday*

The Supreme Court's prescription of 'clear error' as the mode of appellate review[45] meant that the habitual residence determination, key to the District Court's dismissal of the father's petition, was reviewed deferentially, rather than *de novo*, and affirmed by the Court of Appeals for the Tenth District as consistent with *Monasky's* totality of the circumstances standard.

A. The District Court's Judgment

The language and structure of the District Court judgment evidence, quite explicitly, the trial judge's disapprobation that the father should even have considered petitioning for return. Indeed, the judge raised an unnecessary legal question – whether newborns can have a habitual residence at all – instead of the much narrower issue of whether, applying the prevailing habitual residence test, the twins were habitually resident in Brazil immediately before the retention. By the time the District Court actually addressed the latter question, in the second half of its analysis, it was framed in leading terms doubting that the children in question could be considered habitually resident in Brazil since they were US citizens born in the United States to US parents and had never spent a moment of their lives in Brazil.[46] The whole judgment was noticeably shaped by a number of misunderstood or misrepresented elements of fact and law, raising the suspicion of predetermination.[47]

i. Language

The trial judge did not hide his incomprehension that the father petitioned for return and his expectation that the application should be dismissed. In the very

[45] *Monasky* (n 11) 730.
[46] *Pope* DC (n 14) 9.
[47] Predetermination is a form of bias in the sense that the decision is approached 'with a closed mind and without impartial consideration of all relevant … issues' (*Georgiou v Enfield London Borough Council* [2004] EWHC 779, [2004] 2 P&CR 21 (Admin) [31]); predetermination occurs 'by the closing of its mind to the consideration and weighing of the relevant factors because of a decision already reached or because of a determination to reach a particular decision' (*Bovis Homes Ltd v New Forest District Council* [2002] EWHC 483 (Admin) [111]). 'Bias is an attitude of mind which prevents the Judge from making an objective determination of the issues that he has to resolve … Bias can come in many forms. It may consist of irrational prejudice, or it may arise from particular circumstances which, for logical reasons, predispose a Judge towards a particular view of the evidence or issues before him' (*Re Medicaments No 2* [2001] 1 WLR 700 [37] (CA)).

first sentence of the Order, the District Court chose to put the term 'return' in quotation marks considering it a 'bit of a misnomer because the children have never been to Brazil'.[48] Later, having correctly stated that the Convention does not define the notion of habitual residence, the Court considered the Convention text in order to establish a 'valuable context' that could be helpful for the determination of the 'intended application' of the term habitual residence, noting again that 'a child can hardly be "returned" to a place [he] has never been'.[49] This led to the assumption that the acclimatisation test must be favoured. Indeed, in the trial court's view, '[the 1980 Convention] applies to cases where a child is being retained away from the country in which they have *assimilated and developed ties* that have been broken by the removal (sic)', which reinforced its conclusion that 'the Court is not convinced that a newborn is capable, at the moment of birth, of having a place of "habitual residence" as the term is used in the Convention'.[50]

Other elements of language point towards subjectivity in the treatment of the return application. This transpires, for instance, from a long sentence in an early section of the decision in which the Court sums up elements of the father's petition. According to the trial judge,

> [The father]'s position assumes that day – *(or hour- or minute-)* old newborns must have a place of 'habitual residence'[51] … and that the [parents'] actual respective intents at the time of the children's birth must be overridden by any past agreement [they] had regarding where they would raise their *hypothetical*, future, children.[52]

In the first part of the sentence, the addition of the words in brackets, and the use of quotation marks around the term habitual residence reinforce the unarticulated but implicit suggestion that the father's assumption (and, by extension, petition) was without merit. In the second part, the epithet 'hypothetical' conveys the judge's view (further developed later), that the shared parental intentions regarding the children's habitual residence should have no weight as it related to supposedly *hypothetical*, ie, imagined, perhaps not true,[53] beings as opposed to real, conceived, five-month *in utero* children, thereby undermining the father's claim.

[48] *Pope* DC (n 14) 1 *ad notam*.

[49] Ibid 6. This view is at odds with the conventional interpretation of the Hague Convention. As noted by Pérez-Vera (n 23) para 110, the drafters rejected a proposal to the effect that children should always be returned to the country of their habitual residence and preferred to provide courts with some flexibility. As a result, children have been returned to places in the country of habitual residence to which they have never been (eg, *Murray v Director, Family Services* (1993) FLC 92-416 (Australia)) or indeed to third countries (eg, *RB v VG* RfamA (SC)5579/07, 7 August 2007 (Israel). This has recently been confirmed by the UK Supreme Court in *Re C* [2018] UKSC 8, [2019] AC 1 [17]: 'Article 12, in providing for an order for return, does not specify that return must be to the state of the child's habitual residence; it could be to any State'.

[50] *Pope* DC (n 14) 6. This view is at odds with the US Supreme Court position in *Monasky* (n 11) 728: 'a presumption of no habitual residence for infants [would leave] the population most vulnerable to abduction the least protected' and 'would undermine the Convention's aims to stop unilateral decisions to remove children across international borders'.

[51] *Pope* DC (n 14) 4.

[52] ibid.

[53] eg, *Collins Dictionary*: www.collinsdictionary.com/dictionary/english/hypothetical: 'If something is hypothetical, it is based on possible ideas or situations rather than actual ones'; *Cambridge*

ii. Misunderstandings and Misrepresentations

The positions adopted by the trial judge appear to be intertwined with a number of misleading or erroneous statements linked to the Court's view that the issue at stake was fundamentally a custody matter in the resolution of which a US court must have a determining voice.

First, the trial judge acknowledged, *in limine*,

> after considering the arguments made in the briefs, the Court is convinced that this is not a case of children being wrongfully removed or retained within the meaning of the [Hague] Convention, but rather a custody dispute that ought to be decided by a court with jurisdiction over these matters.[54]

Later, reinforcing the idea that the denial of the return petition was both inevitable and unquestionably correct, the Court noted:

> [W]hile [the father] describes this case as an 'invitation for forum shopping at its worst', let us be clear what denial of this petition will mean for him and [the mother]. They, two US citizens, will litigate custody of their US citizen children … in a court in the United States that may well ultimately decide that jurisdiction lies in Brazil.[55]

Such statements encapsulate a double misrepresentation of the role and aims of the Hague Convention. Citizenship (nationality) was one of the connecting factors that the drafters of the Hague Convention chose to reject in favour of that of habitual residence precisely because the criterion of the child's nationality seemed inappropriate to the drafters.[56] One of the reasons why the 1980 Hague Convention was negotiated was indeed to fill gaps in the protection of children left by the 1961 Hague Convention on the Protection of Minors. Indeed,

> the effect of these provisions [of the 1961 Convention] was such that, if the minor was abducted from the country of his or her habitual residence and taken to the country of his or her nationality by a parent … no recourse was available.[57]

The drafters of the 1980 Hague Convention in other words meant to prevent the requested State from 'hiding behind the citizenship of the child to reject the return petition'.[58] Therefore, while citizenship may understandably be *one* of the many

Dictionary: dictionary.cambridge.org/dictionary/english/hypothetical: 'imagined or suggested but not necessarily real or true'.

[54] *Pope* DC (n 14) 4–5. The Court thus expected that jurisdiction be decided under the Uniform Child Custody Jurisdiction and Enforcement Act, as in *Lin Shu-Hsin v Virgin* No117,692 slip op (Okla, 12 February 2019). This reference was however irrelevant and misleading as this case involved a dispute connected to the US and Taiwan, to which the 1980 Hague Convention does not apply.

[55] Ibid, 12.

[56] AE Anton, 'The Hague Convention on International Child Abduction' (1981) 30 *International & Comparative Law Quarterly* 537, 544.

[57] A Dyer, 'International Child Abduction by Parents' in AL Droz, M Pélichet and A Dyer, *La Conférence de Droit International Privé, 25 ans après la création de son Bureau Permanent : Bilan et Perspectives*, vol 168 (RCADI, 1980) 242.

[58] F Monéger, 'Les enlèvements internationaux d'enfants' (1992) GI *JCP* 3605, para 35. According to the latest global statistics published by the HCCH, the country of refuge is predominantly (58%) a

relevant facts that courts will consider as part of the determination of the habitual residence of a child, other aspects were potentially equally relevant, such as the fact that the father was a permanent resident of Brazil,[59] or that the mother, with whom he had a relationship since 2014 and a public deed of stable union under Brazilian law, had been living in Brazil since July 2018.[60] Contrary to the trial court's view, *forum shopping* is still possible where the court seised is the parties' national forum. As acknowledged by Article 16, the Hague Convention's mechanism is meant, albeit indirectly, to determine the competing jurisdiction claims that can be made by two countries,[61] bearing in mind that decisions as to forum, especially in child abduction claims, may well be 'outcome determinative'.[62] Even leaving aside the potential nationalist reflexes of courts handling child abduction cases,[63] litigating in the United States rather than Brazil would in fact have had an impact on the law applicable to the custody determination regarding the twins.[64] Citizenship of the stakeholders alone did not justify giving precedence to the jurisdiction of the US courts in this case as opposed to that of the Brazilian courts, the courts of the alleged family home and of the country in which the parties intended their children to be raised.[65]

Further, the Court never properly assessed the timing of the twins' retention. The Court cursorily rejected the father's allegation that the birth of the children marked the start of the retention on the basis that 'this position cannot be squared with the text of the Convention, which explains that a child cannot be wrongfully retained away from a place unless they were first a habitual resident of that place'.[66] According to the Court,

> the Convention text indicates that it does not apply to all child-custody disputes with an international element. Rather, it applies to cases where a child is being retained away from the country in which they have assimilated and developed ties that have been broken by the removal.[67]

country of which the taking person is a national, *cf* 'Prel Doc No 11 A' (n 8) 3. The previous statistics showed figures ranging from 52% to 60%.

[59] *Pope* DC (n 14) 1.

[60] *cf Pope CA* (n 10) 969.

[61] Pérez-Vera (n 23) para 121: 'This article, so as to promote the realisation of the Convention's objects regarding the return of the child, seeks to prevent a decision on the merits of the rights of custody being taken in the State of refuge'. *Monasky* (n 11) 723: 'the Convention's return requirement is a "provisional" remedy that fixes the forum for custody proceedings'.

[62] Schuz (n 28) 443.

[63] See the contrasting US statistics referred to above (n 17). See generally, A Fiorini, 'Enlèvements internationaux d'enfants – solutions internationales et responsabilités étatiques' (2005) 51 *McGill Law Journal*, 279, 289.

[64] Neither Brazil nor the US have ratified the 1996 Hague Child Protection Convention, nor are they bound by any other bilateral or multilateral instrument harmonising international family law rules: www.state.gov/treaties-in-force/.

[65] The general disregard of the District Court for the fact that the situation was not purely American is evident in footnote 35 which states 'under American law, [the mother] could have unilaterally terminated her pregnancy', ignoring the fact that, under Brazilian law, the law of her habitual residence at least until she left for the US, abortion was illegal, *cf* M Malta et al, 'Abortion in Brazil: the case for women's rights, lives, and choices' (2019) 4 *Lancet* 552.

[66] *Pope* DC (n 14) 8.

[67] Ibid.

In this the Court operated a logical inversion. In its view, the timing of the retention could not be moments after the birth as the children could not possibly have a habitual residence at that point. Yet the determination of the timing of the removal or the retention must instead *precede* that of the habitual residence of the child: according to Article 4, the Convention applies to children who were habitually resident in a Contracting State '*immediately before* any breach of custody or access rights'. The Court should thus have decided if the birth marked the start of the retention *before* identifying where the twins were habitually resident at that point. Having deemed the alleged timing legally impossible rather than factually incorrect, the Court did not properly assess when the breach of custody rights had allegedly taken place. The Court simply expressed its disapproval of the identification of the twins' birth as the relevant point by noting that the father

> talks in terms of a wrongful removal when he describes [the mother]'s actions as an 'abduction' and as 'her deception in sneaking away from the marital home, lying to her husband regarding her intentions, and secreting herself and the unborn children from him until she gave birth and thereafter'.[68]

The Court did not draw any conclusions from what it presented as 'undisputed [facts] that after leaving Brazil for the United States, [the mother] ended her relationship with [the father], remained in the United States, and intends to remain in the United States'.[69] If the parents indeed separated[70] during the pregnancy and the father knew then that the mother would not return to Brazil after the birth, the retention would have predated the children's birth, rendering the Convention inapplicable. If the parents' relationship had deteriorated but they were still willing to try family life together in Brazil at some point after the birth, then the answer might be different. If the parents only separated around the time of the birth and the mother only manifested her decision not to return to Brazil at that point, then the retention would perhaps be at the time claimed by the father. Yet the facts surrounding the period between the mother's travel to the United States and the return petition were not investigated by the Court. The Court's inconsistency regarding the relevant point led it to contradict itself by stating 'the question is thus: Where did the children regularly or usually live *just prior to their birth*' and then noting as part of the answer that '[the parents] have never *during the children's short lifetimes* agreed on a place of residency' even though intentions post retention were irrelevant to the habitual residence determination.[71]

Lastly, having overcomplicated the issue by questioning first if newborns can even have a habitual residence at birth[72] and then having hypothesised reluctantly

[68] ibid, 3 *ad notam*.

[69] Ibid, 11.

[70] The father actually disputed that fact, as noted by the Court of Appeals (n 10) 972.

[71] *Pope* DC (n 14) 7 and 11–12. The emphasis is our own.

[72] To justify its view that newborns may not be capable of having a habitual residence at birth, the Court referred to some cases (ibid, 9 *ad notam*) which had contemplated that the children *in question* might have no habitual residence at the relevant time or had positively concluded that they did not. This reference confuses *de facto* absence of habitual residence of a specific child with *ex lege* impossibility for children to have a habitual residence at birth and is at odds with *Monasky*; see above (n 50).

that this may be the case, the Court reasoned that 'there was never shared parental intent with respect to the children because they did not yet exist at the time of the alleged agreement'.[73] For the Court, accepting that habitual residence could be determined by an *in utero* agreement was problematic because 'first, it render[ed] an agreement as to where to raise a child irrevocable unless superseded by a new agreement'[74] and 'second [the father]'s position ignore[d] everything that has happened since the alleged *in utero* agreement'.[75]

As shown above, other courts in the United States had, until *Monasky*, relied on shared intentions before birth to determine the habitual residence of very young children. Considering that the habitual residence of a neonate may be determined by an *in utero* agreement does not mean they are any more irrevocable than post-birth agreements. By nature, the last shared intent standard, when used to establish a child's habitual residence[76] implies that the courts enquire into the shared intent at the last time that it was shared before the removal or retention. If there was an early agreement but the parents jointly changed their mind, the earlier agreement would naturally be replaced by the later one. However, no new agreement about where to raise the children could emerge from purely unilateral actions,[77] regardless of whether the initial joint intentions were established pre-birth or post-birth. The District Court should thus have considered whether the parents had jointly changed their plans (regarding where the twins would live once born) between the uncontested *in utero* agreement and the start of the retention rather than asserting that the 'shared parental intent that existed 19–20 weeks *in utero* is not sufficient to override every other undisputed [unilateral] fact of this case'. Indeed, the unilateral acts of the mother after the moment of the last shared intent pointing towards the United States were no more relevant than the unilateral acts of the father after the last moment of shared intent pointing towards Brazil. If however the parents, acknowledging that their initially shared intentions were put into question by the deterioration of their relationship, were discussing, 'negotiating' alternative plans, such as the family living in the United States in the early stages of the twins' lives, then this would have impacted on the habitual residence determination.[78] On the other hand, contrary to what the Court noted, it was entirely irrelevant that the parents had never agreed on a place of residence since the birth of the children, as any facts happening *after* the start of a retention should have been immaterial to the determination of the twins' habitual residence for the purposes of the return petition.

[73] *Pope* DC (n 14) 10.
[74] ibid.
[75] ibid, 11.
[76] Shared parental intentions are no longer a dispositive factor post *Monasky* but only one of many circumstances to consider.
[77] eg, *Rath v Marconi*, 2016 US Dist LEXIS 167685, 55.
[78] cp *Diagne* (n 8).

B. The *Pope* Appeal

Following *Monasky*, an appellate court will reverse for clear error only where 'although there is evidence to support it, the reviewing court on the entire evidence is left with the definite and firm conviction that a mistake has been committed'.[79] For all the shortcomings evident in the judgment as regards the reasoning of the trial court, the Court of Appeals for the Tenth Circuit found that the denial of the father's petition was the correct outcome.

Applying the deferential review standard to the *Pope* case, the Court of Appeals found that the first order, though decided 'without the benefit of the Supreme Court's [decision] in *Monasky*',[80] was consistent with the 'totality of the circumstances approach'.[81] The appellate court summarised the background, noting important facts that had not been mentioned by the trial judge[82] and nuancing other findings,[83] traced key aspects of *Monasky* and determined it could 'not conclude that the District Court clearly erred in determining that Brazil was not the infants' habitual residence'.[84] Neither the father's assertion that a newborn's habitual residence was where the parents last agreed it would be, nor the mother's emphasis on the fact that the twins had never been present in Brazil was decisive as the Supreme Court ruled that 'there are no categorical requirements for establishing a child's habitual residence'.[85] The Court of Appeals, whose judgment is expressed in a much less emotional language than the District Court order, first rejected the father's argument that the trial judge had erred in concluding that newborns cannot have a habitual residence on the basis that 'all the [trial] court said was that it was not convinced' that they did.[86] It thus primarily focused on the twins' habitual residence determination before addressing the question whether the District Court had denied the father due process by deciding the petition without holding an evidentiary hearing.

The Tenth Circuit found the District Court ruling to be consistent with *Monasky's* 'totality of the circumstances' test as a 'wide range of factors'[87] had been considered which it summarised in a series of quotes from the trial court's order. In so doing it reproduced two errors initially made by the trial court: the reference to the entirely irrelevant situation after the birth (ie, after the start of the retention)[88]

[79] *United States v US Gypsum Co*, 333 US 364, 394–95.
[80] *Pope* CA (n 10) 970.
[81] ibid, 972.
[82] The Court of Appeals noted, eg, that the parents had a deed of stable union under Brazilian law (ibid, 969), or that the mother had taken her pet cat when she left Brazil (ibid, 970).
[83] The Court of Appeals acknowledged that in the Autumn of 2019 the parents' relationship was 'strained' (ibid), rather than accepting the trial court's view that the mother had ended her relationship with the father, a point contested by the petitioner (ibid, 972).
[84] ibid, 971.
[85] *Monasky* (n 11) 726, 728.
[86] *Pope* CA (n 10) 970.
[87] ibid, 972.
[88] ibid. And *Pope* DC (n 14) 11–12.

and the confusion between inapplicability of the 1980 Hague Convention because the children did not have their habitual residence in the requesting State and the wrongfulness of the retention[89] (contrary to Article 3 of the Hague Convention which defines wrongfulness in terms of a breach of actually exercised custody rights). Nonetheless, the Court of Appeals found the trial judge's findings to have had 'support in the record' and thus was 'not left with a definite and firm conviction of a mistake'.[90]

The trial court had also decided that an evidentiary hearing was not needed because it had reached its conclusion based 'solely on the facts alleged in the petition and taking as true [the father]'s contention that he and [the mother] had an *in utero*, pre-estrangement agreement that they would reside in Brazil with their future children'.[91] It is accepted that district courts have 'a substantial degree of discretion in determining the procedures necessary to resolve a petition filed pursuant to the [Hague] Convention'[92] and its implementing legislation. All that due process requires is that the parties are given a 'meaningful opportunity to be heard'.[93] Given the requirement for expeditious action in Hague Proceedings,[94] affording discretion to the court in deciding whether to hold an evidentiary hearing appears entirely reasonable as the usefulness of such a hearing will vary depending on the circumstances of the case and the nature of the facts that are contested. The Court of Appeals considered that the trial judge had acted within his discretion because the father had put forward and evidenced many facts, which were assumed as true by the judge, and failed to identify any specific additional evidence he could have presented. However, even assuming that all the relevant factual elements were within the purview of the Court, an evidentiary hearing may still have had the important merit of testing the credibility of submissions from both sides, for example regarding the start of the children's retention. In addition, if elements of fact or evidence in favour of one of the parties are overlooked[95] or afforded no weight,[96] can one truly say that party was given a *meaningful* opportunity to be heard? Ultimately, however, the trial judge's doubt that newborns can have a habitual residence, which had coloured his decision both regarding the twins' habitual residence and the lack of need for an evidentiary hearing, could

[89] *Pope* CA (n 10) 972: 'the infants were not habitual residents of Brazil and, accordingly, [the mother] did not wrongfully retain them in Oklahoma'. And *Pope* DC (n 14) 8.

[90] Ibid, 972.

[91] *Pope* DC (n 14) 5.

[92] *West v Dobrev*, 735 F 3d 921, 929 (10th Cir, 2013).

[93] ibid, 932.

[94] 1980 Hague Convention, Arts 2 and 11.

[95] The father disputed that the mother had ended their relationship before the birth and intended to remain in the US. In response, the Court of Appeals noted 'the very existence of this litigation supports this conclusion'. However, as previously shown, the timing of this separation was crucial for the determination of the petition.

[96] While the District Court claimed to be taking as true the fact that there was an *in utero* agreement (*Pope* DC (n 14) 5) it subsequently entirely dismissed its value in stating that 'there never was shared parental intent in respect of the children' because they did not yet exist at the time (ibid, 10).

not be redressed given the limits of the deferential standard of review.[97] Indeed, is it really possible to note, and draw consequences from the fact, that considering a 'range of factors' is not the same as considering 'the totality of the circumstances', even in situations in which a strong subjectivism appears to have guided the first court, without engaging in a *de novo* appreciation of the case?

A brief study of child abduction cases which considered the habitual residence of very young children after *Monasky* confirms the tentative conclusions drawn from *Pope* that the deferential standard of review, coupled with the nature of the new habitual residence test, leave fertile ground for subjectivism and may promote a lack of decisional harmony.

IV. Putting *Pope* in the Context of Other Post *Monasky* Cases

In all cases regarding habitual residence in child abduction cases where *Monasky* was decided between the trial court's and the appellate court's decisions, appellate courts have, like the Tenth Circuit in *Pope*, systematically affirmed the initial order. In *Minkiewitz*, a Californian state court of appeal affirmed the return order of a child on the basis that the child, who had spent a year in Mexico, was habitually resident there under both the parental intention and the acclimatisation test.[98] In *Smith*, the US Court of Appeals for the Fifth Circuit affirmed a judgment dismissing a return petition to Argentina of children who had spent over two years there before being allegedly wrongfully retained in the United States.[99] Similarly, in *Farr*, the US Court of Appeals for the Ninth Circuit affirmed a trial court decision dismissing the return application of three-year-old children who had spent two years in Mexico before being removed to Arizona.[100] In *De Carvalho*, in stark contrast to the *Pope* decision, a court of appeal in Florida affirmed a return order to Brazil of a neonate born in the United States who was one month old and had only lived in Florida prior to their retention.[101] The great variety of outcomes could be explained by factual differences relevant to each case but also by the very limited review involved in the clear error standard, especially when combined with the fact that the Supreme Court in *Monasky* did not entirely break from the past when establishing the correct habitual residence test.

The totality of the circumstances test means that elements of the tests hitherto applied by all Circuits in the United States, are still in part relevant: circumstances regarding the child's integration in a social and family environment and

[97] On the high threshold of the clear error test, see below, section IV.
[98] *Minkiewitz v Becker*, 2021 Cal App Unpub LEXIS 892 (11 February 2021).
[99] *Smith v Smith*, 976 F3 3d 558 (5th Cir, 2020).
[100] *Farr v Kendrick*, 824 Fed Appx 480 (9th Cir, 2020).
[101] *De Carvalho* (n 10).

parental intentions, and which hitherto 'may ultimately [have caused] a judge to reach opposite conclusions regarding a child's habitual residence when examined separately'[102] are, along with any other relevant aspect, now meant to be balanced as part of the determination of the child's habitual residence. Since all Circuits 'consider[ed] *both* parental intent and the child's acclimatisation, differing only in emphasis',[103] it can be assumed that the parties involved in appeals pending at the time of *Monasky*, would have already put forward to the trial court the facts that were now relevant to the *Monasky* test so that instances in which a trial court clearly erred will be less frequent than in cases in which a completely new test would have been introduced.

Where all potentially significant facts have been mentioned and evidenced by the parties, a trial court will have identified those it deems particularly pertinent regarding the (now 'old') test it was supposed to apply, and focus on those. If other facts are acknowledged in passing but were not deemed relevant in the context of the initial enquiry, it is naturally unlikely they will have emerged sufficiently strongly for an appellate court to find that the trial judge made a clear error in the context of a new test that combines the old standard and additional circumstances, and given the 'limited guidance'[104] from the Supreme Court regarding the respective weight to be afforded to relevant factors.[105] Indeed, the threshold for clear error is high. According to the US Supreme Court 'a finding is "clearly erroneous" when although there is evidence to support it, the reviewing court on the entire evidence is left with the definite and firm conviction that a mistake has been committed'.[106] 'If the district court view of the evidence is plausible in light of the entire record, an appellate court may not reverse even if it is convinced that it would have weighed the evidence differently in the first instance',[107] bearing in mind that 'where there are two permissible views of the evidence, the factfinder's choice between them cannot be clearly erroneous'.[108] In addition, in many habitual residence in child abduction cases crucial facts will understandably be disputed and trial courts may be influenced by testimonies that are perceived as more sincere or believable. This again will reinforce the strength of findings made by the trial court for

[102] MA Kucinski, 'The Future of Litigating an International Child Abduction Case in the United States' (2020) 33 *Journal of the American Academy of Matrimonial Lawyers* 31, 38.

[103] *Redmond* (n 38). This analysis was confirmed by the majority in *Monasky* (n 11) 726. See also, AL Estin, 'Where is the Child at Home? Determining Habitual Residence after Monasky' (2020) 54 *Family Law Quarterly* 127, 137.

[104] Estin (n 103) 134. See also, AG Spector, 'Proceedings Under the Hague Child Abduction Convention: 2020' (2021) 54 *Family Law Quarterly* 325, 327. Before it was even endorsed by the Supreme Court, *Abou-Haidar v Vazquez*, 945 F 3d 1208, 1220 (DC Cir, December 27, 2019) termed the totality of the circumstances test 'relatively unguided'.

[105] *Monasky* (n 11) provided clear but minimal guidelines that 'no single fact … is dispositive across all cases' (727); adding the 'bottom line: There are no categorical requirements for establishing a child's habitual residence' (728).

[106] *Gypsum* (n 79) 394–95.

[107] *Brnovich v Democratic National Committee*, 141 S Ct 2321, 2349 (2021).

[108] *Anderson v Bessemer City*, 470 US 564, 574 (1985).

> when findings are based on determinations regarding the credibility of witnesses, Rule 52(a) [Federal Rules of Civil Procedure] demands even greater deference to the trial court's findings; for only the trial judge can be aware of the variations in demeanor and tone of voice that bear so heavily on the listener's understanding of and belief in what is said.[109]

Interestingly, the study of abduction cases turning on habitual residence determinations regarding very young children which went to court since *Monasky* shows similarly disparate outcomes. For example, in *Dumitrascu*, the District Court for the District of Colorado considered the return petition regarding a child whose parents, initially established in the United States and planning to live there permanently with the child, had gone to Romania for the birth of the child and a few months thereafter. When the child was 10 months old, the father took her to the United States for six months with the consent of the mother but did not return her as agreed. The Court granted the return petition on the basis that the child had been habitually resident in Romania when the retention became wrongful.[110] In *Schwarz*, the District Court for the Eastern District of Wisconsin refused to consider a baby born in Mexico and who had lived there until he was allegedly wrongly removed at three months to be habitually resident in Mexico.[111] In *Oliva*, a California District Court dismissed a return petition to Mexico concerning a three-year-old child who had been born and lived in Mexico until the family went to the United States, and whose alleged wrongful retention had begun two months after the arrival in the United States.[112] In *Meng-Jung Ho*, an Illinois District Court ordered the return of a 21-month-old child whose family, initially established in the United States, had spent four years in New Zealand where the child was born and had lived until his alleged retention in the United States.[113] In *Harm*, the Court of Appeals for the Fifth Circuit affirmed a trial judge's refusal to order the return to Ireland of a child who led a peripatetic life but whose parents had made Ireland their 'home base' for a year prior to the start of the alleged wrongful removal.[114] In *Garcia*, a Texas District Court ordered the return to Spain of an allegedly wrongly retained two and a half year-old child, born in the United States, who had lived in Egypt for 16 months and then in Spain for 10 months until the father went to Mexico for work. After a while the mother and child had visited him there for three months, then instead of travelling to Egypt to visit family, the mother and child had stayed in the United States.[115] In *Kenny*, the Court of Appeals for the Ninth Circuit affirmed a trial court's decision denying the return petition regarding a child who had been born and lived a year in Ireland until the family relocated

[109] ibid, 575.
[110] *Dumitrascu* (n 42).
[111] *Schwartz* (n 8).
[112] *Oliva v Espinoza*, 2021 US Dist LEXIS 192114.
[113] *Meng-Jung Ho v Ho*, 2021 US Dist LEXIS 129173.
[114] *Harm v Lake-Harm*, 16 F 4th 450 (5th Cir, 2021).
[115] *Garcia v Ramsis*, 2022 US Dist LEXIS 17025 (ED Texas, 31 January 2022).

to Alaska and lived there for four months until the start of the alleged wrongful retention.[116]

Of course, 'locating a child's home is a fact-driven' enquiry and the above snapshot does not convey the 'unique circumstances of the case' that each court had to be 'sensitive to'.[117] But some courts, while trying to apply the post *Monasky* habitual residence test, appear to have continued to be overly influenced by the formerly prevailing standard. In post *Monasky* cases involving very young children, a number of decisions show that the importance of aspects that were outcome determinative in the previous test and should have become just *one* of the circumstances relevant to the new standard, continue to be magnified despite the Supreme Court's prescription that no factor should be dispositive. In *Oliva*, for example, although the trial court was at pains to note that it was applying the *Monasky* test rather than the shared intent test hitherto applied by Ninth Circuit courts, the Court's analysis remained largely focused on the fact that the parents had moved to the United States with a view to making it their habitual residence.[118] In *Kenny*, and *Schwartz*, the appellate decisions similarly concentrated on the parental intentions to establish the habitual residence of the children.[119] It is possible that, in time, the totality of the circumstances test will be more strongly established (and more influential than previous tests on the judicial mind). Meanwhile, these contrasting outcomes at least exemplify how hybrid tests, such as the totality of the circumstances test, grant judges what appears to be 'unbridled discretion'[120] in 1980 Hague Convention child habitual residence cases, potentially leading to confusingly diverse results due to a varied interpretation of similar facts by different judges that cannot be controlled in the absence of independent appellate review.

V. Conclusion

This chapter has not argued that considering that the twins were not habitually resident in Brazil at the time of their alleged wrongful retention and dismissing

[116] *Kenny v Davis*, 2022 US App LEXIS 4466.

[117] *Monasky* (n 11) 727. This had already led a commentator to predict that 'in many cases, in all of the circuits, the evidence and analysis will not change significantly as courts embrace the new standard', Estin (n 103) 139.

[118] *Oliva* (n 112) 18: 'all of the facts taken together indicate that Petitioner and Respondent, with [the child], intended to make the United States their habitual residence'.

[119] *Kenny* (n 116) 3: 'When aggregated, these facts can properly be construed as indicating that [the parents] made their home in Alaska, so the district court did not clearly err in making its factual finding that Alaska was the child's habitual residence immediately before [the start of the retention]'. *Schwartz* (n 8) 7–8: 'even though [the parents] shared an address in Mexico for 5 years and the children spent most of their young lives in Mexico [the father] has not established by a preponderance of the evidence that the children are habitual residents of Mexico. The record suggests that [the parents] did not have a shared intent to abandon the United States for Mexico'.

[120] *Office of the Children's Lawyer v Balev* [2018] 1 SCR 398 (Supreme Court of Canada) per Coté & Rowe JJ (dissenting) [152].

the return petition was necessarily the wrong outcome. Rather, it seeks to suggest that by raising misleading questions and providing answers guided by personal intuition more than legal rigour, the Court's decision, though reasoned, was not as convincing as it should have been. After all, *Pope v Lunday* was as much or indeed as little about whether US twins born in the United States to US parents could be habitually resident elsewhere as about whether twins born abroad to a family settled in Brazil could be *not* habitually resident in Brazil. Yet, applying the clear error review standard, the Court of Appeals had little choice but to affirm the trial court's decision.

In this *Pope* may, beyond its individual flaws, also be illustrative of broader risks in habitual residence cases. 'Judges' decisions are a function of what they prefer to do, tempered by what they think they ought to do, but constrained by what they perceive is feasible to do'.[121] In US 1980 Hague Convention habitual residence cases, the deferential standard of appellate review – impacting on what trial judges may perceive as feasible[122] – mixed with a habitual residence test promoting indeterminacy and judicial discretion[123] – (barely) shaping what judges think they ought to do – means that few external (legal and institutional) factors constrain judicial decision-marking. Partially hidden by the fact-intensive nature of the habitual residence enquiry, this combination gives scope for personal preferences and subjectivity strongly to influence decisions, a most unsatisfactory result in an area where international families deserve predictability.[124]

[121] JL Gibson, 'From simplicity to complexity: the development of theory in the study of judicial behavior' (1983) 5 *Political Behaviour* 7, 9 and 32.

[122] It has already been suggested that *Monasky* should now reduce the number of appeals in habitual residence in child abduction cases, Estin (n 103) 136.

[123] *Balev* (n 120) [153]. See also Spector (n 104) 327.

[124] *Balev*, ibid. On the key importance of predictability, see PE McEleavy, 'La résidence habituelle, un critère de rattachement en quête de son identité: perspectives de common law' (2008–10) 19 *Travaux du Comité français de droit international privé* 127. The lack of predictability in this area is all the more unpalatable that habitual residence is a ground for refusal in a quarter of Hague return applications worldwide: see 'Prel Doc No 11 A' (n 8) 3.

14

Private Divorces and Brussels IIb: Three Questions for the New Article 65(1)

ANATOL DUTTA

I. Introduction

It is by now a well-known trend – also within Europe – that the dissolution of marriage by divorce is no longer an act exclusively performed by the courts but is also achievable by an autonomous legal act of the spouses, be it by agreement or by unilateral declaration. To differentiate clearly between private divorces and divorces pronounced by a court can, however, be difficult, at least from a functional perspective: what defines whether a state authority pronounces the divorce in its own capacity or merely assists the spouses in autonomously dissolving their marriage? The dividing line is hard to identify since private divorces often involve acts performed by state authorities such as formally drawing up or registering the spouses' declarations and thereby providing them with the requirements of form.

The European legislator recently introduced a new provision in Article 65(1) of the Brussels IIb Regulation[1] in reaction to the widespread confusion following the decision of the Court of Justice of the European Union (CJEU) in the *Sahyouni* case.[2] Said decision does not answer clearly, inter alia, whether the provisions on recognition and enforcement of foreign judgments provided by the Brussels IIa Regulation apply to private divorces performed in other European Member States like France, Greece, Italy, Portugal, Romania, Slovenia and Spain.[3] Sentence one of

[1] Council Regulation (EU) 2019/1111 of 25 June 2019 on jurisdiction, the recognition and enforcement of decisions in matrimonial matters and the matters of parental responsibility, and on international child abduction, [2019] OJ L178/1 (here referred to as Brussels IIb).

[2] Case C-372/16 *Soha Sahyouni v Raja Mamisch* (CFEU, 20 December 2017). In its decision, the CJEU referred for the cross-border effects of private divorces to the responsibility of the European legislator, *cf* para 47.

[3] This was answered in the affirmative by the Berlin Kammergericht in respect of a private divorce under Italian law, see KG 30 March 2020 – 1 W 236/19, [2020] *Zeitschrift für das gesamte Familienrecht* 1215.

the newly introduced Article 65(1) of Brussels IIb now provides: 'Authentic instruments and agreements on legal separation and divorce which have binding legal effect in the Member State of origin shall be recognised in other Member States without any special procedure being required'. According to the second sentence of the provision, this 'recognition' shall be governed by the rules on the recognition of judgments in Article 30 et seq of Brussels IIb.

Article 65 of Brussels IIb has a complex legal nature and is innovative in many respects. Consequently, the provision prompts several questions – three of which shall be addressed in this chapter[4] commemorating Jonathan Fitchen (see also section V below), a great European private international lawyer who contributed much to our understanding of authentic instruments and their cross-border effects.[5]

II. Question No 1: Which Types of Private Divorces are Covered by the New Rules?

The material scope of the newly introduced recognition rule in Article 65(1) of Brussels IIb covers authentic instruments and agreements on legal separation and divorce which have binding legal effect in the Member State of origin.

The reference to 'authentic instruments' and 'agreements' restricts the scope of Article 65(1) of Brussels IIb to private divorces whose formal validity is based on the involvement of a state authority in the Member State of origin. The latter can either involve formally drawing up or registering the spouses' declarations in an 'authentic instrument' according to Article 2(2) No 2 of Brussels IIb or registering these declarations as an 'agreement' according to Article 2(2) No 3 of Brussels IIb. An 'agreement' in that sense is 'a document which is not an authentic instrument, has been concluded by the parties in matters falling within the scope of this Regulation and has been registered by a public authority as communicated to the Commission by a Member State.' All types of private divorces currently permitted by the Member States require some sort of official documentation and should therefore fulfil the formal requirements set out by Article 65(1) of Brussels IIb. The reference to 'agreements' on legal separation and divorce seems to be targeted at private divorces under Article 229 et seq of the French Civil Code. This type of private divorce is formally valid after the lawyer of either party has signed the document, which is afterwards deposited with a notary public.

Furthermore, an authentic instrument or agreement documenting the private divorce needs to have 'binding legal effect' in the Member State of origin (this is the Member State in which the authentic instrument was formally drawn up or

[4] Which is based on an earlier paper: 'Privatscheidungen und Brüssel IIb: drei Fragen an den neuen Art 65 Abs 1' [2020] *Zeitschrift für das gesamte Familienrecht* 1428. I thank Charlotte Wendland, research fellow at my chair, for her valuable assistance.

[5] J Fitchen, *The Private International Law of Authentic Instruments* (Hart Publishing, 2020).

registered or the agreement was registered).[6] The 'binding legal effect' addressed in the provision does not refer to the ability of the document to provide evidence as this is a general effect of authentic instruments governed by the applicable procedural law. Therefore, the European legislator does not explicitly refer to the 'binding legal effect' of an authentic instrument, where the object of recognition is solely the document's function as a piece of evidence.[7] For Article 65(1) of Brussels IIb it is, however, decisive whether the private divorce that is contained in the authentic instrument or the agreement has binding legal effects in the Member State of origin. This is the case if it has the effect of divorcing the couple or legally separating the spouses. Thus, Article 65(1) of Brussels IIb applies only to authentic instruments or agreements originating from a Member State whose domestic law allows private divorces.

The wording of Article 65(1) of Brussels IIb does not use the term 'private divorce'. Thus, at first sight, judicial decisions on divorce and legal separation could be governed by that provision, too, if they are contained in an authentic instrument and are legally binding. However, Article 30 et seq of Brussels IIb contain specific rules on the recognition of foreign judgments that override Article 65(1) of Brussels IIb.[8] Nevertheless, the difficulty remains to decide how much involvement of state authorities in the legal act of divorce will turn the divorce into a decision as defined by Article 2(1) of Brussels IIb. This question was discussed intensely before the recast of the Brussels IIa Regulation[9] by the Brussels IIb Regulation. For example, the Berlin Kammergericht, a regional court of appeal, characterised the private divorce under Italian law as a decision in the sense of Brussels IIa and applied the provisions on the recognition of judgments;[10] and the German Bundesgerichtshof has asked the CJEU for a preliminary ruling in this case in the meantime.[11] The

[6] Art 2(2) No 4 of Brussels IIb.

[7] *cf* Regulation (EU) 650/2012 of the European Parliament and of the Council of 4 July 2012 on jurisdiction, applicable law, recognition and enforcement of decisions and acceptance and enforcement of authentic instruments in matters of succession and on the creation of a European Certificate of Succession, [2012] OJ L201/107, Art 59 (here referred to as the Succession Regulation); and Council Regulation (EU) 2016/1103 of 24 June 2016 implementing enhanced cooperation in the area of jurisdiction, applicable law and the recognition and enforcement of decisions in matters of matrimonial property regimes, [2016] OJ L183/1; and Council Regulation (EU) 2016/1104 of 24 June 2016 implementing enhanced cooperation in the area of jurisdiction, applicable law and the recognition and enforcement of decisions in matters of the property consequences of registered partnerships, [2016] OJ L183/30, Art 58 (here referred to as the Property Regulations).

[8] Similarly, M Sonnentag and J Haselbeck, 'Divorce without the Involvement of a Court in Member States of the EU and the Brussels IIbis- and the Rome III-Regulation' (2022) 1 *Praxis des Internationalen Privat- und Verfahrensrechts* 29.

[9] Council Regulation (EC) 2201/2003 of 27 November 2003 concerning jurisdiction and the recognition and enforcement of judgments in matrimonial matters and the matters of parental responsibility, repealing Regulation (EC) 1347/2000, [2003] OJ L338/1.

[10] Above (n 2).

[11] See BGH 28 October 2020 – XII ZB 187/20, [2021] *Zeitschrift für das gesamte Familienrecht* 119. This paper was finalised before the (problematic) decision of the CJEU in Case C-646/20 *Senatsverwaltung für Inneres und Sport, Standesamtsaufsicht v TB* (CFEU, 15 November 2022), where the CJEU came to the conclusion that the provisions of the Brussel IIa (and – least obiter – Brussels IIb) Regulation on the recognition of court decisions apply also to private divorces at least under Italian law.

fact that Article 65 of Brussels IIb now contains a specific provision for private divorces should, however, lead to a narrower interpretation of the term 'decision'. When drafting the Brussels IIb Regulation, there was – at least according to reports by persons familiar with the negotiations – universal agreement among the Council that the existing rules on recognition did not cover the types of private divorce that recently emerged in Europe mentioned already (in section I). Only the application of Article 46 of Brussels IIa to authentic instruments documenting private divorces was discussed.[12] This suggestion was refused by the majority due to the lack of enforceability of these documents, at least regarding divorces which do not require any enforcement but rather dissolve the marriage affected *ex lege*. Thus, Article 65(1) of Brussels IIb was designed to close the legislative gap that was identified on the basis of this restrictive interpretation. The intention to close this gap supports the view that the term 'decision' – at least under the Brussels IIb Regulation – is to be construed narrowly. However, agreements negotiated by the spouses that were approved by the judiciary should still be characterised as decisions in the sense of Article 2(1) of Brussels IIb and therefore fall outside the scope of Article 65(1) of Brussels IIb.[13]

Article 100(1) of Brussels IIb clarifies the temporal scope of Article 65(1) of Brussels IIb. The provision applies to all private divorces formally drawn up or registered in an authentic instrument on or after 1 August 2022 or which are contained in an agreement that was officially registered on or after that date.

III. Question No 2: What is the Scope of 'Recognition' in the Sense of the Provision?

There is some uncertainty as to the precise legal consequence triggered by Article 65(1) of Brussels IIb. This uncertainty is closely intertwined with the hybrid legal nature of the provision. It seems to be a mixture of international procedural law and international private law since the provision simply states that the authentic instrument or agreement shall be 'recognised' in other Member States.

Authentic instruments or agreements as mere documents are facts and, in this capacity, cannot be subject to recognition. Thus, the obligation to recognise imposed by Article 65 of Brussels IIb refers to a duty to recognise the legal effects of the document. As explained above, these effects can either be the evidentiary value of the authentic instrument or agreement or the content of the document.

Recognition of the *evidential effect* of an authentic instrument or an agreement would mean to expand the evidentiary value this document possesses in

[12] On this discussion, see, eg, C Mayer, 'Scheidung ohne Gericht – Europäische Entwicklungen' [2018] *Das Standesamt* 106, 112.

[13] *cf* Recital 14 sentence 2 of Brussels IIb. For more details, see J Antomo, 'Ausländische Privatentscheidungen im Standesamt' [2020] *Das Standesamt* 33, 43; C Mayer, 'Verfahrensrechtliche Anerkennung von gerichtlichen Entscheidungen, Urkunden und Parteivereinbarungen – insbesondere von Privatscheidungen nach der neuen Brüssel IIb-VO' [2020] *Das Standesamt* 193, 199.

the Member State of origin to other Member States – a process similar to that commanded by Article 59 of the European Succession Regulation and Article 58 of the European Property Regulations for spouses and registered partners respectively. However, the wording of Article 65 of Brussels IIb differs considerably from said other provisions. While Article 65 of Brussels IIb demands 'recognition', Article 59 of the Succession Regulation and Article 58 of the Property Regulations use the term 'acceptance' of an authentic instrument. And while Article 65 of Brussels IIb does not specify the object of the demanded recognition, the other provisions explicitly refer to the 'evidentiary effects' of the authentic instrument to be accepted in the other Member States. Thus, if the EU legislator wished to restrict the recognition of private divorce documents to their evidentiary effects, they would probably have employed terminology similar to that in Article 59 of the Succession Regulation and Article 58 of the Property Regulations.

Therefore, Article 65 of Brussels IIb can only be understood as ordering the Member States to recognise the *content* of the authentic instrument or agreement, thus the legal act embodied in that document – ie, the private divorce. Recital 70 of Brussels IIb provides an argument for this construction. The Recital provides that authentic instruments and agreements should be treated as equivalent to 'decisions' for the application of the rules on recognition. Foreign judgments are recognised comprehensively, meaning that not only the evidentiary effects of the document in which the judgment is embodied are recognised, but also the legal effects of the judgment. Thus, recognition of a foreign decree of divorce means expanding the legal effects of that decree – ie, the dissolution of marriage – to other Member States. Article 65(1) of Brussels IIb awards the same effect to private divorces. The provision adopts a concept that German private international law discourse discusses (and criticises) under the term '*Anerkennung einer Rechtslage*', ie, recognition of a legal status or situation.[14] The concept resembles that of Article 34 of the European Commission's Proposal for the Succession Regulation, which demanded mutual 'recognition' of foreign authentic instruments, however, was not adopted in the Regulation due to opposition from some Member States.[15]

What are the exact implications of this new form of recognition? It would be too much to assume that the *abstract legal effects* described in the authentic instrument or agreement – the dissolution of the marriage – should be recognised irrespective of the material and formal validity of the actual legal declaration by the spouses. Such a formalised approach towards recognition is adopted in some proposals for

[14] For further information on this concept, see D Coester-Waltjen, 'Anerkennung im Internationalen Personen-, Familien- und Erbrecht und das Europäische Kollisionsrecht' [2006] *Praxis des Internationalen Privat- und Verfahrensrechts* 392, 393 et seq; H-P Mansel, 'Anerkennung als Grundprinzip des Europäischen Rechtsraums, Zur Herausbildung eines europäischen Anerkennungs-Kollisionsrechts: Anerkennung statt Verweisung als neues Strukturprinzip des Europäischen internationalen Privatrechts?' (2006) 70 *Rabels Zeitschrift fur ausländisches und internationales Privatrecht* 651, 712 et seq.

[15] As to the content of the Commission's Proposal and the criticism it received, see, eg, A Dutta, 'Art 59 EuErbVO' in *Münchener Kommentar zum Bürgerlichen Gesetzbuch*, 8th edn (CH Beck, 2020) para 3.

the law of names that suggest recognition of a registered name irrespective of a correct registration.[16] This approach, however, does not fit the purposes of private divorce recognition since it could cause the effects recognised in a foreign country to exceed the legal effects the divorce actually has in its country of origin. If in the Member State of origin the drawing up or registration of the spouses' declarations is only indicative as a (rebuttable) presumption or only provides factual evidence for the spouses' declarations,[17] the same should count in other Member States. It would be too far-reaching to require the other Member States to recognise the authentic instrument or agreement as a legal act unconditionally changing the legal status of the spouses if that is not the case under the law of the Member State of origin.

Thus, only *the actual legal effects of the spouses' declaration* formally drawn up or registered will be recognised in the other Member States. Consequently, Article 65(1) of Brussels IIb is a '*Quasikollisionsnorm*', ie, a quasi-conflict rule that designates the law of the place where the document was formally drawn up or registered as the law applicable to the private divorce embodied in the authentic instrument or agreement.[18] Admissibility, substantive validity and legal effects of a private divorce are governed by the law of the Member State of origin, including its conflict of law rules.[19] Thus, the authentic instrument or agreement is merely the 'crystallisation point' for recognition.[20] Authorities of Member States recognising the authentic instrument or agreement are bound by the private declarations embodied in the document to the same degree that the courts and state authorities in the Member State of origin are according to their domestic law. Thus, the recognition according to Article 30(1), (2) and (5) in combination with Article 65(1) sentence 2 of Brussels IIb, requires foreign authorities or courts to examine the

[16] *cf* Art 12 of the draft European Regulation on the law applicable to names – see A Dutta, R Frank, T Helms, K Krömer and W Pintens, 'One Name Throughout Europe – Draft for a European Regulation on the Law Applicable to Names' (2013–14) 15 *Yearbook of Private International Law* 31.

[17] If the drawing up or registering of the spouses' declarations by a Member State authority has the effect to directly change the spouses' legal status under the applicable law, one should not characterise this legal act as a private divorce but as a decision in the sense of Art 2(1) of Brussels IIb, to which Arts 30 et seq of Brussels IIb are applicable.

[18] Not in favour of this characterisation but regarding the provision as a procedural rule of recognition, eg, C Kohler and W Pintens, 'Entwicklungen im europäischen Personen-, Familien- und Erbrecht 2018–2019' [2019] *Zeitschrift für das gesamte Familienrecht* 1477, 1479 et seq; Antomo (n 13); Mayer above (n 13); M Kramme, 'Private Divorce in Light of the Recast of the Brussels IIbis Regulation' [2021] *Zeitschrift für das Privatrecht der Europäischen Union* 101, 105 et seq; and Sonnentag and Haselbeck (n 8).

[19] In the same direction, Mansel above (n 14) 720.

[20] P Mayer, 'Les methods de la reconnaissance en droit international privé' in *Le droit international privé: esprit et méthodes, Mélanges en l'honneur de Paul Lagarde* (Dalloz, 2005) 562, speaks of 'point de vue concret susceptible de reconnaissance a été "cristallisé"'; sceptically from a legal policy point of view, whether a formally drawn up agreement should suffice for the recognition of a legal status, eg, Coester-Waltjen (n 14) 397 et seq; Mansel, above (n 14) 716; as far as the object of the recognition is an 'agreement' Art 65 (1) Brussels IIb indirectly refers to a registration (which is necessary according to the definition in Art 2(2) No 3 Brussels IIb) – this should suffice according to Coester-Waltjen above (n 14) 397 et seq.

validity and effects of a private divorce with reference to the law of the Member State of origin. However, this examination is permissible only up to the extent that the authorities and courts of the Member State of origin would be competent to examine the validity and effects of the spouses' declarations embodied in such documents. The prohibition of a *révision au fond* does not alter this interpretation.[21] Articles 40 and 71 of Brussels IIb establish this prohibition for the recognition of foreign judgments. Based on the cross-reference in Article 65(1) sentence 2 of Brussels IIb, this prohibition is – at least formally – also applicable to the recognition of authentic instruments and agreements on private divorces. However, the object of recognition is not the authentic instrument or the agreement itself but the effects of the spouses' declarations they embody. If the authentic instrument or agreement does not bind the courts and authorities in the Member State of origin, the power of the courts and authorities in the other Member States to check the declarations' validity and effects is not a prohibited *révision au fond*.[22] Regardless, the cross-reference in Article 65(1) sentence 2 of Brussels IIb is restricted by the words 'unless otherwise provided for in this Section'. Characterising Article 65(1) of Brussels IIb as a conflict rule does not require courts and authorities in the recognising Member States to *always* examine the validity and effects of a private divorce with reference to the applicable law. In the majority of cases, the law of the Member State of origin will consider the existence of a formally valid document as an indicia or evidence for the substantive validity and effects of the divorce.[23] In contrast, courts and authorities in the recognising Member States should conduct investigations as to the validity of the private divorce whenever there are specific reasons to doubt the validity of the agreement, for example, if one of the spouses lacks legal capacity. However, investigations are only permissible to the extent that they could equally be carried out by the courts and authorities in the Member State of origin based on the applicable law.

Characterising Article 65(1) of Brussels IIb in the above-described way as a conflict rule prompts the question whether the provision is *located in the right Regulation*. The provision demands for an application of the law of the Member State of origin to evaluate the cross-border effects of a private divorce. Thus, it could easily fit into the Regulation on the law applicable to divorce and legal separation – the Rome III Regulation.[24] Incorporating the rule into the Brussels IIb Regulation was nevertheless a sensible decision, at least from a pragmatic point of view. First, a reform of the Brussels IIa Regulation was already on the agenda. Secondly, the Brussels IIb Regulation binds all Member States,

[21] Differently, however, Kramme (n 18) 105.

[22] Equally critical is Mayer, above (n 13) 200, who suggests an analogous application of Art 59(2), 59(3) of the Succession Regulation or Art 58(2), 53(3) of the Property Regulations.

[23] This will especially be the case if one of the parties hands in a certificate in the sense of Art 66(1)(a) of Brussels IIb.

[24] Council Regulation (EU) 1259/2010 of 20 December 2010 implementing enhanced cooperation in the area of the law applicable to divorce and legal separation, [2010] OJ L343/10 (here referred to as the Rome III Regulation).

while the Rome III Regulation does not. Thus, the EU legislator could regulate cross-border private divorces much more efficiently by introducing the rule into the Brussels II regime. In addition to that, a solution in the Rome III Regulation would have had the disadvantage that the same mechanism would be adopted in relation to private divorces from non-Member States.[25] Extending the solution of Article 65(1) of Brussels IIb to private divorces from third states would probably go too far. Furthermore, the incorporation of private divorces into the Brussels II system can be justified from a systematic point of view: it has a positive, coordinating effect of regulating the recognition of private divorces in the same legal act as classic divorces (ie, decrees of divorce handed down by courts),[26] whose effects are extended to the other Member States by this Regulation. Consequently, Article 65(1) of Brussels IIb is a conflict rule camouflaged as a procedural provision. Before German courts this rule therefore overrides, for example, the national conflict rules adopted to close the *Sahyouni* gap (see section I above), that is Article 17(2) of the Introductory Act to the German Civil Code[27] and its cross-reference to the Rome III Regulation.

IV. Question No 3: How do the New Rules Prevent a Private Divorce Tourism within the European Union?

The wording of Article 65(1) of Brussels IIb indirectly allows spouses to choose the applicable law of any Member State that provides rules for a private divorce. This is possible as the Regulation does not determine which Member State is competent to draw up or register an authentic instrument or to register the agreement of a couple willing to divorce. In particular, the uniform rules on jurisdiction in Article 3 et seq of Brussels IIb do not *directly* apply to private divorces. At first sight, spouses willing to divorce could request the state authorities of any Member State to formally draw up or register their private divorce, irrespective of the existence of a close connection to that Member State. Consequently, the spouses could indirectly choose the applicable law.

However, the European legislator has established a filter that *indirectly* restricts a private divorce tourism within the European Union. According to Article 64 of Brussels IIb, private divorces within the meaning of Article 65(1) of Brussels IIb are only recognised if the courts of the Member State of origin would have jurisdiction for a classic court divorce or legal separation of that particular marriage under Article 3 et seq of Brussels IIb. This cross-reference to the provisions on international jurisdiction ensures a minimum of connection between the spouses and the law applicable to the private divorce. Article 64, furthermore,

[25] *cf* Art 4 of the Rome III Regulation.
[26] *cf* Art 68(1)(b) and 68(1)(c) of Brussels IIb.
[27] Einführungsgesetz zum Bürgerlichen Gesetzbuche, 1994.

safeguards the application of the priority principle by extending the application of Article 20(1) of Brussels IIb to private divorces. Article 64, however, does not prevent state authorities of a Member State lacking jurisdiction for a judicial divorce, to offer a private divorce to (foreign) spouses. The provision merely ensures the effects of a private divorce in a non-competent Member State being extended to the other Member States by Article 65(1) of Brussels IIb.[28] This is also stressed by Article 66(2)(a) of Brussels IIb. This rule only allows a Member State competent under the jurisdictional rules of the Regulation to issue the certificate required for the recognition of the authentic instrument or the agreement. This indirect jurisdictional filter is to be checked by the courts and authorities in the other Member States when recognising the foreign private divorce, notwithstanding the fact that Article 68(1) of Brussels IIb does not mention the jurisdiction of the Member State of origin as one of the grounds for refusal of recognition. Article 64 of Brussels IIb is a provision on the scope of the section on the cross-border effects of authentic instruments and agreements which is to be applied by all courts and authorities in the Member States if the recognition of authentic instruments or agreements is in question. To which authorities is Article 64 of Brussels IIb otherwise directed? That the authorities in the Member State of origin issuing the certificates for the recognition abroad are bound by jurisdictional rules is already expressed in the special provision in Article 66(2)(a) of Brussels IIb.

An alternative recourse to the private international law of the Member States – if the preconditions of Article 65(1) of Brussels IIb have not been met, for example, because the Member State of origin lacked jurisdiction – is not permissible for private divorces originating from another Member State. This exception from the '*Günstigkeitsprinzip*', ie, the application of the most recognition-friendly regime, that traditionally shapes the law of recognition[29] can be justified by the position adopted in this chapter that Article 65(1) of Brussels IIb is a conflict of law rule specifically designed for private divorces originating from other Member States. Only private divorces from third states are subject to domestic private international law rules.

V. In Memoriam Jonathan Fitchen

Jonathan and I have met at various academic occasions, and I have always admired his work. Apart from his impressive scholarly achievements he remains in my heart as one of the kindest colleagues. Some years ago, I sent him off-prints of rather insignificant contributions. A couple of weeks later I received a CD – instead

[28] A Schulz, 'Die Neufassung der Brüssel IIa-Verordnung' [2020] *Zeitschrift für das gesamte Familienrecht* 1141, 1148 and fn 86, who calls Art 64 Brussels IIb a novelty ('*Novum*').

[29] See, for the Brussels II regime, the obiter dicta in Case C-256/09 *Bianca Purrucker v Guillermo Vallés Pérez* [2010] ECR I-07353, para 92.

of an 'academic thank you present' as Jonathan wrote, hoping, that it 'if you do not already have it (or detest it) might prove to be of some amusement'. The disk contains a recording of Richard Wagner's *Die Meistersinger von Nürnberg* which was missing in my collection so far. When working at my desk I listen to this addictive music frequently – and then I always remember you, Jonathan, wherever you are.

INDEX

www.ingramcontent.com/pod-product-compliance
Ingram Content Group UK Ltd.
Pitfield, Milton Keynes, MK11 3LW, UK
UKHW020800290926
15470UKWH00003B/873

9 781509 956647